GREEK, MESOPOTAMIA, EGYPT & ROME

FASCINATING INSIGHTS, MYTHOLOGY, STORIES, HISTORY & KNOWLEDGE FROM THE WORLD'S MOST INTERESTING CIVILIZATIONS & EMPIRES

(4 BOOK BUNDLE)

HISTORY BROUGHT ALIVE

© **Copyright 2021 - All rights reserved.**

The content contained within this book may not be reproduced, duplicated, or transmitted without direct written permission from the author or the publisher.

Under no circumstances will any blame or legal responsibility be held against the publisher, or author, for any damages, reparation, or monetary loss due to the information contained within this book, either directly or indirectly.

Legal Notice:

This book is copyright protected. It is only for personal use. You cannot amend, distribute, sell, use, quote, or paraphrase any part, or the content within this book, without the consent of the author or publisher.

Disclaimer Notice:

Please note the information contained within this document is for educational and entertainment purposes only. All effort has been executed to present accurate, up-to-date, reliable, complete information. No warranties of any kind are declared or implied. Readers acknowledge that the author is not engaged in the rendering of legal, financial, medical, or professional advice. The content within this book has been derived from various sources. Please consult a licensed professional before attempting any techniques outlined in this book.

By reading this document, the reader agrees that under no circumstances is the author responsible for any losses, direct or indirect, that are incurred as a result of the use of the information contained within this document, including, but not limited to, errors, omissions, or inaccuracies.

FREE BONUS FROM HBA: EBOOK BUNDLE

Greetings!

First of all, thank you for reading our books. As fellow passionate readers of History and Mythology, we aim to create the very best books for our readers.

Now, we invite you to join our VIP list. As a welcome gift, we offer the History & Mythology Ebook Bundle below for free. Plus you can be the first to receive new books and exclusives! <u>Remember it's 100% free to join.</u>

Simply scan the QR code to join.

Keep up to date with us on:

YouTube: History Brought Alive

Facebook: History Brought Alive

www.historybroughtalive.com

CONTENTS

ANCIENT EGYPT: DISCOVERING FASCINATING HISTORY, MYTHOLOGY, GODS, GODDESSES, PHARAOHS, AND MORE FROM THE MYSTERIOUS ANCIENT EGYPTIAN CIVILIZATION

INTRODUCTION 2

CHAPTER 1 12

SETTING THE STAGE 12

   Many Rivers, One River 12

      Inundation 16

      The Red Land 19

CHAPTER 2 23

EGYPT AT THE DAWN OF HISTORY 23

   What Came Before 23

   The People of the Black Soil 32

      Social Structure 32

      At Least it's Work: Occupations in Egyptian Society 35

CHAPTER 3 49

GODS AND GODDESSES 49

   The Great Paradox of Ancient Egypt 54

   Speech, Fiction, and the Birth of a Civilization 58

   The Cognitive Revolution of *Homo Sapiens* 59

   The Gods of Chaos 61

      The Ogdoad 61

   The Creator Gods 63

- Amun and Amunet 63
- Atum 64
- Ra, the Sun God 64
- Ptah 66
- Khnum 68
- The Created Gods: the Ennead of Heliopolis 69
  - Shu 69
  - Tefnut 69
  - Geb 70
  - Nut 70
  - Osiris 71
  - Isis 76
  - Seth 77
  - Nephthys 79
  - Horus 80
  - Horus, the Child 81

CHAPTER 4 83
MYTHOLOGY OF ANCIENT EGYPT 83
- Toward a Worldview 83
- Mythology: A Moving Target 87
- In the Beginning 89
  - Chaos 90
- Creation 93
  - The Ogdoad 93
  - Alternative Creator Myths 95
  - Male and Female: He Created Them 97

Death and Resurrection 101
    Osiris and Isis 101
On Earth, as it is in *A'aru* 103
To *Duat*, the Underworld 105

CHAPTER 5 108
THE DRAMA UNFOLDS 108
    The Outline 111
    Cast of Characters 113
        The Early Kingdom Period 113
        The Middle Kingdom Period 114
        The New Kingdom Period 115
        The Ptolemaic Period 119
    Prologue 120
    Act I 123
    First Intermission 127
        First Intermediate Period (2181-2040 BCE) 127
    Act II 129
    Second Intermission 132
        Second Intermediate Period (1782-1570 BCE) ... 132
    Act III 133
    Epilogue 134
        The Late Period (1070-332 BCE) 134
        The Ptolemaic Period (323-30 BCE) 135

CHAPTER 6 138
PIT GRAVES TO PYRAMIDS 138
    It's the *Pits*, Man! 138

The Great Pyramid of Khufu...140
How to Build a Pyramid.. 143
    Choose the Right Man for the Job 143
    Pick the Site Carefully 146
    Find your Bearings 147
    Make it Level, Larry! 149
    Get the Teams Together 150

CHAPTER 7 154

I'M NOT YOUR MUMMY! 154

CONCLUSION 163

INTRODUCTION 166

GREEK MYTHOLOGY: EXPLORE TIMELESS TALES OF ANCIENT GREECE, THE MYTHS, HISTORY & LEGENDS OF THE GODS, GODDESSES, TITANS, HEROES, MONSTERS & MORE

CHAPTER 1 170

WHY GREEK MYTHOLOGY IS STILL RELEVANT TODAY... 170

    What Were the Greek Myths?...171

    What Did These Myths Teach and Do Their Teaching Still Hold Relevance? 173

    Why Is Greek Mythology Still Studied? 174

CHAPTER 2 177

GREEK MYTHOLOGY AND ITS REVOLUTION THROUGH THE AGES..177

    How Greek Mythology and Myths Influenced Ancient Greek

Society 178

How Philosophers Challenged Greek Mythology and Worship of the Gods 183

CHAPTER 3 187

THE HISTORY OF THE WORLD ACCORDING TO GREEK MYTHOLOGY.. 187

The Children of Chaos and Gaea 188

The Tyrant Rule of Uranus 189

The Titan Ruler Cronus..................................... 190

The Return of Zeus..191

The Final Hurdle the Gods Versus the TItans 192

The Creation of the Human Race According to Greek Mythology... 194

CHAPTER 4 197

THE ANCIENT GREEK WORLD: WORSHIP OF THE GODS, ILLUSTRIOUS TEMPLES, AND THE MANY GREEK FESTIVALS 197

Greek Mythology as a Pagan Religion............................. 198

Temples Built in Honor of the Greek Gods.....................202

Temple of Olympian Zeus in Ancient Athens, Greece 204

Temple of Poseidon at Sounion in Athens, Greece..... 205

Temple of Hera in Samos..207

Ancient Greek Festivals and Athletic Games to Honor the Gods...209

The Olympic Games 211

The Spring Festivals of Anthesteria and Mounukhion 212

The Summer Festivals................................... 214

 The Autumn Festivals 217

 The Winter Festivals.. 218

CHAPTER 5 .... **219**

THE GREEK PANTHEON OF MT. OLYMPUS **219**

 The Olympians 220

  Zeus... 221

  Hera 223

  Apollo 226

  Artemis... 228

  Hermes 230

  Aphrodite 231

  Poseidon... 234

  Athena 238

CHAPTER 6... **242**

THE MANY LARGER THAN LIFE FIGURES OF GREEK MYTHOLOGY **242**

 Nymphs... 243

 Centaurs.. 244

 Satyrs 247

 Demigods.. 249

  Herakles 250

  Achilles... 252

  Theseus 254

  Perseus 256

  Helen of Troy 258

CHAPTER 7 .... **261**

GREEK MONSTERS THAT TERRIFIED A NATION AND THREATENED THE GODS 261

- Medusa 262
- The Hydra 263
- Typhon 266
- Cerberus 268

CHAPTER 8 272

MYTHS THAT WITHSTOOD THE TEST OF TIME AND DEFINED A MYTHOLOGY 272

- Pandora's Jar 273
- The Myth of Icarus 274
- The Abduction of Persephone by Hades 276
- The Love Story of Eros and Psyche 279

CHAPTER 9 289

BATTLES AND CONQUESTS: THE TROJAN WAR AND ALEXANDER THE GREAT 289

- The Trojan War 290
- Alexander the Great of Macedonia 297

CONCLUSION 302

THE MYTHOLOGY OF MESOPOTAMIA: FASCINATING INSIGHTS, MYTHS, STORIES & HISTORY FROM THE WORLD'S MOST ANCIENT CIVILIZATION. SUMERIAN, AKKADIAN, BABYLONIAN, PERSIAN, ASSYRIAN AND MORE

INTRODUCTION 310

PART I: THE HISTORY 316

CHAPTER 1
KINGSHIP DESCENDS FROM HEAVEN 317
(CA. 5400-2350 BCE) 317

- Temple Rule 317
- The Flood 320
- A New Order 324
  - The Lugal of Kish 327
  - From Lugal to Monarch 330

CHAPTER 2
THE FIRST EMPIRE 335
(CA. 2350-2150 BCE) 335

- Prelude: The Conquests of Lugalzagesi 335
- Sargon of Akkad 338
- The Rise and Fall of Gods 343

CHAPTER 3
SUMER RESTORED 349
(CA. 2119-2004 BCE) 349

- The Third Dynasty of Ur 354
- Ideology and Personality 358
- The Fall 363

CHAPTER 4
OLD BABYLON 365
(CA. 2000-1600 BCE) 365

- King Hammurabi's Code 369
- A New Society 371
- The Fall of Old Babylon 376

CHAPTER 5 378
ASSYRIA 378
(CA. 1800-700 BCE) 378
    The Merchant State 379
    From Mercantile to Military 384
    A New Culture 388
    The Military State 394
CHAPTER 6 401
THE END OF AN ERA 401
(AFTER CA. 700 BCE) 401
    The Decline of Culture 401
    The Decline of Power 404
PART II: THE MYTHOLOGY 409
CHAPTER 7 410
ENUMA ELISH 410
CHAPTER 8 417
THE MYTH OF ADAPA 417
CHAPTER 9 421
THE MYTH OF ETANA 421
CHAPTER 10 426
THE ATRAHASIS MYTH 426
CHAPTER 11 431
THE EPIC OF GILGAMESH 431
CHAPTER 12 442
THE DESCENT OF INANNA 442
CHAPTER 13 447

THE CURSE OF AGADE 447
CONCLUSION 450
ROMAN EMPIRE: RISE & THE FALL. EXPLORE THE HISTORY, MYTHOLOGY, LEGENDS, EPIC BATTLES & THE LIVES OF THE EMPERORS, LEGIONS, HEROES, GLADIATORS & MORE

INTRODUCTION 456
   Author Bio 456
   Roma Victrix 456

CHAPTER 1 462
TIMELINE 462
   The Three Periods of Ancient Rome 462
      The Founding of Rome 462
      The Legend 463
      How Rome Was Born 464
      Expansion 465
      The Seeds of the Empire 466
      Caesar, Pompey, and Crassus 468
      The Rule of Caesar 470
      The Assassination of Caesar 471
   The Time of the Emperors 471
      The Second Triumvirate 471
      Battle at Sicily 472
      Pax Romana 473
      Caligula 475
      Christianity in Ancient Rome 475

- The Five Good Emperors 477
- End of the Pax Romana 477
- The Third Century 479
- East and West 480
- The First Christian Emperor 481
- The 4th Century and the Decline and Fall of the Empire 482
- The Invasion of the Huns 484
- The Decline, Invasion, and Fall of Rome 485
- Life After the Empire 485

CHAPTER 2 487
THE GEOGRAPHY OF ROME 487
- Rome's Place in the World 487
  - The Boundaries and Divisions of Rome 487
- The Geography of the City 488
  - The Location of Rome 488
  - Geographical Features That Allowed Rome to Thrive 489
  - The Role of the Environment in the Early Development of Rome 490
  - The Mountains Of Rome 491
  - The Strategic Advantage of Topography 493
- Roman Roads 494
  - Types of Roads 494
  - Management of Roads 496

CHAPTER 3 498
THE MAIN FIGURES IN ROMAN HISTORY 498

Political Figures 498
   Emperors 498
Famous Writers 505
   Some 1st Century Roman Writers 506
   Some 2nd Century Roman Writers 508
   Some 3rd Century Roman Writers 510
   Some 4th Century Roman Writers 512
Poets, Artists, and Musicians 513
   Famous Roman Poets 513
   Roman Music 514
Famous Military Figures 516
Gladiators 522
   Carpophorus 523
   Flamma 524
   Gannicus 524
   Spiculus 525
   Marcus Attilius 525
   Commodus 526
   Tetraites 526
   Priscus and Verus 527
   Crixus 527
   Spartacus 528

CHAPTER 4 529
ROMAN LIFE 529
Roman Food and Cooking 529
   Roman Food Habits 529

- Everyday Foods 531
- Roman Drinks 533
- Popular Dishes 533
- Food for the Rich 535
- Food for the Poor 535
- Ways of Cooking 536
- Roman Jobs 536
- A Typical Day 539
  - Life in the City 539
  - Life in the Country 539
- Family 540
- School 541
- Clothing 542
- Entertainment 543

CHAPTER 5 545

MYTHOLOGY 545

- The Mythological Origin of Rome 545
- Roman Gods 546
- Other Cultural Myths 550
- Paganism in Ancient Rome 555

CHAPTER 6 556

ROMAN MILITARY 556

- Structure 557
- Logistics 558
- Legions 559
- Training 560

- Training Infrastructure 562
- Romans Soldiers in Everyday Life 563
- Benefits of Roman Army Training 564
- Navy 564
- Weapons and Tactics 566
  - Weaponry 566
  - Siege Equipment 567
  - Tactics 570
- Famous Battles 575
  - Punic Wars 575
  - Teutoburg 576
  - Catalaunian Fields 577
  - Actium 579
  - Corinth 580

CHAPTER 7 582
DECLINE AND FALL OF THE ROMAN EMPIRE .. 582
- The Beginning Of The End Of The Roman Empire 582
  - Factors That Led to the Empire's Decline 583
  - The Timeline for the Decline 588
  - The Fall of the Empire in 476 589
  - Aftermath 590

CONCLUSION 592
ABOUT THE AUTHOR 596
REFERENCES 597
OTHER BOOKS BY HISTORY BROUGHT ALIVE. 622

ANCIENT EGYPT

DISCOVER FASCINATING HISTORY, MYTHOLOGY, GODS, GODDESSES, PHARAOHS, PYRAMIDS, AND MORE FROM THE MYSTERIOUS ANCIENT EGYPTIAN CIVILIZATION

HISTORY BROUGHT ALIVE

INTRODUCTION

What does your bucket list look like? No matter your circumstances in life, it's there if you allow yourself even a moment to dream. Chances are, you're thinking about it right now! The bucket list is our repository of dreams. A to-do list not of things we feel we should do, like the New Year's resolutions we struggle to keep, but of the things we want to accomplish, given an opportunity, before we die. It speaks to the secret yearning of our hearts: A yearning to make or renew connections with others, to overcome our innermost fears, to escape the mundane day-to-day of our workday lives, or, just once, to experience the far-flung or the exotic. The stronger that heart's desire, the closer we place that dream to the top of our list. Your bucket list might include 20 things, or 100, or only one. No matter, it's yours. So, let me ask again: what's on your bucket list? If you're like the thousands—affectionately labeled "Buckaroos"—who responded to that same question on bucketlist.net, you might have included some once-in-a-lifetime adventure like skydiving, zip-lining, scuba diving, or swimming with dolphins. Or perhaps your dream is more personal and long-term, such as getting married, buying a house, even getting a tattoo! But I'll wager that, like the vast majority of Buckaroos out there, somewhere near the top of your bucket list of longing is this: travel. And not just any kind of travel. Northern lights? The Grand Canyon? Nice. But that's not it. A cruise? You're not "feeling it." So let me tell you one thing (maybe the only thing) that I'm sure is on your list: you want to see the pyramids in Egypt. How do I know? No, I'm not psychic! I know because you picked up this book. And here's another thing of which I'm sure: You'll be glad you did!

Let us tell you why.

The pyramids rank among the largest, most majestic calling cards on earth. More than 13 million tourists from around the world flocked to the Nile Valley in 2019 to experience the tombs, temples, and treasures of Egypt, in particular, the last remaining of the Seven Wonders of the Ancient World, the Pyramid of Khufu. Until the completion of the Cathedral Church of the Blessed Virgin Mary of Lincoln (aka the Lincoln Cathedral) in northeastern England in 1311 CE (the Common Era), this aptly-named Great Pyramid of Giza held the distinction of being the tallest free-standing man-made structure on the planet. Its iconic profile dominated the earthscape for somewhere between 3851 and 3871 years! We'll get up close and personal with this and other pyramids in chapter 6. Suffice it to say that these glorious artifacts are the lodestone which draws us inexorably toward that mysterious, magnificent world of ancient Egypt with its gods and goddesses, kings and queens, temples and tombs, mythology and ritual, history, hieroglyphs and, running through it all, a river–the river–the source of all that was and is Egyptian civilization. In chapter 1, we'll journey together down this river through time and space to understand the meaning of Herodotus' words, "Egypt is the Nile, and the Nile is Egypt" (Gemmill, 1928, p. 295). Ancient Egypt, the second-oldest civilization on earth, endured and thrived for more than 3,000 years! You want to get closer to that fantastic, colorful, and mysterious time–to pull back the curtain and catch a glimpse of what it was really like back then. The problem is that you don't know where to begin. You're overwhelmed! You want more than a superficial, watered-down Wikipedia rehash. Yet, you haven't the time or energy to dig through a mountain of scholarly tomes written by Egyptologists, or to navigate some tortuous maze of footnotes. You're searching for that one book, the starting place of that bucket list dream to experience the ancient Egyptian civilization which produced the pyramids and so much more.

This is that one book. Within these pages are the kind of vibrant, exciting, and memorable characters, places, and events that put flesh on what might otherwise be the dry bones of ancient Egyptian history. That's because we at History Brought Alive share a passion for presenting rigorously factual, meticulously researched, and thoroughly enjoyable history and culture in an easy-to-digest style that keeps you turning the page until the very end. It's what sets us apart from the competition!

What sets this book, in particular, apart from others is its unique approach to unfolding the successive eras of Egyptian history. The traditional editorial strategy has been to distill that history into conventional and sometimes monotonous timelines, chronologies, alphabetized glossaries, and so on. Granted, navigating the lives and reigns (sometimes concurrent or, at least, overlapping) of almost 200 pharaohs requires that historians impose some sort of structure on the facts! The first to grapple with that monumental task was a 3rd century BCE (Before the Common Era) Egyptian priest named Manetho, who grouped the pharaonic succession before Alexander the Great into 30 dynasties. To his credit, that convention has endured to the present day. Modern historians have further organized these dynasties into periods so that, for example, the reigns of the eight kings of the First

Dynasty (2950-2750) and the eight or more of the Second Dynasty (2750-2650) become part of the Early Dynastic Period. So, the question is: Are you bored yet or, worse, having flashbacks to your tenth-grade history class? We hear you. These scholarly conventions are extremely useful, but they don't fully deliver on our History Brought Alive promise to make your journey through ancient Egypt exciting and memorable. Allow us, then, to take a slightly different approach: a dramatic approach. Yes, there will be names and dates too. But we promise that when you've finished reading this book, you'll not take away a kitbag of dusty facts—you'll own the experience as if you've lived it yourself! So then, think about this: The timeline of ancient Egyptian history is precisely like the script of an epic theatrical production when you examine it from a bird's-eye view.

Egyptian history as high drama? Nothing could be closer to the truth! In the coming chapters, you'll become familiar with the broad outlines and the key players in that drama played out over millennia on what might just be the world's grandest outdoor stage. But it requires the proper perspective to appreciate it. So here's an analogy drawn from the very geography of Egypt: Though ancient Egyptians had never seen their country from above, they imagined the course of the Nile River, from where they believed it originated in the underground caverns of Hapy, god of the inundation, near the First Cataract, to the lazy, slow-moving Delta where it drained into the Mediterranean Sea, to resemble a papyrus stalk in full flower; and its most northerly tributary, which ends in the Faiyum Lake, a new shoot growing from that stalk (Wilkinson, Toby, 2015). It was only when I saw a satellite image of that same country, as the camera panned slowly southward from lower to upper Egypt (remember, the Nile flows from south to north), that I could see, from miles above, the papyrus-flower, the new shoot, the slightly crooked stalk, precisely as those ancient Egyptians had pictured their homeland with their feet in the sand. Now I'll remember that perspective of Egypt for as long as I live. I own it. We'll be able to say the same of the broad sweep of the history of Egypt when we approach it from a similar vantage point.

I've drawn upon the chronology set forth by Professors Bob Brier and A. Hoyt Hobbs, which breaks Egyptian political history into nine eras (Brier & A Hoyt Hobbs, 2013) with their approximate periods and dynasties. I say approximate because, before the year 624 BCE, dates can fluctuate by 50-100 years, and many can only be inferred by comparing religious texts, inscriptions from the tombs of specific rulers, even the hieroglyphs on the walls of palace and temple ruins scattered throughout upper and lower Egypt. This inference creates some discrepancies between the chronologies of different historians. Nonetheless, the vast majority of experts are in agreement with the broader brushstrokes of the following Egyptian chronology, to which I've added a theatrical twist:

- Prologue

The Predynastic Era (before 3150 BCE) - Prehistory to Dynasty 0

- Act I

The Early Dynastic Era (3150-2686 BCE) - Dynasties I-II

The Old Kingdom Era (2686-2181 BCE) - Dynasties III-VI

- First Intermission

The First Intermediate Period (2181-2040 BCE) - Dynasties VIII-XI

- Act II

The Middle Kingdom Era (2040-1782 BCE) - Dynasties XI-XII

- Second Intermission

The Second Intermediate Period (1782-1570 BCE) - Dynasties XIII-XVII

- Act III

The New Kingdom Era (1570-1070 BCE) - Dynasties XVIII-XX

- Epilogue

The Late Period (1070-332 BCE) - Dynasties XXI-XXXI

The Ptolemaic Period (332-30 BCE) - Dynasties XXXII-XXXIII

The Late and Ptolemaic Periods taken together represent an era of gradual decline in Egyptian history, when foreign powers (Libya, Nubia, Persia, Greece, and, finally, Rome) began to assert direct influence, if not control, over pharaonic governance and the reshaping of cultural and religious norms. For this reason, some historians omit them altogether from chronologies which focus on indigenous ancient Egyptian political history. Instead, we have taken a broader view. While we will not detail this later period of Egyptian history, we consider it an appropriate epilogue to the classic Egyptian story. First, then, we'll look briefly at the famous last Pharaoh before the demise of ancient Egypt. Ultimately, with the death of Julius Caesar's widow, Cleopatra VII, in 30 BCE, and the murder of her son and co-regent Ptolemy Philopator Philometor Caesar ("Caesarion"), the last king of Egypt, that same year, the paradigm of pharaonic rule ends: The country becomes a mere province of the Roman Empire under Augustus, and the curtain falls forever on this 3100-year historical drama we have come to know as ancient Egypt.

We'll follow the intrigues of Caesar and Cleopatra, Mark Antony, Caesarion, and his great-uncle Octavian (later to become Emperor Augustus) through to the last scene at the end of chapter 6. But we mustn't get ahead of ourselves. Before Caesarion and Cleopatra; before the foreign rulers of ancient Egypt; before the Pharaohs; before Osiris, Isis, Horus and the host of Egyptian deities (chapter 3); before Amun, the "self-created," sitting cross-legged on the ben-ben which had risen from primordial waters, or any of the myriad myths which shaped the worldview of that civilization (chapter 4); before even the first representative of the genus *Homo* had stood on the rocky outcropping above the First Cataract and gazed down upon the future Land of the Pharaohs (chapter 2), there was a river.

As successive species of man moved through that river valley over hundreds of thousands of years–first, *erectus,* then *heidelbergensis, neanderthalensis,* and lastly, *sapiens*–they came to identify it as *the* river: *Iteru,* in the ancient Egyptian language of the modern humans who hunted and gathered on its floodplains and who later herded domesticated livestock and planted crops in its fertile alluvial soil. It was not until the Greeks under Alexander the Great conquered Egypt in 332 BCE and inaugurated the 300-year dynasty of the Ptolemies that their language gave *Neilos,* "the river," the name we recognize today: the Nile. Whether *Neilos, Iteru,* or another name given before the dawn of Egyptian history, this is the grand and glorious stage upon which we witness the birth, flourishing, and decline of earth's second-oldest civilization.

CHAPTER 1
SETTING THE STAGE

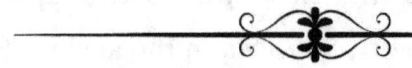

Many Rivers, One River

"Without the Nile, there would be no Egypt" (Wilkinson, Toby, 2015, p. 3). That statement would seem bold were it not absolutely true. The river, iteru in the ancient Egyptian language, has dominated and defined the East African landscape since before the arrival of the first human species, Homo erectus, in Africa more than 700,000 years ago. The Egyptian segment of the Nile River follows a roughly straight, south-to-north course from modern Aswan to Cairo and the Delta. Seen from above, the river's course resembles the iconic papyrus reed with its slender stalk and flowering head—and, like that iconic water plant, was integral to ancient Egyptian civilization and thought. So true was this that the glyph for Egypt was simply a horizontal line (representing the flat floodplain) with three black circles beneath (signifying clumps of the black alluvial soil left behind after the annual inundation).

The waters of the river, and particularly of the annual inundation, were the lifeblood of Egypt. According to Harvey Cox, "the annual flooding of the Nile...provided the framework by which the society was held together" (Harvey Gallagher Cox, 2013, p. 27). Yet, ironically, no Egyptian in the nation's 3,000-year history ever knew the actual geographical source of the Nile, recognized today as the world's longest river at 4,130 miles (Liu et al., 2009). Nor would the average Egyptian citizen have acknowledged the need to know. Instead, an all-pervasive polytheism, which ascribed divine agency to every aspect of human experience, including the life-sustaining flow of the river, framed their worldview. "Sun gods, river goddesses, and astral deities abounded. History was subsumed under cosmology, society under nature, time under space. Both god and man were part of nature" (Harvey Gallagher Cox, 2013, p. 27).

That worldview convinced Egyptians that the river's life-giving (or sometimes life-taking) waters flowed from an underground cavern beneath the First Cataract, adjacent to the Elephantine Island, close to Egypt's southern border with Nubia (modern Sudan). This underground cavern was the abode of the god Hapy—not the god of the Nile itself, but the annual inundation. Though no one had ever seen Hapy, pictograms depict this deity as a big-bellied, droopy-breasted figure of nonspecific gender who wore a ceremonial beard (Wilkinson, 2003). This depiction speaks to the Egyptian belief that Hapy (like the waters of iteru itself) was the source of fertility and prosperity. Nothing is more expressive of their conviction than the following excerpt from the "Hymn to Hapy (the Nile Flood)," originally written in Middle Egyptian and believed to have been composed during the Middle Kingdom period (c. 2060-1782 BCE):

Hymn to Hapy: Hail flood! emerging from the earth, arriving to bring Egypt to life, hidden of form, the darkness in the day, the one whose followers sing to him, as he waters the plants, created by Ra to make every herd live, who satisfies the desert hills removed from the water, for it is his dew that descends from the sky—he, the beloved of Geb, controller of Nepri, the one who makes the crafts of Ptah verdant...

If he is greedy, the whole land suffers, great and small fall moaning. People are changed at his coming; the one who creates him is Khnum. When he rises, then the land is in joy, then every belly is glad, every jaw has held laughter, every tooth revealed.

Of course, we need only consult a map to understand the reality which was literally beyond their comprehension: the one iteru, or river, of Egypt, the only Nile they knew, was the product of several major and minor tributaries which commingled far south in regions once occupied by ancient Nubia, the semi-mythical Land of Punt, and beyond the 'end of the world' as the Egyptian people knew it. The main branch of the Nile, called White for its heavy clay deposits, begins in a stream, the Ruvyironza, which flows out of Mount Kikizi in southern Burundi (Godfrey Mugoti, 2009) and empties into Lake Victoria. From Jinja, Lake Victoria, it flows into Lake Albert and then continues its northward journey until it joins the Blue Nile at Khartoum in Sudan–a distance of some 2,300 miles from its source. The Blue Nile, on the other hand, originates at Lake Tana in the highlands of modern-day Ethiopia and flows some 900 miles through Ethiopia and Sudan. It has historically provided at least 80 percent of the fresh water and silt in the Nile during the North African monsoon season between June and October. A third major Nile tributary, the Atbara River, called the Red Nile, starts its journey 500 miles southeast of the White Nile, in the mountains 30 miles north of Lake Tana in Ethiopia, as little more than a stream. However, like the Blue Nile to the south, it swells dramatically during the late summer rains, contributing to the surge of the annual inundation in the Nile

Valley. The Yellow Nile, a former tributary that flowed from eastern Chad to its confluence at the southern point of the Great Bend of the White Nile between c. 8000 BCE and c. 1000 BCE (Keding, 2000), became extinct at roughly the same time as ancient Egyptian civilization was subsumed into the Roman Empire.

So, there were many rivers, with many sources, each bearing her gifts–fresh, clear water, clay, black silt–in a happy marriage of currents, rushing through steep gorges and past red sandstone cliffs and, finally, tumbling around the crags of the First Cataract in Upper Egypt and on toward the Great Green, as Egyptians used to call the Mediterranean Sea. I think the ancient Egyptians would have smiled with pleasure had they been aware that the several tributaries of the White Nile (Blue, White, Red, and Yellow, among others), seen from above, resemble the roots of their beloved and iconic papyrus plant!

Inundation

We'll return to the importance of the annual inundation throughout this book, as fundamental as it was to ancient Egypt's economic, social, political, and even religious development. But, if you're like me, you can't help but ask the question: What was it like? Reach out with your imagination to that distant time. Can you get a sense of the mystery—and for every Egyptian, it was indeed that—of the inundation? Consider the words of New Zealand filmmaker John Feeney:

Flowing out of a barren desert, from a source "beyond all known horizons," the Nile had baffled the world for thousands of years. Regular as sun and moon, in the middle of burning summer, without a drop of rain in sight, when all other rivers on earth were drying up, for no apparent reason at all, the Nile rose out of its bed every year, and for three months embraced all of Egypt (Feeney, 2006, par. 1).

Feeney and his Egyptian crew set out in 1964 to capture on film the last Nile flood and the last Egyptian inundation before the completion of the Aswan High Dam. He and his crew are the only persons in history to have followed the flood from its source in the Ethiopian highlands, all the way to Cairo, and to have documented the journey. His words are a stirring, if bitter-sweet, in memoriam to the singular event which shaped and defined a civilization:

With a name that means "roaring fire," the Tisisat Falls must be one of the loneliest places on Earth, little known and rarely seen by outsiders.... We first heard the murmur and then the roar as we got our first glimpse through the trees.

Then we stood transfixed before the answer to the riddle that had baffled the world for thousands of years. There before us, pouring forth with the sound of thunder in one colossal fuming torrent, the Blue Nile was anything but blue, plunging from its source in Lake Tana above, down into a deep dark abyss that was the beginning of its great journey to Egypt (Feeney, 2006, par. 16-17).

He goes on to say that,

By August, the most colossal Nile flood of the century was pouring out of Ethiopia. We followed the surge as it moved like a slow-motion tidal wave across the deserts of eastern and northern Sudan into Egypt (Feeney, 2006, par. 19).

With the arrival of the inundation, dry land became lakes; basins filled and overflowed, filling adjacent basins. Villages, built on high ground, became islands (reminiscent of the Primordial Mound of creation, surrounded by turbulent, chaotic water), and neighbors visited one another in boats. The sounds of singing and celebration echoed throughout the

Nile Valley. At last, when the waters had receded,

In the soft sediment left by the floodwaters...the farmers of Egypt...set about planting their crops of beans, wheat, and barley as they had done for thousands of years (Feeney, 2006, par. 24).

Theirs was an organic relationship with iteru, the river which carried life and happiness to the Egyptian people through waters that were not the country's own but came as gifts from afar.

The Red Land

While the narrow strip of fertile land known as Kemet, "black land," was said to be the gift of the Nile, the surrounding desert, Deshret, "red land," would have been considered the opposite. Egyptians recognized that the western and eastern deserts presented a formidable (though not impenetrable) natural barrier to intruders, creating significant cultural isolation in which the unique Egyptian civilization could develop. Nonetheless, they viewed the red land as largely inhospitable. After all, they were the People of the Black Soil, and the fertility of the Nile Valley was the blessing of Hapy. The desert was dry, hot, and dangerous. It was also the abode of foreigners—Libyans to the west, nomadic tribes, and expanding empires like those of Babylonia, Assyria, and Persia to the north and east—who posed a threat, both real and perceived, to the security of ancient Egypt. That the Egyptians were willing to cross the unfamiliar and treacherous desert to exploit its natural resources, particularly gold, turquoise, lapis lazuli, and other precious materials, indicates how strong the attraction was to the elite of ancient Egypt. However, aside from its distant, buried treasures, the two obvious features of the Red Land that found meaning within the Egyptian worldview, and therefore ensured its enduring significance, were its aridity and location.

The Red Land was a desert adjacent to the western bank of the Nile and yet beyond the reach of the yearly inundation. As we'll see in chapter 8, this made it the ideal place for Egyptian burials. Remember our previous examination of the sand-pit graves of the Predynastic Period and before? Modern humans, who lived for millennia not only in the Nile Valley but in the broader surrounding desert lands, buried their dead in shallow pits dug into the sand, which served to desiccate, preserve, and, to some extent, naturally mummify the remains. Even when the mastaba, a sloped, four-sided stone structure resembling a bench, became a prevalent funerary structure, the body within was still buried in that same sandpit, often covered with wooden planks which were themselves buried under a layer of sand. It was only later in the Old Kingdom as beliefs in the nature of the Afterlife evolved that the elite members of society—Pharaoh, his family, and wealthy citizens—began to construct tombs for above-ground burial.

Egyptian cemeteries were therefore deliberately established to the west of the Nile, on the fringes of the western desert. But the preservative effects of the desert sand were not the whole story of Egyptian burial practices. The Osiris-Isis mythology evolved into a paradigm of the preparation of the deceased for a conscious, physical existence in the Afterlife. First, the Pharaoh and, later, the Egyptian people as a whole, came to identify their death/rebirth experience with that of Osiris, Lord of the Underworld. He was called the Lord of the Westerners, the temporarily disembodied spirits of the deceased who waited in "the West" for an imminent rebirth into their previously preserved or mummified bodies. Egyptian burial customs reiterated and reinforced the belief that resurrection would come from the west, the Red Land direction. Bodies of deceased individuals were transported by boat from the west to the east bank of the Nile, where they were placed in the hands of embalmers. Then, following an intricate preparation process, tailored to the family's financial resources, the mummified body was transferred once again to a boat and carried across the Nile, toward the west, where the family enacted a ritual drama before the interment of the remains. It is ironic that, while the life of every Egyptian came from the Black Land, Kemet, the new life which all eagerly sought for and anticipated was believed to come from Deshret, the Red Land.

CHAPTER 2
EGYPT AT THE DAWN OF HISTORY

What Came Before

Artifacts uncovered in and near the narrow floodplain which hugs the eastern and western banks of the Nile, from the rocky, turbulent First Cataract in the south to the broad, fan-shaped delta in the north attest to an early human presence in, and dependence upon, the land. The unique geography of the world's longest river (Liu et al., 2009) facilitated the dispersion of Homo erectus ("upright-walking man"), as early as 700,000 years ago, through eastern Africa into the Levant (modern-day Israel, Palestine, Lebanon, Syria and much of southeastern Turkey), India, and eventually to Java, where the most recent H. erectus fossils have been found. Unfortunately, no such fossilized remains have yet been uncovered in the region, which later would be known as Egypt. However, the discovery throughout the Nile Valley of distinctively pear-shaped, flaked, flint hand-axes believed to be associated with H. erectus suggests that these early nomadic hunter-gatherers passed through the valley over thousands of years. At that time, the terrain surrounding the river more closely resembled savannah than the arid, desertified climate we know today, and large populations of gazelle, hartebeest, giant buffalo (pelorovis), and other grazing mammals provided ample food supply.

Homo heidelbergensis, which exhibited some features of H. erectus, but which possessed a larger braincase, coexisted with its possible ancestor for at least a half-million years, until around 200,000 BCE, and must have transited the Nile Valley since evidence of its presence in the Levant dates back to 790,000 BCE (Smithsonian's National Museum of Natural History, 2010). H. heidelbergensis may have been more communal than its predecessor, building hearths and demonstrating the earliest human control of fire. They were likewise more innovative: more significant refinements to the flint hand-ax, and the manufacture of wooden spears, speaks to the evolution of early human skill with hunting. Thus, H. heidelbergensis has the distinction of being the first big game hunter.

Around 400,000 BCE, while H. heidelbergensis endured

colder nights and frigid winter temperatures in Europe and the northern Mediterranean area, subtle evolutionary genetic processes were at work. One outcome of these processes was another branch of the Homo family tree: a robust and resourceful species called H. neanderthalensis, or Neanderthals as we have come to know them. Neanderthals were distributed through Europe (their name comes from the Neander Valley in Germany, where their remains were first identified) and in parts of southwest and central Asia (Smithsonian's National Museum of Natural History, 2010), where the discovery of their more sophisticated stone tool technology, called Mousterian as opposed to the archaic Acheulean hand-ax technology of H. erectus, attests to their presence there (Mousterian Pluvial, 2021). Neanderthals exhibited a somewhat more refined, but not radically different, way of life than their ancestors. They lived in a community, built shelters, controlled fire, and hunted big game using spears. Forensic examination of Neanderthal skeletal development shows that they used these spears by thrusting, not by throwing, from which we can infer two things: Neanderthals must have routinely gotten up close and personal with their prey, and they must have hunted collaboratively, that is, in larger groups, to succeed.

Neanderthal tool technology–particularly scrapers, used to

remove animal flesh from hides–uncovered in the Western Sahara, close to the Nile Valley, points to Neanderthals' presence from around 70,000 BCE until 43,000 BCE. Unfortunately, the conspicuous absence of Neanderthals from the Nile Valley region after that time coincides with the arrival of the first modern humans (Brier, 1999), the outworking of whose earlier Cognitive Revolution (Harari, 2014) equipped them to out-compete their genetic cousins, driving them to extinction. There is no evidence of H. neanderthalensis in the fossil record, anywhere in the world, after about 30, 000 BCE.

Where did these new kids on the block come from? The Omo Valley of southern Ethiopia evidence what has proven to be the watershed moment in the history of the world, close to 200,000 years ago, with the first appearance of Homo sapiens, called 'Anatomically-Modern Humans', to differentiate them from later, post-cognitive-revolution Homo sapiens sapiens, called modern humans, who appeared between 70,000 BCE and 30,000 BCE in Eastern Africa. The former shared many of the cultural characteristics of their H. heidelbergensis ancestors, yet seemed to make hardly a ripple, as it were, on the genetic pond until the Cognitive Revolution (Harari, 2014). "But then," says Harari, "beginning about 70,000 years ago, Homo sapiens started doing very special things." (Harari, 2014, p. 19). Concerning those who remained in Eastern Africa after the departure of H. sapiens bands during the second "Out-of-Africa" event around 65,000 BCE (University of Cologne, 2021), and who migrated into the Nile Valley around 43,000 BCE, archaeological evidence bears witness to dramatic advances in tool technology and manufacture, hunting practices, crafting of pottery, the grinding of pigments for cosmetic and ceremonial uses, and burial of the dead (I. Shaw, 2000).

At approximately the time of the Out-of-Africa migration, around 65,000 BCE, the Western Sahara was lush with vegetation thanks to cyclical climatic and environmental processes, which turned the once-arid landscape into green savannah. When H. sapiens first arrived in the Nile region, that cycle had reversed itself, bringing the return of arid and less habitable conditions beyond the fringes of the valley. Climatic changes reduced the Nile River flow throughout this time, but evidence supports that men used fishing to provide food for their families. The people lived together in smaller bands of 25-50 persons. They were still hunters and gatherers, but their larger brains and cognitive hard wiring enabled them to innovate in terms of how those subsistence methods were carried out and the technology they used. For example, men had moved away from cutting chert blanks, which would later be fashioned into rudimentary axes and blades, favoring more durable and sharper materials such as obsidian, flint, or quartzite. During this time, men had discovered how to make a sickle, presumably to harvest wild grains. The agricultural revolution was thousands of years in the future!

However, the most extraordinary development thus far had come about simultaneously with the Cognitive Revolution: the bow and arrow. Archaeologists place the invention of the bow and arrow at somewhere around 70,000 BC–coincidentally, about the same time as development of our species. It represented a significant step forward in hunting technology. Do you remember that we discussed previously how Neanderthals, for instance, developed an exaggerated skeletal structure on one side of their bodies? It came from repeated thrusting of their spears to capture and kill their prey. Neanderthals, it seems, could not grasp the concept of a projectile, something that left your hand on its way to take down your dinner. After all, they were concrete thinkers; they literally could not imagine such a sophisticated hunting tool as a bow. Neanderthal physiology would suggest that they hadn't figured out the idea of throwing their spear instead of thrusting. H. sapiens figured everything out. Arrow points no larger than a thumbnail ("micro-points") has been discovered at Kom Ombo on the south-central Nile, which attests to H. sapiens' advanced skills.

Hunter-gatherers lived in and around the Nile Valley over the next 30,000-35,000 years, through cycles of aridity and greening of the deserts and fluctuations in the Nile River flow. Identification of their cultural developments centered on the particular regions or ancient cities where archaeologists found their artifacts, mainly pottery. However, the names of their bands or tribes are lost to time. The Nile Valley seems to have been uninhabited for 2,000 years or more, between approximately 11,000 BCE and 9,000 BCE when the river experienced extreme flooding. As a result, people were forced into the Western Desert, which was still more habitable during this period. When the waters receded, people moved back into the lower valley and settled around the lake formed by a natural basin known as the Faiyum depression. Their culture is known as Faiyum A (c. 9000-6000 BCE). Domestic cattle, sheep, and goats were introduced into Egypt late in this period, where the people had before subsisted by hunting, gathering, and fishing. They built reed huts with underground grain storage cellars and crafted distinctive pottery. Bans of nomadic hunter-gatherers settled around Faiyum lake, forming communities with centralized government by tribal chieftains.

The Faiyum period in Lower Egypt gave way to the Merimda

(c. 5,000 BCE-4,000 BCE) and, later, the El-Omari, Ma'adi, and Tasian cultures (c. 4,000 BCE). More durable pole-framed huts with windbreaks, organized into rows, replaced the reed huts of the Faiyum period. Later still, villagers used walls of plastered mud to construct oval huts with woven floor and wall coverings. The ceramic design continued to flourish. People developed more extensive and more secure grain storage facilities. Around this time, cemeteries were more widely used to bury the dead.

When the Merimda culture was at its midpoint in Lower Egypt, the Badarian culture (c. 4,500 BCE - 4,000 BCE) flourished further south, becoming Upper Egypt. These were farmers, supplementing their primary grain diets with hunting. Perhaps their location closer to the Nile headwaters favored a more substantial flow of water to reach further inland and a significantly higher proportion of alluvium. They lived in tents after the fashion of their nomadic ancestors. Domesticated animals provided food and materials for shelters. Like their northern contemporaries, the Badarian people buried their dead in cemeteries, atop mats of reeds, or covered with animal hides. Unlike them, however, the people of Badarian culture included food offerings and personal belongings, presaging the burial practices of the Early Kingdom period.

The following 850 years saw the rapid development of predynastic culture in Upper Egypt through the Naqada I (c. 4,000 BCE - 3,500 BCE), Naqada II (c. 3,500 BCE - 3,200 BCE), and Naqada III (3,200 BCE - 3,150 BCE) periods. More sophisticated dwellings with hearths and possibly windows progressed to sun-baked, mud-brick homes. Mummification began around 3,500 BCE, and graves were becoming more ornate. Abydos, north of Naqada, became a significant and vital burial center for people all over the country. Future power centers were developing at Thinis, Naqada, and Nekhen, and people wrote a prototypical hieroglyphic language at Abydos. As these smaller communities grew into "nomes," tribal centers under the authority of "nomarchs" or chieftains, war broke out between the nomes at Thinis, Naqada, and Nekhen. The nomarch of Thinis believed to have been Menes/Narmer, and his tribe defeated that of Naqada and subsequently assimilated Nekhen. The Scorpion Kings I and II waged war against Menes/Narmer and an individual named Ka. Narmer defeated these predynastic kings to establish a politically unified Upper and Lower Egypt, ruled from Thinis where he had previously been nomarch, inaugurating the First Dynasty of ancient Egypt. Archaeology supports this sequence of events: A study of pottery fragments from digs in Lower Egypt reveals a dramatic and complete transformation in manufacturing style around Narmer's victory, from the localized Tasian culture to that of Upper Egyptian Naqada III (I. Shaw, 2000).

The People of the Black Soil

Social Structure

We must not impose our western concepts of social structure upon ancient Egyptian society. There was no recognizable class system, with its upper, middle and lower strata, though, even in the Predynastic Period, we see evidence in Egyptian burials of a developing hierarchical structure based on wealth. Instead, the fabric of Egyptian society was woven upon a framework of rights and freedoms, the nature and extent of which defined the social category to which an individual man or woman belonged. The real possibility of upward (or, at times, downward) movement between categories is a distinguishing feature of ancient Egyptian civilization, in stark contrast to the modern-day caste system of some eastern cultures, which is rigid and inflexible. Of the four categories of ancient Egyptian social structure, defined by the relative possession of these rights and freedoms, the ones that offer the slightest chance of mobility are slaves and royalty.

Royalty

Royalty was the narrowest social category, encompassing the

immediate family of the reigning Pharaoh, his parents, and full aunts and uncles. The chief of Pharaoh's many wives was considered royalty as well; his other wives were not. A commoner who married to become Pharaoh's chief wife was granted royalty, as was the common wife of an individual who assumed the throne after their marriage. The royal family was given full economic support while they lived together in palatial accommodations, yet they retained the right to work if they chose. The granting of power to royal family members was not automatic; many had to work to demonstrate proficiency and earn promotions. Work most often involved government positions, from which the family member or Pharaoh himself could exercise leverage over government departments. This was especially true of Pharaoh's sons, all of whom would be groomed so that one or another—usually, but not always, the eldest—could succeed his father in the pharaonic dynasty, either reigning concurrently with or upon the death of his father.

Free Citizens

Two things defined free Egyptian citizens: the right to travel and the right to enter into contractual arrangements such as buying or selling property or other possessions, buildings, or animals. Free citizens, therefore, exercised some control over their own lives, unlike serfs and slaves. They could also enter into marriage contracts with the parents of a prospective spouse. In this regard, men and women enjoyed equal rights under the law while, on the other hand, occupations were strictly gender-defined: women performed all the duties of managing their households, while men engaged in outside occupations such as farming, herding, craftsmanship, or business. It is estimated that slightly under half of the Egyptian population consisted of free citizens by the Middle and New Kingdom Periods.

Serfs

Serfs did not control their lives but were completely controlled; they had no freedom to initiate legal, contractual arrangements, including marriage, though they could choose to live with a partner and raise children. However, a free citizen could decide to marry a serf, whom the master must first free. According to Brier, "serfs belonged to the land, hence changed masters only as the land changed hands" (Brier & A Hoyt Hobbs, 2013). Masters expected absolute obedience from their serfs, who were considered their property. Nevertheless, serfs could, and did, attain the status of free citizens through the good graces of their masters who might elevate them to positions of responsibility and authority. Or a serf might distinguish himself on the battlefield, meaning his freedom in that way.

Slaves

Slaves, like serfs, were under absolute control and could be bought, sold, and traded like chattel. They had no rights and no freedoms. Slavery, like serfdom, was a hereditary status; the children of slaves were automatically slaves themselves. Because only foreigners captured in war could be slaves, there were no slaves in the Early Kingdom days of Egypt since she had not yet flexed her military muscle against other peoples and taken captives. However, once Egypt had undertaken numerous military campaigns, the ranks of slaves grew and could be utilized in hard or dangerous labor situations, particularly mining or quarry work.

At Least it's Work: Occupations in Egyptian Society
Farmers

If Egypt is the gift of the Nile, then it is equally valid that farmers who cultivated the soil and grew their crops according to the clockwork regularity of the inundation were the gift of Egypt. Egyptians constructed their calendar entirely around the natural rhythms of the inundation and, therefore, of agriculture. Egypt had only three seasons, each consisting of four 30-day months. The first season of the year was called Akhet, the time of the inundation (Haney, n.d.). The first day of the new year corresponded to the arrival of the floodwaters at the First Cataract adjacent to Elephantine Island, in the far south of the country. Government clerks would watch for the water to surge around the rocks out of supposed underground caverns in which, according to Egyptian belief, the God of inundation, Hapy, lived to favor the people with this annual gift. From the first day that the waters began to rise—Egypt's New Year's Day—officials would periodically measure the height of the surge on a "Nilometer" that measured in cubits the magnitude of the inundation. Such officials communicated the information gathered to Pharaoh and his government officials, who devised estimates of the coming year's agricultural productivity. These estimates, in turn, formed the basis for the taxation of the people of Egypt at harvest.

Egyptians used two different types of Nilometer in ancient Egypt, depending on the location along the river. The first was portable and could be repositioned to zero every year to account for increased water height due to the previous flooding sedimentary deposits. The second type of Nilometer was fixed rather than portable: It resembled a narrow stone staircase whose risers were carved with numbers to measure the height of the Nile in cubits. The lowermost stair indicated the zero point—the average level of the Nile before inundation. Unfortunately, less than thirty fixed Nilometers have been found intact from one end to the other of the Nile Valley.

Based on accumulated information from previous years, officials could estimate the success or disaster of that year's crops. If the water was too high, Egyptian people could anticipate extreme flooding, possibly losing life and income. If the Nile surge was lower than usual, it could mean ensuing famine. Reflecting upon the Nile's variability, Wilkinson quotes the Roman historian, Pliny, who observed that.

An average rise is one of sixteen cubits [twenty-seven feet]. A smaller volume of water does not irrigate all localities, and a larger one by retiring too slowly retards agriculture...in a rise of twelve cubits [Egypt] senses famine, and even at one of thirteen it begins to feel hungry, but fourteen cubits brings cheerfulness, fifteen complete confidence and sixteen delight. (Wilkinson, Toby, 2015)

As the inundation swept through the Nile Valley, making farming impossible, farmers would use the opportunity to repair their homes and tools and prepare for the next season, named Peret, or emergence (Haney, n.d.). Egypt had developed a system of irrigation canals to take the precious alluvial soils of the inundation further inland to cultivate a larger area of crops. Unfortunately, the sometimes-torrential waters of the inundation might have disturbed or damaged the canals or filled them with silt. Therefore, the first step of emergence was to dig out, repair, and reconstruct all their irrigation canals. When the water had finally receded, leaving behind the rich black soil that gave Egypt the name Kemet (Haney, n.d.), farmers would return to their fields to plow, then to break up the clods of moist earth, and finally to scatter seed into the furrows. If a farmer were fortunate to own cattle, they would do the work of pulling the plow while he leaned his weight on the back to ensure deep furrows. Usually, a son walked before the team, guiding it in straight lines. If a farmer had no cattle, two men would take their place in the traces to do the hard work of pulling. Once the women had scattered seeds into the furrows, they tossed straw over the top, encouraging their sheep to mash the seeds into the soft soil with their hooves. A period of waiting and anticipation followed planting, while farmers performed the strenuous daily task of nurturing their crops to harvest. Water needed to be drawn from the Nile in buckets and emptied into the canals. There were regular chores to occupy them while they waited for their crops to ripen—and, of course, there were always weeds to pull!

Finally, everyone welcomed the third and final season of the year, Shemu, the harvest (Haney, n.d.). Government officials would pass through the Nile Valley, measuring the fields and taxing them at the rate established months before on the first day of inundation. Once the officials' assessment was complete, entire families would move into the fields to harvest their crops before weather conditions or animals could affect them. Egyptian farmers utilized the same harvesting process 5000 years ago as is currently employed in many parts of Africa and the Mediterranean region today. First, grain heads were cut off, gathered into piles, and bound into sheaves. Next, the men loaded these sheaves onto donkeys to be carried to the threshing floor, where they were thrown down and trampled by oxen. This process threshed, or separated, the heavier heads of grain from the lighter chaff so that it could be winnowed, that is, tossed into the air with large scoops, allowing the wind to carry away the chaff and leave the grain behind. Heads of farming households then distributed the gathered grain among their farming families according to how many sheaves each had brought to the threshing floor. Then farm families would take the opportunity to rest, repair their tools, and await the next sign of inundation, sometimes within days of harvest. Since the Egyptian year was 365 days long and the three seasons occupied 360 of these, a short five days' respite from the work was their only downtime. The annual cycle of Akhet, Peret, and Shemu defined Egyptians' existence and depended for its clockwork regularity upon the ability of its citizens to predict the inundation of the Nile which sustained them. So dependent were they on the inundation that any severe or prolonged reduction in the river's flow that occurred throughout the Old Kingdom (Bell, 1970) and likely through some or all of the First Intermediate Period, spelled economic, social, and political disaster.

Scribes

Given the enormous size of Egypt's government and religious bureaucracies, it is no surprise that the category of the scribe is second only to that of farmers in size. Scribes were employed on many levels, both in the public and private sectors, and were thereby exposed to opportunities for advancement. Those who worked as freelancers would sell their services to local patrons or priests. In contrast, others more fortunate could find lower-level government positions that held the possibility of promotion depending upon the scribe's skill. Because their training involved advanced courses in mathematics and basic building practices, they could be employed in government building projects, such as characterized the Early Kingdom or 'age of the pyramids,' indeed a productive time at all levels of trade and commerce. Unlike that of farmers, the schedules of scribes were dictated more by their patrons on an as-needed basis.

Once a scribe had completed his training, he was allowed to wear the uniform of a scribe: a long skirt instead of the traditional kilts of other professions. He would also be seen carrying a stone palette with two carved depressions which served as inkpots, one black and the other red, and writing brushes to perform his duties. The function of the two colors of the ink becomes quite apparent by analogy with another document. For example, you may be familiar with specific editions of the Judeo-Christian Bible, which highlight the words of Christ in red while the bulk of the biblical text is printed in black. Egyptian scribes used black ink for body text and red for chapter headings or highlighting a pertinent word or phrase. A perfect example of this is the "Hymn to the Nile Flood," written on papyrus in Middle Egyptian, presumably during the Middle Kingdom Period (Hymn to the Nile flood, 2002). The scribe who recorded the lyrics used red ink for the first words of the first verse, which comprise the title, "Hymn to Hapy." The rest of the verse is written in black ink. Successive stanzas display this same distinction.

All scribal duties were predicated upon one crucial condition: The scribe-to-be must be literate. Masters expended great effort teaching their apprentices the minutiae of writing hieroglyphics. Once a student had successfully learned the Egyptian language in its hieroglyphic form, he still had two other forms, more cursive than pictorial, to learn. As with any acquired skill, tremendous effort produced better results and more significant opportunities. Mediocrity in learning the written Egyptian language consigned the overtly successful scribe to a life of humble clerking and accounting duties. Achievers could envision a future more attractive and even more lucrative than that of their average classmates.

Craftsmen

It was essential for the craftsman working in Egyptian society to find pleasure and pride in what he produced, for society afforded him little respect. He could not read like the scribe. His products couldn't feed multitudes or fill the green storage bins of the Egyptian people. The tools with which he worked were rudimentary, and yet, with those tools, he could make precious works of art, some of which have survived to this day. Craftsmanship was most often carried out under a system of patronage. The crafting of jewelry, statues, or other works of art required a supply of raw materials out of the reach of an independent craftsman. The most precious jewels and metals were reserved for the pharaoh and his government officials. Private patrons or estates could hire an artisan on an ad hoc basis to create a particular piece of art or jewelry; patrons would be responsible for providing the raw materials for their projects and accommodation, food, and the like. Some artisans were fortunate enough to be taken on permanently and were employed full-time by their patrons. The quality of their lives depended upon the goodwill of their patron, and patrons had the right to demand time and effort from their craftsman. Under these circumstances, the lives of craftsmen were not their own. It was possible, in theory, for an artisan in an unsatisfactory patronage relationship to seek out another patron, but chances were not always suitable for success in that venture.

Artisans learned craftsmanship in an apprentice/master relationship. No instruction manuals existed because the knowledge required to know the trade was securely in the mind of the master. The work of artisans was usually passed from father to son through successive generations. Once the sun had attained the appropriate skill level, he was obligated to make his way and, hopefully, secure a good patron or a good position. The most fortunate craftsman in Egyptian society ended up working for the royal court, where their working conditions and the supply of raw materials was exemplary. But like the pyramids themselves, the opportunities for such positions at the top were smaller than at the bottom.

Businessmen

Business people occupy a smaller proportion of the working

population in Egypt than in other trades and professions. In large part, this was because the wealthy could afford their own workshops and buy their materials so that they did not need the goods of independent businessmen. There was little left over to barter in the local marketplace for lower-income clients, who had barely enough to provide for their own needs. Nor could independent business people exchange goods with foreign visitors since that avenue of trade was entirely under the control of central government agencies and their brokers. On the whole, it was not a profession with any kind of job and economic security.

Quarrymen and Miners
When we gaze with awe and amazement at the achievements of Egypt, in particular, the glorious monuments of the Early Kingdom, known today as the Age of the Pyramids, it would be easy to lavish praise on the builders and architects who devised and designed these wonders, who orchestrated supply chains and the building of pyramid towns such as the one at the foot of the Giza plateau, or who coordinated the efforts of tens of thousands of workers from all over the Nile Valley, for twenty years of non-stop production.

These workers deserve their share of praise. But then I think of these statistics for the Great Pyramid of Khufu: 2,300,000 blocks of limestone, averaging 2 tons in weight, to be moved into place on successive courses, dressed, then positioned at the rate of one block every two minutes, 10 hours per day, seven days a week, over 7,300 or more days. Even if crews worked shifts of several days with rest days in between, the work must have been crushing. Do many hands make light work under such circumstances?

It is telling that there are no records (of which I'm aware) of the numbers of quarrymen who suffered heat stroke, broken or mangled limbs, back injuries, or death at the lowest levels of the production hierarchy. Given the nature of this and many other building projects in the glory days of ancient Egypt, quarrymen were essential workers. No limestone equals no building. Yet their tools were rudimentary, barely sufficient for the magnitude of their responsibilities. Yes, the limestone they quarried was of the softer variety, unlike that which supported the foundations of the pyramids. Still, their chisels were made of copper or bronze, the edges of which were quickly dulled, likewise the points of their picks. Lucky quarrymen worked the open pits to free their massive blocks, only to watch their counterparts have to pull them up the slope of the plateau on sleds and move them up the courses of the pyramid.

Quarrymen did all this work, day after day, for 20 years, under the harsh and unforgiving Eye of Ra, a scorching sun in a country with no clouds nor any rain. The 'resurrection machines' of the pharaohs could rightly be considered monumental tributes to the workers who risked their lives only to disappear into the sands of time.

Herders

Since the introduction of domestic livestock to the Nile Valley in the sixth millennium BCE, herders have occupied a vital role in the economy of the Egyptian people. The description of their job bears little difference to that of a herdsman in our day: Some cared for smaller herds on farm estates, their own or others while larger herds were attended by more nomadic herdsmen who roamed the plains with thousands of cattle, sheep, and goats. These herdsmen lived and moved with their herds: watching out for predators, seeking fresh pastoring areas and water sources, and tending to injured animals. And like the ranchers and herders of our day, roundups, last sewing, and branding were the herders' stock in trade. Briar and Hobbes point out another similarity with our day: Cattle were branded on the right shoulder to identify their owners. The only difference? The brand was in hieroglyphics!

Marshmen

Marshmen, it seems, were the unsung heroes and free spirits of ancient Egypt. Their privilege was to gather precious papyrus, the nation's national vegetation, from the papyrus marshes of the Delta, which they called Mohit. Almost one-third of Egypt was covered with water throughout the year, providing plenty of work and shelter for this unique niche of the working population. Their work outfit consisted of little more than a loincloth or, in some cases, no clothing at all.

Papyrus was a vital national commodity, given that all official writing was inscribed on its pages. In addition to providing the raw materials for elite scribal work, papyrus could also be used to manufacture the boats used by marshmen and for their homes. Stocks of papers could be lashed together at specific links to form a lightweight craft that marshmen could pole through the papyrus thickets. Those same bundles of papyrus bound together and patched with mud became the walls and roofs of their homes. Papyrus stems grew to upwards of 10 feet high. Marshmen could pull their boats through the thickets, cutting the papyrus stalks below the waterline, stacking them, and bundling them for personal or commercial use. If the papyrus were destined to become writing material, the bundles would be delivered to papermakers who sliced the stems lengthwise into thin strips;

cut the fibers into roughly one-foot lengths; and then layered them in alternating horizontal and vertical directions.

The stacks of papers were beaten with a wooden mallet, compressing the fibers and extruding their juices which, when dry, formed a kind of glue that held the layers together, producing a fine writing surface for the scribes. To finish their work the scribes trimmed the edges of the sheets and smoothed them with a polishing stone. Individual sheets could be glued together to form scrolls. In addition to papyrus harvesting, marshmen enjoyed the freedom to hunt and fish in the marshlands of the Delta. What a contrast to the narrow economy and precarious position of an Egyptian businessman!

CHAPTER 3
GODS AND GODDESSES

Egyptian religion didn't germinate from the literary creations of some great author such as Homer, as did the religion of the Greeks, or from a syncretistic process of assimilation such as that of the Roman empire, which adopted the gods of the conquered and latinized them. Instead, with the possible exception of Sumerian religion and Mesopotamian culture, the development of the Egyptian religion follows an entirely original trajectory: it developed directly and organically out of the human evolutionary process known as the Cognitive Revolution.

However, as *H. erectus* moved away from the trees to walk upright on the Savannah, it likely shared the primitive characteristics of its primate forebears (think of chimpanzees living in troops, caring for their young, asserting dominance, and demonstrating the hierarchical organization which enabled them to survive and to thrive). Still, at this early stage, there is no evidence of ritual, certainly not of religion. *H. heidelbergensis*, a likely descendant of *H. erectus*, demonstrated developed tactical and survival skills, the refinements in tool manufacture and hunting skills, and advances related to the ability to coordinate survival efforts within the larger community: the building of 'group homes,' rudimentary wood and hide shelters with hearths to control fire, to cook, to warm themselves against the cold, to protect against predators. These abilities were evidenced on the north coast of the Mediterranean Sea as early as 400,000 BCE (Terra Amata (archaeological site), 2021) at precisely the same time as their siblings roamed southern and eastern Africa. From a grave dated to around that time unearthed in what is now Germany, there is a suggestion of the first evidence of ritual behavior by *H. heidelbergensis*. Thirty bodies were thrown into a pit, together with several artifacts and one well-crafted, double-edged hand ax (Smithsonian's National Museum of Natural History, 2010).

The digging of a pit to inter human remains, rather than simply to leave them to the natural processes of decay and predation, may seem of little consequence. But, as we begin to see from those pit burials unearthed around the Nile Valley in the mesolithic and particularly in the Neolithic period, by which time early *Homo sapiens* had arrived on the scene, there is a progression in ritual connected to the internment of human remains which leads directly to the complex burial rituals and, yes, to the pyramids of historical Egypt.

We will return to this subject in chapter 7, discussing Egyptian burial practices and the building of the pyramids, and in chapter 8, when we unravel the mysterious process of mummification. But here is one tantalizing hint of the direction in which *Homo* was moving in prehistoric Egypt: Many of the buried remains thus far uncovered were found in shallow pits, in a contracted or fetal position, lying on their left side, head pointing to the south and facing to the west. Why so intentional a burial regimen? This question intrigues us. It beckons us to get inside the head of those who cared for their buried dead in such a purposeful, if obscure, way. Some bodies were wrapped, or at least covered, with hides or, in the early Neolithic period, with woven mats or both (I. Shaw, 2000). *Homo neanderthalensis* was discovered to bury its dead deliberately and to leave grave markers, even flowers, on top of the graves. This was the first such ceremonial behavior in the *Homo* family tree (Smithsonian's National Museum of Natural History, 2010). The earliest known mummy associated with Egyptian culture was a young *Homo sapiens* female "wrapped in linen and fur" who died around 3500 BCE

(Geggel, 2017). She was buried more than 300 years before Menes/Narmur conquered the northern kingdom, taking the Red Crown of Upper Egypt and the White Crown of Lower Egypt as the first historical ruler of the unified country.

Likely by the time our young, linen-and-fur-wrapped lady was buried, and before the creation of that unifying government under Narmur in 3150 BCE, Egypt possessed, according to Bob Brier, "all the characteristics of a country except one" (Brier & A Hoyt Hobbs, 2013, p. 10). The most significant of those characteristics (aside from strong centralized government), he implies, is that the Egyptian people "spoke a common language and shared similar religious beliefs" (Brier & A Hoyt Hobbs, 2013, p. 10). Though we can, of course, infer the existence of verbal communication, and possibly some primitive form of language from the physiology of the hominid (pre-Sapiens), remains discovered thus far in the Nile Valley, it was the Cognitive Revolution which set *Homo sapiens* apart from its predecessors, according to Yuval Harari (Harari, 2014). Our species was able to coordinate its efforts, to work collaboratively, and to communicate effectively on a scale impossible for its smaller-brained predecessors to achieve and, ultimately, to dominate the entire world. We'll unpack Harari's claims later in this and the following chapter because they hold the key to our understanding of how stone-age people such as the Egyptians could establish a civilization that endured and thrived far longer than any other since.

For the first time, humans could give voice to more than the immediate, concrete facts of daily life—how to recognize an edible plant, where to locate a herd of gazelle or giant buffalo, when to light a fire for warmth or how to fashion a flint into a hand-ax. They could appreciate the abstract and the intangible, and grapple with ideas of past and future, not merely the present moment. *H. sapiens* could frame universal questions of existence, such as: where did we come from? Why does such-and-such happen? What happens when we die?

The answers they came up with and the stories which framed those answers, shared around the hearth-fire after a day of hunting or whispered to a child as they lay on their sleeping mat under a warm fur blanket or intoned at the graveside of a departed elder—these answers and these stories became the vessels for an emerging Egyptian worldview, in which the gods and their interaction with man and his world were foundational to human existence. We will read some of the essential stories in chapter 5. Now, from our vantage point of five millennia of history, we call these stories myths. But to the Egyptian people, from serf to Pharaoh and everywhere between, these stories described the most profound and significant realities. If we are to appreciate these stories as did the ancient Egyptian people, we must set aside our modern-day perspectives and prejudices and try to see the world as they might have seen it. As we do, we will come face to face with what Bob Brier has labeled the "great paradox of ancient Egypt" (Brier & A Hoyt Hobbs, 2013).

The Great Paradox of Ancient Egypt

In the introduction to their book, *Ancient Egypt: Everyday Life in the Land of the Nile* (2013), Bob Brier and Hoyt Hobbs enumerate some of the multitudes of accomplishments that exemplify ancient Egyptian culture, from engineering and architecture to strong government and military might, from clothing and diet to medicine and art. Then they make this bold and insightful statement: "Their buildings, architecture, clothing, food, and medicine may have been thousands of years ahead of their time, but their view of the world was closer to a prehistoric caveman's than to ours" (Brier & A Hoyt Hobbs, 2013).

It seems from that statement that Brier and Hobbs find the crux of their paradox in the primitive nature of the Egyptian worldview rather than in the magnitude of their accomplishments. However, we want to turn that thinking on its head! Instead of asking how a civilization boasting of such accomplishments as Egypt has produced could be so primitive in its worldview, we should ask ourselves how the Egyptian civilization, birthed directly out of the New Stone Age and retaining her Neolithic mindset, could achieve the precocious marvels for which she is known. The answer to that question may very well be the key to understanding how this precocious, infant civilization endured well beyond any other in history. For clues to that answer, we will look, in a moment, to Yuval Noah Harari and his discussion of the power of stories (Harari, 2014).

We have seen previously how the unified nation of Egypt sprang, seemingly fully formed, from the evolutionary river of the Paleolithic and Neolithic eras. There was no Nilotic civilization that existed before Egypt and from which it could arise. There was no science to inform and explain the Egyptians' world (Brier & A Hoyt Hobbs, 2013, p. 43). But the occurrence of natural phenomena demanded an explanation. If that explanation were not visible and apparent to the watching eye, then it must be invisible–invisible and powerful. The welcome and sometimes deadly heat of the sun, or the desirable but sometimes disastrous arrival of the inundation, must be the manifestation of some hidden agency. It was not a great leap for people to ascribe the workings of nature to powerful, unseen deities.

The inhabitants of the Nile Valley were recent descendants of those who chose to settle while others of their species departed, with all or most of their Neanderthal cousins, in the Out-of-Africa migration around 65,000 BCE. Geographically isolated and insulated at first from any significant outside cultural influence by the pre-existing cultures of the Fertile Crescent, the People of the Black Soil entered history as those "who looked both forward and back," manifesting "a paradoxical combination of startlingly modern accomplishments with incredibly ancient thought processes" (Brier & A Hoyt Hobbs, 2013, p. 2). Of these ancient thought processes, Brier and Hobbs write:

They saw the universe as inhabited by a panoply of gods—spirits that controlled every natural phenomenon and left an Egyptian feeling powerless, dependent on prayers and offerings to entice gods to accomplish what he could not do on his own. Rather than individuals pursuing their own destiny, ancient Egyptians acted like helpless pets waiting for whatever their masters, the gods, might provide (Brier & A Hoyt Hobbs, 2013).

At the zenith of their civilization, the Egyptian people collectively worshipped as many as 1,000 gods and goddesses–truly a panoply. Unfortunately, the scope of this book prevents us from meeting all of them. Still, in chapter five, we will have an opportunity to greet many of the lead actors later in this chapter and consider their roles in the most significant myths of Egyptian culture. Whether the Egyptians' incredibly ancient thought processes, specifically their well-developed belief in the power and unseen presence of this multitude of gods who controlled every aspect of their lives, left them feeling powerless, dependent or helpless, seems to border on conjecture. We cannot see their feelings, no matter how knowledgeable we have become regarding their civilization. What we can see is the outworking of their beliefs: the tombs and their inscriptions; monumental temples like that of the sun-god at Karnak, and lesser temples scattered throughout the land; religious literature such as the Pyramid and Coffin Texts; and the massive network of priests and religious workers who administer the rites of Egyptian religion on behalf of the people, in service to the gods and Pharaoh, god-on-earth. Despite Egypt's history of achievement followed by periods of internal strife, even civil war, and of increasing conflict with foreign aggressors, Egyptian civilization's single most significant galvanizing force has been its shared beliefs.

Speech, Fiction, and the Birth of a Civilization

Earlier, we heard Brier and Hobbs speak of the emergence of Egyptian civilization at the end of the Neolithic period (c. 3150 BCE) and how it "possessed all the characteristics of a country except one," namely, a unifying central government (Brier & Hoyt Hobbs, 2013, p. 10). The victory of Narmur secured the latter. Now there may be any number of characteristics which, taken together, define a country, yet, interestingly, Brier and Hobbs enumerated only two: the speaking of a common language and the sharing of similar religious beliefs (Brier & Hoyt Hobbs, 2013). Most fascinating is that the development of precisely these two elements—the capacity to conceive of fictions, not merely to understand concrete facts, and the ability to share them via a common language—characterizes what Yuval Noah Harari has dubbed the Cognitive Revolution of *H. sapiens*. These modern humans occurred between 70,000 BCE and 30,000 BCE (Harari, 2014). When we pull apart Harari's argument for the extraordinary, earth-changing impact of this singular evolutionary event, we'll discover the profound significance of communal belief in the gods, goddesses, myths, and traditions which inhabited the worldview of ancient Egyptian civilization.

The Cognitive Revolution of *Homo Sapiens*

Harari makes the intriguing and straightforward observation that "beginning about 70,000 years ago, *Homo sapiens* started doing very special things" (Harari, 2014, p. 18). I can't help but imagine a slight upturn to the corner of his mouth, at the humor of such a massive understatement. Within 5,000 years or so (the blink of an eye in evolutionary time), representative modern humans would depart East Africa to take over the world! In the process, they would eradicate *H. erectus,* their evolutionary grandfather, *H. heidelbergensis,* their father, and *H. neanderthalensis,* their sibling, with whom their species had shared the planet for almost 200,000 years. Thus, a multi-species mankind would be reduced, by around 40,000 BCE, to one species: *my kind.*

The keys to this 160,000-year process of bringing the whole world under *sapiens* domination could be found in two places, that is, on their tongues and in their imaginations. As Harari says, "The appearance of new ways of thinking and communicating, between 70,000 and 30,000 years ago, constitutes the Cognitive Revolution" (2014, p. 19). The upshot of this revolution was that, for the first time, man was free to conceptualize, dream, *imagine* things beyond the empirical scope, and share these things with others.

[T]he truly unique feature of our language is not its ability to transmit information about men and lions. Rather, it's the ability to transmit information about things that do not exist at all. As far as we know, only Sapiens can talk about entire kinds of entities that they have never seen, touched, or smelled (Harari, 2014, p. 23).

Harari categorizes these "kinds of entities," including "legends, myths, gods, and religions," as types of fiction which enable us to imagine things "*collectively*" (2014, p. 23) and "to cooperate flexibly in large numbers." These fictions, he says, were the product of the Cognitive Revolution (2014, p. 24). Putting aside for the moment Harari's atheistic bias, we might ask the question, at what point in time did modern humans living in the Nile Valley first begin to entertain the fiction of a divine realm, populated with such a diverse and colorful cast of characters as the gods and goddesses of Egypt? How and with whom did they share their stories? We can never know for sure. If we were to use our imagination, however, we might soon find ourselves sitting quietly inside a fringe of warm hearth-glow, where a young father stirs ashen embers with a pointed stick. At the same time, the mother speaks in hushed tones to the child sitting in her lap, blanketed with furs and wrapped snugly in her arms. She has been telling story after story of those very gods and goddesses. If we listen carefully, we might be able to hear some of those stories for ourselves. Let's listen, then...

The Gods of Chaos

The Ogdoad

Let me tell you about the Eightfold, or Ogdoad, who existed from primordial times and were worshipped from antiquity. The Ogdoad was a group of primordial gods and goddesses who embodied the qualities or characteristics of the primordial chaos from which arose the *benben*, or primeval mound of creation. The word primordial refers to a time before time and space, an indefinite period before the world's creation. The central location for their worship was initially called Eight Town but was later changed to Hermopolis Magna (Pinch, 2004). The Eightfold is therefore often referred to as the Ogdoad of Hermopolis. The Ogdoad consisted of four male deities and their female counterparts, each pair representing a particular quality of the primordial chaos. Bob Brier maintains that, concerning myths and the deities they involve, we know that they are not meant to be taken literally, but we can understand the realities they represent (Brier, 1999). So, for example, one of the divine pairs of the Ogdoad is the god Nun and his counterpart Nunet, who personify the primordial waters out of which the mound arose.

Amun, whose name means the Hidden One, and Amunet, his female counterpart, likely represent the formlessness of the primordial state. Amun was sometimes described as part of the Eightfold and as the one who brought the eight into existence together with the world. When he and Amunet are absent from the Eightfold, their place is most frequently occupied by the divine pair, Nia and Niat, representing the primordial void from which all things sprang. Kek and Keket embody darkness. Notice the striking parallel between this personified description of the primordial chaos and that of the Judeo-Christian creation account: "Now the earth was formless and void, and darkness was upon the face of the waters" (Gen. 1:2, KJV). The Ogdoad was either represented in temple carvings in human form or else with the males having frog heads and the females, snake heads. According to Geraldine Pinch, "the Ogdoad seem to be forces that the creator has to subdue before the work of creation can begin. In others, they simply seem to die after bringing forth life" (Pinch, 2004).

The Creator Gods

Amun and Amunet

Amun, the creator god, is portrayed as either one of the Ogdoad of Hermopolis or as the creator god of the Eightfold. In his capacity as creator, he stands apart from, and exercises his power over, the qualities of chaos represented by the four pairs of gods he speaks into existence at the beginning of creation. When Atum is depicted in the role of the creator god, Amun and Amunet form the fourth pair, representing headedness or invisibility of the primordial chaos. His origins are somewhat obscure. In the Pyramid Texts Amun and Amunet are divine protectors of the king. Amun was the chief God of the Theban religion by the Middle Kingdom, believed to rule as a divine pharaoh from his cult temple at Karnak. His new consort there was named Mut and his son Khonsu. Unlike other Egyptian gods, Amun was not tethered to any locality or even to a divine realm. Instead, Egyptians imagined him as omnipresent, close at hand, and ready to aid his human children, be they pharaohs or servants. He seemed, in a sense, to be more approachable and involved in the lives of his creation.

Amun was most often portrayed as a bearded man in the prime of life. Later, in the New Kingdom, mythology brought his latent virility to the forefront. Amun was purported to unite sexually with the queen of Egypt to produce divine-human offspring. Amun may have been linked with the ram during the Middle Kingdom to embody male virility and sexual potency. When united with the sun god Ra, Amun became the originator of all life. Perhaps, though, his name is most familiar to our ears as the latter part of the name of one of the most famous pharaohs in our western experience: Tutankhamun!

Atum

Atum, whose name means completion or totality, is the preeminent deity among the Ennead, or Nine, of Heliopolis. Atum is the first of gods, the Self-Created, having risen from the surrounding waters with the *benben*, or primordial mound. Alone and lonely, Atum is said to have masturbated and then swallowed his semen, creating two offspring, the twins Shu and Tefnut. Atum is depicted as representing the setting sun. Egyptians believed him to embody the potential for all life.

Ra, the Sun God

It is entirely straightforward to characterize Ra, god of the sun: all that the Egyptian people perceived the sun over their heads to be, and to do, are the most apparent characteristics of Ra himself. The sun is the bringer of light, and the giver of life, particularly to the crops planted out of the inundation which depended upon it to bring them to fruition. Without the light of the sun, men could not work to feed their families and their animals. Without its heat, they would suffer, even perish. The regular appearance of the sun at dawn and its setting at dusk represented the order of Maat which pushed away chaos and gave security to the Egyptian people. As it traveled from horizon to horizon, it dominated the upper sky and was the brightest light therein, outshining all other lights. The sun traveled in its visible arc across the upper sky, which was the realm of Horus. So, Ra became associated in the people's minds with Horus and was called Ra of Horus of the Two Horizons. He was sometimes depicted with the body of a man and the head of a falcon, representing Horus, crowned with a coiled cobra. The cobra imagery represents the Eye of Ra, which looks down upon the earth, and the manifestation of Horus himself, whose two eyes are said to be the sun and the moon.

The Eye of Ra also had a negative connotation under certain circumstances. For example, when the Nile failed to rise and the land became parched, the unmerciful Eye of Ra could be seen above, sending its scorching heat to cause famine and death. It would have been difficult for the Egyptian people not to infer from Ra's divine judgment for their sins and failures.

Their mythology already contained stories of Ra sending forth his eye to exact punishment upon his creatures who were said to be created from the tears of that same Eye.

The cyclical journey of Ra, the visible sun, over the earth, across the upper sky, and through the Underworld, Duat, every 24 hours evidenced his power and rule over all creation. Ra, therefore, came to be understood as the greatest of all gods. The rise of the sun cult toward the end of the Early Kingdom was a tacit acknowledgement of this shift in Ra's status. The pharaohs increasingly sought to identify with Ra instead of Horus to bolster their claims to divinity by the end of the Fifth Dynasty. This tradition continued throughout the rest of ancient Egyptian history. Thus, Pharaoh came to be regarded as the son of Ra, ruling with the absolute power of his divine Father.

Ptah

Ptah was a vital creator God of Egyptian mythology whose worship was centered in the Egyptian capital of Memphis. The city of Memphis in ancient times radiated outward from the central temple of Ptah. The image of Ptah was that of a bearded man with beautiful blue skin, wearing an artisan's cap and cloak. He carried a scepter whose symbols combined the ideas of dominion, stability, and life. He was said to bestow these on the pharaohs, often crowned at his temple in Memphis.

Ptah was said to have made the world with his heart and his tongue, the heart being the center of thought and purpose and the tongue, the instrument of power, speaking a word that made things come to be. By the Middle Kingdom era, Ptah's creative power as a divine craftsman gave him the ability to craft the bodies of humans and the new bodies of the dead. Ptah was recognized as the patron of metalworkers and sculptors. Ptah was intimately linked to Osiris and, by extension, the Egyptian mummification process. In the Middle Kingdom and later, spells and incantations were inscribed inside the lids of the coffins of the deceased as helps in the afterlife. These were appropriately called 'Coffin Texts.' One of these Coffin Texts relates how Ptah helped Horus to break open the mouth of Osiris so that he could breathe. This event had its practical counterpart in the opening of the mouth ceremony performed at every funeral for the people of Egypt. One of the last steps in the ceremony was performed by a priest of Ptah who, using a small silver instrument, symbolically opened the mouth of the mummified deceased by touching the lips and reciting a prayer over the body. This last and most important right of burial could only be performed and orchestrated by a priest of Ptah.

Later conceptions of Ptah, such as in Memphite theology, position him as the self-created creator. He made everything with his heart and tongue. That is, his thoughts and speech. Ptah has also been associated with the Ogdoad, particularly Nun and Nunet, which gave birth to Atum. Ptah is similarly portrayed as taking the place of Shu in the separation of earth and sky to open up a space for creation to occur.

Khnum

Khnum was usually depicted as a man with the head of a longhorn ram. Khnum was responsible for the creation of human and animal bodies and giving them life and health. He was often portrayed sitting at a potter's wheel crafting the bodies. This divine creation of human and animal life was understood not as an event never to be repeated. It was an ongoing process for Khnum to craft human and animal life all the time, every day. His work is never done.

Khnum was believed to control the inundation, and he personified the life-giving force of the annual flood. He was a chief God of the First Cataract adjacent to Elephantine Island beneath which, people believed, were twin caverns containing the inundation water.

The Created Gods: the Ennead of Heliopolis

Shu

Shu is one of the twin offspring of Atum and one of the nine primordial gods of the Ennead of Heliopolis. He is often depicted wearing a feather on his head. Shu is the god of dry air and sunlight who separates the earth from the upper sky. After Atum had masturbated and then swallowed his own semen to recreate himself, he sneezed out Shu and spat out his twin sister Tefnut. After Shu had sex with his sister, she gave birth to two children: Geb, god of the earth, and Nut, goddess of the sky. When Shu later discovered his children, Geb and Nut, locked in a passionate embrace, he separated them. That act of separating the sky above from the earth below opened up a space that enabled creation to proceed.

Tefnut

Tefnut is "the greatly beloved daughter" (Pinch, 2004, p. 197) of Atum and the twin sister and sexual partner of her brother Shu. Tefnut may have some association with moisture, perhaps the morning dew, according to Pinch (2004, p. 196). She has the distinction of having given birth to Geb, god of the earth, and Nut, goddess of the sky, whom their father Shu was forced to separate because of their physical indiscretions.

Geb

Geb is a pivotal figure in Egyptian mythology. God of the earth, Geb, is the son of Tefnut by her brother-mate Shu and brother of Nut, goddess of the sky. Geb and his sister-mate Nut represent the third generation of divinities that comprise the Ennead of Heliopolis. The forcible separation of Geb from his sister Nut while they were in each other's arms has given rise to one of the iconic creation stories of Egyptian mythology. Despite their interrupted passion, Gen and Nut became the parents of five of the most important divinities of Egyptian myth: Osiris, Isis, Nephthys, Horus the elder, and Seth. Geb was often depicted as human in keeping with his preeminent role as God of the earth. His skin was occasionally painted green to represent the vegetation that springs from the world, and he personifies the ground upon which living creatures can crawl.

Geb was considered the leader of the Ennead and the king of all kings of the earth. To be a pharaoh was to sit on Geb's throne, a position of absolute earthly power (Pinch, 2004).

Nut

Nut is the goddess of the sky, the sister-mate of Geb, and the daughter of Shu, God of the air, and Tefnut, his mate. She is frequently depicted as a naked woman, her body stretched arch-like over the earth, just as is our sky. Though separated from her brother and mate, Geb, Nut gives birth to five of the most significant deities in the Egyptian pantheon. The drama of these five siblings is pivotal to our appreciation of Egyptian mythology and the establishment and governing of the nation of Egypt in the time of the pharaohs. We will consider these five and their complex inter-relationship in the next chapter. The role of Nut is pivotal to mythological explanations of the rising and setting of the sun and moon and the appearance of the stars in the night sky. I appreciate the imagery of the role of Nut within the created order as outlined by Pinch below:

In the day, the sun god sailed along the "sea below the belly of Nut." Each evening, the sun god was swallowed by Nut and passed through a perilous inner sky inside her. At dawn, Nut gave birth to the sun, her blood turning the sky red. At the same time, she would be swallowing the moon and the stars to give birth to them again at dusk (Pinch, 2004, p. 174).

Osiris

The myth of Osiris and Isis may very well be the most important in all of Egyptian mythology. Their story is as banal and as bloody as any late-night drama. Yet the lessons it teaches or, perhaps, the questions it was crafted to answer are among the most fundamental questions of human existence. What happens to us when we die? Oh, that is the first question in every generation of humankind. What happens to my body? Is there such a thing as a soul? If so, what does it look like? Will my body stay dead, or will it somehow have the chance for life again? Does my soul live after death? If so, where and how does it live? What kind of life is it that I can experience after my body dies?

I could continue asking more such questions, but I know you understand what I'm saying because, admit it, you've asked those questions yourself and more at some point in your life. No, the Egyptians lived when there were no certainties, no science, no atoms or DNA. These fundamental human questions demanded answers. It remains unclear where, when, and how Osiris became the answer to those questions. Still, sometime between the unification under Narmer and the fifth dynasty in the middle of the third millennium BC, Osiris seems to have risen to prominence in the world view of the Egyptian people. One of the earliest primary sources for the story of the birth, death, and afterlife of Osiris is the Pyramid Texts. Remember that, as with all Egyptian myths, the details can change from dynasty to dynasty and era to era. But we can speak with reasonable certainty about how Osiris was depicted. And since every aspect of Egyptian burial and mummification derives from the story of Osiris, it is no surprise that he is described as a mummified pharaoh wearing a crown and carrying a crook and flail, the traditional symbols of kingly rule and power. Portraying his skin as either green or black has been suggested by some to represent decomposition. Still, it came to be associated through his myth with the endless cycle of death and rebirth, which was integral to the Egyptian worldview.

Who was Osiris? If there were a human figure behind the story, it would be virtually impossible to determine. There is no historical evidence for an actual king or other historical figure being the first Osiris. But of the mythical Osiris, we have already learned a little in the previous chapter. Osiris was one of five children of the earth god Geb and his sister-mate Nut who, as the story goes, were discovered by their father so close together in a passionate embrace that there was no space between them. Their father, Shu, was forced to separate them as far as the upper sky is from the earth to create a space for the creation of men and creatures of the planet. Osiris and Isis, his sister-mate, ruled Egypt together until the events of the Osiris myth occurred, when his brother Seth struck him down out of jealousy, causing Isis to use her powers of magic to reanimate him. Having been resurrected by Isis, Osiris is overcome by passion and impregnates his sister, and for most Westerners, he gives birth to Horus. Horus in turn will become the God of the living while his father Osiris became the God of the Dead.

Wrapped up in the mythical person and work of Osiris are the ideas of the afterlife, judgment, truth, or Maat, as the Egyptians termed it. Moreover, the myth of Osiris is the genesis of the burial practice of mummification, which typifies Egyptian civilization from our perspective. The sarcophagus of the pharaohs is a physical representation of the wooden box designed by Seth to entomb his brother. It was a box made to the exact specifications of its inhabitant. Sealed with lead or other material, the mummification process was an extension of the Isis and Osiris mythology, which necessitated that Isis reassemble her brother-mate's dismembered body before she could reanimate it. The underlying belief contained in that story is that a body must be intact as it enters the afterlife for that body to be resurrected. The resurrection of Osiris himself is a type of experience that every Egyptian desired. Osiris is termed Lord of the Westerners. The term "westerner" refers to the deceased spirits over whom he rules in the afterlife. Resurrection has always been associated with the west in Egyptian thinking. That is why burial ceremonies bring the mummified remains of the deceased across the Nile River in a boat from east to west so that the body can be buried on the west side of the Nile.

Osiris' experience in the afterworld is also a pattern or an archetype of that experience. Every Egyptian could anticipate thorough judgment on the way to the next life. As Osiris had to face a determination of truth, each soul must undergo that same experience over which Osiris himself will preside. Those judgments determined if, in a literal sense, one's heart was true. Another way of expressing that would be the judgment of Osiris that one was a possessor of *Maat*, being the principle of truth, justice, and order in opposition to chaos, which is untruth, disorder, and injustice. With the aid of Isis, Horus, and other deities, Osiris argued his case in the Hall of Double Truth before a tribunal of 42 gods, and, as we say, he passed with flying colors. Osiris was vindicated, and his death was deemed to be unjust. For that reason, the creator God allowed Osiris to leave his mummy and reign in the underworld. He was given a new name: Wennefer. According to Pinch (p. 179), the actual raising of Osiris seems to be accomplished by Horus presenting the power of his eyes to Osiris. Though Osiris' new name was originally believed to mean "the one whose body did not decay," it later came to be understood as "the beneficent one." (Pinch, 2004).

Isis

It is not clear from the earliest accounts of Osiris and Horus what role she played or its significance. By the New Kingdom era, however, Isis had been elevated to a position of reverence and respect, causing her to be worshipped more widely than any other Egyptian deity. That's quite impressive, given the mythological company she kept. But perhaps her elevation is entirely understandable, given that the Osiris-Isis myth depicts her as a loving and devoted wife and protective, nurturing mother. According to some texts, she will stop at nothing to avenge her husband's murder at the hands of their brother Seth. Specific texts indicate that Isis's hatred for her brother Seth is boundless and eternal. Isis was a tender mate and mother but a fierce opponent. There is much to admire about such an individual.

What do we know of Isis herself? We know that, like Osiris and Seth, she was among the five children of Geb, lord of the earth, and Nut, goddess of the upper sky. These five children represent the fourth generation in the Ennead of Heliopolis. She is typified as the throne goddess, such that the iconography of her Egyptian name is the throne symbol. In that role, she was recognized as the mother of every Egyptian king. Isis is portrayed furthermore as having the same maternal tenderness for humanity that she does for her children, Horus, and, by extension, for all of humankind. It would have been hard not to love her! What is interesting about the position of Isis is that her mythology grew up amid a male-dominated, patriarchal society. There were comparatively few female pharaohs throughout the history of Egypt, and yet, over them all, this remarkable woman, wife, and mother reigned. I wonder at the parallels between this god-mother and mother of a god and another more familiar to our western experience, the Mary of Catholic tradition, which is titled "Mother of God." She sits on a throne in the heavens presiding over God's representative on earth, his vicar, the pope. But that's just speculation and not germane to our Study.

Some Egyptian texts emphasize the power of Isis to work magic and highlight her cleverness, cunning and determination. By the later New Kingdom, a cult had developed around the person of Isis, which honored her as the guide and guardian of sailors, the inventor of agriculture, and the giver of the blessing of the annual inundation. It is not difficult to see how Isis could become the center of the Egyptian worldview and religion.

Seth

Does every family have a black sheep? If that were true, the divine family would be no exception. Seth is the bad boy brother of Osiris, Horus the Elder, Isis, and Nephthys, and a fourth-generation member of the Ennead of Heliopolis. He is described as tumultuous and thoughtless, portrayed as a brute with incredible strength, like the enforcer in a powerful and dysfunctional family. The cult of Seth seems to have originated in upper Egypt (Pinch 192). In the early dynastic period of Egypt, Seth was alternatively identified with the gods of the despised Redland, the eastern desert, and Western Sahara. Dangerous desert conditions and wild animals were associated with the presence and activity of Seth. He is depicted as an unsavory imaginary creature. Egyptians believed him to masquerade as various animals, all of them destructive in one way or another.

Seth is a god of perpetual strife, conflict, and jealousy, whose battles with Horus are represented in several Egyptian sources. But, of course, Seth is perhaps best known for his pivotal role in the unfolding drama of Osiris and Isis. In that central myth, Seth is the deceiver and the murderer of his brother Osiris. Seth is, in this way, a catalyst for the cycle of death and rebirth and, like the antiheroes of other fictions, is acknowledged as necessary to move the plot forward, in this case, to a happy ending. Without Seth, one might say that there would have been no Osiris the resurrected Lord of the

Westerners. And so, while it is easy to dislike the character of Seth, we recognize that we can't disown him from the family. We can undoubtedly resonate with his sister's hatred for him. So what is the reality behind Seth? There's no way that we can say for sure. All we can do is think about the possible questions that his character will answer. I suggest, perhaps, that one of those questions that ring true in every generation on earth is: Why do horrible things happen to good people? That seems an appropriate question, and Seth, the deceiver, seems like a reasonable answer, at least to the Egyptian mind.

Nephthys

In how many stories do we have two siblings, one of whom is accomplished, beautiful, and famous while the other is inconspicuous? Are we growing up in the shadow of our beloved sibling? That story seems as old as time. And, yes, it is the story of Nephthys and her sister Isis, the throne goddess. Isis would have been a tough act to follow, and it seems Nephthys knew this. She is mainly portrayed as a devoted sister but a woman of little significance and few accomplishments. If the Pyramid Texts indicate her status, then to describe her as "an imitation woman with no vagina" (Pinch, 2004, p. 171) is probably the worst insult one could level. By today's standards, she was a spinster who, having been raped by her brother Seth, chose to move in with Osiris and Isis. The pictorial representation of her name represents "lady of the manor." According to some texts, she slept with the Lord of the Manor, Osiris, much to Isis' chagrin, and gave birth to Anubis, with whom many will be familiar even if they know little about Egyptian mythology. Anubis, the jackal-headed god, is the master of the dead and oversees the embalming and burial rights of Egyptian practice.

Nephthys, the devoted sister, shared with her sister Isis searching for their brother, Isis' mate, Osiris. After finding the body, Isis and Nephthys were on hand while Anubis mummified their brother's body. Nephthys is associated with the linens used for wrapping the mummified body since she is recognized as one of the goddesses of weaving. Nephthys and her sister Isis were portrayed as the protectors of the mummified corpse of their brother and later came to typify the gods' protection over the remains of the dead.

Horus

We must distinguish at the outset between two Horuses. There is the child Horus, the son of Isis by her brother-mate Osiris; and the Horus of whom we speak now, the Elder, the brother of Seth against whom he engaged in constant struggle. The falcon represented this elder Horus, the lord of the sky, whose wings spanned heaven and whose two eyes were the sun and the moon. In this capacity, Egyptians believed him to be the child of a sky goddess, either Nut or Hathor. Egypt's earliest kings were frequently typified as hawks praying on their enemies, an allusion to the role of Horus, the embodiment of pharaoh's rule. Some parts of the mythical cycle describe a time when the gods ruled directly on earth. In these, the reign of Horus is seen as the perfect paradigm of earthly rule, the pattern and prototype for future pharaonic reign.

The rulers of the Early Dynastic Period sometimes took as many as four "Horus names" for their official designations to identify the attributes for which they most desired to be remembered. They included the symbol of Horus in the glyphs, which represented their public names. Pharaohs of later dynasties moved away from identification with Horus to embrace the cult of the sun god Ra, of whom they claimed to be the sons (or daughters, in some cases), and therefore divine.

Horus, the Child

Horus, the child, is the son of Isis, conceived by her brother and mate Osiris after his reanimation and given birth to after his father's descent into the underworld to reign there as Lord of the Westerners. Horus, the child, is, strangely enough, portrayed as a young Egyptian boy, naked, his head shaved save for one braided side lock. When shown as the third member of divine triads in mini temples throughout Egypt, he is the preeminent one. His role as child-god is to represent the renewal of the world. The birth of a child heralds hopes for the future, and so must Horus the child have been recognized. And the pregnancy of Isis was said to have been ten months along, and her delivery exceptionally difficult and painful. Isis was forced to hide little Horus in the papyrus thickets of the Nile delta to protect him from his uncle Seth.

Images of the innocent Horus child were especially appealing to the pharaohs who acknowledged their dependence upon the gods in the same way that an infant depended on his mother for protection, nourishment, and growth.

CHAPTER 4
MYTHOLOGY OF ANCIENT EGYPT

Toward a Worldview

Let's indulge in a thought experiment. Let's think back to our childhood, wherever and whenever that was, before the invasion of digital media, google, iPads and cell phones, and the Hubble space telescope. For some of us, that's a long journey, and for others, just a few short steps. If you were born after Apple and Microsoft windows, you might find this experiment a challenge. No matter. Now try to remember the first time you stood outside late on a clear night and gazed up at the sky. Are you with me? Questions were bouncing around inside your head, weren't they? Questions like: Where did all this come from? What are those lights in the sky and how did they get there? You look around and ask yourself: How did this get here? Mommy, and daddy, and crazy aunt Edna who could never fail to pinch your cheek every time she saw you. How did they–how did I–get here? And those are just a handful of all the questions that you and I have. Now imagine for a moment and ask yourself this question: What if there was no one and nothing in my world to which I could turn for the answers? No Wikipedia, no Google search, no science at all. Don't imagine, at this point, that you know these things exist but that you simply don't have access to them. Instead, imagine that these things don't exist at all.

Could you do it? Well, then, congratulations! You've just experienced, for the briefest moment, what it was like at every moment of every day, for each man, woman, and child walking this narrow strip of Black Land as the Stone Age gave way to the Pyramid Age.

You are that late Neolithic child, looking around at your world, your head filled with those questions we've asked ourselves. Life is ok, you guess, but not easy. Father came back today looking sad, only two fish in his fishing basket. The nearby river that was so full last summer that it took away your little brother is now so low that you can almost cross it without getting your knees wet. And little water means no black dirt. Mother's garden looks dry, and nothing wants to grow. Father turns his face to the sun, and his face is angry. The bright, hot sun looks angry too. What can you do? Do you feel helpless?

Afraid? You ask father why this is happening to us, but all he can say is, "I don't know."

"Why are there no more fish?"

"I don't know."

"When will the black dirt come back so mother's garden can make more to eat?"

"I don't know."

"Why is mother's belly getting round again? Will I get another brother?"

"Go ask your mother."

Our *H. sapiens* brains, hot-wired between 70,000 and 30,000 years ago during the Cognitive Revolution, began to think and communicate in new ways. We need to know and to understand not just some things but everything. If we don't know, if we can't know, we're inclined to fill in the blanks.

I'll bet that, before the Cognitive Revolution, our species didn't ask many questions. Concrete thinking, characterized by our *Homo* ancestors before 70,000 BCE, observes that "Todd was killed by an elephant yesterday." Post-Cognitive Revolution, that would never happen. "Why did Todd have to get stepped on by that elephant yesterday? Who is responsible for that elephant wandering into our back yard so it could kill Todd?"

Every parent has experienced the interminable questionings of their children. Their questions, we believe, require answers. When we don't know the answers—when there is no possible way to know—and when, at the same time, we must provide them, we tell stories. We fill in the blanks. We weave tales. And those stories, told and re-told, shared with other children and recounted by their parents, then passed on from generation to generation down through the ages, become the myths that characterize our times and the worldview which permeates our culture.

And so, somewhere back in time, inside a wattle-and-daub hut close to *iteru*, a little child, tucked beneath a fur blanket on her palette near the glowing hearth, looked up at her mother and asked the question: Why? And that mother began to weave a story of a time when there was only water, dark and churning, full of all the possibilities of life, and of how the Primordial Mound began to rise from the water, and sitting atop that mound, Atum, the self-created, the source of life, alone, and lonely.

Mythology: A Moving Target

Egyptian mythology was born out of millennia of oral tradition in the late Neolithic era. Modern humans living in the Nile Valley had not yet developed a system of writing. Like many cultures, their truths and traditions were passed from fathers to their sons, mothers to their daughters, and generation to generation. These stories were memorized and recited, creating what we might think of as an oral corpus, or body of work. There was no existing method of codifying and collecting the stories of the culture we call myths today in that predynastic Egyptian culture. This reality of predynastic and dynastic Egyptian culture meant that the stories were free to change and develop over time, though fixed in their essentials. They were influenced by evolutionary, social, and political forces around them. As a result, you can find many Egyptian myths in several versions. With the unification of Egypt under King Narmur, the local myths of the villages of Upper and

Lower Egypt became national myths. Over time, the events and even the names of the individuals involved morphed. Any attempt to capture Egyptian mythology in some westernized and codified way is frustrating, if not impossible. We cannot impose our Greek logic and rationality onto what is essentially an oral tribal tradition. The Greeks, by the way, had the good fortune of a prime position amid the stream of civilization: their writing was well-established. Authors such as Homer could craft their stories of Greek gods and goddesses who created the world, who controlled the movement of the planets, who hurled their lightning bolts and shook the earth, and could capture them for posterity with the stroke of a pen.

While we find it easy to pick up a volume of Greek mythology and read virtually the same stories in the exact words from many different sources, we cannot as quickly compile and organize Egyptian myths into clear and logical units. The stories were written inside the lids of coffins, on the walls of tombs and temples, in palaces and passageways and papyri over the thousand miles of monuments that comprised the Nile Valley. So we'll talk about some of these Egyptian myths in this book instead of sharing them in story form. The opportunity exists for some future Egyptian scholar, or latter-day Homer of Egyptian mythology, to gather these stories into a form that could be read by parents to their children, just as was done around the hearths of ancient Egypt. But that is not this book! Instead, I encourage you to chase some of the references from the bibliography at the end of this book and read more of the fascinating world of Egyptian mythology.

In the Beginning...

"The origin of the universe," according to Geraldine Pinch, "was an intellectual problem that came to fascinate the Egyptians." (Pinch, 2004). Many of the gods and goddesses we've come to know in the previous chapter are directly or indirectly related to the origin of the universe and the creation of the things that constitute our world. Atum, for example, was already an ancient player in primordial creation stories by the time of the early Kingdom. While no writing exists before Narmur and his famous palette, we can infer that Atum's story comes from ancient oral tradition. Atum and the Ogdoad, or Eightfold, could read the first chapter of the Egyptian worldview in much the same way as the first chapter of the book of Genesis defines the worldview of Hebrew and Christian cultures. We have encountered bits and pieces of this creation story in the brief biographies of its divine participants. Let's consider it now as the story unfolds. Let's remind ourselves of the perspective suggested by Bob Brier, that we do not take the stories literally but rather try to see how those stories might provide answers to the questions we ask of the world around us.

Chaos

In our quest to decipher the intricacies of Egyptian mythology, it behooves us to remember that the non-negotiable details of that mythology, that is, the things which remain the same over time, afford us the closest glimpse into the worldview of Egyptian culture. I suggest that the one belief that undergirds Egyptian mythology, like a mathematical constant, is that before there was anything, there was *isfet*: chaos, or disorder. The Egyptian understanding of chaos provides a counterpoint to order and its pursuit, which was intrinsic to Egyptian culture. As we've seen previously, the recognition of and the striving toward order as an antidote to chaos pervades, perhaps defines, the ancient Egyptian psyche. Numerous historians have remarked that aside from what we might call microevolution in the culture of Egypt over 3000 years, from a macro view, she remained the same through that whole time. As much as the worldview of the Egyptians was tuned to the obtaining and preserving of order in their universe, it was just as much a desire to prevent a return to chaos. The history of Egypt displays this duality of thinking. A unified kingdom with its central government, religious structure, and fixed social organization came from the chaos of predynastic history. The universe demanded that life be lived by rules which upheld its internal order. When those rules and those structures were honored, the country underwent periods of stability and growth. Egyptian society maintained balance. The early Middle and New Kingdoms were evidence of the restoration of order and the maintaining of balance. The average Egyptian would perceive those times between, which historians had labeled the first, second, and sometimes third intermediate periods as times when the balance was disrupted, and chaos ruled. But what is the true nature of chaos?

The Egyptian worldview saw things ordered in pairs: light and darkness, earth and sky, life and death, male and female. In this case, primordial time was when only one thing existed: Chaos. There was not yet an order to balance the universe. It would take the emergence of the creator to create that order. The word chaos evoked an image of a dark and formless infinite watery void. This was the primordial water from which all life springs. Egyptians called it Nu, or Nun. The Nu was conceived of as containing all the potential for life and existence. From the Nu, these primordial waters, the first land arose: the primordial mound, or *benben*. The primordial waters continue to surround the mound even after creation and were believed to be the ultimate source of the Nile, according to Pinch (2004). Sitting cross-legged upon the primordial mound as it arose from the chaotic primordial waters was Atum the "unique one in the Nu" and as "one who is in his egg," alone until he creates the Ogdoad, the Eightfold "by speaking with the nun" (Pinch, p.59).

Atum is understood to have created another eight gods whom we know as the Ogdoad by speaking with the Nun. These eight may represent the previously hidden elements of chaos which Atum speaks into existence, possibly by saying their names. To have one's name spoken, in Egyptian thought, was to avoid the second death in the afterlife. Some authors suggest that it is this reason that pharaohs, in particular, took for themselves several names and ensured that these names were inscribed in texts, tombs, monuments, and temples. The underlying idea is that there is power in the speaking of a name. You can read more about the Ogdoad in the previous chapter. Often included in the Ogdoad were the gods Amun and Amunet. Amun was identified as the hidden one or the invisible. Later accounts separated Amun from the Eightfold and made him the creator God who spoke the others into existence. Different imagery exists to describe the moment of that first creation. Some sources describe that first sound as a loud cry, a heavy sigh, or even the honking of a goose. Atum/Amun is often called the creator sun god because Egyptians believed that the first appearance of the creator brought the first light and power of the sun to support life. Some accounts have a tomb cry out or whisper to drive back the primordial waters and to expose the first land, the primordial mound, to provide a place for him to begin his work.

Creation

The Ogdoad

The relation between the creator god Atum or Amun and the Ogdoad varies among different texts and sources. We have seen that the creator God arose from the primordial waters simultaneously with the primordial mound and then spoke the other eight gods into existence or separated their properties from the undifferentiated chaos. Specific texts would say that the eight came together, perhaps by "some primitive instinct" (Pinch, 2004, p. 177), to make the primordial mound upon which the creator emerged. As Pinch says, "the Ogdoad merged in the primeval waters to allow the creator to come into being." This paradoxical chicken-and-egg scenario only highlights that Egyptian thinking and orientation in time were not necessarily linear. The Ogdoad could be said to be the fathers and mothers of the Creator God. And yet, it could also be noted that the creator is the father of the fathers and mothers. We should not spend much effort trying to unravel what is fixed in time over 5000 years. It should simply serve as an example of the challenge of understanding the thinking of a culture so removed in time and space from our own.

We met the Ogdoad in the previous chapter. Still, it serves our purposes to remind ourselves of the names of these dualities and the qualities or principles and body. The first pair representing the primordial waters themselves are Nun and Nunet. When included within the eight, Amun and Amunet represent the hidden or invisible within chaos and possibly the invisible breath of life. When they are absent from the eight, when creation is ascribed to Amun himself, another pair, Nia and Niat, takes their place. This pair represents the chaotic void. Kek and Keket, The third pairing represent the darkness of a chaotic state. The fourth duet is somewhat harder to identify in its characteristics, for they do not appear in most texts and sources. Finally, Tenemet or Heh as he is otherwise known, and his partner Hehet, are thought to represent chaos itself, and the strong and turbulent currents of the primordial waters, respectively.

The purpose of the Ogdoad in the process of creation seems as murky as the primordial waters themselves. Yet, this account answers the question: what was it like before there was anything? The Ogdoad, which personifies the qualities or characteristics of primordial chaos, represents the time when things were formless or invisible, dark, void, turbulent, and yet containing the invisible breath of life.

This thought would coincide with Pinch's statement that "the Ogdoad seem to be forces that the creator has to subdue before the work of creation can begin" (176). In those contexts where they are seen as coming together to give life or allow the creator to come into being or make the primordial mound upon which creation can proceed, the primordial mound becomes their tomb. For once the chaos has been subdued, there is room for order to be established.

Alternative Creator Myths

A possible source of confusion to our western minds is that various texts were written at different times in different locations throughout Egypt, which ascribe the creative act to gods other than Atum or Amun. Naturally, our rational minds want to label such occurrences as contradictory, but there was no sense of contradiction in the minds of the ancient Egyptian people. Whether to say that it was Amun atop the primordial mound who spoke other gods into existence and from there the world, or to ascribe that act to Ra (or Amun-Ra, or Ra-Atum), Shu, Ptah, Khnum, the goddesses Neith, Hathor or Isis, caused no consternation to them. These were all pathways two some understanding of the invisible, intangible, and perhaps incomprehensible. If the creator god wore another face or was called a different name, the principle was the same. An all-powerful, unknowable reality beyond us was responsible for bringing the world into existence. And this is the truth behind the story.

The primary order of creation from the starting place of the primordial mound was, first, to create the deities who inhabited the invisible divine realm; then, to generate lesser creatures, namely people and animals, to inhabit the world.

The divine separation of Geb and Tefnut, that is, earth and sky, is one of the critical stages in the creative process. The space between them is where humans and animals, and lesser things can live. Likewise, the creation of gender out of an undifferentiated genderless state was essential to the process of creation. Some could be their own fathers or mothers. But in the created realm, it was necessary to establish a duality of male and female. Once the creator god completed that creative act, living beings could procreate and thrive in the home made for them. That brings us to the third most crucial step in the divine creative process. Having banished chaos and created both divine and mortal creatures, the creator still needed to establish order. This need implies that the absence of disorder does not mean the presence of order. These are intentional, deliberate actions. This principle carried over into the Egyptian worldview, where one must be intentional about not simply avoiding the state of chaos but establishing and preserving order or balance in one's own life and that of others.

Male and Female: He Created Them

If, as Yuval Harari claims, myths are the fictions we invent and share which become universally believed by groups or even nations, then the story of Atum, Shu, and Tefnut, and the creation of male and female genders deserves to win an award! Imagine for a moment the scene: a boy comes to his mother and father and asks, "Why are boys, boys, and girls, girls?"

Mother replies, "Because that's the way God made us."

"And where did he get that idea? Does God have kids of his own?"

"Well, yes, as a matter of fact, he does."

"And did their mommy push them out of her tummy as you pushed me out?"

"Well, no, not actually...."

"So, where did the kids come from?"

At this point, his mother says, "Go on, Fred, tell your son where God's kids came from?" Mother leaves the room, looking embarrassed. "Well, dad? How did God get kids if they had no mother?"

Now it's father's turn to be embarrassed. "Well, um, you see... It's like this...." *Should I go all in or not,* father asked himself.

"Heck, here goes... You see, son, before he had kids God wasn't a boy or a girl. It was like he was both. But he still had "parts", do you know what I mean?"

The little boy nods, not sure he wants to hear the rest. But there's no stopping now.

Father says, "So, one day he decides he wants children; in fact, he wants twins, a boy, and a girl. But nothing like that has ever been done." Father takes a deep breath. Here it comes. "So, Johnny, he starts touching himself down there, do you understand? He does that until stuff comes out. He puts that into his own mouth and swallows it. And then he coughs or sneezes, or maybe both, and out pops his two kids, Shu, his son, and Tefnut, his daughter."

Johnny's eyes are enormous. Father says, "Do you understand?"

Johnny just turns around and walks away. But the next day at recess, boy, does Johnny have a story to tell!

I can't speak for you, dear reader, but I know I will never forget the story of Shu and Tefnut and their father, Atum! That, my friends, is the incredible power of the story. As Harari points out, it's not only necessary to tell stories but to tell good stories. The difference is that average stories are likely to be dismissed or forgotten and fail to have their desired impact. But, on the other hand, good stories, remembered, retold, and shared from generation to generation, become the myths of our culture, which have the power to shape and define that culture.

We've examined some of the stories of Shu and Tefnut in the previous chapter. They became the first God and Goddess of the pantheon since all other gods before them were not distinguished in gender. When Atum gave them new names and new identities, he introduced foundational concepts into Egyptian thinking. In speaking their new names, he brought the qualities associated with those names into existence. Shu, his son, became Ka, which means "life force or vital essence." Ka became the god who sustains life. Atum's daughter Tefnut became Maat, the principle of truth, justice, and especially order. Maat is the antithesis of *isfet*, chaos. Maat became the favorite daughter of the creator and a source of joy. Maat was the guiding principle of the created world and its people. All Egyptian governors, especially Pharaoh, strove to establish and preserve Maat on earth "as it was in the First Time" (Pinch, 2004, p. 65).

We considered some of the events of this First Time in our brief study of Shu and Tefnut. In Shu's act of separating his children Nut and Geb, the sky and the earth, Shu made life possible and enabled the sun to manifest for the first time as the sun god, Ra. Pinch also mentions that "as part of establishing the divine order, Shu and Tefnut also become two different types of time. Shu is eternal recurrence, and Tefnut is eternal sameness" (2004, p, 65).

Because of this principle of Maat or eternal sameness, Egyptian civilization hardly changed in over 3000 years. Thus, innovation and change were contrary to the principle of Maat.

Death and Resurrection

Osiris and Isis

We come to the most important and foundational story in the canon of Egyptian mythology: the sad and happy tale of Osiris and his sister-mate, Isis. You've met this couple before–the fourth generation of the Ennead of Heliopolis, the children of Geb, lord of the earth, and his sister-mate, Nut, goddess of the sky. The product of their parents' passionate embrace, so close that there was no room between them for creation to occur, yet they could not resist each other's affections. Osiris, the eldest, loves Isis, and she loves him. But their brother Seth is jealous of Osiris. There is murder in his heart. So brutish, reckless Seth devises a plan to take Osiris away from his sister for good. While Osiris sleeps, Seth measures the exact dimensions of his brother's body. Now Osiris must travel into the world for some time to bring agriculture and the domestication of animals to the world as a whole. Seth seizes the opportunity to hatch his plan.

Seth commissions an artisan to craft him a wooden chest, made to his brother's exact shape and dimensions. When Osiris returns home from the world, Seth announces that he will throw a massive banquet in honor of his brother. The evening's entertainment will be a contest, and the prize? A beautiful wooden chest. Each man will have the opportunity to win that prize, and the competition is simple. Each man, in turn, will lay down inside the chest, and the lid will be closed. Whichever man fits perfectly into the chest will get to keep it for himself. Of course, Osiris, the guest of honor, must go first! Seth removes the lid from the chest, and Osiris climbs inside. Seth slams the top down on the chest, seals the chest with molten lead, and throws it into the Nile, where a tributary carries it away from Egypt.

Isis is heartbroken and vows to find her husband and to bring him home for burial. She and her sister Nephthys search across the world, hoping to find their brother. When both are ready to give up the search, Isis finds her lover's wooden chest in Byblos in Lebanon. The wooden chest had washed up onto the shore and grown into a tree, and the owner cut down that tree and made it a pillar in his home. Isis breaks open the box to find her Osiris dead! She and Nephthys bring the body back home and give their brother a proper burial.

Seth is angry that his plans have been thwarted! He digs up the grave, removes his brother, and hacks him into fourteen pieces, which he scatters throughout Egypt. When Isis discovers what her brother Seth has done, she searches through Egypt to gather the pieces together. Isis manages to find thirteen out of fourteen of Osiris' body parts, but his penis is gone, thrown into the Nile, and eaten by fish. Isis, a magician, fashions him another and then, changing into the form of a bird, hovers over him until he comes back to life. Filled with passion, he impregnates his wife before returning to the underworld to become Lord of the Westerners.

On Earth, as it is in *A'aru*

Egyptians conceived of their world as containing three realms: *A'aru*, the divine realm in the upper sky described as the Field of Rushes, where its inhabitants would live an idealized version of their earthly farming life; the *Duat*, most often referred to as the Underworld though, in Egyptian thought, it was considered part of the created world and not separate; and the earth, at the center of which stood the nation of Egypt (Pinch, 2004). It appears that the creation of man to inhabit the space between Geb (earth) and Nut (sky) was seen as a more peripheral event than the creation of the Universe, the gods, and pharaoh, a god on earth. His life took on an almost magical significance. By comparison, the average lives of ordinary citizens must have seemed insignificant, except insofar as they participated in and preserved Maat, the divine order. That is not to say that the creator cared nothing for his creation. Coffin Texts 1130 delineates the "four good deeds" which the creator has performed on behalf of man:

"To create the four winds to give the breath of life to everybody, to make the annual Nile flood so that everyone would get enough food, to create everyone with equal potential, and to make every person's heart remember the West." (Pinch, 2004, p. 67)

It was not until the Middle Kingdom that Egyptians imagined stories to answer how humans came to be. Pinch quotes Coffin Text spell 1130, where the Lord of all claims to have created deities from his sweat and "people from the tears of my eye" (2004, p. 66). It is uncertain how much weight to give to the observation, but the ancient Egyptian words for "tears" and "people" sound almost identical. Perhaps the history of Egypt and, by extension, of the world bears out that exciting parallelism.

We observed in the previous chapter that Egyptians recognized the gods Khnum and Ptah as those who crafted the bodies of the gods and people, the former out of precious materials and the latter out of mud or clay. Khnum is depicted as using a potter's wheel to fashion the creatures of the earth. Khnum would, in fact, fashion two bodies for each individual: one body before birth and a second to house an individual's vital essence, or Ka.

To *Duat*, the Underworld

Duat is many things in Egyptian mythology, but the most evocative word to our western minds is Underworld—not to be confused with the Judeo-Christian concept of Hell or Hades since the Hebrew and Greek scriptures which reference these concepts would not be written for more than two millennia. Nor should we think of Duat as being somehow removed from creation, like an alternate but invisible dimension. On the contrary, the ancient Egyptians believed that Duat was the lowermost of three realms of creation, the other two being the earth and the upper sky. Duat, therefore, was still part of the world, nearer than we might conceive. It was believed to be the realm of the dead and the residence, in fact, of several gods, the most important by far in Egyptian belief being

Osiris, Lord of the Underworld. Osiris was the pattern for all to follow. He was the first mummy and the first to be reborn from his mummified condition as a reward for having passed the weighing of the heart, the final ritual of the judgment of one's life.

Duat represented the journey of the soul of the deceased through various ordeals on its way to final judgment and the prospect of an afterlife in A'aru. Osiris and different resident gods appeared to the departed soul, often accompanying it on portions of its journey. Sometimes grotesque, demon-like figures appeared, trying the soul on its journey. The deceased had to face a tribunal of 42 judges, each of whom evaluated a different aspect of the soul's spiritual fitness to continue the journey. The dead must persuade each of the judges, in turn, that he is innocent of a total of 42 specific sins or that circumstances should enable him to be excused if he has committed any. If successful in his persuasion of the judges and the passing of the many ordeals and challenges, he would stand before Anubis, who would weigh his heart against the feather of Maat, standing for truth and justice. If the soul's heart were heavier than the feather, it was rejected and then consumed by Ammit, the devourer of souls. There was no hell in the Egyptian worldview—the deceased, in this case, was denied an afterlife altogether and ceased to exist.

Duat was not merely the setting for the journey of deceased souls on their way to judgment and either life in A'aru or extermination. Divided into twelve sections, it represented the twelve hours of the night through which the sun god, Ra, traveled from sunset (west) to sunrise (east). From the vantage point of Atet, the solar barge which floated on the Primordial Waters, Ra passed through the hours of the night, shining his rays on the souls of the deceased who slept and reviving them for that one hour. At the same time, throughout the night, Ra fought to defeat Apep or Apophis, the serpent who represented chaos, so that the sun–himself–would rise the following day. At his rising, Ra manifested himself as the youthful god of sunrise, Khepri, while at sunset, he embodied the aged creator god Atum. Between these two points, he was Ra, god of the noonday sun.

CHAPTER 5
THE DRAMA UNFOLDS

In chapters 1-3, we have explored ancient Egyptian society from the outside looking in. In our mind's eye, we have glimpsed the world of Egypt as it might have been. Our vision may correspond at least in part to the reality of that old place and time. But this reality is more like an enormous jigsaw puzzle, complete at the edges but missing many of its connecting pieces and without the benefit of the box lid. We study the pieces we have, wanting to see the whole picture. Nonetheless, we recognize that "evidence for lives and events so distant from our own time will, regrettably, forever remain incomplete" (Shaw, 2014), and so will be our understanding. Yet the lure of the mysterious and the unknown continues to hold us in its grip.

Our first glimpse of that far-away culture has been from the bank of the Nile, which defines the country and its people. In that river, we discover a connection with the past. The eternal Nile remains, despite the onrush of modern civilization, while the former glories of Egypt are in ruins. The river itself fuels our imagination. From that vantage point of creativity, we have imagined the rich black soil of *iteru* between our bare toes and strained our ears to hear the first rush of water as the inundation arrives in the summer season. We have stopped for a moment to witness the everyday activities of freemen, slaves, and serfs in their kilts who work the fertile alluvial soil–the gift of Hapy, the god of the inundation–as *iteru* recedes, planting crops of barley and wheat, or graze their flocks of sheep and goats and pasture their cattle on the narrow, flat floodplain.

We have listened to the gaggle of commerce as government businessmen trade stories and haggle the price of goods with swarthy traders from across the Red Land or as lone hawkers barter the surplus goods of their estate masters. We have seen scribes in their long skirts, carrying wooden palettes with writing brushes and ink pots, returning to their homes from work in government positions or as clerks or accountants. We have remarked on the distinctive appearance of the Wab priests, hairless, clothed in their linen robes and papyrus sandals, approaching the entrance to their temples in service of local or national deities. We have caught the measured, almost rhythmic, sound of artisans transforming gold, silver, and copper, turquoise and lapis lazuli into breathtaking designs for wealthy patrons or the royal court, or else shaping wood, stone or bronze with rudimentary tools into the forms of animals, persons, even gods; witnessed the dangerous and backbreaking efforts of miners, mining treasures they will never possess, and quarrymen cutting massive blocks of limestone (or sandstone during the New Kingdom) with astounding precision for tombs, temples, and pyramids; and listened to the gentle lapping of the waters of Mehit, the Delta, against the sides of marshmen's punts as they weave through papyrus stands with their knives ready to harvest one of Egypt's most significant natural commodities.

We have encountered Pharaoh—not yet the individual men and women who rose to absolute power throughout successive dynasties, first as incarnations of Horus and later as sons and daughters of Ra but, instead, the idea of Pharaoh as the lead actor in a massive spectacle, whose primary role evolved through the Predynastic era (before 3150 BCE) and was first realized in the person and reign of Narmur at the beginning of Egyptian history. Finally, we have glimpsed Pharaoh at the pinnacle of an enormous civil and religious structure that promised order and prevented chaos, like the gods themselves in primordial times.

We have been introduced to many gods and goddesses who were believed to inhabit the invisible world and manifest their power and presence in our own. And in listening to the stories of their actions and their exploits, and of the beliefs which shaped the human journey from birth to death and beyond, we have drawn a little closer to understanding the worldview of the People of the Black Land.

The Outline

Now, imagine yourself a famous director. Your producer has just spun out to you her idea for a stage play—not some one-night-only, off-Broadway kind of production. This idea has epic written prominently on every page. Egypt. Ancient Egypt. You've spent several cups of coffee listening as she unravels the backstory: the Nile at the inundation, kingdoms at war, victory and unification, prosperity, pharaohs, and priests, gods and goddesses, myths and magic, death, the Underworld, rebirth. Her hands are waving in the air. You know she's excited about the whole thing. Frankly, so are you.

"Pyramids?"

"Yep, she says."

"And mummies?"

"It wouldn't be Egypt without mummies," she says, leaning in. You're hooked, and she knows it. Reaching into her bag, she produces a document, not thick but well-worn, with a single staple, upper left corner. You recognize it: a planning outline for a three-act play (much like you see below). It's not the script—too soon for that. This will give you an idea of the flow, she says, the main characters, the highlights. Standing up, she pushes the outline across the table.

"Read it," she says. And she walks away.

You reach for the manuscript, fold the dog-eared corner to page one, and begin to read...Narmer, the first king of unified Egypt.... Your imagination soars. The stage is set. In your mind's eye, the characters assume their roles and take their positions. The curtain is ready to come up on the first act in Egyptian civilization's grand historical drama.

Cue the lights, you whisper, and… action!

Cast of Characters

The Early Kingdom Period

Narmer (c. 3150 BCE): he ruled during the Naqada III period in Upper Egypt. He conquered Lower Egypt c. 3150 BCE to establish the First Dynasty of a unified ancient Egypt. Narmer led from Thinis.

Khasekhemwy (c.2704-2686 BCE): last ruler of the Second Dynasty, an obscure period in Egyptian history. Khasekhemwy ruled from Thinis. He is believed to have been the father of **Djoser** (see below).

Djoser (c. 2686-2668 BCE): first ruler of the Third Dynasty. Djoser may have been responsible for moving the capital of Egypt from Thinis to **Memphis.** In addition, he designed step pyramids at Saqqara, where he was buried.

Sneferu (c. 2613-2589 BCE): first ruler of the Fourth Dynasty. He experimented with step pyramid design, ultimately building the first true smooth-sided pyramid.

Khufu (c. 2589-2566 BCE): second ruler of the Fourth Dynasty. He built the Great Pyramid at Giza, the last remaining of the Seven Wonders of the Ancient World, over 20 years.

Khafre (c. 2558-2532 BCE): the fourth ruler of the Fourth Dynasty, and son of **Khufu,** built the third of three pyramids on the Giza plateau, beside the Great Pyramid.

Unas (c. 2375-2345 BCE): believed to be the last ruler of the Fifth Dynasty. He built a smaller pyramid at Saqqara, the burial chamber boasting the first hieroglyphic inscriptions of any pyramid, the Pyramid Texts.

Pepi II (c. 2278-2184 BCE): second last ruler of the Sixth Dynasty and the Early Kingdom altogether, he ruled for 94 years. During his reign, pharaonic power crumbled, leading to the First Intermediate Period within three years of his death (c. 2181-2041).

The Middle Kingdom Period
Mentuhotep II (c. 2060-2010 BCE): sixth ruler of the

Eleventh Dynasty, put down an insurrection at Abydos, reuniting Upper and Lower Egypt to end the First Intermediate Period to the Middle Kingdom. Mentuhotep II ruled from Thebes.

Amenemhat I (c. 1991-1962 BCE): first ruler of the Twelfth Dynasty. He worshipped the local deity of Thebes, Amun, the creator god, and the "Hidden One," who would become the principal deity of Egypt. He ruled from It-towe, 10 miles south of Memphis.

The New Kingdom Period

Ahmose (c. 1570-1546 BCE): the first ruler of the Eighteenth Dynasty and the New Kingdom period, he crushed both Hyksos and Kushite kingdoms, reunifying Egypt. He ruled from Thebes.

Tuthmosis I (c. 1524-1518 BCE): third ruler of the Eighteenth Dynasty. Tuthmosis I was a commoner who married the eldest royal princess to obtain the throne. He was known for his extensive military conquests and establishing the Valley of the Kings for his own and successive underground burials. Tuthmosis I ruled from Thebes.

Hatshepsut (c. 1498-1483 BCE): the "Foremost of Noble Ladies," as her name is translated, was one of four children of Pharaoh Tuthmosis I and grew up in the royal household. While she was still a child, her two brothers and sister died, making her an only child. Her father, wishing to secure the dynasty for his own family before he died, married Hatshepsut to a half-brother who later became Tuthmosis II. Her husband was sickly, however, and died without an heir. As a result, Hatshepsut seized the role of regent when the 10-year-old son of a lesser wife was crowned pharaoh **Tuthmosis III** (see below). Two years later, Hatshepsut took for herself the title of Pharaoh and reigned for 22 years until her death. She chose to dress like a pharaoh, and she even wore the ceremonial beard and short kilt of her male counterparts. Moreover, she claimed to be the daughter of the ancient creator god Amun.

Tuthmosis III (c.1504-1430 BCE): the sixth ruler of the Eighteenth Dynasty, he distinguished himself through extensive military campaigns over his 54-year reign. His father died when Tuthmosis III was only two or three years old, yet he was officially crowned Pharaoh. His aunt, Hatshepsut, assumed the role of regent and, within two years, took for herself the title of Pharaoh. When Hatshepsut died after 22 years, Tuthmosis II ascended the throne. He is distinguished for his military prowess and for leading more than 17 campaigns. He conquered hundreds of cities and expanded the Egyptian Empire to include Nubia in the far south and Canaan and southern Syria in the Levant.

Amenhotep IV/Akhenaten (c. 1350-1334 BCE): the eleventh ruler of the Eighteenth Dynasty, attempted to replace the ancient Egyptian religion with the monotheistic worship of *Aten*, the visible orb of the sun. He ruled from Akhetaten, near modern-day Tel Amarna.

Ramesses II (c. 1279-1212 BCE): called "The Great." He was the second son of Pharaoh Seti I and a member of the royal household, though his older brother was next-in-line to the throne. Unfortunately, that brother died when Ramesses II was 14 years old so that Ramesses II became the Prince of Egypt. He took for himself two wives, Nefertari and Isetnofret. Nefertari became Ramessses' chief wife when he ascended the throne of Egypt at 25 years of age, upon the death of his father Seti I, and Nefertari ruled beside him during his 66-year reign. Ramesses II was the third ruler of the Nineteenth Dynasty of the New Kingdom Period.

After the expulsion of the Hyksos from the northern Delta

where they had established a stronghold during the Second Intermediate Period, the pharaohs recognized the critical need to establish buffer zones at their borders to prevent future invasion. Ramesses II eagerly pressed this agenda with a series of aggressive military campaigns against Nubians to the south, Libyans across the Red Land, and Syrians and Hittites northward in the Levant. He led the 20,000-strong Egyptian army, equipped with some 5,000 chariots, against a Hittite force more than twice as strong at the Battle of Kadesh, the oldest recorded battle in history. The battle ended with a stalemate, and later a peace treaty, with the Hittite nation which lasted for the duration of Ramesses II's reign.

Ramesses II distinguished himself as a great warrior and military leader. His military achievements were chiseled into stone from one end of the Nile Valley to the other. Ramesses II was also known for having the names and glyphs of former pharaohs removed from records of their achievements and replaced with his own! Moreover, Ramesses II was responsible for a multitude of building projects featuring his own likeness, including the giant statue at his Mortuary Temple on the west bank of the Nile near Thebes, and a series of four giant, seated statues of Ramesses II which adorn the temple facade of Abu Simbel. Ramesses II also built a new capital city which was used during his reign but was later abandoned: Pi-Ramesses. Pharaoh Ramesses II died at around 90 years of age, and was initially buried on the western bank of the river, in the Valley of the Kings. His mummy was later moved to protect it from tomb robbers. The mummy of Ramesses II the Great now resides in the Grand Egyptian Museum at Giza, just outside Cairo.

Ramesses III (c. 1182-1151 BCE): second ruler of the Twentieth Dynasty, led a mighty land and sea battle in the Delta, turning away invading tribes to save Egypt. He built a great temple on the west bank of the Nile opposite Thebes. His reign was marked by a gradual decline, leading to the Late Period (c. 1070-332 BCE).

The Ptolemaic Period

Alexander the Great (c. 332-323 BCE): As Alexander the Great expanded his empire throughout Europe, Asia, and the territories of the Persian Empire, he took control of Egypt by sheer military might. From Egypt, Alexander sought to expand his Empire eastward, towards the Indus Valley. Alexander was eventually undermined by his own troops, who desired to return to Greece. He died of fever during the return journey at the age of 33.

Ptolemy I Soter I (c. 304-284 BCE): first ruler of the Thirty-second, and last, Dynasty. He had commanded Alexander the Great's personal guard, until the latter died in 332 BCE. After nine years of ensuing turmoil, Ptolemy seized control of Egypt, founding an all-Greek dynasty which endured until its thirteenth ruler, **Cleopatra VII** (see below), committed suicide, bringing ancient Egypt's independent history to an end.

Cleopatra VII (51-30 BCE): the last pharaoh of the Thirty-second, or Ptolemaic, Dynasty and of ancient Egypt itself, and the favorite daughter of Pharaoh Ptolemy XII, Cleopatra VII grew up in the royal household with all its privileges, including education. She could speak, read, and write Greek since her father and the entire Ptolemaic Dynasty before him were of Greek descent. But her education included at least six other languages, including Egyptian and Latin. She was intelligent, capable and ambitious for herself and for her son, Caesarion, whose father was Julius Caesar.

Prologue

Setting: the ancient city of **Thinis**, believed to have been located near Abydos. Thinis had been the center of a confederacy of tribes in Upper Egypt until its leader, Narmer, conquered Lower Egypt and united the Two Lands. Thinis then became the capital city of unified Egypt.

Time: The Early Dynastic Era (3150-2686 BCE)

Synopsis: The earliest known example of a story utilizing the Egyptian writing system we know as hieroglyphics is called the Narmer Palette, after Narmer (believed to be the same person as *Menes*), the ruler of Upper Egypt who conquered Lower Egypt to unite the Two Lands under one government. A six-inch stone palette was commonly used in early Egyptian culture to mix cosmetic eye shadow. This palette, however, was two feet tall, carved on both sides with rudimentary writing and bas-relief sculpture, and was intended to tell a story: the story of Narmer's victory and the establishment thereby of the First Dynasty of a centralized Egyptian government. Incidentally, this palette marks the beginning of Egyptian history. It is ground zero for the civilization which spanned 31 centuries!

Not much more is known for sure of Narmer, though other archaeological finds corroborate the evidence of the Narmer Palette. Narmer was believed to be the ruler of a southern tribal confederacy. One side of the palette shows Narmer wearing the "White Crown of the South" and "leading a procession of tiny figures carrying banners" (Brier & Hoyt Hobbs, 2013, p. 11) which are believed to represent the various tribal allies. The reverse of the Palette displays Narmer wearing the Red Crown of the North and wielding a mace to strike down his enemy. Archaeologists found the macehead depicted on the palette in the same dig as the palette itself, which, moreover, is inscribed with the name Narmer.

Narmer consolidated power to find the First Dynasty of Egyptian civilization. Relatively little is known of his successors, whose reign spanned the First and Second Dynasties of the Early Dynastic Period. There seems little overt significance to their individual accomplishments until the rule of Khasekhemwy, the last ruler of the Second Dynasty and of the Early Dynastic period itself. He is credited with restoring order and unity to Egypt after a period of unrest, possibly civil war, between rival devotees of the Horus and Set cults. His royal glyph or insignia, unique in Egyptian history, includes the symbols for both names.

Khasekhemwy also initiated several building projects during his reign, the most significant of which is a vast mud-brick enclosure called Shunet El Zebib, or "raisin barn" in Arabic, built at Abydos c. 2700 BCE. Its original purpose is unknown, but details of its structure evoke the later step pyramids built by Khasekhemwy's son, Djoser. In light of these similarities and of the imminent boom in the building of royal tombs and mortuary temples, beginning in earnest with Djoser's step pyramids, we may safely infer that Egyptians were thinking more deeply, and asking themselves more pointed questions, about death, the Afterlife, and what ought to be done by the living to prepare for these. By the living we mean, of course, the pharaohs, since the Egyptian cosmos afforded little room for consideration of the plight of average mortals. It turns out that the Third and Fourth Dynasties would supply concrete answers to such questions.

Act I

Setting: Memphis, a city at the mouth of the Nile Delta 12 miles south of Giza in Lower Egypt. Its origin predates the unification of Egypt, and legend ascribes its foundation to Menes/Narmer. Memphis became the capital of Egypt around the beginning of the Third Dynasty.

Time: the Old Kingdom Era (2686-2181 BCE)

Synopsis: This period is rightly called The Age of the

Pyramids, though Djoser deserves credit for the original thought which precipitated the building frenzy. The idea of containing a sand-pit burial within a sloped, rectangular enclosure, called a *mastaba*, was not new (see chapter 7). Enclosing several elaborate burial and storage chambers inside a mastaba 397 ft. x 358 ft. sq at the base, rising in six layers like "a 200-foot-high facsimile of a wedding cake" (Brier & Hoyt Hobbs, 2013, p.179), was novel. The architectural genius who designed this remarkable structure was Imhotep, chancellor to Pharaoh Djoser and high priest of Ra, who later in Egyptian history was given the status of a god. Imhotep's forward-thinking and design failed to prevent robbers from emptying the tomb, however.

Snefru, the first pharaoh of the Fourth Dynasty, set out to improve upon the innovative step pyramid of his predecessor in designing his tomb. We would recognize his concept as a true pyramid in design. Unlike that of his successor Khufu, Snefru's pyramids—he constructed three in total—were simply modified step pyramids. He filled in the steps of successive courses with dressed stone to render the smooth-sided appearance we recognize today. Snefru could not finish his first attempt because its sides were too steep and unstable for its soft limestone casing. The second, or bent, pyramid started too steep, and its builders had to use a shallower wall angle from the halfway point to prevent its collapse. The third and final attempt was a success: That same shallow slope angle and broader base ensured that the pyramid would stand the test of time. It still stands today, at Saqqara, as the earliest extant example of a true pyramid.

The history of the Fourth Dynasty reached its zenith with the construction of what became known as the Great Pyramid of Khufu, Snefru's son, on the Giza plateau a short distance from the capital, Memphis (see chapter 7). There had been pyramids of various kinds before, as there would be after (Khufu's son, Khafra, for example, would build a pyramid almost as glorious as that of his father, beside the Great Pyramid; it is recognizable for the iconic 200-foot long Sphinx guarding the tomb). But Khufu's tomb stands alone. It was the tallest free-standing structure on earth for almost four millennia. And, once considered one of the Seven Wonders of the Ancient World, it remains a Wonder to this day. To think of Egypt is to think of the pyramids, and in particular of the Great Pyramid. What was once designed as the "resurrection machine" of Pharaoh Khufu has become the singular memorial of a great ancient culture.

The long reign of Pepi II (c. 2278-2184 BCE), the second-to-last ruler of the Old Kingdom, coincided with the gradual breakdown of stable, centralized political authority. Bureaucrats sought to entrench themselves and their families in positions of power, often away from the national capital. Nomarchs vied for control of their own and other nomes throughout Upper and Lower Egypt. The leadership base of the country was fragmented. Some might be tempted to blame Pepi II for what they assume was weak and ineffectual rule, as though he allowed things to get out of control. And yet the longevity of a 94-year rule—perhaps the longest reign of any pharaoh in Egyptian history—should be the hallmark of stable government. What other factor might have contributed to Egypt's drifting into the period of anarchy following the death of Pepi II? Cox holds the key to this mystery: "The annual flooding of the Nile...provided the framework by which the society was held together" (Harvey Gallagher Cox, 2013, p. 27). Barbara Bell has described how the level of the annual Nile inundation began to drop by the end of the First Dynasty, and continued to fall throughout the Second to at least the Fifth, according to the oldest existing records (Bell, 1970). By the reign of Pharaoh Sahure (c. 2490 BCE), the inundation had risen only 2.48 cubits, or 4.33 feet (Bell, 1970). Remember that, according to the Roman historian Pliny, "in a rise of twelve cubits, [Egypt] senses famine" (Wilkinson, Toby, 2015). Many historians agree that progressively lower annual inundations over several centuries of the Early Kingdom, up to and including the reign of Pepi II, must have precipitated serious famine and the subsequent collapse of the "framework by which the society was held together" (Cox, 2013, p. 27).

First Intermission

First Intermediate Period (2181-2040 BCE)

This 141-year period in ancient Egyptian history, sandwiched between the glories of the Old Kingdom—the unification of Upper and Lower Kingdoms under Narmur, and the construction of numerous pyramids both at Saqqara and on the Giza plateau—and the restoration of political and civil order under the Mentuhotep, Amenemhat, and Senusret pharaohs during the Middle Kingdom, epitomizes the chaos which was so repugnant to the Egyptian psyche. According to Manetho, the 3rd century BCE priest mentioned earlier who introduced the concept of dynasties to lend structure to the span of Egyptian history, no less than 140 individuals laid claim to the title of pharaoh during this time of weakened royal authority, political maneuvering, and civil war. Since it seems unlikely, if not impossible, that the country had a new pharaoh every year over several average Egyptian lifetimes, we can safely infer that more than a few of these "ephemeral kings" (Wilkinson, 2013) ruled simultaneously and from different capitals. Manetho identified at least three different dynasties in his reckoning of this turbulent and uncertain time.

With the absolute rule of the pharaohs weakened and diluted in this way, government and civil administrators seized the opportunity afforded by the resulting power vacuum to expand their influence significantly and to secure their own and their families' futures. Appointed positions gradually became hereditary possessions without a stable, higher authority to provide necessary checks and balances. Furthermore, Egyptian infrastructure and economy were driven, as we saw in chapters two and three, by the ability of the pharaoh, the Son of Ra and the incarnation of Horus, to mobilize the entire population of Egypt in unquestioning obedience to his divine will and with promises of favorable treatment in the next life, where he would once again be their pharaoh. In the absence of that one clear voice of command and comfort, the building of monuments, tombs, and temples all but ceased.

This unfortunate episode in the history of Egyptian civilization deserves the epithet Dark Age. Brier and Hobbs reference the following excerpt from a papyrus written by some unnamed eyewitness to the crisis which characterized this period, as follows:

The bowman is ready. The wrongdoer is everywhere. There is no man of yesterday. A man goes out to plow with his shield. A man smites his brother, his mother's son. Men sit in the bushes until the benighted traveler comes in order to plunder his load. The robber is the possessor of riches. Boxes of ebony are broken up. Precious acacia wood is cleft asunder. (Brier & A Hoyt Hobbs, 2013, p. 20).

We can hardly appreciate to what extent the inner turmoil of gods-fearing Egyptian citizens might have mirrored that without, given what we know of their worldview, unless we attempt to reach across the millennia with the eyes of our imagination. Yet can we not hear a faint echo from this turbulent past in the midst of the noise of our today? It reminds us that the drama of these people, upon whose lives the curtain has long ago fallen, is not merely an ancient Egyptian drama–it is a *human* drama, after all. And as with any drama, it is just at that point when all hope seems lost, that we eagerly await a hero who will set things right.

Act II

Setting: Thebes, capital city during the Eleventh Dynasty; and It-towe, ten miles south of Memphis, which became the new capital city of Egypt under the reign of Amenemhet I, at the beginning of the Twelfth Dynasty.

Time: The Middle Kingdom Era (2060-1782 BCE)

Synopsis: The Egyptian people found their hero in Mentuhotep II (2060-2010 BCE). Previous rulers, all bearing the name Intef, had tried unsuccessfully to restore Maat, order, to the Two Lands. What the country needed was not a diplomat or a politician, but a strong warrior, someone with whom the war god ("Mentu") is pleased ("hotep"). Mentuhotep II took for his Horus name the descriptor, "He Gives Life to the Heart of the Two Lands," and, later, "Uniter of the Two Lands." Historians point out that his statues display his "brute power" but are "crude and poorly worked" (Brier, 1999), suggesting that the artistry and craftsmanship of the Early Kingdom were lost during the time of chaos. What may also have been lost, for the time being, is that belief in pharaohs who depicted themselves as immortal and above the rest of humanity. 141 years of very human struggle led the Egyptian people to appreciate real men of bone and sinew, men who could fight and bleed for the sake of reunifying their country. The records of Mentuhotep's valiant efforts are scattered up and down the Nile. His sons who succeeded him were likewise men of action, undertaking great expeditions for the sake of rebuilding their country.

Amenemhet I (c 1991-1962 BCE), the first ruler of the Twelfth Dynasty, was "a commoner who did great things" (Brier, 1999, p. 38), including establishing a new capital, It-towe or Binder of Two Lands, strategically placed in the Faiyum instead of at Memphis or Thebes. His successors took measures to increase agricultural production there, including the building of a 30-mile long canal to bring the Nile's water to the Faiyum. Amenemhet I's reign inaugurated what is considered to be the Golden Age of the Middle Kingdom Period; it was a time of stability and expansion, particularly south into Kush (as far as the Second and Third Cataract) and north into southern Canaan in the Levant.

During this amazing period of Egyptian history, art evolved in elegantly realistic directions, some of the most refined literature in the Egyptian language was produced, and building projects displayed a level of skill and refinement that still speaks for them to this day.

Second Intermission

Second Intermediate Period (1782-1570 BCE)

Have you heard the familiar refrain: second verse, same as the first? That describes perfectly this second period of chaos and turmoil in ancient Egypt. The quelling of civil war and the social upheaval which followed in its wake by Mentuhotep II, which inaugurated the Middle Kingdom period, must have offered Egyptian citizens a renewed sense of hope for the rebirth of their nation after the disastrous events of the previous 140 years. Whole generations had passed into Duat, the Farworld of departed souls seeking passage to the Field of Reeds, while their familiar and comforting social and political order had crumbled. They had needed some strong deliverer to re-establish that order, and Mentuhotep II had accomplished that heavy task.

Now, 400 years later, the Egyptian people found themselves in a similar, yet at once even worse, situation than before. Over more than 200 years, Egyptian rule once again became fragmented, with more than 160 individuals from three dynasties vying for the pharaonic throne. Weakened from within, they found themselves beset by powerful foreign invaders who had emigrated from the Levant and established a power base in the far northeast of Lower Egypt at Avaris. These infiltrators, Indo-Europeans who called themselves

Hyksos, adopted many of the features and practices of Egyptian culture. Yet, they did not fool the proud and insular Egyptian people: to the Egyptian, these immigrants were despicable foreigners. They should be driven out of the country. That task would fall to the rulers of what became the 17th dynasty and, ultimately, to the pharaoh Ahmose, the first king of the 18th dynasty, whose victories opened the door to the glories of the 500-year New Kingdom (1570-1070 BCE).

Act III

Setting: Thebes, during the Seventeenth Dynasty; the first of the Eighteenth Dynasty until the succession of Akhenaten; the rest of the Eighteenth Dynasty after Akhenaten, and the first portion of the Nineteenth Dynasty until the succession of Rameses II the Great; Akhetaten, the new capital city under the reign of Akhenaten; Pi-Ramses during the reign of Rameses II in the Nineteenth Dynasty; and Memphis, following the death of Rameses II and throughout the Twentieth Dynasty.

Time: the New Kingdom Era (1570-1070 BCE)

Synopsis: The New Kingdom witnessed the transformation

of Egypt from an isolated country to a vast empire, through the military conquests and political alliances forged by a series of powerful and dynamic leaders. Increased wealth spurred grand building projects, including the Temple of Luxor at Thebes and major expansion of the Temple of Karnak. Ramesses II chiseled his name and accomplishments over much of Egypt, and erected massive monuments to himself, including the Temple of Abu Simbel, which boasts four massive seated statues of the pharaoh across its facade. Hatshepsut built a spectacular Mortuary Temple carved into the base of a mountain. The pharaohs of the Eighteenth, Nineteenth and Twentieth Dynasties wanted to be sure that their names and deeds would never be forgotten. It seems they achieved that desire. And the Valley of the Kings, for 500 years the burial ground of New Kingdom pharaohs, has yielded up unimaginable treasures in the early 20th century which would forever secure its place as among the most iconic and memorable features of ancient Egypt.

Epilogue

The Late Period (1070-332 BCE)
This was a time of decline, from the glorious days of the New Kingdom Period, during which other nations occupied Egypt and brought with them foreign speech, different customs, and the gradual dilution and disintegration of indigenous

Egyptian culture. This and the Ptolemaic Period which followed are absent from the chronologies of some historians, who feel that the true Egypt perished with the invasions of Nubian, Libyan, Kushite, Persian and Greek peoples over more than 700 years. However, the role of Pharaoh did not disappear from history until the death of its last representative, Cleopatra VII.

The Ptolemaic Period (323-30 BCE)

The Ptolemaic Dynasty had ruled ancient Egypt for more than 250 years when Cleopatra VII was born. Cleopatra's father died when she was 18 years old, having left the throne to her and Ptolemy XIII, her 10-year-old brother. The two married and together assumed the throne of Egypt; but, given their age difference, Cleopatra could assert more authority than her brother, becoming the de facto Pharaoh. The younger Ptolemy was not pleased with his sister's apparent usurping of authority. When he was 13 years old, Ptolemy expelled Cleopatra from the palace and assumed the throne as Pharaoh.

Julius Caesar arrived in Egypt in 48 BC, and Ptolemy XIII welcomed him to the palace. While Caesar was there, Cleopatra allegedly snuck back into the palace inside a rolled-up carpet and enlisted his aid to overthrow her brother.

Caesar defeated the Egyptian army at the Battle of the Nile, and Ptolemy XIII drowned in the river while attempting to escape. Cleopatra once more took the throne as Pharaoh, co-ruling with another brother, Ptolemy XIV. Cleopatra VII strengthened the Egyptian economy, establishing lucrative trade relations with surrounding nations and increasing Egypt's prosperity, which contributed to her popularity with the Egyptian people. Despite her relationship with Caesar, and notwithstanding that she was Greek, and the descendant of Greeks as far back as the days of Alexander the Great, Cleopatra VII may have considered herself Egyptian, and wanted to preserve her country's independence.

Cleopatra and Julius Caesar became lovers, and he fathered a son by her, named Caesarion. This son would eventually become the last king of Egypt, co-ruling with his mother. Cleopatra had visited Rome and was staying in one of Caesar's country houses when he was assassinated on March 15, 44 BCE. Cleopatra returned thereafter to Egypt where, in 41 BCE, she met Mark Antony, one of the Roman leaders who were vying for power after Caesar's murder. Cleopatra fell in love with Mark Antony and enlisted his support against Caesar's legitimate heir, Octavian, desiring instead to put her own son Caesarion on the throne of the Roman Empire. Mark Antony had declared Caesarion to be Caesar's legal heir, pitting himself against Octavian in a contest for control of the Roman Empire.

The combined armies of Cleopatra and Mark Antony clashed with Octavian's forces at the Battle of Actium. The two were defeated and fled to Egypt. Antony made another attempt to defeat Octavian but realized that he would once again be defeated and taken prisoner by Octavian's superior forces. In the midst of battle, Antony heard the false report that Cleopatra was dead, and took his own life. When Cleopatra heard that Antony was dead, she committed suicide, possibly by self-administering some kind of poison or by exposing herself to the bite of a venomous snake. Later that year, Caesarion, the son of Cleopatra VII and Julius Caesar, was murdered. Ancient Egypt was dead, absorbed into the Roman Empire of Octavian who took the name Augustus as the first Emperor of Rome.

CHAPTER 6
PIT GRAVES TO PYRAMIDS

It's the *Pits*, Man!

We've witnessed the development of an Egyptian worldview centered upon the Afterlife, particularly upon resurrection–the reanimation of the deceased person, the reunion of his body with *Ba*, the soul, and *Ka*, the vital essence, and the prospect of eternal life within that body. I'm convinced that the germ of this worldview came from at least as far back in time as the Predynastic period and the resettlement of modern humans in the Nile Valley eleven millennia ago. Do you remember the most basic form of burial discovered by archaeologists throughout the Valley? Think of its elements: a body placed into a shallow sandpit; legs contracted into a fetal position; the body laying on its left side, its head pointing south so that the body faces to the west. At first, the body is simply covered with warm sand. Later, we see the body covered by an animal hide, perhaps laying on a reed mat. Later still, we see a young woman in that same kind of sandpit, in the same position, but now she's wrapped in linen cloth and fur. Instead of a solitary grave, there are cemeteries. Graves become more ornate, and offerings of food, clothing, and other personal effects are placed within. Some of the deceased were wealthy: their tombs are larger still, more elaborate, while the graves of the poor are humbler.

Egyptian prehistory has supplied us with ample clues regarding the *why* of these aspects of death and burial, which shine a light on the embryonic worldview of Egypt. The bodies of loved ones (not enemies–these were dumped, unceremoniously, in mass graves) needed to be positioned carefully to face the west. Why? The more fully-developed worldview of later centuries suggests that the west was the source of rebirth or reincarnation. The disposition of the dead body was somehow connected to the disposition of the soul. The evolution of preservative techniques confirms this thinking that the physical body was essential to the Afterlife experience. Bodies needed to remain intact (a nod here to the Osiris-Isis myth and the consequent need for Isis to fashion an artificial phallus for her husband) while that which animated them was on the other side. Natural mummification by sand-pit burial progressed to the wrapping of the body with furs and, later, with strips of linen. Yet, the Egyptians could still not prevent the process of decay. At some point, they must have made the connection between the presence of the soft organs and the decomposition process (remember, the Egyptians had no science–only best guesses). The answer? Remove the soft organs before burial. Then, too, if sand possessed some preservative properties, salt would be far better! Enter natron, a salt combination found in only one place in the world–Egypt! Remove the internal organs, bury the body in natron for a lengthy period, remove the desiccated body and clean it, and then–that's right, wrap it in strips of linen! There we have the deliberate mummification process, a logical outcome of the developing Egyptian worldview. We'll look more closely at the details in the next chapter. For now, let's consider the development of what we might consider the "mummy house."

Sandpits have been topped with one mastaba, then another, and another. So, there you have, the step pyramid of Djoser! Nice, but we can do better! What if we were to make it bigger, taller, and smooth out the sides? Why, of course, then you'd have…

The Great Pyramid of Khufu

It's not customary to tell a story by starting at the end.

Nonetheless, we need to keep the following nutshell summary at the forefront of our thinking as we approach the question:

How on earth did they do that?

The statistics associated with the great pyramid of Khufu are humbling: 2,300,000 blocks of stone, each weighing an average of 2 tons, set in place at a rate of one block every two minutes for 10 hours a day over a period of at least 20 years; alignment to true north with an error of only one-twentieth of a degree; and a finished height of 481 feet, making it the tallest building in the world until the construction of the great European cathedrals (Wilkinson, Toby, 2015).

That's the end of the story! But let's travel in our imaginations to the other end, that is, to the beginning of the project – indeed, before the project began. Imagine that you are the king's nephew, Hemiunu and that you've been commissioned to oversee what by rights is the grandest and most ambitious construction project known to man. After consulting the gods and collaborating with the royal engineers, you've selected a site atop the rugged limestone plateau of Giza, within spitting distance of the great monuments of previous dynasties at Saqqara. From where you stand, you can see the pyramids in the distance. An impressive effort, no doubt, but the scale of this undertaking will leave them all behind. And so, there you stand on that limestone plateau as the sun is setting. And you begin to see the faint twinkle of the Polar Star. This will be the destination of your resurrected pharaoh. But so that he does not lose his way after that resurrection, he looks to the structure to orient him in space. Your pyramid must be ideally situated and precisely aligned with the North star. There can be no room for error. The afterlife of your pharaoh depends upon it. Perhaps, your own life depends upon it as well. But how to be sure? You've crunched the numbers with your best engineers and mathematicians. Do you know roughly the quantity of stone you're going to need to build such a monumental structure? By all calculations, you'll need over 2 million blocks of limestone retrieved from nearby quarries, hauled on wooden sleds up watered ramps to be finished and put into place. But as you look around in the twilight of that empty plateau, the magnitude of the job seems almost overwhelming. And yet glory awaits the completion of this unrivaled masterpiece.

You line up your thumb before your face with that North star, and before you leave, you offer a silent prayer to the gods for guidance, and protection, and safety–and to allow you to live to see the completion of this task. You have a little over 20 years.

Can you feel the weight of such an enormous task? It must have felt like being crushed under one of those limestone blocks. And yet...what if you *could* do it?

How to Build a Pyramid

It's a truism that, to finish well, one must start well. With a project as ambitious as this, the earliest decisions and actions can make the difference between resounding success and crushing failure. We know that the building of Khufu's Great Pyramid was successful on a scale unmatched by any other edifice on earth for more than three millennia, and no other single structure has outlasted it, or likely ever will. The decisions made and the steps which Khufu took more than four millennia ago were the right ones. If Khufu wished to create a monument with an enduring sense of permanence, this would be it. So, what were those decisions and those steps? We'll consider each of these in turn as we learn from the best how to build a pyramid.

Choose the Right Man for the Job

In the brief imagination exercise above, I attempted to convey that choosing the right man is indispensable to success.

Hindsight is always one hundred percent for us who look back from the vantage point of the future. We can easily say, *I knew all along that would work.* There were no such assurances before Khufu embarked on his ambitious plan, no matter how strong his belief in the soundness of it. All he had was the advice of his trusted officials and advisors—and, I believe, his capacity to be a good judge of character. There was no mistaking that good character was the primary requirement for this undertaking. There was no one whose resume included pyramid-building—nothing of this magnitude had ever been done before!

Khufu's choice of Hemiunu, thought to have been his nephew, to oversee the entire project from top to bottom proved to be the good first decision we discussed a moment ago. We don't know much about the man except that he was accomplished in several diverse administrative roles. He must have had the pharaoh's complete trust and confidence to be selected for a position of such consequence (Wilkinson, 2013). We must remember that the pyramid was not designed to serve as a giant memorial, like some elaborate, gargantuan tombstone. That sort of thought is merely the overlay of our 21st-century mindset upon a vastly different culture. Egyptian culture was obsessed with the Afterlife, and especially with the prospect of resurrection. No, the pyramids in general, and this Great

Pyramid in particular, were not designed to be grave-markers—they were intended to be resurrection machines! Bob Brier emphasizes that "when the dead pharaoh was resurrected, as the religion of the ancient Egyptians foretold, his new self would travel to the Polar Star, situated directly north" (Brier & A Hoyt Hobbs, 2013, p. 218). Tom Wilkinson reminds us that "the efficiency of the pyramid as a means of resurrecting the king after his death depended on the accuracy of its orientation" (Wilkinson, 2013). The newly resurrected Khufu would, it seems, use the pyramid as an earthly guidepost, pointing his potentially disoriented new self to his new, eternal home.

There could be no mistakes and no margin of error when the pharaoh's eternal destiny hung in the balance. Khufu needed someone he could trust with his life—and so he chose Hemiunu. The result? We can say nothing about the pharaoh's potential, or actual spiritual resurrection, though we know that his physical remains have never been found. What is certain is that he could never have been misguided by an improperly oriented resurrection machine such as the Great Pyramid at Giza—Hemiunu accomplished its "alignment to true north with an error of only one-twentieth of a degree" (Wilkinson, Toby, 2015)!

Pick the Site Carefully

Just as the wrong choice of overseer for such a grand project as Khufu's pyramid could spell disaster, so, too, could choosing the wrong site. After all, the platform for such a massive structure would need to be capable of supporting over 2 million stones, each weighing between one and two tons. That's more than 4,000,000 tons of limestone–a mind-boggling figure! But Khufu had chosen the best man for the job, and Hemiunu's choice of a platform for this monumental structure would be an excellent choice over the next 4,500 and more years. The Giza plateau contains a large vein of hard grey limestone, known by geologists as the Mokattam Formation.

It was upon this extremely stable bedrock that Hemiunu chose to erect the pyramid. The site had several other distinct advantages: it stood within a short distance of the step pyramids of Saqqara, visible to and from them as seemed appropriate for a royal monument; it was close to fast supplies of local building materials, notably softer limestone deposits which could be quarried and transported more quickly and easily to the plateau; there was room in the vicinity of the Giza plateau to erect what Bob Brier describes as a virtual Boomtown (2013) to house, feed, and care for the tens of thousands of workers who would spend the next 20 years building the pyramid. It was a relatively short four miles from the Giza plateau to the banks of the Nile. Though workers would have to excavate a canal to float supplies to the plateau from up the river, the location ensured that during the inundation every August and September, boats could reach the plateau's base easily, providing an uninterrupted supply chain for this massive undertaking. The digging of the canal necessitated the dredging of a harbor on the river and the building of docks to accommodate the increased number of boats and barges required.

Find your Bearings

As we noted earlier in this chapter, the orientation of the future pyramid needed to be exact. The resurrected life of the pharaoh himself depended on it! Suppose the engineers' calculations caused the pyramid to deviate by even a minuscule amount from true north. In that case, those deviations could be magnified in the finished structure to produce a pyramid that was unusable. According to the pharaoh's timeline, there would be no opportunity to build a second pyramid should the first fail to meet the exacting standards required by Egyptian religion. Unlike Zoser with his step pyramids at Saqqara, there would be no second chance.

There were several methods by which Egyptian engineers

could determine precisely the orientation needed for the pyramid's foundation with fair precision. Each technique involved the position of the building relative to the north pole or star, which was always visible to the Egyptians. This was the same polar star to which if the building program was more successful, Koufos resurrected spirit would fly. And the first method of determining orientation two true north involves the use of a plumbline. Two stars rotate in a regular pattern around the celestial polar star. It was discovered that when those two stars are perfectly vertically aligned with the polar star and a plumbline suspended in the plane of their orientation, true north could be established as the basis to orient the building. Another method involved the planting of a stick so that it would cast no shadow at noon. If engineers marked the stick's shadow at a specific interval before and after noon, the point halfway between those marks indicated true north. A third method involved building a temporary wall with its top edge as level as possible and facing as closest possible to the north. The builder would observe the rising of a particular star, mark its position on the top of the wall, and later make a similar mark at the place where that same star set, the point halfway between was sure to be as close as possible to true north.

What is remarkable is that the orientation of a massive

structure like the Great Pyramid, which is so critical, in the Egyptian worldview, to the king's future, could be made using rudimentary tools and methods. The Egyptians did not need advanced mathematical principles or the assistance (as some have claimed) of aliens! Everything they needed was within their grasp.

Make it Level, Larry!

To be fair, there was no manual written in Egyptian or any other language to instruct architects, engineers, and builders in the knottier points of pyramid construction, such as guaranteeing a level foundation that would measure 756 feet square at its base. Nor I suspect, would such an instruction manual be appreciated or even needed. Nevertheless, through a process of trial and error, Zoser managed, within his lifetime, to build a step pyramid that has stood the test of time and still stands today. And while, for at least the first three dynasties of the Early Kingdom, Egyptian civilization still had one foot firmly planted in the lower Neolithic age, it is beyond dispute that they were fundamentally masters of stone. Thus, it is not surprising that their most iconic structures were raised during this period. Moreover, the sheer number of Egyptian tombs, temples, and even the pyramids scattered throughout the land is a testament to their deep knowledge of and facility with stoneworking.

It should come as no surprise, then, that the elevation of the Great Pyramid from corner to corner, over a length of 756 feet, deviates by less than one inch (Brier & A Hoyt Hobbs, 2013, p. 219). The question remains: How did they accomplish such a feat? The answer may be simpler than you think. Brier and Hobbs (2013) have suggested that the engineers may have cut a shallow trough around the pyramid's perimeter and filled it with water to function as a giant level. Workers would excavate any spot where the ground was unlevel until the level was achieved.

Get the Teams Together

By now, you may be wondering what sort of workforce was needed to build the great pyramid of Giza? First, we've considered the raw numbers of material and the pace at which the pyramid would need to be created: over two million stones, weighing anywhere from one to two tons each on average, to be placed at an average rate of 30 blocks per hour, seven days a week, 350 days a year, for 20 years. Many of the workers employed in this venture were farmers who couldn't work their fields for weeks or months after the inundation. They constituted a transient workforce since they must have returned home to plant their fields once the waters had receded. Pharaoh's recruitment officers roamed the land enlisting those strong and able-bodied enough to endure the backbreaking work of pyramid construction. Egyptologists are of two minds regarding the nature and outcome of this recruitment process. Bob Brier (Brier & A Hoyt Hobbs, 2013) believes that the workforce pressed into service for Pharaoh was composed primarily of freemen and patriots willing to serve their king and their country–more like a partnership than a proscription. However, Toby Wilkinson sees a darker side to the workforce management of ancient Egypt. Imagined living conditions in the pyramid town adjacent to the Giza plateau, and similar pyramid towns built during later dynasties, suggest that far from being willing participants, the workers who worked 10 hours a day seven days a week to make the pyramids did not enlist but were instead drafted into a rigorous and disciplined working structure. They were provided with crude dormitory accommodation and seem to have eaten communally. The evidence of refuse dumps from these pyramid towns indicates that food was a significant preoccupation for these workers, understandable because of the nature of the work they performed. Perhaps the men were not slaves as portrayed in classic movies, but again, there was likely not a volunteer arrangement sealed with a handshake.

I refer again to Toby Wilkinson, who has done the math of which I speak. I suspect that his calculations for the size of the workforce and organizational structure are based upon the sleeping capacity of dormitories in the pyramid town. A bunkhouse or dormitory can sleep up to 40 men (20 on each side of the long building). So then, it is likely that the basic workforce unit consists of a team of 20 men with one team leader. Teams will compete against one another and pace one another, enabling greater productivity. Ten teams comprise a division or, in Greek, a phyle. Five phyles would make up a gang of 1000 workers, and two gangs with unique identities and comraderies made a crew–the largest unit. The larger units of such a workforce are allegedly attested in surviving inscriptions, but Wilkinson does not identify the source of these.

He goes on to say, "calculations and practical experiments have shown that just two crews, or 4000 men, would have been sufficient to quarry, haul, and set in place more than 2 million stone blocks used to build the pyramid" (Wilkinson, 2013).

Wilkinson suggests that perhaps the same size of the workforce would have been needed to construct and maintain the vast ramps, leading from the main quarry to the pyramid and then up the sides of the monument as it grew in height; however, Brier and Hobbs dismiss the outside pyramid ramp idea as being impractical and costly both in time and resources. Briar and Hobbs' suggestion is that workers may have built a shorter, shallower ramp to reach the first few courses as the pyramid grew but that afterward, the stones would have been moved up ramps on the inside of the pyramid structure, expanding the hallways as they move forward to each successive course. Indeed, this idea is intriguing. Wilkinson discusses the "army of workers" working behind the scenes to keep the machine running, as it were. He concludes with this statement, that "the number of people employed at any one time on the pyramid project may not have risen much beyond 10,000 at any one time" (Wilkinson, 2013). If pyramid construction took place 350 days out of a year and if sickness, injury, and death were as significant as they may appear, Wilkinson's numbers may be conservative. A workforce of free men and patriots? Given the nature of the work, I am not sure, but that may be a rosier picture than the reality, driven by a divine imperative of absolute and unquestioned obedience to a god-king.

CHAPTER 7
I'M NOT YOUR MUMMY!

As we have seen in previous chapters, the history of ritual care for the bodies of the deceased has a long history, stretching back into neolithic and even Palaeolithic times. You may remember that I raised the intriguing question: Why is it that many human remains were uncovered in the Nile Valley in shallow burial pits in the sand, curled into a contracted or fetal position, laying on their left sides, with their heads pointing south and their faces pointing to the west? I mentioned then that we might never know the answer to the why of that seemingly ritual behavior. But there can be no coincidence in the repeated performance of that minor ritual. Perhaps it is part of the human psyche to treat the dead with a measure of reverence and respect. But, of course, that is not necessarily true when the deceased was one's enemy. There is evidence, relatively recent in the archeological record, of bodies having been thrown into a mass pit or grave together, having had their throats slit most unceremoniously. Such instances might represent rudimentary human sacrifice, but the motivations will remain forever hidden since neither the dead in those pits nor their killers can reach out from their graves to enlighten us.

Nonetheless, in classic post-unification Egypt, there is a progression in burial rights until, as Bob Brier has said, "preserving the physical body after death became, over the centuries, a kind of Egyptian industry" (Brier & Hoyt Hobbs, 2013). All the instances, in Paleolithic and Neolithic times, of sandpit burial failed to preserve the body as well as its attendants may have desired. Of course, the dry sand would serve as a desiccant to dehydrate the body and create what we think of as "natural" mummies. By 3500 BC, however, as we saw in a previous chapter, thought had been given to treatments to preserve the body, such as wrapping in strips of linen cloth and covering with fur, the first instance in the archeological record of intentional mummification. Now, this was nothing like the detailed and meticulous procedures which developed in civilized Egypt. But it does point tantalizingly forward to the early days of united Egypt when burials became more elaborate. As with other cultures to come, bodies were placed in rock-cut tombs much like the mausoleums of today. Still, these bodies would soon decompose without the benefit of sand's dehydrating properties, especially in a hot climate. It became clear to the Egyptians that some artificial means were necessary to preserve the deceased's body before burial. They believed that the spirit of the deceased would require that body to carry them on their journey through the Underworld, hopefully–though by no means certainly–to eternity in paradise, called the Field of Reeds.

In ancient Egypt, embalming shops were situated on the east side of the Nile River and burial sites on the west. This practice was a deliberate and strategic choice, necessitating a ritual boat ride first toward the east and then back across the river to the burial site on the west bank. The intent of this was to symbolize the deceased individual's journey through the Underworld toward resurrection in the west. Thus, a family who had no means to provide their own boat would need to rent a special funerary boat to transport their loved one's remains to the embalming shop. Then, in a scene reminiscent of the cultures of the Middle East in our day, female mourners would be commissioned to lament the passing of the soul into the far world. They would weep and wail, and in an eastern Mediterranean style, pour sand on their heads in mock remorse.

The mummification process involved several well-orchestrated steps:

- removal of the moist organs, those most likely to cause decomposition
- removal of the organs from the torso to be stored in special containers
- preparing the body with a mixture of various salts to dry the body completely
- washing and packing of the body cavities, specifically the abdomen and the chest
- padding of the face with linen in the cheeks and under the eyelids
- anointing the body with precious oils and lotions while a priest recited prayers
- the extraordinarily meticulous and painstaking bandaging of the body to prepare for the journey to the underworld.

Let's look at each of these steps in a little more detail to appreciate the process.

The first step of the mummification process removed the soft tissues, which would cause the body to decompose quickly. And as is true of each step in the process, the techniques used and the extent to which they were employed were tailored to suit the budget of the surviving family members. The costliest method to accomplish this first step involved inserting a long, needle-like instrument through the nostril to pierce the brain cavity, followed by a thin tool resembling a coat hanger or perhaps a crochet hook, when rotated, would break the brain into pieces. Next, the corpse was placed in a prone position so that the brain matter would drain through the nostrils. Egyptians gave no thought to preserving the brain because the seat of the soul, in their belief, was not the brain but the heart.

The next organs to be removed were the stomach, liver, spleen, and intestines, all removed through a tiny incision in the abdomen on the left side. The heart was left untouched and in place. It was believed in the Egyptian worldview to be the center and seat of human thought. Since the deceased would have to remember and recite specific magic spells on the other side to be reanimated, the heart must stay where it was. The other organs, once removed, were placed into particular jars, each of whose lids were carved in the shape of one of the four sons of Horus: Mesti, with a human head; Duamutef, who resembled a jackal; Hapy, represented by a baboon; and Qebesenef, a hawk.

Before the embalmers sealed the jars, they poured a preservative liquid over the organs inside. They sealed the jars while priests recited prayers.

The next step in the process was the preparation of the body for drying. And this involved covering the body with a naturally occurring alkaline mixture called natron. The salt mixture consisted of sodium bicarbonate, sodium chloride, and sodium carbonate. Depending upon the size of the body, after the embalmers shoveled 600 pounds and possibly more of natron over the body to cover it entirely, the body was left to desiccate for 40 days.

At the end of that time, the body was removed from the natron. Its cavities were cleansed with wine and aromatic spices and packed with linen soaked in resin to preserve the body's natural contours. Of course, cheaper burials involved cheaper stuffing, typically sawdust and bags of onions. The cheeks and nose sockets are padded with linen as well so that the face maintained a lifelike appearance. Finally, the body was anointed twice with oils containing a mixture of frankincense, cedar oil, Syrian balsam, and oil of Libya. As the oils were being administered, a priest would recite specific prayers. The wrapping of the deceased body was intricate and purposeful. Bandages could be provided by the family and were usually scraps of linen or the bedding of the deceased. These were torn into strips 4 inches wide, and as much as 15 feet long, and rolled to be applied according to a fixed ceremony and ritual. Each finger and toe was wrapped separately, then the head bound tightly so that one could recognize the contours of the face. This was governed by strict and unwavering rituals and presided over by priests to ensure that the individual could see and breathe in the afterlife. The extremities were last to be bandaged. Usually, magic amulets were woven into the wrappings for protection until the body's resurrection.

The most crucial resurrection ritual awaited the deceased's return with their family and friends to the tomb on the west bank of the Nile. Once servants had stocked the tomb with furniture, food, and other necessities for their family member's journey through the Afterlife, a highly ritualized drama was enacted before the grave, officiated by a priest who dictated the order of service. This was the opening of the mouth ceremony as summarized by Bob Brier, an expert in the lost art of mummification:

The ground on which the play was to be performed was purified with water from four vases representing the four corners of the earth. Actresses, often members of the family, portrayed Isis and her sister Nephthys; males acted as the guardians of Horus and a central character called "The-son-who-loved-him." After incense was lit and various gods invoked, a calf was slaughtered to commemorate the battle in which Horus avenged the murder of his father, Osiris. (In the continuation of the Isis and Osiris myth, Seth's conspirators, attempting to escape the avenging Horus by changing into various animals, were caught by Horus and decapitated.) Special animals were ritually killed, including two bulls (one for the north and one for the south), gazelles, and ducks. One leg from the bull of the south was cut off and, along with its heart, offered to the mummy (Brier & Hoyt Hobbs, 2013, p. 65).

The final step in this ceremony involved a priest touching the deceased on the mouth with a special implement while reciting the following prayer, after which the tomb was sealed, and the funeral party shared a meal:

Thy mouth was closed, but I have set in order for thee thy mouth and thy teeth.

I open for thee thy mouth; I open for thee thy two eyes. I have opened thy mouth with the instrument of Anubis, with the iron implement with which the mouths of the gods were opened....

You shall walk and speak, your body shall be with the great company of the gods....

You are young again, you live again.

You are young again, you live again. (Brier & Hoyt Hobbs, 2013)

CONCLUSION

The history of ancient Egypt began with conflict, and with a king who unified the Two Lands, creating a civilization that would endure for 3,000 years. It ended with war, and with a queen whose death was the dissolution of that 3,000-year-old civilization. Between these two markers, we've witnessed the birth, maturing, and decline of earth's second-oldest civilization. We have seen Neolithic hunter-gatherers gradually exchange their nomadic ways for a sedentary, agrarian social structure. Tribes have become villages; villages, cities; and cities, a nation. A tribal chieftain has become the ruler of the Two Lands of Upper and Lower Egypt. His successors would build tombs–called pyramids–on a scale unrivaled in history until the 14th century BCE. Stories shared around the flickering hearth of a tiny wattle and daub hut became a religion that defines a civilization. That civilization's rulers aspired to divinity, calling themselves sons or daughters of a deity. The gods themselves dominated every aspect of ancient Egyptian society, presiding over life and especially over the death of its people. And isolated, insulated Egypt grew in military might and by territorial expansion until it became the Egyptian Empire, rivaling Babylonia and Assyria for world power and domination. Eventually, that empire faded and ultimately disappeared.

Yet the river, *iteru*, the Nile, lives on. Egypt is no longer Kemet, the Black Land. The inundation of Hapy no longer reaches the Nile Valley, its way barred by the Aswan High Dam. But late every summer, as has happened for thousands of years before, towering storm clouds rush in from the Atlantic Ocean and disgorge their contents in a deluge of water over the Ethiopian highlands, filling the Blue Nile to overflowing in a roaring torrent that rushes on as if unaware that ancient Egypt, who's lifeblood it ever was, is no more. The one who has ears to hear, let him hear–hear, and remember.

GREEK MYTHOLOGY

EXPLORE THE TIMELESS TALES OF ANCIENT GREECE, THE MYTHS, HISTORY & LEGENDS OF THE GODS, GODDESSES, TITANS, HEROES, MONSTERS & MORE

HISTORY BROUGHT ALIVE

INTRODUCTION

Greek mythology is filled with fascinating myths, epic battles, awesome folklore, interesting customs, traditions, beliefs, and captivating gods and goddesses. It is sometimes seen as a daunting task to sink your teeth into something as immense and rich as Greek mythology, however, that is where *History Brought Alive* comes in. Throughout your captivating read, we will help you venture on a discovery to unpack all the secrets, customs, beliefs, myths, stories, and gods this fascinating ancient belief system has in store. At *History Brought Alive,* we are history and mythology enthusiasts. We hope you feel the same joy and excitement we do when venturing back thousands of years in the past. Join us on an adventure to discover the path of Greek mythology and learn what life was like in Ancient Greece. All the secrets of one of the most fascinating civilizations the world has ever known lie within these pages.

Throughout your read, we will not simply rehash the ancient Greek myths of the time, but rather uncover the context and background behind these myths and the Ancient Greek world. We want to make sure that you cannot only enjoy these fascinating myths but understand what they were like when they were told thousands of years ago. Through context, background, and discussion, we are able to take a peek at what life was like during ancient Greece and how life during that era was influenced by the vast array of myths. Throughout the book, we will be peeling back layers of a complex history that surround these fascinating myths to take a peek at the accurate accounts of the myths, beliefs, costumes, and traditions as they actually were.

We will uncover the creation of the universe, the gods, and the humans from the perspective of Greek mythology. We will unpack the notorious war between the gods and the Titans to understand how the gods of Greece came into power and ended up the rulers of all that the ancient Greeks knew. There are complexities to this story, family conflict, power struggles, and a lot of different agendas about who should be the ruler of the universe. Understanding the creation of the universe and the great Titan war is critical to give us context of why Ancient

Greece society operated as it did as well as the origin and importance of the Greek pantheon.

The gods played a significant role in all aspects of Ancient Greek society; thus it is pivotal that we examine how the gods influenced the Ancient Greek world. We will unpack the ancient temples dedicated to the gods, the festivals that honor the gods, the sacrifices the Greeks made in securing favor from the gods, and how the Greeks went about their daily lives with the Greek pantheon forever weighing on their minds.

However, understanding how the Greeks worshiped the gods and how the gods played a significant role in all aspects of society is one thing, but understanding who the Greek gods and goddesses were another. We will look at all of the major gods and goddesses such as Poseidon, Hera, Ares, Hermes, Apollo, Artemis, Aphrodite, and many more iconic gods. Who they were, what they represented, the role they played in Greek society, and the myths that surrounded their legacy will all be uncovered.

Just as the gods need to be uncovered, so do the monsters, hybrids, minor deities, and demigods. We will highlight many characters that play a role in Greek mythology to get a greater understanding of the myths for all they were. Just like the gods, the other characters of Greek mythology will be highlighted in terms of who they were, what they represented, the role they played in Greek society, and the myths that surrounded their legacy.

The mythology is more than the gods and the monsters. We will discuss many myths and epic battles, highlighting all the fascinating tales that make Greek mythology an interesting belief system. Although Greek mythology is no longer followed religiously in the 21st century, there is so much we can learn from the ancient religion. The epic tales and myths are filled with lessons, philosophies, cautionary warning signs, and golden nuggets about life. It is still an important academic topic that merits study and understanding to this day.

The legends, myths, and stories are all here just waiting to be read. Everything you need to know about the Ancient Greeks and the Greek pantheon is neatly wrapped up in one single read. All that is left to do is for you to uncover the secrets of the Ancient Greek world. Discover what life was like thousands of years ago in the Mediterranean and what governed these people's customs, traditions, and beliefs.

CHAPTER 1
WHY GREEK MYTHOLOGY IS STILL RELEVANT TODAY

There is a reason why mythological beliefs are still studied to this day. These myths were not just stories and epic tales, but were a guiding system of humanity for hundreds of years that provided lessons, morals, hope, comfort, and played a crucial role in developing how we shaped modern thinking.

If there is one subject of history that is still taught today and has stood the test of time, it is Greek mythology. Greek mythology is not just taught as a part of the literature curriculum in high school, but also forms part of most history lessons to uncover the hidden secrets of humanity's past.

Many people may be wondering how mythology as ancient as Greek mythology still lingers on the world's collective mind. Many may view the ancient Greek myths as nothing more than stories that were told thousands of years ago and believe they hold no value in modern society. However, if you stop and look at the vast amount of influence Greek mythology has had on popular culture such as countless movies, TV shows, and books it quickly becomes clear that Greek mythology still fascinates the modern world.

Throughout this chapter, we will highlight why the Greek myths have withstood the test of time, still remain relevant, and will remain relevant for centuries to come.

What Were the Greek Myths?

To many people the ancient Greek myths will simply only be viewed as epic tales of the Greek pantheon gallivanting around the earth, going on crazy adventures, and achieving all sorts of supernatural feats. This is true, but only on the surface. If you only view these tales with tunnel vision, then you will only believe them to be ancient fairytales. However, if you look beyond the bloody tales, epic battles, and the supernatural, you will see that these myths are more than simple legends. A deeper look will help you uncover the lessons, morals, philosophies, and even warnings that these myths taught the ancient Greek world and quite honestly still teaches modern civilization to this day.

Take note that very few of these stories have happy endings, which is something the world has become very accustomed to today. There are often no happy endings in Greek mythology as they were not stories that were written for the purpose of entertainment. Instead, they were stories to teach, understand the world, and a model for ancient Greeks to ensure their actions were in line with.

These stories, or myths, were not designed to tell a story for the sake of telling a story, but, instead, played a crucial role in ancient Greek society to impart knowledge from generation to generation. The stories open windows for us to see into the past and their lessons are still true today. It allows us to catch a glimpse of what the lives of the ancient Greek populace were like back then.

What Did These Myths Teach and Do Their Teaching Still Hold Relevance?

These myths were passed down by the ancient Greek populace from generation to generation. They were told with the purpose to help Greeks realize the difference between what is right and what is wrong. In an era where Greek mythology was at its pinnacle, law and order were not, and thus the differentiation between what is right and wrong was critical. Even today the understanding between what is right and what is wrong is an integral cog in a functional society.

The myths also taught the Greeks the importance of humility, selflessness, caring for those you love, and never thinking of themselves as being immortal as they would be punished for such foolishness. It taught the Greeks to always remain pure of heart and resist the urges of temptation and corruption, as Zeus would punish the corrupt and disobedient with great wrath. All of these teachings are still very prevalent in the modern world.

The myths also told the Greeks about the tales of heroes and how true greatness would be achieved by those who dared and lived life courageously. However, these same tales showed the flaws of these very same heroes, signifying that everyone has flaws and nobody is perfect, no matter how they may seem. These lessons remain true to this day.

Any person from the 21st century who hears or reads about a Greek myth is almost guaranteed to see the relevance of some of the lessons these ancient stories taught humanity. Anybody, no matter who they are, who picks up a book on Greek myths is likely to learn a thing or two other than simply being entertained.

Why Is Greek Mythology Still Studied?

The truth is reading and hearing about Greek mythology and the ancient myths is one thing, however, studying the matter is another. Thus, the question that many may have is why are these mythological beliefs still being studied in the 21st century? The answer is to learn. Plainly put and said, we still study Greek mythology in the 21st century as we want to know how the Ancient Greeks lived. Studying to understand how the Ancient Greeks lived is no different than an anthropologist studying how the Khoi-san people of South Africa live. We study ancient cultures not only to understand the culture but to learn from it too.

After all, after studying culture as progressive as the ancient Greeks and breaking down how they lived and what they believed in, you really can't help but learn a thing or two. These myths are time capsules. They show the modern human how humanity's concept of the world compares to their own. It allows 21st century humans to glance at the past, see what the ancient Greeks considered important, how their civilization operated, what their moral compass looked like, and how they viewed the world with what extremely limited scientific explanations they had access to. What's more, studying ancient Greek myths has helped us understand classic literature. Greek mythology has also contributed and influenced many box office hits, TV shows, modern literature, comics, and more.

It has been said by experts that by studying, or even simply reading, Greek mythology that people tend to have more control of their actions and utilize more rational thinking before they act due to the teachings of the myths (Smith, 2020). This is an interesting claim as many of the Greek myths communicate tales about how humanity's stupidity, follies, and hubris constantly lands humankind in danger. Perhaps being versed in the myths makes you second guess your actions' consequences. What is ironic is that people to this day still tend to be guided by foolishness, give in to temptation, make selfish or stupid decisions, and possess excessive pride despite the warnings and teachings of Greek mythology. It is quite humorous to witness just how accurately the ancient Greek myths still capture the essence of human behavior and is relevant to how the 21st-century human behaves.

CHAPTER 2
GREEK MYTHOLOGY AND ITS REVOLUTION THROUGH THE AGES

Greek mythology, as with many other cultures and beliefs at the time, was used as an instrument to help humans understand the world and environment on a grander scale. This greater understanding that Greek mythology bestowed upon ancient inhabitants of Greece provided insight regarding how humankind lived, the natural phenomenon the world experienced, as well as the passing of time as day turned into night and days, turned into weeks, months and years.

What we now call mythology was a collection of stories, beliefs, and traditions designed to help the citizens of Greece lead happy, fulfilled lives. They sought to explain the origins of the gods, the origins of man, and where the deceased souls depart after death. Myths were also used as a form of documentation to re-tell historical events to the greater public so that the citizens of ancient Greece could remain and sustain contact with their ancestors, the wars Greece fought, and the lands that the Greeks explored.

How Greek Mythology and Myths Influenced Ancient Greek Society

In modern society, the term "myth" is largely associated with negative connotations and is often believed to be a rumor or story that lacks sufficient authenticity or reliability to be considered factual. However, when Greek mythology was flourishing during 3000 B.C.E. to 1100 B.C.E., myths were whole-heartedly believed by many. However, as with everything, especially with a religious or non-written source, there would always be those who believed and those who discounted the authenticity of the source.

The myths were largely used for educational and religious purposes to help mankind get a greater grasp of the world around them. However, it is important to realize that myths played a large part in influencing entertainment at the time in Ancient Greece. Much of what we know today about Ancient

Greece and Greek mythology is due to the many forms of artistic representations of the myths themselves. It is evident that the myths of ancient Greece were incredibly popular and familiar to a wide section if Greek society due to the common representation of the myths through art, such as paintings, sculptures, and pottery.

Literacy was not common in ancient Greece, thus myths were relayed orally amongst Greek citizens. Famous Greek bards, such as Minoan and Mycenaean, from the 18th Century B.C.E., and onwards, were often found passing the myths of Greek mythology through song. Due to the fact that the myths of Greek mythology were often passed on orally, there was a large possibility that, with each re-telling of the myths, they would be embellished and improved upon. The myths themselves would evolve as they were passed on through the ages largely due to word of mouth. The evolution of the myths could largely boil down to the stories being told in such a way to improve an audience's interest, relating the story to the era they were being told in, and incorporating local events and prejudices into the myths.

It is also likely that the re-telling of myths in the world of art and storytelling in Ancient Greece followed a particular set of rules of presentation. This is because a knowledgeable audience may not be as willing to accept an ad hoc adaptation of the myths they were familiar with. However, over centuries of the citizens of Ancient Greece having increased contact with other city-states and trading amongst each other, it is hard to imagine that the myths and local stories did not get muddled up with one another thus leading to myths with several diverse origins.

The next major development at the time was around the 8th century B.C.E., when the presentation of myths took place in the form of poems, with epic poems being written by brilliant poets such as Homer and Hesiod in Ionia.

This was revolutionary because this was the first time the myths had been presented in written form as literacy levels in Greece began to rise. Homer's epic poem *Iliad* presents the final stages of the Trojan War. The Trojan War is incredibly significant to the Ancient Greeks as it is an amalgamation of various conflicts between the Greeks and many of their neighboring Eastern borders. The Trojan War took place between 1800B.C.E. to 1200B.C.E. during the late stages of the Bronze Age. In *Odyssey,* written by Homer, the poem recounts the protracted voyage home of the Greek hero Odysseus following his fierce battle in the Trojan War.

Other significant poems at the time were written by Hesiod and included *Theogony* as well as *Works and Days*. In the poem of *Theogony*, Hesiod provides the world with a genealogy of the Greek gods for the very first time in written form. Hesiod's *Works and Days* poem retells the story of the creation of man from a Greek mythological perspective. What is incredibly interesting about these poems is that the gods themselves are generally described with typically human feelings and faults, but in the end, heroes are created and born.

After poetry had been introduced as a form of representation of the gods and myths, the next introduction to the retelling and documentation of Greek mythology came in the form of pottery from around the 8th century B.C.E. onwards. Ancient Greece often utilized pottery as an art form to portray the gods and myths with a myriad of mythical scenes frozen in time as they were decorated on ceramics of all shapes and sizes. The pottery that came out of Ancient Greece at the time was absolutely breathtaking. These beautifully crafted pots spread the myths through art to a wider audience and relayed the stories of the gods throughout Ancient Greece thus the myths evolved once again through a new medium.

Throughout the centuries, the myths continued to be popular and had a major influence over society. As a result of the surging popularity and influence, many major temples were built in honor of these stories and legends. These included the Parthenon in Athens, the Temple of Zeus in Olympia, and the Temple of Apollo in Delphi. However, there were many more examples of beautiful temples built in the name of the gods. These grand architectural marvels of the world were decorated with larger-than-life sculptures to represent and celebrate the legendary scenes of Greek mythology and the myths that had been passed down for centuries.

In the 5th century B.C.E., the myths were represented in a new format. The myths were now beginning to be told in the theater in the form of plays. The theatre provided an opportunity for the myths to be presented in a theatrical display and were largely told by three major tragedians: Aeschylus, Sophocles, and Euripides.

Just before the introduction of the theater, the myths started to see skepticism of their authenticity in the 6th century B.C.E. The first rejections and skepticism of the myths had been documented in writing and thus began the era of pre-Socratic philosophers. These philosophers wanted to gain a greater scientific explanation for natural phenomena and events.

Finally, in the 5th century B.C.E., the pioneers of modern history, Herodotus and Thucydides, began to document phenomena to a greater degree of accuracy (as accurate as they possibly could at the time) and bestowed it upon themselves to take a less subjective view of phenomena and events. Due to this shift in thinking, and a new approach to understanding the natural world with a greater scientific approach, the subject of history was born.

How Philosophers Challenged Greek Mythology and Worship of the Gods

In Ancient Greece the gods were all-powerful and they all admired beings of the universe. However, during the 6th century B.C.E., a new wave of thinking took place and the age of Greek philosophy was born. The philosophers, unlike the majority of the Greek populace at the time, looked to challenge the beliefs of the Greek pantheon and wanted to view the world from a more scientific perspective. This movement began during the period of the Ionian philosophers, particularly due to the work of one of the founding fathers of philosophy, Anaximander. Anaximander was the first scholar to have made a map of the inhabited world and developed a theory of the creation of the world without the influence of the Greek pantheon. Anaximander came up with a theory of the origin of the world known as the concept of the Apeiron.

Anaximander explains this theory as "the first principle and element of existing things was boundless . . . he has creation take place not as a result of any of the elements undergoing qualitative change, but as a result of the opposites being separated off by the means of motion, which is eternal," (Decibelboy, 2012).

Anaximander's views of the creation of the world through the concept of Apeiron is the first time that somebody had taken the perspective of the creation of the world as, if not scientific, at least a perspective that is non-mythic. However, having said this Anaximander's attempts to explain the realities of the world the Ancient Greeks were living in were still tied within a mythic context as it seemed he still considered the Aperion to be a result of divine intervention. However, what is important was that it completely ignored the influence of the Greek pantheon.

Anaximander's views birthed a new revolution and led to the inspiration of countless philosophers. Another great philosopher around the same time as Anaximander was

Xenophanes. He too had his own theory of the universe outside of the influence of the Greek gods. Xenophanes' ideas were strongly linked to a reason. He was known to challenge the ideas of the anthropomorphic gods.

However, at the pinnacle of the use of reason, scientific perspective, and logic to challenge the ancient Greek myths was the legendary philosopher Socrates. Socrates himself did not write a single word, however, his teachings were used extensively by the Greek philosopher Plato. Thanks to Plato's work, we can learn from Socrates' beliefs through the dialogues Plato had documented. Through this documentation, we are able to learn about how Socrates challenged the gods and are left to see how many holes in the myths of Greek mythology have been prodded upon through arguments of science, reason, and logic.

However, Socrates' story does not end well, as the ruling classes of ancient Greece took a dislike to the teachings of Socrates and would sentence the philosopher to his death. This is an incredibly important event in the evolution of Greek society and the progression of classical mythology. Before the philosophers, the myths of the ancient Greek world were used as a means to understand and explore the realities of the world. However, at this point in history, it seems it was the first time that the myths' power as tools of explanation had been credibly challenged. These challenges to the ancient myths represented a desire among the Greek populace to escape from what they had been brought up to believe and move towards a more logical explanation of the realities of the world.

The ruling bodies of the ancient Greek world were not fond of this idea and realized that if this was left unpunished, problems would occur from Socrates' new logical thinking. The ruling bodies believed that if Socrates was allowed to continue expressing his views it would change their society and everything in it which the ruling classes would not accept. Instead, they would act, by labeling all philosophers as criminals, to ensure that the myths stay intact to shield the majority of the Greek populace from this new form of thinking. Thus, this marked the age where there was a divide in belief between those who believed in the gods and those who desired to seek a more logical and scientific explanation of the world.

CHAPTER 3
THE HISTORY OF THE WORLD ACCORDING TO GREEK MYTHOLOGY

In Ancient Greece, the Greek populace created myths that helped them understand and explain the world around them and help them to better understand the human condition. In Greek Mythology, the world began with one entity known as Chaos, the first goddess of the known world according to the Greeks. Chaos was believed to be a gaping whole of emptiness that gave birth to the world as we know it. Out of Chaos's dark and empty formless void sprang forth three more deities known as Gaea, the goddess of the Earth, Tartarus, the dark abyss of the Underworld, and Eros, the god of love. When Eros was born, the two goddesses, Chaos and Gaea, were able to procreate and bring life into the universe and thus the known Universe began to take shape.

The Children of Chaos and Gaea

The great poet, Hesiod, wrote an epic poem during the 8th century B.C.E. about the creation of the world, titled *Theogony*. According to Hesiod's poem, three crucial elements played a role in the creation of the world. These elements included Chaos, Gaea, and Eros. In the poem of *Theogony*, it is stated that Chaos slept with Eros and gave birth to Erobus, the god of darkness, and Nyx, the goddess of the night. Chaos's children Erobus and Nyx formed a romantic union and gave birth to Aether, who was the bright upper air of the world, and Hemera, who brought the daytime. Nyx would go on to have twelve more children, each representing other parts of nature and life. Nyx's twelve children included the hateful Moros (fate), Hypnos (sleep), Momos (blame), Philotes (sexual pleasure), Apate (Deceit), Eris (Strife), Oizus (pain), Nemesis (Revenge), Ker (Doom), Oneiroi (Dreams and Nightmares), Geras (Old Age), Thanatos (Death), and Hesperides (the daughter of the evening).

While Chaos and Nyx had their own children, Gaea gave birth to Uranus (who created the story sky) and Oceanus (who created the oceans). Uranus was appointed as Gaea's protector, and over the years the two of them became lovers and were the first gods to rule over the world as we know it. Uranus and Gaea had eighteen children. Twelve of these children would be born as Titans, three of these children were born as Cyclopes, and three were known as Hecatoncheires (monstrous giants with 50 heads and 100 arms).

The Tyrant Rule of Uranus

However, the union between Gaea and Uranus was not a peaceful one. Uranus was a cruel husband, but an even crueler father. Uranus was threatened by his children's divine powers and was afraid that one day his children would rise up and overthrow him to claim the throne of ruler of the world. In an attempt to ensure his children would never rise above him, Uranus made sure that none of his children were to see the light of day again and imprisoned them in the hidden place of the Earth—Gaea's womb.

At first, Gaea agreed to this unjust punishment as a result of being heavily manipulated by her husband. However, as the years passed, Gaea could not sit idle any longer. Gaea devised a plan to rid her children from their abusive father's clutches, in doing so Gaea handed over a sickle to her youngest son, the Titan Cronus. After giving her son the sickle, Gaea arranged a meeting between Cronus and Uranus. Cronus used the sickle to cut off Uranus' genitals. The seed of Uranus fell into the ocean, creating Aphrodite, the goddess of beauty. The blood that fell from Uranus's severed testicles created the Fates, the Giants, and the Meliad nymphs.

The Titan Ruler Cronus

Uranus's fears turned into reality and his son overthrew him to take the throne. As the new ruler, he imprisoned his Cyclopes and Hecatonchires siblings in the prison of Tartarus (the Underworld), guarded by a fierce dragon. Cronus married his Titan sister, Rhea, and freed all of his siblings. Once all of Cronus's siblings were freed from their earthly prisons, Cronos shared his kingdom with them. All of Cronus's brothers and sisters were given duties and responsibilities they needed to fulfill. His brother, Oceanus, was given the responsibility to rule over all the oceans, seas, and rivers. Another of Cronus's brothers, Hyperion, was responsible for the sun and the stars.

Cronus and Rhea had five children of their own. According to Greek mythology experts, it is believed that Cronus's parents, Gaea and Uranus, prophesied that Cronus would also be overthrown by one of his sons, just as his father was. Haunted with fear, history repeated itself and Cronus imprisoned his children.

Cronus eventually decided that the best way to deal with this problem was to swallow all his children the moment they were born. Like Gaea, Rhea was horrified and would not stand for the mistreatment of her children and devised a plan to save her children. Rhea tricked Cronus by wrapping a stone in infant clothing and presenting it to Cronus as the sixth child. Cronus fell for the deceit, and swallowed the stone whole thinking he had devoured his newborn son.

Rhea managed to hide Zeus from Cronus and left the newborn god on the island of Crete, where he was raised by the Nymphs of Mount Dikte. When Zeus was growing up, the Kouretes (Creatures who worshiped the goddess Cybele with drumming and dancing) would clash their shields together and dance to cover up the sound of Zeus crying. Years passed and Zeus entered manhood and gained unparalleled strength.

The Return of Zeus

Zeus had grown into an extremely handsome and powerful adult. The time had come to return to his homeland to defeat his father and free his siblings from his clutches. Zeus left Crete and unbeknownst to him asked his future wife, the Titan Metis, the god of wisdom, for advice on how to defeat his tyrant father. Metis replied with a seamless plan. She told Zeus to prepare a poisonous drink that was indistinguishable from Cronus's favorite wine. This drink would be designed to make Cronus vomit and slowly poison him. Zeus was delighted with this plan and executed it to perfection. Zeus disguised himself as one of the Kingdom's cupbearers and successfully slipped Metis's drink into Cronus's glass of wine.

The plan worked like a charm and Cronus began vomiting uncontrollably. As Cronus began to vomit, each one of Zeus's five siblings were expelled from their tyrant father's stomach. Zeus was united for the first time with his siblings Hestia, Demeter, Hera, Hades, and Poseidon. Zeus's siblings were overwhelmed with gratitude and immediately recognized Zeus as their leader who would bring down Cronus's tyrannical rule.

The Final Hurdle the Gods Versus the TItans

Although Zeus had managed to free his siblings from his father's imprisonment, Cronus was still in command and was yet to be defeated. However, thanks to Zeus, the Titan ruler was greatly weakened. As it stood, Cronus was too old to protect himself from the onslaught of his progeny, so he enlisted the help of his most faithful Titan soldiers and followers. The war between the Titans and the Olympians lasted for an entire decade and is remembered by generations as the Titanomachy. Cronus enlisted Atlas as the Titan's leader in arms and he led the Titan army to many victories. In fact, for a long stage of the war, it seemed that the Olympians would lose and all of Zeus's efforts would be for nothing. However, Zeus was approached by Gaea who advised him to visit Tartarus and release the imprisoned Cyclopes and Hecatoncheires. Zeus listened and freed the prisoners, and in gratitude the Cyclopes gifted Zeus with his legendary thunderbolt. The Cyclopes also provided Poseidon with his trident and gifted Hades with the helmet of invisibility. With these new weapons and equipment, the tables had turned and Olympians were well on their way to victory.

Greek mythology is filled with stories of cunning succeeding over brute strength. The final battle between the Titans and the Olympians was no different. The victory for the Olympians was the result of a cunning, little trick, credited to the Titan Prometheus. Armed with boulders, the one hundred armed Hecatoncheires set an ambush for the Titans. Zeus retreated his army to draw the Titans into the Hecatoncheires trap, in which the Titans would be met with a storm of boulders plummeting to the ground from the sky. The Titans fell for the trap. Hundreds of boulders rained down on the Titan troops with such fury that the Titan army thought that the entire mountain range was falling down upon them. The Titans retreated and surrendered. After ten long and bloody years of war, the Olympians were awarded victory and Zeus could finally consider himself the king of the Universe. Zeus immediately exiled all the Titans who fought against him to the depths of Tartarus, however, he made an exception for one. He punished Atlas to an even greater degree as Atlas was sentenced to hold the universe on his shoulders for the rest of eternity.

The Creation of the Human Race According to Greek Mythology

According to the myths, the Olympian Gods thought it would be interesting to create beings in their own image, but as mortals without divine powers, to inhabit the earth. When the mortals were created, Zeus ordered Prometheus and Epitameus, the sons of the Titan Iapetus, to bestow various gifts among the mortals. Zeus ordered these gifts to be given to the mortals as he hoped that the human race would evolve into interesting creatures that would act as a source of amusement for the gods.

Thus, Prometheus and Epitamus began to divide these gifts among themselves and started to give them to the new inhabitants of Earth. It was decided between the two brothers that Prometheus would hand out the first gifts. Prometheus handed out the gifts to the animals first. He handed some animals beauty, some animals were given strength, others were given agility, and the rest were given speed. However, Prometheus left the mortal humans defenseless and did not give them any natural weapons. Prometheus loved mankind and realized the error of his ways, and to make up for his error, he promptly distributed his own gifts to mankind in the form of superior intellect and reasoning. He stole the gift of reason from the goddess Athena and bestowed it upon man. Prometheus then stole fire from the gates of Hephaestus to make sure that the humans could keep themselves warm and cook. Due to Prometheus taking a liking to mankind, he shared all the knowledge he had with them and became the protector of the human race.

However, Prometheus did not consult Zeus. Zeus was furious. Until that point, fire had been reserved for the use of the gods and Zeus did not want the mortals to resemble the gods. Due to Prometheus's negligence, he was heavily punished. Prometheus was chained up for thirty years on the peak of Caucasus, hovering over the edge of the world. Every day, an eagle would feast on his liver, only for it to grow back the next day. However, after thirty years the seemingly never-ending nightmare came to an end. Herakles (Hercules) relieved

Prometheus from his punishment and he was allowed to return back to the land of the gods.

CHAPTER 4
THE ANCIENT GREEK WORLD: WORSHIP OF THE GODS, ILLUSTRIOUS TEMPLES, AND THE MANY GREEK FESTIVALS

In ancient Greece, there were very specific customs, cultures, worship practices, and traditions that were held within high regard to the overwhelming populace of the time. The Ancient Greeks were famous for demonstrating the utmost admiration for the gods by instilling several rituals and celebrations to honor and appease the gods that they both loved and feared at the same time. They also practiced and instilled these customs as a way to ensure harmony with the gods. Thus, it is fair to say that Ancient Greek culture was a product that was molded from appeasing their many gods. There are various examples of how the Greeks showed their admiration and prayers to the god such as sacrifices, temples, festivals, and even games that were formed to honor the gods.

Greek Mythology as a Pagan Religion

The religion which the Greeks practiced can often be seen as a heavy influence over other Pagan religions who also believed and worshiped several gods instead of simply one divine being. This can be seen in Roman mythology, Egyptian mythology, Norse mythology, and many other polytheistic religions. This is because many of these Pagan cultures and beliefs would overlap with one another due to the various different cultures coming in contact with one another through trade and travel. The citizens of different regions would converse with one another and trade stories about their beliefs and their gods, thus mythological aspects from various forms of mythology were borrowed and adapted. This is especially evident with the Greeks and the Romans who shared a very similar belief system. Both the Greek and Roman myths and tales shared strikingly similar aspects throughout their respective ancient religions.

Greek mythology is classified as a Pagan religion as it was polytheistic. This means the Ancient Greeks worshipped many gods and goddesses, each one representing a piece of the human condition, and were often used as a means to help understand the world. The ancient Greeks believed that by worshipping multiple gods, they were granted an opportunity of a great sense of freedom as they could relate to the gods that they felt most resonated with them. This sense of freedom that Greek mythology awarded the populace of Greece and many other Pagan religions was an aspect that the followers of the mythology treasured.

During the era when Ancient Greece reigned supreme, between 700 B.C.E. and 480 B.C.E., they were well known for their intellectual distinction from other nations of the world at the time and their means of worship played a significant role in that. What was so interesting about the Ancient Greek world was that although they believed in Greek mythology their perception and views on their ancient religion were quite drastically different depending on the region the Greeks lived in. In Greek society, each city-state, also known as polis, was believed to have a specific god or gods protecting and guiding the residents of that region. Each polis had its own set of gods watching over them meant that the belief of common gods in a region would help unify the residents that populated it. What is evident in Ancient Greece was the idea that the Greek populace at the time was yearning for a distinct unity and order in the universe that they inhabited. The Greek citizens took a lot of comforts knowing that the universe was always balanced thanks to the gods they believed in.

It may seem rather contradictory that the Greeks yearned for organization and order while still worshiping multiple gods, as the connotations of multiple gods would generally be assumed to create confusion and disorder. However, to the Ancient Greeks, the gods were not only gods but symbols and representations. Each god would uphold a distinct role of the universe and represent a different part of life thus as a unit they would be known to be the organizing body of the universe if each god was pleased and honored.

Beyond the gods being representations of the human condition, they would also be used as a means to help justify any phenomenon that could not be understood. For example, the Ancient Greeks believed that when thunder and lightning fell from the sky it was because Zeus the god of skies (particularly lightning) was punishing humans as he was irate with them. The Greeks would believe that they had angered Zeus due to some wrong-doing they must have committed or perhaps their worship of the god of thunder was inadequate. However, to ensure that the gods were happy and appeased with humans, the Greeks would participate in activities such as prayer, sacrifice, building temples, and engaging in festivals in the name of their gods.

There was even evidence of the institutionalization of the gods in the form of a hierarchy. The main gods of the Greek pantheon would include the 12 gods of Olympus and below them would be smaller and more minor deities, thus creating the reign of the Olympian gods and forming the Olympian religion. However, as said early not all gods were worshiped equally, and depending on the region or polis that Greeks lived in would play a role in which gods were considered more desirable than others.

The Ancient Greeks, like many other pagan or polytheistic beliefs, viewed their gods as having flaws. The Greek pantheon was not "flawless"; they had their faults and the Greeks recognized them. This is quite contrasting to many other monotheistic belief systems such as Christianity or Judaism who regard their respective God as being all-powerful, all-forgiving, and without flaws. The Greek pantheon was portrayed as human-like figures who would make mistakes and felt human emotions, often succumbing to these emotions at times. The Greek pantheon was known to experience pain, envy, anguish, greed, jealousy, and even greed. These emotions are ever-present in the myths of the Greek pantheon and more often than not the Greek gods and goddesses' emotions that they experienced would dictate their actions.

What separates greek mythology even more from Christianity was that the Ancient Greek religion was ritual-based and was a religion with flexible belief systems without traditional clergymen. Above that, Greek mythology did not institute any real sacred texts or enforce a definitive moral code that the Greek populace needed to abide by. Like many other Pagan religions, the tales and worship of the gods were primarily oral and thus documentation is scarce. This was because religion and culture heavily relied on spoken stories, myths, and tales that survived through the oral tradition of Ancient Greece. Ancient Greek culture was heavily reliant on oral forms of communication as most of the Greek populace was illiterate and thus were unable to accurately document their lives, beliefs, myths, and legends in written form for many years.

Temples Built in Honor of the Greek Gods

In Ancient Greece, many temples were built and acted as a center of worship for the Ancient Greeks to honor and appease the gods. These temples were believed to be the home of gods and goddesses. In each temple, there were servants who would serve the house of the gods and worship their honor through prayer and sacrificial offerings. The sacrifices made in the temples needed to be conducted by higher-ups, as no ordinary man nor woman could enter the temple, as it was forbidden in Ancient Greek customs. Instead, ordinary men and women would have to worship the gods from outside the temples of the gods or more often than not in their own homes. However, if they were to workshop the gods by the temple they would generally have to worship the gods around the Temenos, which was a natural feature that generally surrounded the temple. Temenos was generally a creek or a cave in which the temple of the gods would be built around. Within the Temenos, Ancient Greeks would generally hold festivals as this was an ideal opportunity to worship and celebrate the gods in large numbers of people. Festivals were an opportunity for the Greek populace to show their undying appreciation and admiration for the gods of the Ancient Greek world.

It was evident that temples were a significant aspect of Ancient Greece and were a significant factor that shaped the lives and customs of all Greek people at the time. The Greeks believed that if they provided sacrifices to the gods and if they showed consistent admiration and devotion through prayer that the gods would favor them and provide them with a great fortune in life, safe passage, and even assist them in war. To many Greeks, showing respect to their gods was what they believed their life purpose to be, and temples provided a tangible platform to achieve their desired purpose in life.

Temple of Olympian Zeus in Ancient Athens, Greece

Today only fragments of the illustrious Temple of Zeus in Athens still remain as it is believed most of the temple was destroyed as a result of the earthquakes of AD 522 and 511. Although only a few columns remain of the grand temple of the god of the lightning, it does not take much imagination to realize just how enormous the temple was. The temple of Olympian Zeus was located in Athens and was known as the Olympian, it was a 15-acre building that was just Southeast of the Acropolis. However, in Ancient times, Zeus's temple would be located in a city known as Olympia. In Ancient Greece, the city of Olympia was the center of worship for Zeus, the king of the Olympian gods, and was the home of the cult of Zeus. In Olympia, there were many smaller temples, monuments, altars, theaters, bathhouses, and beautiful statues that were all built in honor of the mighty Zeus. The Temple of Olympian Zeus was also the location where the original Olympic games would be held every four years to honor Zeus and the other Greek pantheon.

The construction of the Temple of Olympian Zeus in Ancient Athens was believed to have started around the 6th century B.C.E. This construction was done during the time Athents was ruled by Athenian tyrants. These tyrants envisaged a temple so large and so grand that it would be known throughout the ancient world. Although the construction of Zeus's temple in Athens was started by the Athenian tyrants, the temple was not completely finished under their rule. The temple in honor of the King of Olympians was completed in the 2nd century B.C.E. Zeus' temple was completed under the rule of the Roman Emperor, Hadrian, and took an astonishing 638 years in total. The end result was a marvelous temple, which was one of, if not the most, impressive temples in all the known ancient world—just how the tyrant Athenian rulers envisioned it to be. Zeus's temple in Ancient Greece stood at an enormous height of precisely 68 feet. The temple was also 95 feet wide and 235 feet long. The size of Zeus's temple was almost unimaginable and was one of the seven wonders of the ancient world.

Temple of Poseidon at Sounion in Athens, Greece

Poseidon was one of the most celebrated gods of the known Greek world and was known to be the god of the ocean. Poseidon was one of Zeus's brothers, thus it is no surprise the Greeks constructed an incredibly beautiful and lavish temple to honor him. The illustrious temple in honor of Poseidon was built on the Greek cape of Sounion, located on the coastline of Athens. This was a very fitting location for a temple honoring the god of the Ocean. This beautiful temple's construction was estimated to take place between the years 444 and 440 B.C.E. The temple was built almost entirely from marble that was sourced from the valley of Agrilesa, about two and a half miles (four kilometers) north of the beautiful cape of Sounion. It is believed that the architect was Ictinus, the same architect who erected the Temple of Hephaestus located in Athens in the Ancient Agora, built the Temple of Poseidon.

Ictinus built Poseidon's temple with 16 columns as he knew that this would help it stand the test of time and would withstand the environmental damage. However, today the temple is only a remnant of its former design. Another clever addition to Poseidon's temple that Ictinus added was to make the Doric columns slenderer at the top so that it would create the impression that the temple was actually taller than it was.

As Poseidon was the god of the ocean, it was only logical that a god considered so powerful and significant would be highly revered and worshiped in a country that is accompanied by over 8,390 miles (13,500 kilometers) of coastline. In Ancient Greece, it was a general belief among the populace, especially sailors, that Poseidon would bring upon treacherous storms as a sign of his wrath when he was displeased with humans. For this reason, Poseidon's temple located at the Sounion Cape was a highly sacred location. It was a temple that many sailors, and the general population, would come to offer sacrifices and gifts in order to appease Poseidon to entice him to provide good fortune for the Greek populace and safe travel upon the oceans.

Temple of Hera in Samos

The goddesses Hera, goddess of fertility, marriage, woman, and family was believed to have four major temples built in her honor, however, the temple dedicated to Hera in Samos is considered the marvel of them all. Hera was the main deity of Samos and it was believed that Samos was in fact the birthplace of the great goddess. For this reason, the Temple of Hera was considered the sanctuary of ancient Samos and was one of the most significant sanctuaries in all of the known ancient world.

The temple is located on the southeast coast of Greece and is approximately four miles (six kilometers) away from the Ancient Island Samos which is today known as Pythagorion, however, the temple was connected to Samos by a road which was known as the "holy road."

The temple began to be constructed around about 540 B.C.E. which was during the rule of the tyranny of Polycrates (538 to 522 B.C.E.). The architects credited for the grand design of Hera's temple were Theodorus and Telecles. The temple was enormous, to say the least, and was almost immeasurable for the time. However, it is believed that the temple in all its glory was 368 feet (112.2 meters) long, 181 feet (55.16 meters) wide, and 70.5 feet (21.5 meters) high. It was a goliath. Hera's grand temple had 155 pillars to hold up the enormous structure in which historians have managed to distinguish those four different types and sizes of pillars were used in the construction of the goddesses' temple. However, due to the temple's age and the harshness of the environment, only one pillar at half the original height remains. Greeks from all regions would come to offer sacrifices, and gifts in honor of the goddess of love and marriage to show their gratitude and attempt to gain good fortune with the goddess.

The location of Hera's temple is also significant as not only is the temple they believed location of the goddess' birth but is also supposedly where Hera and Zeus were married. On top of that, according to Greek mythology, humans found a wooden statue of Hera in this very location, however, it was believed that the wooden statue was not carved by human hands. As a result of this discovery, the populace of Samos was convinced that the presence of the deity was present in these lands. Thus, it was decided that the creation of a temple to represent the sanctuary in honor of the goddess Hera was imperative. This decision was made despite the fact that they knew the area in which the temple would be constructed was not conducive due to the unstable terrain due to the erosion caused by the river Imravos.

Ancient Greek Festivals and Athletic Games to Honor the Gods

In Ancient Greece, festivals and athletic games were a crucial component of the ancient religious practices of the Greeks to honor, respect, and show admiration towards their gods. The purposes of the festivals all differed and played different roles in terms of worship, however, what was common among all the festivals was a common desire to maintain a good relationship with the gods and praise them to bestow great fortune amongst the Greek populace. Festivals were plentiful in Ancient Greece, particularly in Athens, the Greeks would set aside approximately 60 days a year to be dedicated in honor and worship of the Greek pantheon. These festivals and athletic games were forever recurring and were major religious events that would either be practiced annually, every two years or every four years depending on the nature of the festival.

The festivals were strategically organized by the Greeks so that at least one of the festivals or athletic games would fall each year, in truth many festivals were held every year. The oldest and most prominent festival of athletic games were known as the Olympic games which were held in honor of Zeus and were practiced at his temple in Olympia every four years. The Olympic games are still held to this day; however, the nature of the event has evolved significantly and is no longer exclusive to just the Greek populace.

Olympia was one of the Greeks' oldest religious centers and the worship hub of the king of the Olympians, Zeus. So, it was logical that their most esteemed festival would be held in the region of the country where Zeus was worshipped the most extensively. The games would always recur at the same site—the Temple of Olympian Zeus. Other festivals other than the Olympic games were also hosted on a major religious site, such as a temple dedicated to the god or goddesses. For all the festivals and games, there would be messengers who would announce the dates of when the festivals would commence so that everybody across the land could come and partake in the celebrations and worship of the gods.

The Olympic Games

The first-ever Olympic games were held in 776 B.C.E., and unlike its modern iteration of the event, there was only one competition—the foot race. There are two myths that the foot race is representative. The first myth is that the foot race symbolizes how the guardian nymphs of an infant Zeus hosted the first-ever foot race, and the other myth is that the foot race hosted by the first-ever Olympic games symbolizes Zeus's victory over his father Cronus in his race to control the entire world.

The footrace that commenced at the first Olympic games was 600 feet long and was the only event that would take place for the first 13 iterations of the event. However, over time the Greeks decided that it was time for the games to evolve and added the pentathlon (discus, long jump, foot races, wrestling, and javelin) as well as boxing, wrestling as a single event and equestrian contests. These events were strictly only for the Greek populace and any other nationality was restricted to participate in the Games.

It is important to remember that although the Olympic games were an athletics competition, it was also a religious festival held in the honor of the god of thunder, Zeus. As such it was a tradition that on the middle day of the Olympic games that 100 oxen would be sacrificed to Zeus. The athletes that participated in the games would pray to the gods for strength, victory, and good fortune. The athletes and spectators would provide offerings and sacrifices to the gods in the form of produce, sacrificial animals, gifts, and cakes, as thanks for their success and gratitude for the right to participate.

The Spring Festivals of Anthesteria and Mounukhion

Anthesteria was the first spring festival of the Ancient Greek world and was one of the first festivals that the Greek populace practiced in honoring the gods. During this festival, the Greeks would wear garlands and would shower themselves with perfume to symbolize the beautiful smells that the spring solstice brings. The Greeks would also participate in contests and would honor and celebrate Dionysus, the god of the grape harvest, winemaking, and wine, by pouring a libation for him of the last of the wine the Greeks had.

The next major festival in Spring for the Ancient Greeks was Mounukhion, which occurred in the middle of spring to honor Artemis, goddess of the hunt and animals. Participants at this festival would offer cakes with torches stuck inside of them to the goddess Artemis.

However, Artemis was not the only deity honored during this festival. It was believed that April was under the protection of Aphrodite and the month of May was under the protection of Apollo. Due to this, there were hymn-singing contests where both the men and the boy's choirs would compete in honor of the two gods of their respective months. The winner of the contests would win a tripod and would then be offered in the name of the gods in respect to them.

There were two different types of offerings that were associated with the Mounukhion festival which seemingly highlights two sides of the Goddess of Hunt's character. The first offering consisted of a goat that was to be dressed as a girl which would be sacrificed in the name of Artemis. This sacrifice was made to represent the event in which the Athenians killed Artemis's she-bear that entered the goddess's shrine. When the Athenians slaughtered Artemis's she-bear she became infuriated with the Athenian's actions and consulted with her Oracles to relay a message stating that an Athenian must sacrifice their daughter as punishment for their barbaric actions. One Athenian bravely accepted Artemis's demands, however, instead of offering his daughter as a sacrifice he performed a switch at the sanctuary and offered a goat dressed as a girl in his daughter's place. Artemis was satisfied and in return for his brave actions, he acquired the priesthood of Artemis for life.

The second offering that occurred during the Mounukhion festival represents Artemis's affiliation with the moon. The Mounukhion festival always took place when a full moon was present. Round cakes were offered to the goddess as a gift to symbolize the moon. These cakes were known as amphiphontes, which translates to "shining all-round," and in the amphiphontes a dadia (a small torch or candle) was stuck in the middle of the cake. The dadia was in reference to the fact that the amphiphontes would only be offered to Artemis when both the sun and the moon were visible at the same time. The amphiphontes would be offered to Artemis with a special prayer. Many Greeks were not particularly skilled in making animal sacrifices, so instead many opted to make offerings of cakes that were shaped as goats or simply offer Artemis amphiphontes to show their admiration for the Goddess of the Hunt and the Moon.

The Summer Festivals
In Summer, there were many festivals that were hosted by the Greek populace, however, the first festival was known as

Plunteria and was hosted around June. This festival revolved around the washing of the illustrious statue of Athena. In Greece, bathing and washing godly statues was a common custom. The women of Greece would be tasked with the duty of cleaning Athena's temple a few days prior to the start of the festival, this act was known as Kallunteria which translates to "to beautify by sweeping." At the same time as the sweeping, the priest would re-light the candles in the temples to symbolize Athena's eternal flame.

June had another festival known as Skiraphoria and occurred during the season in Greece when farmers would cut and pick the grain. The head priestess of Athena, the head priest of Poseidon, and the head priest of Helios would all band together and go to the Skiron, which according to legend is the location where sewing took place for the time. The priests and priestesses of Athena, Poseidon, and Helios would carry a large white canopy over their heads during the procession of the festival, which was mainly celebrated by women. The festival's purpose was to bring fertility to the populace of Greek women. To honor the gods and receive good fortune and fertility, Greeks would abstain from sexual encounters for the entire day and women would eat cloves of garlic to make themselves undesirable to men. It was also believed that the Greeks would throw offerings in the sacred caves of Demeter.

The next festival that the Ancient Greeks practiced during the season of summer was known as Panathenaia. This festival was considered the celebration of Athena's birthday and was the day the goddess of wisdom, war, and handicraft burst out of Zeus's skull and was given life.

Although the festival was in honor of the goddess Athena's birthday it was also a festival that was in honor of all the Olympian gods as they were all present for Athena's birth. The festival of Panathenaia was a sacred one and was a feast that Greeks believed the humans and gods celebrated together. The festival would be held every four years, much like the Olympic Games, and every four years a new robe would be woven by the Greeks and offered as a gift to Athena. The robe would always incorporate a middle stripe that displayed the battle between the Titans and the gods which would symbolize the gods triumph over the savagery brought upon by the tyrant Titans. Greeks from all over Athens would participate in the festivities and would present Athena with many sacrificial animals, gifts, and, and food.

After the festival of Panathenaia, the Greeks would participate in contests of sport and art for the next three to four days. The winners of the athletic contests would be rewarded with a "Panathenaic amphora," a large vase that contained olive oil that was sourced from the goddess Athena's sacred grove. While the winners of all the artistic contests were given a gilded crown of wild olives and were occasionally awarded prize money.

The Autumn Festivals

At the start of autumn there the Greeks participated in a minor thanksgiving festival in honor of Apollo. This festival was known as Boedromia and was participated by the Ancient Greeks to show their thanks to the god Apollo for being a savior in war.

The next festival to follow in autumn was known as Puanepsia, which was a festival that focused on fruit gathering and was practiced seeking divine blessings for the autumn sowing for the Greek populace. The Puanepsia festival was once again in honor of Apollo as he was the god of the son, but the gods Helios (a lesser-known god of the sun) and Horai (god of the seasons) were also worshiped in this ancient festival.

The Winter Festivals

Lastly, there were the Greek festivals of winter, and they were generally more concerned with raising human spirits and reviving the crops more so than they were about worshipping the gods to return the summer sun. The Greek deities responsible for good harvest, agriculture, and food were generally the gods that were celebrated and honored. In December, minor festivals were held in honor of Poseidon as he was considered the god that provided protection to the humans during that month. The Greeks held a festival known as Posidea to honor the god of the ocean, Poseidon.

CHAPTER 5
THE GREEK PANTHEON OF MT. OLYMPUS

The Olympian gods of Greek mythology were often referred to as the Greek Pantheon. The word pantheon can be understood as a collective group of gods within a particular culture, for example, there would be the Egyptian pantheon of the Norse Pantheon that would consist of those regions' collective gods. The word pantheon comes from the Greek words pan (all) and theoi (gods), thus suggesting all the gods of a particular group or belief system. The ancient Greeks pantheon consisted of the Olympian gods, along with other major deities as well as various other minor deities and demigods.

The Olympians

The Olympians were the principal deities of Greek mythology and consisted of six gods and six goddesses. These gods and goddesses include Zeus, Apollo, Ares, Hermes, Poseidon, Hephaestus, Hera, Aphrodite, Athena, Artemis, Demeter, and Hestia.

According to legend, the twelve most celebrated and worshipped gods and goddesses, the Olypians, would spend their days residing on Mount Olympus, the highest peak in all of Greece. Out of the twelve gods and goddesses of Mount Olympus, Zeus was the most important of all, as he was considered to be the king of Olympians and was known to reign supreme over all known beings of the universe, including all of the major and minor deities. Zeus was all-powerful and was responsible for being the protector of justice, kingship, authority, and social order in the universe in its entirety.

The gods, particularly the Olympian gods, played an integral role in the Greek view of the world. The gods were seen as representations of the most significant ideals and features of the human condition and would represent aspects of life such as wisdom, beauty, justice, knowledge, music, and even the changing of seasons. However, due to the long list of the Greek Pantheon, we will highlight the most significant Olympian gods.

Zeus

Zeus was the son of Rhea and Cronus and the youngest of his six siblings. Zeus had two brothers, Poseidon and Hades, and three sisters, Hestia, Hera, and Demeters. Zeus was the father of all gods and men alike, and the king of the universe. He ruled over Mount Olympus with his golden throne perched on the highest point of the mountain.

Zeus was a sky god, and possessed the power to control the weather and is able to shape the climate and environmental conditions as he pleased. Zeus can also control lightning and bend it to his whim. It was believed that when Earth was blessed with beautiful weather it was because Zeus was in a good mood and was gracefully bestowing mankind with a gift. However, when Zeus was in a bad mood it was believed he would punish mankind with relentless rain, winds, thunder, and lightning bringing disaster upon mortals. Zeus was considered to uphold justice and balance in the universe, and he would punish anybody who lied or broke an oath and reward those who were honest. Zeus was a fair god, and he always tried to maintain balance in the lives of mortals.

Zeus was believed to be a god that loved to laugh out loud and was relatively carefree. Zeus possessed the entirety of the universe's knowledge and was merciful, just, and extremely wise. However, Zeus was known to be extremely unpredictable and could have an extremely brutal and cruel side to his demeanor. Due to this, no god could accurately read his true intentions or guess his decisions he would make.

Zeus was known to have love affairs with mortals. Many kings claimed to be descendants of Zeus, claiming their bloodline came directly from the gods. However, although Zeus slept with many women, be it a goddess, Titan, or mortal, he ended up marrying his sister, Hera, the goddess of marriage and monogamy. Marriage didn't stop Zeus' affairs, and he continued to have countless encounters with women.

Zeus was known for his amorousness, and in order to achieve this amorous design that he assumed with so many women of various different races, he would frequently assume the forms of animals to arouse and seduce women. Zeus was believed to take the form of a cuckoo when he ravished his wife Hera, he took the appearance of a swan when seducing Leda, and the shape of a bull when he carried off Europa to go make love to her. Due to Zeus's incredibly active sex life, he fathered an enormous amount of children. The most notable of Zeus's offspring were the twin's Apollo and Artemis, Helen, Herakles, Athena, Ares, Hebe, Eileithyia, and many more.

In art, Zeus was almost exclusively portrayed as an incredibly handsome humanoid deity with a neatly trimmed beard and shoulder-length black hair. Zeus was incredibly tall and very muscular with an imposing presence about him that demands respect. Zeus was often associated with an oak tree, and with regards to illustrations, Zeus was always a stately figure in the prime of his life. There are many symbols and trinkets that are largely associated with the Greek god of lightning. Zeus was almost always portrayed as being accompanied by an eagle along with either a scepter or his iconic lightning bolt. Zeus was also often associated with either a ram or a lion and is often clothed with an aegis (a piece of armor with a shield). Zeus was often also carrying a goat's horn, also known as a cornucopia, as this symbolizes his years as an infant when he was brought up and nursed by the nymph Amalthea.

Hera

Born after Hestia and Demeter, Hera was the youngest daughter and third child born to Cronus and Rhea. Some sources cite her as both the oldest and youngest daughter.

While she was born from Rhea last, when the siblings were freed from Cronus' stomach, Cronus emptied his stomach in the opposite order in which he devoured them. Hera, as the last daughter, would have been freed before the others, making her the oldest sister after her rebirth.

Based on numerous different accounts from various worship centers, it is believed that Hera was an incredibly ancient goddess who even predates Zeus. Hera was so ancient that it is believed that nobody knows the queen of Olympus's official name. The name Hera was actually a title placeholder, which when translated means lady or mistress.

Hera would go on to marry Zeus and was regarded as the queen of all the gods of Greek pantheon. However, even before she married Zeus, it is believed that she ruled over all the heavens and the Earth, and was why she is often referred to as the Queen of the Heavens. Hera was the goddess of marriage and birth, thus the goddess was the symbol of family and was often associated with providing welfare of mortal women and children. Hera's Roman name was Juno, and thus the month of June was named in honor of her and to this day the month of June is still the most popular time for weddings. Hera and Zeus would have seven children together—Ares, Eileithyia, Hebe, Hephaestus, Eris, Angelos, and Enyo. However, although they had many children together, their marriage was not a happy one. Hera was known to be incredibly jealous of her husband Zeus' extramarital affairs. She would occasionally punish the women seduced by Zeus out of jealousy.

Zeus was a cruel and brutish husband. When she couldn't bear the mistreatment any longer, Hera plotted a revenge plan with her brother Poseidon and the goddess Athena, possibly even a few other cohorts. Hera drugged her husband, and while all others involved bound Zeus to his bed, stole his thunderbolt. However, Thetis (the goddess of water) managed to summon the hecatonchires Briareus to quickly untie Zeus. Zeus was merciless with his punishment for Hera for her role: he hung Hera from the clouds and attached unimaginably heavy anvils to her feet. Hera, desperate to grant herself release from her excruciating punishment, swore to never challenge or rebel against Zeus again. Instead, Hera would turn her anger and hostility toward Zeus's offspring and lovers.

The most notable of Zeus's offspring who fell victim to Hera's jealousy wrath was Herakles. The son of Zeus and a mortal woman, and ironically named in Hera's honor, was a target for Hera on many occasions. Hera sent snakes to kills Herakles as an infant, she raised a treacherous storm to drive Herakles off his course at sea to kill him, and she sent multiple gods with the orders to murder Herakles and those who refused would pay for it severely. Hera was a jealous god who was extremely powerful and vengeful, killing many of Zeus's lovers. Hera was so vengeful that Zeus himself was terrified of her at times.

In art, Hera was generally portrayed as a beautiful, matronly woman. She was often fully clothed with a wreath, or a veil and a cylindrical crown polo perched on her head. Hera would often be portrayed carrying a scepter that was capped with a pomegranate and a cuckoo. The cuckoo was a symbol of fertility in Greek mythology and is the animal form Zeus took to woo his wife. Hera was also sometimes accompanied in art by a peacock, which was the sacred animal of the goddess of marriage.

Apollo

Apollo was considered one of the most important and complex gods in the Greek pantheon. Apollo was the son of Zeus and the Titan Leto. He was also the twin brother to Artemis, the goddess of hunting. Apollo was associated with many aspects of the human condition, namely truth, prophecy, healing, disease, crops, herds, archery, music, dance, and poetry. Apollo was also considered the most Greek of all the gods. He was known to bring ill health with his arrows, but also could heal epidemics. Apollo has a deep connection to art and was also known to be the muse of many artists and composers. A primary symbol of Apollo is the lyre, a string instrument, as he was said to have created string music. Apollo was also credited, along with his sister, to have invented archery. To add to this impressive resume, Apollo was also associated with the sun and light.

Apollo's nature and temperament are obscure, as during the time of Homer and onwards, he was considered the god of divine distance. Ultimately, this meant that Apollo would make mortals aware of their own faults and guilt, but would also assist mortals in healing these faults. Apollo would also preside over the religious laws of mortals and oversee the justness of the constitutions of cities. Apollo was known to communicate his knowledge to the mortals of Earth as well as relay the will of Zeus down to Earth. It was said that even the gods were intimidated by Apollo's presence and that only his parents could feel comfortable in his presence.

In art, Apollo was often portrayed as a beardless youthful man, who often appeared naked. In most depictions of Apollo, he would be accompanied with his iconic symbols, a bow, and a lyre. The bow would symbolize distance, terror, and death. On the other hand, the lyre symbolizes Apollo's gentle side and represents the joy of music, poetry, and dance that the gods shared with the mortals.

Artemis

Artemis was the twin sister of the god of Apollo and the daughter of Zeus and Leto. Artemis was a widely celebrated goddess and was one of the most important goddesses in Greek mythology. Artemis was primarily known as the goddess of hunting, however, she was also credited as being the goddess of all wild animals, chastity, childbirth, and vegetation.

Artemis was especially popular among the rural population of Ancient Greece as she brought them good fortune in terms of crops and game to hunt. In the rural population of Greece, it was believed that Artemis was the favorite of all the Greek pantheons. Artemis was believed to be a goddess who loved and adored nature, she was carefree, and she would dance in the company of nymphs in the mountains, forests, and marshes.

Although Artemis was the goddess of hunting, she did not only kill the game but she would also protect it and nurture it, punishing anybody who disrespected nature. Artemis was especially protective of the young animals and was given the title by the poet Homer as the mistress of animals.

In art, Artemis was often portrayed as a young woman in her prime around the age of 16-17, she is generally very fit, and fleet of foot. The goddess is often wearing a knee-length tunic which leaves her legs free to run through the woods without restrictions. Artemis was very athletic and spent most of her time roaming the woods and forests of Earth. She was a very beautiful woman, however, the exact detail of her appearance and the forms she takes on often vary.

Some of the depictions portray Artemis as a woman with multiple breasts so that the goddess of the wilderness could feed a litter as opposed to a single baby or twin offspring. However, it was believed that Artemis remained a virgin and was unable to bear any children of her own. Artemis' divine powers, appearance, and apparel are believed to be a result of six wishes she asked Zeus to bestow upon her when she was just a child. These wishes included ruling the mountains areas of her domain, having more names than her twin brother Apollo, to bring light to the world, inherit an archery bow and hunting tunic that was crafted by the Cyclopes, inherit sixty nymphs to act as attendants for her hounds, and to never marry throughout existence.

Hermes

Hermes was the son of Zeus and Maia, a daughter of the Titan Atlas and nymph Pleione. Often referred to as "bringer of grace," or "the luck-bringing god," or "the slayer of Argus," Hermes was primarily known as the messenger of the gods. He was a psychopomp, a guide for the dead, and as such, transported the souls of the dead and fallen to the king of the Underworld, Hades.

Hermes was more than just a psychopomp and messenger, he was also the patron god of traveling and travelers, the god of fertility, the bringer of sleep, the ruler of dreams, the god of thievery, and a trickster deity. As both the god of sleep and messenger of the gods, people would offer their last libations to Hermes before bed.

Zeus also decided that Hermes would play the role of god of commerce and music. Hermes was credited with the invention of many devices in relation to Greek mythology; it was believed that Hermes was known to invent many musical compositions, the string instrument kithara, and the fire itself.

Hermes was also known as the god of good fortune and would sometimes provide mortals with gifts. Treasures that were casually found by mortals and any stroke of good luck were considered a gift from Hermes. He was both a helpful god, but also associated with trickery and theft. Other gods viewed him as a thief.

In art, Hermes was often portrayed as a young man in his prime who would wear traveling clothes as well as his symbolic winged flat hat known as petasus. He would also wear winged sandals on his feet as well as being depicted with wings on his shoulders. Hermes would generally be shown holding a caduceus, a winged staff with intertwined snakes. This staff would help him gain access to anywhere in the world. He would also often be depicted with an erect or semi-erect penis in sculptures to symbolize his connection of being the god of fertility.

Aphrodite

Aphrodite was the Greek goddess of love, sex, beauty, and fertility. Aphrodite was considered to be the most beautiful of all the gods and the most beautiful specimen in the universe. Aphrodite's name actually originates from the Greek word *aphros* which translates to "foam." Aphrodite burst forth from the seafoam caused by Cronus throwing Uranus' genitals into the sea. Due to this, Aphrodite is also considered to be the goddess of the sea and protector of those that travel her waters.

Although Aphrodite represents such a soft, gentle, and beautiful aspect of the human condition, she was also considered to be the goddess of war, especially in the regions of Sparta, Thebes, and Cyprus. However, what Aphrodite was known most for was being the god of love, beauty, and fertility and was believed to occasionally preside over mortal marriages. Aphrodite's circle of worship was generally very formal and was often very strict. What is interesting about the goddess of beauty is that she actually had a large following among the prostitutes of Ancient Greece who considered Aphrodite to be their patron. This is quite contradictory to the rest of her formal and strict worshipping circles throughout Ancient Greece.

Aphrodite was married to the blacksmith god, Haphaetsus, however, this was not a happy marriage and Aphrodite was known to have several other lovers, most notably with the god of war, Ares. Perhaps Aphrodite's promiscuity and her association with sex is the reason she had a large following from Greek prostitutes.

Although Aphrodite was worshiped and honored throughout Ancient Greece, unlike her lover, Ares, there were regions that celebrated the goddess of love and beauty more intensely. The regions where Aphrodite's main center of worship circles were situated are Paphos and Amathus. Amathus is on the small island of Cythera, where it is believed among scholars that the worship of the goddess of beauty originated. Paphos, on the other hand, is situated in what is today known as Cyprus. However, within the main Greek inland, the goddess's chief center of worship was in Corinth.

In ancient Greek art, Aphrodite was often portrayed as a fully clothed woman. It was only in the 5th-century B.C.E. that Aphrodite would gain individualistic features and aesthetic characteristics by the hands of Ancient Greek sculptors. Before the 5th century B.C.E., the artistic portrayals of Aphrodite would lack distinguishing features that would separate the goddess of beauty from the rest of the goddesses of the Greek pantheon. Her most famous sculpture, a full-scale nude sculpture of the beautiful goddess, was carved by Praxiteles. Aphrodite is often described in literature as having beautiful skin that had absolutely no blemishes or flaws. Aphrodite was also described as having strawberry blonde hair that was so beautiful it was unparalleled to any being in the universe.

The goddess of beauty is often portrayed in art in her early 20s, and was quite tall in stature, possessing a curvy and sexually desirable figure that overwhelmed mortals and gods alike with lust. Aphrodite's neck is often described as being very soft and tender. The goddess of beauty was often known to wear only the finest clothing and don the most lavish of jewelry.

Poseidon

Poseidon was the god of the ocean, storms, horses, and earthquakes. The name Poseidon was derived from the Greek work πόσις (posis) which can be translated to the words "husband or lord" the other part of the god of the oceans name is derived from the Greek word δᾶ (da) which translates to "Earth." Thus, when Poseidon's name is translated in full it can mean one of two things: "husband of the earth" or "lord of the water."

Poseidon was one of the five siblings of Zeus and was the second born son of Rhea and Cronus. Poseidon was married to the sea nymph Amphitrite. Poseidon had many offspring with many consorts, his most notable children were Orion, Pegasus, Atlas, and Triton.

Zeus was not the only god of the Greek pantheon to be associated with an iconic weapon. Many of the Greek pantheons had their favored weapons. For Poseidon, he was closely associated with his iconic trident, gifted to him by the Cyclopes to help the Olympian gods defeat the Tyrant rule of the Titans. Just like Zeus's lightning bolt, this Trident was pivotal to the Olympian's victory over the Titans. Poseidon would later go on to use the trident as a tool to rule over the world's oceans. Although Poseidon was the god of the ocean, it was all up to chance that he was given this responsibility. According to legend, once the gods beat the Titans the world was divided into three parts, these being the skies, the oceans, and the Underworld. Zeus and his brothers Poseidon and Hades would go on to draw straws to decide who would rule which part of the newly divided world. Legend says that Zeus drew the straw that represented the skies, Hades drew the straw for the Underworld, and Poseidon drew the straw for the Oceans. From that point on the brothers would rule their allocated part of the new world.

Out of the famed Greek pantheon, Poseidon was one of the most powerful and even the most feared gods of Greek mythology. Many Ancient Greeks, particularly sailors, feared Poseidon because he was considered to be the worst-tempered, greediest, and moodiest god of all the Greek pantheon. It was said that Poseidon would often take his fury out on mortals by creating treacherous sailing conditions leading to many Greek sailors' deaths. However, Poseidon was not only feared by mortals but even Greek deities were fearful of the god of the ocean. It was believed that Poseidon could be incredibly vengeful and hostile towards anybody around him, especially towards mortals, when he was insulted.

However, although Poseidon was known to bestow his wrath among the humans of Earth, he had many heated disputes and run-ins with other gods of the Greek pantheon. As mentioned earlier, Poseidon even went as far as to try and murder his brother Zeus by aiding Hera in her exploits, but that was just one of many occasions he acted hostile and violent towards the gods.

Poseidon was a greedy god and that greed led him to obsess over the city of Athens, Athena's main city. As a result, Athena and Poseidon clashed. Poseidon claimed that the great city of Athens would benefit more if he became ruler opposed to Athena. However, it was clear Poseidon had no interest in Athens, he just wanted it for selfish gain. To prove that he would be the greater protector, Poseidon struck a rock with his trident, which produced a beautiful stream of water that encircled the Temple of Erechtheion on the north side of the Acropolis. Poseidon believed that his gift of water would provide the mortals with a source of life in which they could better sustain themselves. However, in reply, Athena planted an olive tree. The gods asked the first king of Athens, Cecrops, to decide who he felt should rule over Athens as their protector. Cecrops decided that Athena's gift of the olive tree would prove more useful as it would provide the citizens of Athens with wood, oils, and fruit, rather than only water. Athena kept Athens, and to this day the olive branch is considered a universal symbol of peace. However, Poseidon never forgave Athena and held an eternal grudge towards the goddesses.

In art, Poseidon was often depicted similarly to Zeus, with a dense beard and long curly hair, and piercing eyes. According to Homer, Poseidon's shriek was as loud as ten thousand men screaming at once. Often Poseidon was portrayed as riding on a four-horse chariot over the waves of the ocean while wielding his iconic trident. Although Poseidon's trident was his most recognizable symbol, it was not exclusive to him as his son, Triton, also wielded it.

It was believed that Poseidon used his trident to create the very first horse by striking a rock. The god of the Ocean also used his trident to break off a piece of the Greek mythological island Kos and create the island Nisyros.

Athena

Athena was one of the major goddesses of Greek mythology. She was primarily known as the goddess of wisdom and war, but was also associated with agriculture, weaving, spinning, navigation, architecture, and needlework Athena was truly a well-celebrated goddess and was among one of the most respected and admired figures in all of the Greek pantheon.

The birth of Athena is quite remarkable and was an epic tale in itself. Athena was said to have emerged as a fully grown goddess out of the skull of Zeus, however, there is an interesting backstory to this. As we know, Zeus had many lovers and one of his lovers included Metis, an Oceanid nymph. A romantic union commenced between Zeus and Metis, resulting in the Oceanid nymph falling pregnant. Zeus became weary of his unborn child and remembered the danger that he posed to his father, Cronus, as well as, how Cronus posed a threat to his father Uranus. Zeus became troubled and he became increasingly wary that history would repeat himself and thus in an effort to ensure that Athena would not overthrow him in the future he swallowed his nymph lover Metis.

However, Metis was still pregnant with Athena and deep within the darkness of Zeus's interior, Metis continued to carry the child. Much time had passed, and Zeus was beginning to suffer from terrible headaches. The headaches were becoming unbearable, so Zeus called upon the god of blacksmiths, Hephaestus (some myths say it was Prometheus instead of Hephaestus), to split his head open. Hephaestus agreed and split the King of the Olympians skull open. Out of Zeus' skull emerged the fully grown Athena in all her glory. Since that day Athena was a proud member of the Olympian gods and goddesses and played an integral role in Mount Olympus.

Although Athena was the goddess of the war, she was very different from her half-brother, Ares. Athena was not associated with the same degree of brutality, violence, or bullying behavior as Ares was, instead Athena was more of a strategist. She was a diplomat who was often summoned by the gods to mediate several disputes and wars amongst the Greek pantheons. Athena was not known to own weapons of her own, but rather known to borrow her weapons from Zeus.

Athena is the patron goddess of the Greeks capital, Athens and named in the goddess' honor. In Athens, the goddess' most famous statue stands in the Parthenon. The goddess Athena was responsible for overseeing all of the physical buildings and structures throughout Greece, not only in Athens. She oversaw that these structures would protect the Ancient Greeks from danger and bring prosperity to the lives of the Greek populace. These structures included fortresses, harbors, and even courts of law.

According to legend, the goddess of wisdom and war was believed to play a pivotal role in the Trojan War and opted to side with the Greeks. Athena was also believed to have assisted many demigods and Greek heroes such as Perseus, Jason, Odysseus, and Hercules. In one instance, Athena gave Perseus the gift of a mirror-like shield that would prove pivotal in Perseus's battle against the Gorgon Medusa. Prometheus was also under Athena's tutorage and was taught architecture, astrology, mathematics, medicine, and navigation by the Greek goddess.

In art, Athena was portrayed as a beautiful, tall woman with golden blonde hair. She was generally portrayed with a physically fit physique and had an athletic build. The goddess of wisdom and war was generally portrayed as clothed in a full set of armor and accompanied with a sword and a shield. Sometimes instead of a shield, she would be wielding a spear. Athena had many symbols that represented her, these included an owl, an olive branch or tree, a clock, a tiger lily, and, occasionally, a lance. In artistic portrayals of Athena, she was generally accompanied by one or a few of these symbols.

CHAPTER 6
THE MANY LARGER THAN LIFE FIGURES OF GREEK MYTHOLOGY

Greek mythology has many other important figures beyond the Olympian gods. There are many other minor gods, demigods, creatures, and other mythical beings that bear great importance on history and culture. Each one has these fascinating creatures and deities have their own myths and lore attached to them. Demigods such as Herakles, Achilles, Theseus, Helen of Troy, and Perseus all make up a significant portion in ancient Greek mythological tales. These demigod's actions are responsible for unfolding major events in Greek mythology and were widely revered and celebrated among the Greek populace. Creatures and minor deities such as nymphs, centaurs, and satyrs are fascinating in their own right and truly give depth to the mythology we all know and love.

Nymphs

Nymphs, also known as nymphai, were any minor goddess which was associated with nature in one way or another. Nymphs could only be female and were largely considered as a class of inferior female divinities. The nymphs populated the earth mainly the wilderness, wild plains, and forests. Although the nymphs were considered to lie beneath the gods on a hierarchical scale, they were still summoned to grace the presence of the gods and attend all of the assemblies the gods would host on Mount Olympus. The nymphs were responsible for watching over and ruling all sorts of different natural phenomena such as the clouds, the natural springs, the meadows, the beaches, the caves, the trees, and much more. The nymphs were also considered to be the responsible entities for ensuring the wellbeing and care of all the plants and animals of their domain. Due to this, the nymphs were especially close to the Olympian gods who were associated as being gods of nature such as Hermes, Artemis, and Poseidon.

Nymphs were also associated with fertility, good harvest, and water. Nymphs, unlike other gods and deities, were not immortal. They could die, however, they tended to live exceptionally long lives. Nymphs were distinguished between the spheres of nature in which they represented. There were many different spheres, however, it is important to highlight the major spheres to which the nymphs were connected to. The Oceanids were sea nymphs who inhabited only saltwater, while Nereids were nymphs that could inhabit both freshwater and saltwater. Other spheres of nymphs included the Naiads who would watch over and protect the springs, rivers, and lakes. The Oreads were nymphs who presided over the mountains, while the Napaea and Alseids were nymphs who protracted the glens and groves of Earth. Lastly, there were the Dryads, also known as Hamadryads, who would preside over all the forests and trees across the world.

Centaurs

Centaurs, otherwise known as kentauroi, are mythical creatures in Greek mythology who are half-man and half-horse. These unusual creatures were believed to have lived in the mountains and forests of the region known as Thessaly. Ancient Greeks believed centaurs to be primal creatures who would exist in tribes and make their homes in caves. They were also believed to be hunters who would hunt wild animals and arm themselves with spears made of tree branches and sharpened rocks at the tip.

There are many origin myths that surround the legacy of these hybrid creatures, one of these myths says that the mortal King

Ixions son, Centaurus, fornicated with a cloud nymph by the name of Nephele. It is said that Nephele was created by a jealous Zeus who created the nymph in the image of his wife, Hera. Centaurus impregnated Nephele and as a result, the cloud nymph gave birth to a flock of centaurs. However, this is just one of the many origin stories of the mythical beasts.

Centaurs were believed to have been followers of the god of wine, Dionysus. The Centaurs earned the reputation, just like the god they followed, as being rowdy, boisterous, and savage creatures. According to legend, the centaurs were governed by their animal half as opposed to their human half, and as a result, were bestial in nature. Centaurs were creatures that were believed to be representative of chaos and barbarism. These traits of the mythical creatures were frequently described in Greek sculpture, stories, myths, art, and pottery. However, although these beasts boasted a barbaric and chaotic reputation it was believed that centaurs would only display these treacherous traits when they had consumed alcohol. This could simply have been a metaphor the Greeks would tell to act as a cautionary tale of the barbaric tendencies alcohol can unleash in man if alcohol was used irresponsibly.

According to myth, the centaurs were invited to attend the wedding of Pirithous, who was the King of Lapith, and who also happened to be the centaurs half-brother. It is said that the centaurs got uncontrollably drunk at the ceremony and tried to carry female guests back home with them. One centaur tried to even carry off the bride. However, the demigod Theseus was also present at the wedding and aided King Pirihous in battle in which most of the centaurs were slain.

The most famous of all the centaurs was known by the name of Chiron. Chiron was considered the most civilized centaur and incredibly wise. His wisdom was so great he tutored and advised many legendary demigods including Achilles, Jason, and HeraklesHerakles. Chiron's family is interesting, to say the least. Chiron was the son of the tyrant Titan, Cronus, and an ocean nymph, Philyra. Thus, he was technically the half-brother of Zeus and many other prolific Olympian gods and goddesses. Chiron married the nymph Chariklo and lived in the deep forest of Mount Pelion.

Although a minor figure in Greek mythology, played a big role. Chiron was responsible for the demigod Achilles' education and gifted Achilles with a Pelian ash spear, which Achilles would famously use in the Trojan War. What is more intriguing about Chiron was that he would never drink, thus, according to some legend, would not give in to his bestial nature. Chiron was also not part of the same lineage as the other centaurs and is believed by many to be the very first centaur ever birthed.

Satyrs

Like centaurs, satyrs are also hybrid creatures who are interesting characters in Greek mythology. Satyrs were half-man and half-beast who inhabited the forests and hills of Earth. They are generally depicted as having a human upper body and below their waist they have the hooved legs of a horse or a goat. They were also believed to have pointed ears and have horns protruding from their forehead.

Satyrs were the offspring of mountain nymphs and goats or horses, thus explaining their appearance. However, some legends say that satyrs were the sons of Hekaterides, which were five nymphs who were associated with a popular dance that was practiced in rural areas of ancient Greece.

The ancient Greek poet Hesiod described the satyrs as brothers of the nymphs. His words held strong credibility with regards to the beliefs of ancient Greek society as his range of influence in Greece was immense. Hesiod would go on to describe the satyrs as "good-for-nothing" and "mischievous" creatures. The satyrs, like the centaurs, were also known to be the followers of the god of wine, Dionysus. Thus, because the satyrs were always in an environment where alcohol was abundant, they had a reputation for brutishness and drunkenness, just like the hybrid centaurs.

Satyrs were not all the same in grand design and as such there were different categories of satyrs. The panes were satyrs that had the legs of goats and were considered to be associated with the god Pan. Although these satyrs differ ever so slightly from other satyrs in appearance, they were sometimes considered in some regions of Greece to be separate from the species of satyrs completely. Another variant of the satyrs included the seilenoi. The seilenoi were older versions of satyrs and would often be depicted as having fat stomachs and long white hair. The seilonoi were often known to be in the company of the god of wine, Dionysus, and were talented in both winemaking and art. The last variation of satyrs included the tityroi. These were the bards of the satyr community and were known to play musical instruments known as a shepherd's pipe. The tityroi were considered to be the local satyr's of the island of Crete.

Demigods

Demigods were the offspring of a mighty deity and a mortal, thus they were half-gods. Demigods were renowned by the Ancient Greeks as entities that were incredibly courageous and strong. Many of the Olympians and other Greek gods, like Zeus, were known to get involved in love affairs with humans and as a result of this union, many demigods were birthed. As demigods were half-man and half-god, it was believed that they possessed great power, strength, and abilities and are often regarded as being as powerful as many of the deities within the Greek pantheon. The demigods were the heroes of the Ancient Greeks and were inherently famous for all that they represented. Demigods such as Herakles, Theseus, Perseus, and Achilles were highly regarded among the Greek populace. Thus, the gods were not the only heroes of Ancient Greece, as the legendary tales about demigod heroes and heroines whose exploits still thrill us to this day. There are many myths and epic tales surrounding the demigods of Ancient Greece. Most of these stories were documented in the famous writings of the *Iliad* and the *Odyssey* which were written by the legendary Greek poet Homer. There were many Demigods but the most famous ones included Herakles, Achilles, Theseus, Perseus, and Helen of Troy.

Herakles

Herakles is better known by his Roman name, Hercules, thanks in part to the famous Disney movie of the same name. While that is how we remember him now, we will continue to call him by his Greek name here.

Herakles was a Greek hero in Ancient times and quite possibly the most famous demigod in the modern world. Herakles was the Son of Zeus and the mortal Alcmene. He was also the nemesis of Zeus's wife, Hera, and would often be persecuted and attacked by the goddess due to Hera's jealousy. However, Herakles would always come out on top. Herakles was renowned for always being too powerful for his foes and is known best for his fantastic feats of strength and courage.

One of the more famous tales involving Herakles was the 12 labors. After being driven mad by Hera, Herakles brutally killed his sons and wife. Once Herakles realized the severity of what he had done, he asked Apollo how he could repent. The Oracle of Apollo, Pythia, told Herakles if he really wanted to atone for his sins, he should go and serve his cousin, King Eurystheus, for twelve years. Eurytheus was not a fan of his cousin Herakles, and sent the demigod on twelve seemingly impossible labors that no other man would even dare to attempt.

Herakles' 12 labors would be impossible for lesser heroes but for the son of Zeus, nothing could shatter his determination and courage. Herakles' amazing feats of strength and daringness during his 12 labors included slaying the nine-headed sea-serpent, the Hydra, stealing the girdle from Hippolyta (the queen of the Amazonians), taming Hades' three-headed hellhound Cerbeus, and slaying the Nemean lion.

One of the Parerga (a collection of philosophical reflections) depicts Herakles' battle with a centaur by the name of Nessus. It is thanks to this battle that the Greek hero would meet his demise. The Parerga depicts a scene in which Herakles was traveling with his wife, Deianira. During the couple's travels, Herakles encountered a raging river and a sly, deceitful centaur named Nessus. The centaur offered to help Deianira across the river and Herakles accepted his offer as he saw no harm in his proposal. The centaur helped Deianeria across the river and forced himself on her. Herakles was filled with rage and slew the centaur with an arrow. With the centaur's last breath, he told Deianira that if she smothered Herakles with his blood, Herakles would be forever loyal to her. Deianeira listened to the centaur and saved some of his blood to use on Herakles, if she needed it.

Some time passed and Deianeira believed that Herakles was unfaithful towards her. Not thinking clearly, she remembered the words of the centaur. Deianeira, overwhelmed with jealousy at the thought that Herakles might have another lover other than her, smothered Herakles in his sleep with a tunic smeared in the blood of Nessus. However, the blood did not make Herakles loyal to her. Instead the centaur's blood poisoned Herakles, forcing the Greek hero to live the rest of his days with the pain of a living fire burning inside of him constantly. Nessus's deceit caused Deianeira to sentence Herakles to a life of unimaginable agony. Herakles could not bear the pain and pleaded with his father Zeus to take his life. Zeus accepted and killed his son. Upon death, Herakles was brought to Mount Olympus to live the rest of eternity with his father and the other Olympians.

Achilles

Achilles is yet another highly celebrated Greek demigod. Achilles' father was the mortal king Peleus, who ruled over the Myrmidons and the Nereid. His mother was the sea nymph and minor goddess, Thetis. Achilles was considered as the most handsome, bravest, and most elite warrior of the Agamemnon army who fought in the Trojan War.

Achilles was one of the most famed and respected demigods of the Greek world and it is no surprise that many myths and legends surround the legacy of the Greek hero. Achilles was believed to be almost indestructible. He was the perfect warrior that could not be wounded and was known to have no weaknesses, except for one. Achilles' almost full-proof invulnerability came from a story when Achilles was no more than a baby. It is said that his mother, Thetis, dipped the infant Achilles into a magical river, known as the River Styx. The River Styx would grant the demigod invulnerability to whatever part of the body was submerged underwater. The infant Achillies was fully submerged into the river except for his heels where his mother Thetis held him. Thus, every part of Achilles was invulnerable and could not be wounded except for his heels which would become his only weakness. Achilles' weak heels would become iconic, and to this day the term "Achilles heel" refers to a weakness that a person possesses. This seemingly insignificant weakness would lead to the downfall and death of the famed demigod.

Achilles was a warrior at heart and was one of many great Greek Heroes and demigods that fought in the Trojan War. However, during the iconic Trojan War, Achilles entered into an altercation with Agamemnon, the king of Mycenae. Due to this dispute, the demigod refused to take further part in the

Trojan War. Due to this, Achilles decided to give his armor to his cousin Patroclus, who he loved dearly. He felt it would only benefit his cousin in warfare as Patroclus was still fighting against the Trojans. However, fate had been written in blood for Patroclus, and he would die in battle by the hand of a Trojan warrior, Hector. Enraged, Achilles returned to the battlefield and put aside his differences with Agamemnon so that he could avenge his cousin's life. Achilles had his eyes set on revenge and returned to battle the Trojans, where he swiftly killed his cousin's murderer. Achilles made sure to make a statement to the Trojans as he dragged Hector's bloody corpse across the walls of Troy, leaving a bloody trail behind wherever he dragged Hector's body. Achilles did this to show the Trojans his ruthlessness and that he was out for blood. However, in Achilles' rage, he was careless and the Trojans capitalized on the demigods' lack of focus. Achilles was drunk with rage and exposed his only weakness, his heels, and the Trojan warrior Paris saw this as an ample opportunity to kill the almost invincible demigod. Paris shot a perfectly aimed arrow, guided by the god Apollo, striking Achilles' heel. The arrow and shot took the demigod's life.

Theseus

Theseus was the son of the god of the ocean, Poseidon, and the mortal princess, Aethra. Theseus was considered by many

Greeks as the greatest Athenian hero Greek had ever known and he was also known to pull off the impossible by managing to politically unify Attica under the aegis of Athens.

As a child, Theseus was unaware of his divine origin and was raised by his mother Aethra in the palaces of Troezen. When Theseus reached adulthood, he was told about his origins and how his father was none other than Poseidon. Armed with the knowledge that he was a demigod, he set out to journey forth to Athens. On his journey, Theseus managed to slay and outwit many notorious Greek mythological figures, such as Periphetes (an enormous club bearing Cyclops), the infamous bandit Sinus, Phaea (a giant pig), the outlaw Sciron, Cercyon (the tyrant king of Eleusis), and the bandit Procrustes.

In Athens, Theseus faced much persecution from the goddess Medea, the granddaughter of the god of the sun, Helios. However, Theseus remained untouchable and thwarted all of Madea's attempts to eliminate him. He remained in Athens for several years, during which he would achieve his greatest triumph. Theseus volunteered to be one of fourteen Athenians who would be sent to Crete as a sacrifice to a fierce Minotaur. The minotaur was owned by a king of Crete named Minos and the creature was kept in the confines of a labyrinth. Theseus agreed to be a sacrifice as he knew this would be an ample opportunity to kill the minotaur of Crete within the labyrinth the monster resides in. However, Theseus did not slay the mighty minotaur without assistance. The Cretan princess, Adriane, helped Theseus navigate his way around the labyrinth with a ball of thread. With the help of Adriane's thread, Theseus slew the beast, and set sail back to Athens.

Due to Theseus's triumph in Crete, he was made king of Athens, where he ruled admirably for several years. However, his rule of Athens would be cut short due to an unsuccessful attempt to abduct Persephone from the Underworld. Persephone was the goddess of the Underworld and the daughter of Zeus and Demeter. His voyage to the Underworld resulted in his deposition as King of Athens and the demigod was consequently murdered in torturous fashion by Lycomedes of Scyros.

Perseus

Perseus was an extremely significant figure in Greek mythology. Perseus was yet another son of Zeus and a mortal woman by the name of Danae.

Perseus was sent on an impossible quest by the king of Seriphos. Polydectes sent Perseus to fetch the head of Medusa (a gorgon with wings, a head with snakes in place of hair, and her gaze could turn men to stone). Polydectes sent Persues on this quest thinking it to be impossible to achieve and hoped the demigod would die on his venture. However, the Greek gods intervened and favored Perseus. The Greek pantheon wanted the demigod to succeed on his quest and gifted Persius with magical weapons. The first gift bestowed to Perseus was from Hermes in the form of a curved sword and sandals. Athena provided Perseus with a mirror-like shield. Lastly, to aid Perseus on his epic quest, Hades, the god of the Underworld, gifted Perseus with a helmet that would make the demigod invisible upon wearing it. With these gifts, Perseus was armed and ready to take on any challenge, even a challenge as formidable as the highly dangerous Medusa.

According to legend, the demigod Perseus consulted with a covenant of great witches, known as the Graeae. The Graeae were believed to be three ugly witches who, between the three of them, shared one single eye and one tooth. The Graeae helped Persues to locate the Gorgon Medusa. The Graeae at first were hostile towards Perseus and were hesitant to help Perseus and did not want to tell the demigod the whereabouts of his Gorgon foe. Perseus used his wits and tricked the witches by stealing their one eye and forcing them to tell the demigod where he could find Medusa. The witches knew they had to get their last remaining eye back and were desperate to have it safely returned to them, so they put aside their hostility and submitted to Perseus's request and told him where he could find Medusa. Once the witches told Perseus where he could find the Gorgon, he gave the last remaining eye the witches had between them back to the Graeae.

Perseus now knew where to find the Gorgon menace and the demigod ventured forth to slay Medusa in an epic battle. Perseus was able to kill the Medusa after a fierce battle, but it was largely due to the gifts bestowed to him by the gods. Perseus was victorious. He brought the head of Medusa to Athena, the goddess of war and wisdom, as proof. Perseus later used Medusa's head as a weapon and turned his enemies to stone by forcing them to lock eyes with Medusa's severed head.

Helen of Troy

Helen of Troy is one of the few female demigods in Greek mythology. Helen of Troy's mother was the mortal queen of Sparta, Leda, however, her divine bloodline would come from her father Zeus, who seduced her mother when he took on the form of a swan.

Helen had two siblings, Castor and Pollux. Some myths say Castor and Pollux were also demigods and the sons of Zeus, and according to others, they were simply mortal Spartan warriors. Although what is certain is that Helen of Troy was considered a demigod to the Ancient Greek populace.

Helen of Troy is most famous for the Trojan War fought in her name and beauty. Helen of Troy was considered so beautiful that some regarded her even more beautiful than the god of beauty herself, Aphrodite. Her overwhelming beauty would lead to her misfortune as she would be abducted by Prince Paris of Troy and forced to become his wife. As a result of Helen of Troy's abduction, war broke loose between the Greeks and the Trojans. It is believed that the gods also were involved in the Trojan War and the Greek pantheon split into factions, some representing the Greeks and some assisting the Trojans.

There were many iconic and significant figures in Greek mythology who took part in the Trojan War such as Ajax, Odysseus, Hector, and Achilles.

The Greek pantheon took a great deal of interest in the Trojan War and found it amusing. Many gods were believed to have participated in the war and would even choose sides. It was believed that Poseidon, Athena, and Hera backed the Greeks and would assist them where they could. Meanwhile, Ares and Aphrodite assisted the Trojans in their conquest. Many of the Greek pantheons remained impartial to the Trojan War and did not take sides, such as Zeus and Apollo. The participation of the demigods involved in the Trojan War was well documented in the writings of the *Odyssey* and the *Iliad* and the legendary war between the Greeks and the Trojans has been etched into history for thousands of years. Finally, after nine years the war came to a halt, and the Greeks came out victorious over their Trojan opposition. Helen of Troy had been rescued and returned to Sparta where she rightfully belonged where she would rule as the queen of Sparta with her husband once more.

CHAPTER 7
GREEK MONSTERS THAT TERRIFIED A NATION AND THREATENED THE GODS

The monsters in Greek mythology were the nemesis of the gods and goddesses and would strike terror in the hearts of the Ancient Greek populace. There are so many monsters within the vast mythology of the Ancient Greeks that it is almost impossible to single out all of them, thus only the most famous and significant monsters will be highlighted and discussed. The monsters made up a significant portion of Greek mythology and were ever-present in the myths and tales of the Ancient Greeks, often appearing in legends regarding epic battles between the Greek pantheon and the ferocious monsters.

Medusa

Medusa was one of three Gorgon sisters. Her sisters were named Stheno and Euryale, however, Medusa was by far the most famous of the sisters. Interestingly enough, Medusa was the only one of her sisters to not be immortal. It is sometimes said that the goddess Gaea was the mother of the gorgon sisters, however, according to other sources, Medusa's parents were the early sea deities Phorcys and Ceto. However, what mythologists do agree on is that the gorgons were all birthed at sea.

Medusa is generally thought to have been unmarried, however, he was thought to be the lover of Poseidon. Their union resulted in Pegasus and Chrysaor. Pegasus was a winged horse and Chrysaor was the Greek hero who wielded a golden sword.

According to legend, Medusa, at one point in time, was a beautiful woman. She was believed to be a priestess of Athena and made a vow of chastity, however, upon breaking this vow with her lover Poseidon she was cursed. As a result of her affair, Athena punished her by turning the once beautiful priestess into an ugly monster. Athena would turn Medusa's hair into multiple venomous snakes as well as change

Medusa's once beautiful skin to a greenish hue. Upon this hideous transformation, it was said that anybody who met eyes with Medusa would turn to stone.

In one of the major myths surrounding the gorgon, the demigod Perseus was sent on a quest to kill Medusa in which he was assisted with the aid of gifts by the Greek pantheon. As mentioned in the previous chapter, Perseus was awarded many magical gifts to defeat Medusa one of which was a mirror-like shield, which would prove invaluable in slaying the monster. Perseus managed to fight his foe's reflection thanks to the mirror shield he was given by Athena, and as such defeated the gorgon by decapitating her.

The Hydra

The Hydra was a ferocious monster in Greek mythology and was a formidable foe and posed a deadly threat to the Greek pantheon in many ways. The Hydra was a serpentine beast that donned multiple heads and was one of the guardians of the Underworld. Each one of the Hydra's snake-like teeth contained razor-sharp teeth and he could strike at his foe with all of his heads at once. The Hydra also possessed poisonous breath that would result in immediate death to any human in contact with it. What is worse, though, is that, even if you managed to cut off one of the Hydra's heads, two more would regenerate in its place. He was a truly formidable opponent and so strong that many of the gods were terrified of him. The Hydra did not only have snakeheads but his whole body was snake-like and just like his breath was poisonous it was believed that when he slithered, he would leave a poisonous trail in his wake. The Hydra was large but not as large as one would assume. The Hydra was large compared to other snakes, but he was no means a giant, in fact, it is said that the beast's body was around the size of an average man, however, with the Hydra's multiple heads he could stand quite tall in stature.

The Hydra was known to reside at the Amymone Spring deep within the Underworld. The Amymone spring was located in a cave and provided the monstrous beast with the protection it needed while it slumbered. The Hydra slept most of its life and would only venture out when it needed to feed. The Hydra was believed to feast on townsfolk and villagers. Due to this, the myth of the Hydra struck fear in rural Greece far and wide.

According to legend, it is believed Hera, Zeus's wife, raised the Hydra with the intention of sending the beast to kill Herakles.

Herakles, as we know, was a demigod who possessed incredible strength and was a formidable foe for any creature. However, Hera was certain that the beast would be enough to end Zeus's son's life. Herakles overheard what Hera was plotting and was also aware of the terror the serpent was issuing upon local villagers and townsfolk. Herakles decided he needed to rid Greece of the Hydra menace.

Herakles traveled with his nephew Iolaus to kill the serpent once and for all. Herakles drew the Hydra from its slumber by shooting flaming arrows in Amymone Springs's cave. The Hydra, infuriated, launched himself into battle with the Greek demigod. Herakles sliced the many heads of the serpent. Usually, the Hydra's heads would simply grow back, but Herakles' nephew, Iolaus, sealed the Hydra's severed necks shut with a torch preventing them from regenerating. The Hydra, unable to regenerate its heads, only had one head remaining, in which Herakles sliced off with one, mighty blow. The Hydra was slain, and Herakles buried the serpent under an enormous rock to ensure the beast would forever be beaten.

Typhon

There were many gods and monsters in Greek mythology, but very rarely was a monster also a god. However, that was exactly the case with Typhon. Typhon was described as the most fearsome and powerful creature in all of Greek mythology and it is no wonder that his very name stirred up so much fear among the Ancient Greek populace.

Typhon was the child of Gaea, the goddess of the Earth, and Tartarus, the murderous bottomless pit of the Earth. According to certain myths, Hera desired to create a god that was even more powerful than Zeus and thus had Gaea and Tartarus mate. It could be argued that Typhon is the product of all the hate that existed in Hera's heart and her jealousy towards Zeus personified.

Typhon was a giant so tall that his head was said to have touched the stars themselves. Typhon possessed a torso of a man, however, his legs were made of vipers which would hiss and attack as the giant slithered. Typhon's head was said to have one hundred snake heads hanging off of it and each one would make the sound of different animals. The monster's eyes were blood red that would glow. Almost anybody who laid eyes on the monster would be stunned in terror. Typhon also possessed a savage jaw, which would breathe fire. The monster's body had over one hundred different types of wings and his hands, like his legs, were made of snakes. Some accounts describe Typhon as like a fire-breathing dragon with a hundred heads who would never sleep.

Typhon married Echidna, another half-human and half-snake hybrid. With their union, Typhon was considered the father of all monsters with Echidna as the mother of all monsters. The pair would go on to spawn horrific creatures that would terrorize Greece and bring chaos to the world. Some of their children include Cerberus, the Hydra, the Chimera, the Nemean Lion, Ladon, Caucasian Eagle (the eagle that would eat Prometheus's liver every day for 30 years), and many more.

The greatest myth that surrounds this ferocious monster is undoubtedly his fierce battle with Zeus. Typhon and Zeus had many epic battles. In one of these battles, Typhon destroyed countless cities, threw mountains in his blinding rage, and had his eyes set on demolishing Mount Olympus. Typhon's brute strength terrified many of the Olympian gods and goddesses. They were so scared of the monster that almost all the gods changed into their animal forms and fled from Mount Olympus. Only Dionysus, Athena, and Zeus stayed in their regular godly forms. Athena, at one point in the battle, called Zeus a coward. This enraged Zeus to an unimaginable level. Zeus attacked Typhon before the monster could destroy Mount Olympus to show Athena that he was not a coward. It is said that Zeus attacked Typhon with one hundred lightning bolts which managed to corner the beast in his tracks. Due to Zeus cornering the beast he managed to overpower Typhon and cast the monster in the bottomless pit of Tartarus. Once Typhon was in the bottomless pit of Tartarus, Zeus entrapped the monster by covering the pit with Mt. Etna so that the beast would never be able to escape again.

It was believed that all volcanic eruptions were a result of Typhon trying to escape his prison of Tartarus and the lava that erupted was the fire that the monster would breathe. However, it is important to note that this battle was the last of many battles. Typhon and the Greek gods engaged in a ten-thousand-year war and thus Zeus only managed to end the war thousands of years later by trapping the monster in the same pit that was half responsible for his birth.

Cerberus

Cerberus, also known as the hound of Hades, was a vicious three-headed hound that guarded the gates of the

Underworld. He made sure that the spirits of the dead were allowed to enter the Underworld but were never allowed to leave. Cerberus was a child of Typhon and Echidna (half-woman and half-snake) and was part of a ferocious family of monsters which included the Hydra, the Chimera, and Orthus. Upon guarding the gates of the Underworld, the monstrous hound would only be tricked three times. Once by the strength of Herakles, once by the music of Orpheus, and once by the Sybil of Cumae who tricked the beast with a cake.

To understand Cerbesus one should understand how dogs were perceived in the ancient world. In Ancient Greece, dogs were seen as wild animals who defied domestication. Although many dogs were companions to many Greeks and were often used as guard dogs, there were still many negative connotations attached to their canine companions. Dogs would often roam the streets of Greece in packs and scavenge throughout town and cause havoc. Thus Cerbeus was the embodiment of these negative traits that dogs were perceived to possess. However, the monster Cerbeus did not only possess the traits of the fearful qualities of ancient canines but also possessed a mixture of traits from many other feared animals. Thus, Cerberus was an amalgamation of ancient Greek nightmares.

Although Cerberus is often only described as a three-headed dog there was more to it that surrounded this legend. Cerberus was a monstrous dog that had three heads, a serpent's tail, a mane made out of snakes, and had the claws of a lion. According to some legends Cerberus's heads were meant to represent the past, the future, and the present. However, other legends suggest the hound's heads represented birth, youth, and old age.

The most famous myth surrounding Cerberus involves the demigod Herakles. Cerberus was the last of Herakles' 12 labors. According to legend, King Eurytheus sent Herakles on a quest to capture Cerberus alive. Eurystheus was certain that this quest would be too much, even for Herakles, and expected the hound of the Underworld to kill Herakles. However, Herakles was convinced he would be successful on his quest. Herakles traveled to the Underworld and proposed a proposition to the god of the Underworld, Hades. Herakles asked Hades if he could take Cerberus out of the gates of the Underworld without the use of weapons if he would be allowed to freely leave with the canine. Hades, who would generally never allow anybody to leave the Underworld once they have entered, was amused by Herakles' request and granted demigod permission to leave upon successfully subduing Cerberus.

Herakles found Cerberus on the shores of Acheron and challenged the beast to a wrestling match using only his bare hands. Cerberus agreed to Herakles' challenge and the two began an epic showdown. Herakles had to use every ounce of his strength to subdue the monstrous hound, but ultimately prevailed. Even though Herakles was the strongest man in the universe, he still struggled immensely. After a long battle, Cerberus grew weary and ran out of breath due to a devastating chokehold from the demigod. Finally, Herakles loosened his grip knowing that if he continued Cerberus would surely die. Herakles was successful with his quest and brought back the three-headed hound to King Eurytheus as requested. However, later Cerberus was returned to Hades to watch over the gates of the Underworld once more. Cerberus was one of the very few monsters who fought Herakles and survived.

CHAPTER 8
MYTHS THAT WITHSTOOD THE TEST OF TIME AND DEFINED A MYTHOLOGY

The myths of Greek mythology are truly fascinating, however, due to the immense amount of Greek myths out there, it is often overwhelming knowing where to begin. Up until this point, many of the Greek myths in the previous five chapters have already been discussed. However, even so, there are so many fascinating Greek takes to be told that there is an arsenal of myths still waiting to be highlighted. Each myth is as fascinating, if not more so, than the last. Greek mythology never seems to fail to capture our imagination and provides us with timeless tales that leave us captivated after every read. There are so many Greek myths to uncover and it is impressive how many of these myths have withstood the test of time.

Pandora's Jar

Pandora's box is a common idiom, taken from Greek mythology. While the idiom refers to a box, in the original myth, it was often portrayed as a jar. This myth takes place after Prometheus gave the gift of fire to the mortals of Earth. As mentioned earlier, Zeus did not take kindly to Prometheus stealing the gift of fire from the gods. Zeus also took vengeance on the mortals; he saw the mortals just as guilty for accepting the gift of fire. Zeus ordered Hephaestus, the god of blacksmiths, to create the first mortal woman out of soil and water as the punishment for the mortals as he knew one day she would be responsible for unleashing unspeakable evil on mankind. The name of the woman was Pandora. Each god and goddess was instructed by Zeus to give Pandora a gift. Athena gave Pandora the gift of wisdom, Aphrodite gave beauty, Hermes provided Pandora with cunning, and so on until all the gods had given some gift, no matter how large or small, to Pandora. The name Pandora can be translated from Greek to English as "all gifts."

Zeus told Pandora she was to visit Epimetheus, the brother of the punished Prometheus. Prometheus was fearful of Zeus at this point and believed Zeus was trying to harm his brother as a result of Prometheus's forbidden gift of fire. Thus, Prometheus urged his Epimetheus not to accept any gifts from

Zeus or be seduced by Pandora, no matter how sincere she may seem. However, Prometheus's brother, Empetheus, accepted Pandora as a gift from Zeus. Empetheus fell in love with Pandora and the pair married. All the gods and goddesses attended the wedding, and on Pandora's wedding night Zeus gave her a gift, just like all the other gods and goddesses before him. Zeus gave Pandora a jar. Zeus had warned the mortal women not to open the jar under any circumstance. However, Pandora was forever drawn to the contents of the jar and could not stay away from it any longer.

Epimetheus kept the key to Pandora's jar safe on his person at all times to ensure nobody would open the jar. However, one night when Epimetheus was sleeping, Pandora stole the key from her husband and opened the jar. Upon opening the jar, all evil was immediately released in the world. When Pandora opened the jar, hatred, war, death, hunger, sickness, and all disaster engulfed the world. Once the jar was opened, the contents could not be returned to it, forever dooming mortals to suffer.

The Myth of Icarus

The tale of Icarus and his father Daedalus is one of the most famous Greek myths. Daedalus was a famous engineer and inventor, said to be taught by Athena herself. A king, King Mino, learned of Daedalus' talent and commissioned him and his son, Icarus, to build a great labyrinth to imprison a deadly minotaur. This is the same minotaur and labyrinth that Perseus would later slay.

Upon Daedalus and Icarus finishing their work on the labyrinth, King Minos imprisoned them inside of it to prevent them from spreading knowledge of the labyrinth or minotaur's existence to the public. Night after night, Daedalus and Icarus tried to come up with ways to escape. One night, Daedalus had an idea. Icarus and his father gathered many feathers from birds and glued them together with wax. With the feathers and wax, Daeduls made four large wings for them to escape the labyrinth.

Daedalus warned his son that the wings were fragile, as they were only held together by wax, and he pleaded with his son to never fly too close to the sun as the wings would melt and he would fall to his death. Icarus told his father not to worry, assuring him that he understood. However, as the two of them were passing the island of Delos, in his delight, Icarus forgot his father's warning and flew too high. The heat of the sun melted the wax, as Daedalus said it would, and Icarus fell into the ocean and drowned. Daedalus was absolutely distraught with the death of his son and named the area "Icaria" in honor of his son.

The Abduction of Persephone by Hades

This myth tells the tale of the abduction of Zeus and Demeter's daughter Persephone and can also be seen as an ancient explanation of how the Greeks understood why certain seasons would blossom and others would not.

The daughter of Demeter (goddess of the harvest and agriculture) and Zeus, Persephone, grew to become an incredibly beautiful goddess and was admired by many. This beauty would ultimately lead to much misery for the goddess as Hades, the god of the Underworld, saw what a beautiful woman Persephone had grown into and immediately fell in love with her. Hades had become overcome with lust for Zeus's daughter and decided to abduct her and take her back to the Underworld with him. According to Homer, the story begins on a sunny day where the beautiful Persephone was picking flowers in a field with a few of her closest ocean nymph friends. While searching for the most beautiful flower on earth, Persephone moved away from her companions. Persephone found what she was looking for, and as she bent down to pick the extravagant flower, the Earth opened and out came Hades on his golden chariot. The god of the Underworld snatched Persephone without a second thought and carried Zeus's daughter back to the Underworld while the goddess was in tears.

Demeter was truly distraught about Persephone's abduction and searched across all the known world, day in and day out. Her search was in vain, and Persephone was nowhere to be found. With Perrsephones' absence, the crops and the land of the Earth began to wither away, as the pain of Demeter grew more severe with each passing day her daughter was missing. However, there was a glimmer of hope as there was a witness to Persephone's abduction. The sun had seen what truly happened to Demeter's daughter and felt sorry for the goddess after watching Demeter's painful search. The sun told Demeter the details of Persephone's abduction. Demeter armed with this new information was absolutely infuriated and could not believe what the sun had just told her. In a fit of rage, Demeter marched to her lover and Persephone's father, Zeus, and demanded that their daughter be returned to them at once. As Demeter was the goddess of the harvest and agriculture, she threatened to never let the world blossom again unless Persephone would be returned to her safely.

Zeus listened to his lover's threats and knew that the world could not survive without arable land and thus would demand that Persephone be returned to Demeter at once. Zeus sent Hermes, the messenger god, to demand that Hades release Persephone immediately and if Hades refused, there would be dire consequences. Hades knew that if he were to fight Zeus, he would be no match for his brother and agreed to release Persphone. However, Hades was clever and cunning, and had a trick up his sleeve. Hades would force Persephone to eat six six pomegranate seeds from the Underworld before handing over Demeter and Zeus' daughter to Hermes. Hades knew that if Persphone ate food from the Underworld, she could never truly escape. This was because whether a god, mortal, or any being eats from the Underworld they may never leave.

Although Persephone ate the six pomegranate seeds from the Underworld, she was returned to Hermes, and was reunited with her parents once more. Hermes told Demeter that Hades forced Persophone to eat the fruit from the Underworld. Not surprisingly, Demeter was absolutely furious and distraught. Demeter knew that anybody who ate food from the Underworld could never leave for a sustained period of time without being severely harmed and thus feared for her daughter's safety. However, Zeus was diplomatic and proposed a compromise. Zeus proposed that for every pomegranate seeds Persphone ate, she would spend a month in the Underworld. In other words, for six months of the year, Persephone would live in Mount Olympus and for the other six months, she would live with Hades in the Underworld. Demeter knew she had no other choice and was forced to accept Zeus's proposal. Thus every six months Persephone would travel to Hades in the Underworld, and during those months Demeter would mourn for her daughter and the crops and the land would begin to wither. Demeter would ensure the Earth would blossom once again for six months when Persephone would return home to Mount Olympus and live with her mother Demeter and the other Greek pantheons.

The Love Story of Eros and Psyche

This is a myth of love and how love isn't always how we expect it to be. This myth is about the mortal woman Psyche and Aphrodite's son Eros, who is the Greek version of the Roman Cupid. The story begins with Psyche, whose name can be translated to mean "soul" in English. Psyche was a mortal but she was no ordinary mortal; she possessed beauty that even the gods and goddesses could not parallel. Many mortal men regarded Psyche to be even more beautiful than the goddess of beauty Aphrodite herself.

Greeks from across the land would travel from far and wide to visit Psyche so they could admire and bask in her beauty. Some men stopped worshipping Aphrodite, as they were too awestruck by Psyche's beauty. Aphrodite was not pleased with this situation and the goddess of beauty became overwhelmed with jealousy and fury directed towards Psyche. The goddess of beauty knew she had to put an end to this and decided to punish Psyche. Aphrodite sent her son, Eros, to ensure that Psyche would fall in love with the vilest and most despicable creature in all the known Greek world. Eros, like the Roman Cupid, possessed arrows that could make anybody fall in love with the first thing that they saw once they were struck with the "love arrows." However, just like how the mortals would swoon over Psyche's beauty, so did Eros and Aphrodite fell in love with the mortal as soon as he saw her and thus could not carry out his mother's task.

Instead, Eros decided to do nothing and refused to be the reason Psyche would be forced to love a hideous creature for the rest of her life. Eros remained silent and returned to the company of the Greek pantheon. Years had passed since Eros last saw Psyche, however, with each passing year Eros's love for the mortal woman grew stronger and stronger. What was truly strange was that Psyche remained unmarried even after all these years had passed, even with her unparalleled beauty and lack of intervention of the gods. It was believed that the Greeks would still admire Psyche's beauty but none would ask for her hand in marriage, perhaps they were intimidated by such divine beauty. However, men would go on to marry other women and Psyche with all her beauty would remain unwed. This worried Psyche's parents and they grew concerned about their daughter's lack of suitors. They were afraid that their daughter would remain unwed for the rest of her life despite her overwhelming beauty.

Due to their concern, Psyche's parents decided to seek the guidance of Apollo to help advise them as to what they needed to do. The oracle who watched over Apollo's temple and spoke on Apollo's behalf told Psyche's parents that there was only one way that Psyche will ever be married. Psyche's parent's ears perked up and they were willing to do whatever it took. The oracle said that Psyche would have to wear a black dress and climb the peak of a high mountain all by herself and wait there. According to the oracle, while Psyche waits on the mountain peak, she will be met by a winged-serpent who will take Psyche as his wife. Psyche's parents were horrified about what they were just told, but they were desperate to find a husband for their daughter and believed they had no other choice than to listen to the oracle of Apollo.

The next day, Psyche made her way up the mountain as the oracle told her and waited on the highest peak. While Psyche was waiting at the top of the mountain, she was shaking and crying in fear until, suddenly, the fresh wind of Zephyrus lifted her up and guided her to a magnificent castle floating in the sky. Psyche was confused and frightened, as she had no idea what was happening. At the castle, Psyche was greeted by a soft sweet voice that put her nerves at ease and made her feel welcome and at home.

The voice that she heard was none other than Eros, the son of Aphrodite, who has been in love with Psyche for years ever since he laid eyes on her, but Eros would not expose himself to Psyche and he was nothing but a voice to the perspective of the mortal woman. However, every night in the castle Eros would lie next to Psyche in the dark, but Psyche would never actually see Eros and thus she did not know who was sleeping beside her every night. Although Psyche never actually saw Eros laying beside her night after night, she could feel that it was not a vile monster laying beside her but rather a caring, loving husband that she and her parents had always wished for.

Days turned into weeks and Psyche was joyous and content with her new life. However, as she was living in the castle in the sky, she was far away from her family and began to miss them. Psyche felt sorry for them as she had left them all alone. She decided to ask her new husband if her family could come visit her in the castle in the sky where she now resided.

Eros was skeptical at first but finally submitted to his wife's request and accepted her terms. Eros pleaded with Psyche to not be influenced by her family, otherwise the relationship she has formed with her new, mysterious husband would be destroyed and they both would suffer. The next day arrived and Psyche's two sisters came to visit her in the castle in the sky. Psyche's sisters were carried like she was, by the wind of Zephyrus, to Psyche's new home. Psyche's sisters were incredibly jealous of her, as they believed that Psyche was living a life of royalty and divinity. The two sisters began to laugh at Psyche as Psyche told them that she has never actually seen her husband before. The sister out of jealousy and envy told Psyche that the reason she has never seen her husband was that was in fact the hideously vile monster the oracle of Apollo had prophesied. What Psyche's sisters said to her really hit a nerve and truly overwhelmed the mortal woman. Psyche's sisters left to go back home but their words did not and they lingered in Psyche's mind like a stain that cannot be cleaned. Psyche began to feel truly conflicted and confused as to why after all this time her husband still has not shown his face. Psyche was desperate to find out the identity of her new husband and came up with a plan.

Psyche's plan was that one night, when her mysterious husband was asleep next to her in the dark, she would light a candle to expose the true identity of her husband. She had decided that if the person sleeping next to her every night was exposed to be a monster, then she would kill with a blade. However, if the candle exposed a man she would roll over and happily go back to sleep. Psyche went along with her plan that night. She lifted the candle and revealed it was not a vile serpent or monster, but Eros! Unfortunately, as she lifted the candle over her sleeping husband, a drop of hot oil from the candlestick fell on the cheek of Eros and woke him up. Betrayed, Eros said "love cannot live without trust." Psyche immediately regretted what she had done and felt horrible for her intrusive actions. Eros ran out of sight and could not be found anywhere. Psyche was desperate to find her husband, and despite the fact that Psyche had only seen his face for the briefest of seconds, she immediately fell deeply in love with him. Psyche was at her wits end and decided to approach Eros' mother. Although Aphrodite detested the mortal for her beauty, the goddess said she would help Psyche to reunite with Eros if she could complete four seemingly impossible tasks. Miraculously, Psyche was able to complete these tasks with the help of nature and even the assistance of the gods.

The first task that Aphrodite demanded Psyche to complete was to sort out an enormous stack of wheat, barley, millet, poppy seeds, peas, lentils, and beans that had been mixed together in a heap by Aphrodite. To make this task even harder Psyche only had one day to complete this task. Psyche was overwhelmed and did not have a clue where to even begin, however, fortunately for her a herd of nearby ants felt sorry for the beautiful mortal. These ants managed to secure the help of all the ants across Greece to help Psyche finish Aphrodite's task in time. Psyche completed what had been asked of her but she still had three more tasks she had to complete.

For Psyche's next task Aphrodite demanded that her son's wife gather a clump of golden wool that could only be acquired from a flock of murderous sheep with dangerously sharp horns. Once again, Psyche was overwhelmed and did not know how she would successfully complete Aphrodite's task. However, nature once again helped Psyche and this time a divinely inspired green reed would advise her. The green reed told Psyche that she must wait till the heat of the afternoon before she attempts to steal the golden wool as this is the time that the sheep would be asleep. Psyche was grateful and listened to the advice of the green reed and returned to Aphrodite with a lapful of golden wool. Aphrodite was still not impressed and demanded that Psyche complete another task.

Aphrodite gave Psyche her third task and this time it was even more complicated. Aphrodite demanded that Psyche was to fill a jar with the fresh waters from the deadly river Styx, which could only be recovered from the water that flowed on the top of a distant mountain. The journey alone was incredibly dangerous and Psyche went through great lengths to simply reach the river Styx. However, Psyche pushed through and managed to reach the river, although Aphrodite did not tell her what would be waiting at the river Styx. Psyche arrived at the river only to find an enormous dragon who guards the water of the river Styx against intruders. Psyche froze at the sight of the dragon out of fear. Fortunately, Zeus noticed the fear struck Psyche before it was too late and remembered that he owed Eros a favor. In order to pay off his debt to Eros, Zeus sent down an eagle from Mount Olympus to snatch the empty jar from Psyche's hands and fill it with the water of the river Styx before handing the filled jar back to Psyche. Psyche was saved and was successful with her task.

Aphrodite, furious with Psyche's success, demanded that she complete one final task. Psyche was tasked to go to the Underworld and retrieve a day's worth of Persephone's beauty cream and bring it back. However, the only way to enter the Underworld would mean that Psyche would have to die. Psyche was ready to do whatever it took to see her husband again and thus went up one of the highest towers she could find with the intention of jumping off of it so that she could enter the Underworld. However, at the last moment, the tower she had planned to jump off of was inspired by Psyche's motivation and pure intentions that it told her a better way to enter the Underworld. She followed the advice of everything the tower had told her.

She first went to a hill called Taenarus in the Peloponnese, where she would be able to find a hole that would lead her to Hades. However, she would not go empty-handed as she went on her journey with two coins and two pieces of bread soaked in honey and barley. Psyche used the first of her two coins to pay Charon (the ferryman of Hades) who took her across the river Styx to the Underworld. After Psyche's ride on the ferry, she met Persephone and would refuse any of her meals that she offered her just as the tower had advised her to do. Instead of accepting the food from Persphone, the tower advised Psyche to request a crust of brown bread and a favor. Psyche did just that and asked Persephone for a jar of her beauty cream. Persephone accepted and brought the cream to Psyche as she had asked for. Psyche had got what she came for and returned to Aphrodite by bribing Cerberus to let her out of the Underworld with her honey-soaked bread and paid Charon to take her to the other side of the river Styx with her last coin.

Psyche returned to Aphrodite with all the tasks completed, however, despite Psyche's success, Aphrodite was enraged and yelled at the mortal woman that she would never let her go. The gods of Olympus witnessed this act of injustice and sent Hermes to let Eros know of everything that has happened. Eros loved Psyche and was touched by her love and thus returned to her. From that day on Eros and Psyche had an official wedding and were happily married. All the gods and goddesses attended their wedding and Zeus allowed Psyche to taste the drink of the gods as a wedding gift, granting Psyche immortality. Even Aphrodite was now pleased, as now that Psyche was immortal mortal men would forget about Psyche and once again praise Aphrodite, the true goddess of beauty.

CHAPTER 9
BATTLES AND CONQUESTS: THE TROJAN WAR AND ALEXANDER THE GREAT

One cannot talk about Greek mythology and Ancient Greece without mentioning the legendary Trojan War and the immense significance Alexander the Great played in the Ancient Greek world. These events are critical standpoints not only in Greek history but in world history. The Trojan war, quite possibly the most famous ancient mythological war throughout history, is an epic tale about how mortals and gods fought together to bring down the city of Troy. While the great conquests of Alexander the Great were not clouded in mythological belief, such as the Trojan War was, they were the stories of legends themselves. Alexander the Great was an incredibly influential, if not the most influential, figure in all of Ancient civilization, and the influences his conquests and united empire bestowed upon the known civilized world were revolutionary to say the least.

The Trojan War

The Trojan War is a legendary battle and is arguably the most iconic battle in all of Greek history. However, the myth that surrounds this battle and what caused the tension between the Greeks and the Trojans is quite astounding. According to myth, the origin of the Trojan war started with a golden apple and a few envious goddesses. The myth begins with the wedding of Thetis and Peleus, the goddess of discord. According to legend, Thetis and Peleus invited various gods and goddesses of the Greek pantheon but did not invite the goddess Eris, the goddess of strife and chaos. Eris was greatly offended by the disrespect shown by the soon-to-be-married couple and decided to gatecrash the wedding. Eris made a dramatic entrance to Thetis and Peleus' wedding and tossed a golden apple in the middle of the table in which the gods and goddesses were feasting during the ceremony. Eris announced to all the guests of the wedding that the golden apple was meant to be a gift to the fairest of all the goddesses, as she knew this would create conflict and tension among the Greek pantheon. Eris's golden apple was claimed by not one but three goddesses—Athena, Hera, and Aphrodite. However, as the apple was a gift to the fairest of them all, only one goddess could physically eat the apple. This led to a fueled dispute among Hera, Aphrodite, and Athena. The three goddesses argued for hours but they could not decide who the most beautiful goddess was, so they asked Zeus who Eris's golden apple rightfully belongs, However, Zeus decided to take on a diplomatic approach to the situation and decided that he would not choose who the golden apple rightfully belongs to. Although he would instead bestow this honor to Paris, a human male and the rightful Prince of Troy should decide in his place.

Paris was no more than a humble shepherd living on Mount Ida and was oblivious of his royal lineage. Paris had an interesting past, and as a child, he was abandoned by his parents when he was just a baby. This was because an oracle had prophesied that Paris would be responsible for the destruction of Troy, the very city that he is the rightful prince of.

However, it was now up to Paris to decide who out of Hera, Aphrodite, and Athena was the fairest of them all. The three beautiful goddesses appeared before Paris and demanded that he choose who he felt was the most beautiful. Paris was now faced with a daunting task and was overwhelmed with the decision he was expected to make. At first, the rightful Prince of Troy was hesitant, and the goddesses noticed Paris's indecisiveness. Each of the three goddesses offered him a gift to entice him to choose them. First up was Hera, who offered Paris kingly power. The next goddess to offer a gift to the rightful Prince of Troy was Athena, who offered him wisdom and glory among all mortals. And finally, the goddess of beauty, Aphrodite, offered Paris the love of the most beautiful woman on Earth. Based on what the three goddesses had offered Paris, he made his decision with no hesitation. Paris gave Eris's golden apple to Aphrodite and from that day, Aphrodite continuously offered counsel to Paris and led the shepherd to Troy, informing him about his royal lineage and what was rightfully his.

Thus, it can be said that the events of Eris's golden apple were the catalyst to the epic Trojan War, because as promised, Aphrodite would secure the "love" of the most beautiful woman on Earth—Helen of Sparta. At the time, Helen of Sparta was considered the most beautiful woman in all the known world. She was married to the King of Sparta Menelaus, and it was declared by Aphrodite that Helen of Sparta was to be given to Paris and she was his for the taking. Paris listened to Aphrodite and abducted Helen and would forcefully make her his wife. Paris refused to return Helen under any circumstances to the king of Sparta, Menelaus.

Due to Paris's treacherous acts, the Trojan War was born. The Spartan king, Menelaus, and his brother Agamemnon waged war against the Trojans and gathered an enormous army of Greeks soldiers to sail to Troy. The formidable Greek army that was assembled by Menelaus and Agamemnon would gather at Aulis, a port town in Ancient Greece. According to legend, many of the greatest Greek heroes participated in the Greek army against the Trojans and included demigods and formidable warriors such as Achilles, Patroclus, Ajax, Odysseus, Nestor, and many others. As mentioned earlier in Chapter Four, the Greeks were also aided by many gods, however, other gods were also assisting the Trojans.

The Greek army's ships were not sailing as they should and were standing idle due to the fact that Artemis had refused to provide the wind needed for the fleet to sail. This was because Agamemnon killed Artemis's sacred deer. The Goddess demanded that he pay a price and atone for his sins and if he refused the Greek fleet would not be able to sail. Artemis proposed a compromise and said she would only provide the wind the Greeks needed if Agamemnon sacrificed his daughter, Iphigenia. Artemis demanded an eye for an eye;

Agamemnon's daughter's life for her sacred deer's life. Agamemnon agreed, and once the sacrifice was made, granted the wind needed for the ships to set sail.

The majority of the Trojan War was fought as a protracted siege by the Greek army on the city of Troy. According to experts, the war was said to have lasted for over nine years and of those nine years, the Trojans managed to resist the Greek army's invasion of the city of Troy, except for one fatal siege which will shortly be discussed. The reason the Trojans were able to withstand the onslaught of the Greek army was that, according to legend, the walls that surrounded Troy were built by the gods Poseidon and Apollo. This was Apollo and Poseidon's punishment by Zeus many years before the Trojan War due to an act of impiety from the two gods in question. Apollo and Poseidon were ordered by the King of the Olympians Zeus to the Trojan King, Laomedon, for an entire year, during which they built the impressive fortifications of Troy.

Throughout the nine-year battle of the Trojan War, there were many battles between the Greeks and the Trojans, however, they were almost exclusively fought outside of the impenetrable wall of Troy. Most times, the battles were fought by soldiers engaging in battle on foot with swords and shields, although on occasion, battles would be fought with chariots. The Trojan War seemed like there would be no end as for nine years the war waged on back and forth across the plains of Troy and it seemed to be a stalemate Greek Heroes and demigods such as Achilles and company fought valiantly and managed to strike fear in the Trojan's hearts. However, the wall was the Trojans' protection and not even the might of demigods could break down Troy's fortification. The Trojans knew as long as the wall stood, they would be safe regardless of how fierce the heroes of Greece fought. Although the war waged on for nine years, it was the final year of the war that featured the greatest battles and highlights. The ninth year of the Trojan War was the year of the Trojan horse.

As the war waged on, the Greek hero Odysseus had a genius idea that would put an end to the Trojan War and see the Greeks victorious. Odysseus proposed that the Greeks built an enormous, hollow wooden horse and a small group of warriors would hide within to strike the Trojans when their guard was down. The Greeks loved this idea and were immediately on board with Odysseus's genius strategy. Thus the Greeks implemented their new flawless plan the next morning. As the Trojans noticed that an enormous wooden horse was standing outside of the gates of Troy, they were confused as they had no idea where this wooden horse had come from. Out of curiosity, the Trojans took the horse within the walls of Troy, despite the warnings of many residents of Troy.

However, the Trojans did not listen to the pleading warnings of their citizens and took the giant wooden horse inside the walls of Troy. The Trojans began to celebrate with music and wine as many thought it to be a gift from the Greeks as a sign of a truce. Little did the Trojans know they were about to be bombarded by an enormous Greek army flooding inside the walls of Troy. When the Trojans went to sleep, the soldiers inside the hollowed-out wooden horse crept out and opened the gates of Troy. With the gates of Troy open, the Greek army could now finally enter the interior of the indestructible wall of Troy. Thus, the Greek army entered Troy without any resistance. The Greeks slaughtered the Trojans with a surprise attack and Troy fell. The battle was not without Greek casualties. The hero Achilles was shot in the heel by Paris, killing him in the battle. Nevertheless, the Greeks won the war, and Helen of Troy was retrieved and returned back to Sparta, where she would rule as a queen with her husband Menelaus.

Alexander the Great of Macedonia

Alexander the Great is one of the greatest figures in world history and it is no surprise that he left an enormous mark in Greek society during his reign. Alexander the Great was born in the year 356 B.C.E. on the 20th of July to King Phillip II of Macedonia in the city of Pella. When Alexander the Great was a young teenager, his father hired the great philosopher, Aristotle, to tutor his son. Through Aristotle's tutelage, Alexander developed a love for science, particularly medicine and botany. However, Alexander the Great was best known for his highly successful reign as a conqueror. Alexander the Great would conquer most of the known civilized world at the time.

Alexander the Great was a man of unparalleled ambitions that were so frightening they even overwhelmed him. He even thought of himself a god, not a man, due to his accomplishments and ambitions. There were even those that thought he was the son of Zeus, and it's possible that Alexander the Great made this claim himself. He is one of the earliest to have the word "Great" attached to his name. Others would go on to use this title, such as Constantine the Great and Charles the Great, however, no other conqueror managed to personify greatness like Alexander.

Alexander the Great is arguably the most successful and skilled generals and conquerors in all of known history. The ruthless general managed to gain control and conquer the Persian army in its entirety. The Persian Empire was an enormous amount of land and the very thought of bringing down the Persian Empire seemed to be an impossible feat, yet this did not stop Alexander the Great from bringing the Persian Empire to its knees. The Persian Empire included a large portion of Asia, Syria, Egypt, Babylon, and of course Persia itself. Along with being history's greatest generals, he was also one of history's most powerful personalities and responsible for starting the Hellenistic Age. The Hellenistic Age was highly significant as it was the platform that spread Ancient Greek culture throughout most of the civilized world.

As mentioned earlier, Alexander was from, and the king of, Macedonia. The Kingdom of Macedonia consisted of Greece, Bulgaria, and all of the former Yugoslavia Republics. In a period of about ten years between the years 334 and 324 B.C.E., Alexander the Great built Macedonia from the ground up and ensured that it was the leading power of the known world.

Alexander the Great conquered an impressive amount of land and in those lands, established a network of military settlements, many of which were to be developed into major cities. The most significant of these cities was known as Alexandria, Egypt, which Alexander the Great founded and named in honor of himself. Alexander the Great had the tendency to name every city after himself, and, in total, there were over 70 cities with the name Alexandria after his conquests. Only Alexandria in Egypt remains, however.

Alexander the Great stabilized the entire Mediterranean economy by establishing a system that utilized coins on a silver standard. This introduction revolutionized trading in the Ancient world and strengthened trade throughout his conquered regions. When Alexander circulated a mass amount of silver throughout his conquered lands from the treasures he seized in Persia, the economy strengthened even further. His conquests united the known world, which at the time was made up of three continents—Europe, Africa, and Asia. Through his conquests, he ensured trade was made possible with these lands. Prior to Alexander's Empire, this would never have happened as all the continents were fearful, suspicious, and full of contempt towards one another. Alexander the Great was also responsible for spreading knowledge throughout his Empire. As mentioned earlier

Alexander the Great had an inherent fascination with science thanks to his tutor, Aristotle. Alexander spread his knowledge of science, geography, and botany and through his personal interest in these topics, huge advances in these fields were realized.

Because the lands were part of one empire, movement and information was more accessible and less dangerous. He ensured that information could flow freely and regimes that did not permit it were abolished. Thus knowledge between people and lands was more accessible. He also removed political barriers that prevented individuals from other places coming into contact with each other. For example, a citizen from Greece could travel freely into Babylonia and vice versa. For the first time, people from different regions and backgrounds were able to see eye to eye, and their different ideas were no longer restricted in the confines of their own nations. Alexander the Great's unified empire was revolutionary as now people were able to make long-distance voyages without having to worry about entering hostile territories of rival countries. Ideas and knowledge were far more accessible, leading to the age of renowned scholars. For example, in the field of mathematics, the revolutionary teachings of Pythagoras and Euclid could spread across borders and educate the civilized world. Alexander the Great was truly an outstanding figure and his influence on the Greek and Ancient world cannot be understated.

CONCLUSION

Ancient Greece and its fascinating mythology are truly a marvel of human history and one that has stood the test of time. The Ancient Greeks practiced a polytheistic belief system which is filled to the brim with captivating tales, myths, gods, goddesses, customs, traditions, and stories that still capture our imagination all these thousands of years later. Throughout our read, we have peeled back the many layers of a complex history that surrounded Ancient Greece and its polytheistic beliefs. In doing so, we have learned a great deal of Ancient Greek culture. We have truly encapsulated what life was like for an Ancient Greek citizen with regards to how their beliefs and numerous gods shaped their society and everything in it. All that we need to know about the Greek pantheon and Ancient Greece has been neatly wrapped into one fascinating read. Throughout our read, we have traveled back in time and peeked through a window to show us what the world was like for the Greeks thousands of years ago.

We covered it all, starting with the creation of the universe, the Titans, the gods, the goddesses, the Cyclopes, and the Hecatonchires. We unpacked how the world began with Chaos, a gaping hole of emptiness, and out of Chaos sprang three more primordial deities. These deities gave birth to many children. These families would go on to have unimaginable conflict leading to terrible tension and horrific actions among one another. A tyrannical rule would come to pass in the form of the Titan Uranus, who would imprison all of his children to ensure they would never overthrow them. Gaee would not stand for such cruelty and freed the youngest Titan child, Cronus, from his father Uranus's grasp. Cronus would go on to slay his father and free his siblings. Cronus had ended the tyrant rule of his father Uranus, but history would repeat itself. The Titan Cronus who took over from his father as the ruler of the world was also a tyrant and just like his father, he would imprison his children by devouring them as he feared they would overthrow him. The Titan Cronus would devour five of his six children but fail to devour his sixth child, Zeus, as a result of being tricked by his wife Rhea. Zeus grew into an unimaginably strong god and defeated Cronus while freeing his imprisoned siblings in the process. However, that was not the end of the Titans or Cronus. Zeus and the other Olympian gods fought the Titans for an entire decade. Zeus and the gods of Olympus defeated the Titans and thus Zeus claimed his throne as ruler of the world and shared it with all the other Greek pantheons.

We further unpacked how the Greek pantheon influenced society. Greek mythology led to countless temples built in the god's honors, as well as many festivals being practiced year in and year out. These temples were grand, and they were all dedicated to a single god as each god had its own city they would watch over. Greeks from far and wide would bring offerings, gifts, and sacrifices to appease, admire, show respect and gain favor from the gods. Festivals were held for many occasions and there were constantly festivals being held in the name of the gods. There were festivals for all the seasons. Whether it was in summer, spring, autumn, or winter it didn't matter as each season hosted an array of festivals. The festival that is still practiced to this day is the Olympics, but the Olympics of today is far removed from what it was. The Olympics during Ancient Greece were many Greeks' favorite festivals filled with athletic games, feasts, and sacrifices in honor of all the gods, but particularly in honor of Zeus. As the Greek world evolved and time began to pass the gods began to be questioned and Greeks started to attempt to debunk the myths, thus the age of the Greek philosophers began. However, despite the attempts of the philosophers trying to propose new explanations about the reality of the world, the majority of the Greek populace still found comfort in their ancient mythological beliefs.

The significance of the gods was evident as seen with all the festivals, sacrifices, and temples built in their honor. It was clear that the Greek pantheon played a significant role in shaping almost every aspect of Ancient Greek society. Thus, it is important that we unpack and highlight the very gods that the Ancient Greeks worshiped and respected so intensely. The Olympian gods were the main gods of Greek mythology. They were made up of 12 gods (six gods and six goddesses) which included Zeus, Hera, Apollo, Hermes, Artemis, Ares, Poseidon, Athena, Demeter, Hestia, Hephaestus, and Aphrodite. They felt human emotions and would often be seen succumbing to them. The Greek pantheon was forever present in the minds of the Ancient Greeks. The Greek pantheon left an enormous legacy behind in human history.

The Olympian gods were not the only significant figures in Greek mythology; there were many minor gods, demigods, mythical creatures, and monsters. Demigods such as Herakles, Achilles, Theseus, Perseus, and Helen of Troy played a significant role in Greek mythology and Ancient Greek society. Minor deities such as the nymphs were also incredibly significant figures and were constantly mentioned throughout the myths of Ancient Greece. Mythical creatures such as centaurs and satyrs also play a part in providing depth to the vast lore of Greek mythology.

What would the Greek myths be without monsters? The monsters were fierce and ferocious and were ever-present in epic battles between them and the Greek pantheon. The monsters of Greek mythology are fascinating, and they come in all shapes and sizes. They provide a sense of danger to the myths and forever capture our imagination with their descriptions, powers, and presence. There are thousands of monsters in Greek mythology, although we only unpacked four of the most legendary monsters in all of Greek mythology—Medusa, the Hydra, Typhon, and Cerberus. Throughout our read, we were exposed to many myths and legends. Some of the most interesting myths include the myth of Icarus, Pandora's box, the abduction of Persephone, and the love story of Eros and Psyche. Throughout our read we have covered so many myths that it is hard to simply pick which are the best ones as each myth is as exciting, if not more exciting, than the last.

In Greek mythology, many battles were fought, but few can argue any battle more significant, famous, and legendary than the epic Trojan War. We unpacked how the conflict began and what the catalyst for the war between the Greeks and the

Trojans truly was. Turned out it was a golden apple and three vanity-fueled goddesses. However, the Trojan War was truly an epic battle and is a story that will be told until the end of time. Other battles that were truly influential included the many conquests of Alexander the Great. Alexander the Great was one of, if not the most, influential figures in human history, and his influence over Greece and the Ancient world was revolutionary.

Greek mythology is fascinating, and it is no surprise that the ancient myths from thousands of years ago are still being studied and told today. These myths might be thousands of years old but they still have great relevance today. These myths were not just stories, they were lessons and held many secrets regarding how the Ancient Greeks lived their lives. If there is one thing we can take away from our read through it is the immense influence the Greek pantheon played in Ancient Greek society and how the Greeks were inherently influenced by the epic tales and myths that surrounded this fascinating polytheistic belief system. The Greek pantheon may not be worshipped anymore but their legacy will live on forever and have a stained history for hundreds of years to come.

THE MYTHOLOGY OF MESOPOTAMIA

FASCINATING INSIGHTS, MYTHS, STORIES & HISTORY FROM THE WORLD'S MOST ANCIENT CIVILIZATION. SUMERIAN, AKKADIAN, BABYLONIAN, PERSIAN, ASSYRIAN, AND MORE

HISTORY BROUGHT ALIVE

INTRODUCTION

We go through our lives with an overall sense of permanence. Perhaps it is due to our living only a short span in a world which, while ever-changing, continues to function around the same basic principles of society and culture. Life is, for the most part, relatively predictable. Human society seems like a constant, even if it changes shape from time to time. Our ability to think, to dream, to build, and to create, is so deeply ingrained into the human psyche that we feel they must always have been there. Genuinely comprehending a time when we were incapable of these things is difficult.

But it was not always so. We were not always the builders of great civilizations, the creators of art and war. There was a time when our grandest congregations were merely small villages, and times before that when we wandered from place to place, living off the land, not unlike all other animals. Everything has a beginning, and everything that occurs has a *cause*, a reason for its genesis. When it comes to civilization, the reasons are many, and they are uncertain. But there is one key similarity between each of the early Eurasian civilizations, which sprung up independently of one another, spread across the globe.

Across Europe and Asia were four of the "cradles of civilization," and each of these four was built along a river. On the banks of the Nile, the great civilization of Egypt rose, dominating the Mediterranean until Alexander's conquests several thousand years later. In the mid-lower basin of the Yellow River, the earliest Chinese civilization rose to regional prominence. Along the Indus, in modern-day Pakistan, the mysterious Indus Valley civilization emerged. But perhaps most significant of all early civilizations was that whose foundations were laid in the fertile lands between the Euphrates and the Tigris in modern-day Iraq and Syria—the Mesopotamians.

The term 'Mesopotamian' is made up of the ancient term *meso* meaning between, and the word *potamos* meaning river, literally translating to "between the rivers." As in Egypt, China, and Pakistan, it was these rivers and the fertile valley which lay between them that allowed the civilization to progress first from Palaeolithic hunter-gatherer societies to an agricultural, village community, and finally through the urban revolution and into a city-dwelling culture. This transition from farm to city was perhaps one of the most significant changes in human history, surpassed only by that from hunter-gatherer to agricultural community coming before it. While this occurred across Eurasia and even in Mesoamerica and Peru around similar periods, what makes Mesopotamia particularly interesting is the fact that it happened there first. As such, despite the independent rise of cities in other areas, Mesopotamia represents the true origins of what we now call 'civilization,' and it is this fact that makes it enormously significant to the narrative of human history.

Mesopotamia is also interesting for many other reasons. First is the creativity of the era—cuneiform writing, the wheel, and an enormous list of other creations over their extraordinarily long period of dominance in writing, construction, science, law, literature and poetry, music, and the building of empires. They have given us an immense number of global 'firsts': the first schools, historians, lullabies, legal precedents, pharmacopeias, aquariums, libraries and library catalogues, the first almanacs, the first animal fables, and the first literary debates. From Mesopotamian culture we inherited the love song, paid employment, moral idealism, tax reductions, bicameral governments, tales of apocalyptic floods and resurrections, and even the first cases of juvenile delinquency. They provided the entire framework for modern civilization. Without their contributions, we could have never reached the social, political, cultural, and technological heights of today.

Another area of interest is the lack of any dominant ethnicity. Mesopotamian civilization, made up of several major empires, numerous cities, spread across an extended period of history, was not merely made up of a local dominant race but of hundreds of different groups of people—immigrants and outsiders were no less significant than the Semitic and non-Semitic locals, and many even rose to prominent positions of power or even kingship. The civilization grew and continued over thousands of years, while the ethnicity of those running and living within it was varied and changing.

Lastly, there is the incredible longevity of the Mesopotamian civilization. From the invention of cuneiform around 3,000 BCE to the conquest of Babylon by Cyrus the Great of Persia in 539 BCE, the independent Mesopotamia lasted somewhere around 2,500 years. If you take the beginning not from the invention of writing but instead from the founding of Uruk around 4,500 BCE, that number increases to 4,000 years. For context—there were around 2,500 years between the conquests of Cyrus and the modern-day. The independent

Mesopotamian civilization ruled the area for upward of half of human history. During this time, empires rose and fell, certain cities or regions within Mesopotamia gained dominance and lost it, but the civilization itself stood strong. In fact, not only was the region independent for such a long period but its culture was also preserved remarkably well. Languages, music, writing systems, scientific and religious traditions were maintained throughout the civilization for its duration, and while changes will have occurred with time, they remained recognizable and understandable from the beginning until the very end.

Mesopotamia, while fascinating, is poorly represented in popular history, dwarfed by Rome or Classical Greece, or even Egypt. For a long time, the only way to understand Mesopotamian history, culture, and mythology has been through dense, academic, or semi-academic sources. This is in part due to the huge time frame, the rise and fall of various empires, and the lack of easily understood ancient sources. The inaccessibility of information about this remarkable civilization means that many people know little about it, and what they do know may be skewed in the direction of pseudo-history and alien-overlord conspiracy theories, derived from very specific interpretations of ancient mythological sources. As such, it is essential to bring the knowledge and history of

Mesopotamia into the light, making it accessible to all, allowing everyone to benefit from the fascinating insight of the very first human civilization.

In this book, we will be discussing the history of Mesopotamia from the urbanization and the rise of Uruk to the fall of Babylon to the Persians in 539 BCE. We will delve into the Sumerians, the Akkadians, the Assyrian Empire, and the Babylonians, discussing their culture, technology, leadership; their art and their war, their rise, and their fall. We will then take a look at some of the Mesopotamian epics and mythological stories, including the famous *Epic of Gilgamesh* and the Babylonian creation myth, the *Enuma Elish*. Through careful, accurate examination of both archaeological sources and the academic work of expert historians, the tales of Ancient Mesopotamia will be carried forth from the fog of time. For too long now, information on this fascinating period has been too sparse, too dense, inaccessible. It is time for the history of Mesopotamia to be brought alive.

PART I: THE HISTORY

CHAPTER 1
KINGSHIP DESCENDS FROM HEAVEN
(CA. 5400-2350 BCE)

Temple Rule

It is important to remember that Sumer was not an empire, nor even a nation, but simply a civilization—a collection of cultural practices, social attitudes, rituals, beliefs, and technology shared between a group of people. Technically speaking, civilization is usually underlined by a writing system and record-keeping, the cultural developments associated with the written word. That said, to understand the rise of Mesopotamia we must delve back beyond the advent of cuneiform, the alphabet used to write Sumerian and other local languages, and explore instead a period prior.

The early cities of southern Mesopotamia first emerged in the fifth millennium BCE, with Eridu, the city of the god Enki, being founded sometime around the year 5000 BCE, followed around 500 years later by the city of Gilgamesh, Uruk. While it is uncertain how the cities were founded, it is likely that the move from agricultural villages to city life evolved around the foundation of religion or belief—this is evident in the early city structure of Sumer, where rather than a monarchy, the first cities were instead defined by temple rule. It is suggested that the early cities of Mesopotamia were founded in locations of regular congregation. In the agricultural era of human history, there would have been times when migration to certain areas was beneficial or even necessary due to plentiful food or fertile ground. People would gather in such areas and, at some point, may have left a monument of sorts in a solid, permanent material, such as baked-clay bricks, a sharp contrast to the typical, temporary huts. This anchor for humanity would stand for generations and may have encouraged others to come and see it. Archaeological evidence suggests that within, and beneath, the immense temples of the Sumerian cities lay the foundations of progressively smaller structures. In a sense, the city radiated out from this central point, as did civilization itself.

The rise of Eridu was followed shortly by the rise of Uruk. According to Sumerian mythology, the god Enki ruled Eridu yet kept the *Me* (pronounced *Meh*, a difficult word to translate, but meaning something similar to divine decrees for culture and the basis of civilization), hidden, only for use by him and in his city. His daughter, Inanna, another god, stole the *Me* from Enki and brought them to her own city of Uruk, thus spreading civilization to her people. Sometimes referred to as the first 'true' city, Uruk was the location of several huge advancements in human society.

By far the most important invention of Uruk, however, was writing. Beginning with logographic symbols many years prior and being used to record simple bureaucratic and administrative notes such as payments of grain, the first full writing system was in use by around the year 3200 BCE. It was around this time that, according to the traditional definition, 'civilization' truly began.

The invention of writing was of extreme importance to Uruk and Sumer as a whole. Not only did it make the recording of administrative notes much easier, but it also developed the sense of personal identity in the city, something that went on to have immense effects on the future of Sumer as a whole and contributed to the transition from temple rule to kingship.

Archeologists have uncovered numerous cylindrical seals, or *kishib*, from around this period which were used for signing documents or for labeling personal property. The *kishib* represented an immense change in the ideology of the people of Sumer, as it became a symbol of personal identity and branding. The importance of the individual was, before this point, overshadowed by that of the community. The prevalent use of the *kishib*, however, demonstrated the newfound importance of the individual within the collective community. It is this, in part, that would lead to a dramatic restructuring of Sumerian society as a whole.

The Flood

The Bible tells us of Noah and the apocalyptic flood sent by the Hebrew God to wipe most of humanity from the planet. While some take this as fact and others consider it biblical fiction or a metaphor, it is not merely the Bible that tells this story of an apocalyptic flood.

Floods, both in the past and in the future, are common in mythology. The obvious is Yahweh's Flood in *Genesis*, but in the Hindu texts *Satapatha Brahmana* and *Puranas*, Vishnu warns the first man of an impending flood and asks him to build a boat; in the Gun-Yu myth of ancient China, an enormous flood occurs which lasts two generations; even Plato describes a flood-myth in his dialogue *Timaeus*, where Prometheus tells Deucalion to build an ark in preparation for Zeus' incoming flood. Norse, Polynesian, Irish, and Mayan mythology, among others, also tell of floods. But the Mesopotamian tale of the Flood, as told in the *Epic of Gilgamesh* and the Akkadian *Atrahasis*, is perhaps the earliest Flood story that we know of.

The *Gilgamesh* version of the Flood story is the one closest to that in the *Book of Genesis*, and of the versions of the epic, it is the 700 BCE Babylonian copy that appears most similar. Considering that *Genesis* was believed to be written at a similar time, it may have been influenced by the Babylonian *Gilgamesh*, which in turn appears to have drawn from the Akkadian *Atrahasis* from the 18th century BCE. Regardless of the edition, however, it is hard to date the Flood to a certain period in history, though it is most certainly a long time before the tales were written. That said, at some point around the year 3000 BCE, the social and political structure of Mesopotamia changed dramatically, and it is believed by many that "the Flood" is less a historical deluge and more a metaphorical representation of dramatic societal change.

Historian Paul Kriwaczek (2010) suggests that "the Flood" may be representative, at least in part, of the change in the Urukian society and also the fall of temple rule. As discussed, the people of Sumer and Uruk, in particular, were moving away from the basic, collective social structure they had developed, one that was headed by the rule of priests in central temples. Theocracies rarely last long before being supplanted by more pragmatic forms of governance, and it is unsurprising that as Sumerian society developed, it outgrew its original leadership.

The soil around Uruk was rich in minerals and salt, in part due to the nature of the two rivers. This was not necessarily a good thing and could prove disastrous regarding irrigation. Over the centuries, the people of Sumer learned to deal with the problems posed by the mineral-rich water by leaving the fields fallow, allowing the soil time to recover. As such, the fields would generally produce crops every two years, and with a growing population, this may not have been seen as enough. It is not hard to imagine priests and religious figures, ruling the city from their temples and knowing little of the farming life, ordering the people not to leave the soil fallow as they had done, and thus (in theory) producing twice the resources. It would have been an inevitable disaster; according to the

Atrahasis, "the black fields became white, the broad plain was choked with salt" (Kriwaczek, 2010).

Civilizations structured around an ideology or belief, and figure-headed by a representation of that belief (as is seen in temple-rule society) are easily toppled in periods of instability. It is not difficult for an ideology to prove incorrect, and when that illusion has been shattered, there is little one can do to repair it. A disaster such as this, bringing with it disease, famine, and death, would prove the end of temple rule, destroying the ideology that had sustained it.

While supreme god Enlil and Hebrew God Yahweh may have had differing motives in their respective tales, the floods they brought were an attempt to wipe humanity from the planet. They represented a dramatic change in the social order, to the point where the history of such civilizations can be divided into pre- and post-deluge eras. Mythology and ancient history are rarely literal—whether there was a genuine flood or not, the deluge is used as a representation of widespread change. Brought about in part by the advent of writing, in part by famine or disease, and most certainly by the faltering of ideology, "the Flood" became a convenient symbol separating the old Sumer from the new. The old was rejected, faith faltered, and the Urukian period of domination was coming to an end. The *Sumerian King List* puts this quite simply at the end of the first section, a hard line dividing the old period from the new: "Then the Flood swept over" (Livius.org, 2020).

A New Order

It is from ruins that great things arise. It has been this way for millennia—change, new orders, need not only a reason to form but a space to form within. When things are working well, people adopt a conservative attitude toward life and toward change. When things are falling apart, it is the progressive attitude that wins out, the creativity of those who seek to cast down the failing relics of times before and instead erect a grand new experiment, something designed to, theoretically, overcome the flaws of the past. So, like the proverbial phoenix rising from the ashes of temple rule, a new form of leadership and governance came into being across the lands of Sumer.

This was by no means an immediate change. Even the best ideas need time to grow organically, to flesh themselves out, and to reach their full potential. Kingship in Sumer was not bestowed overnight. Instead, in the power gap left by the diminishing temples, new men stepped forward, and those new men slowly but surely consolidated power in their cities.

It began, as so many major historical events do, with a change in Sumerian socioeconomic structure, although this term may suggest a more complex system than what they had in place at the time. Ultimately, the growing importance of the individual within society had led to the emergence of a new class structure, one that would lay the foundations for millennia to come—and the entire process began with barley.

Barley is a good crop for areas with high levels of salt and minerals in the soil. As discussed above, the land between the Tigris and the Euphrates had high levels of salinity, and the disastrous effects of poor crop management may have led to this becoming an even more pressing issue. As such, the regular growth of wheat was simply out of the question, and barley grew to become the staple of the Sumerian diet for all classes and members of society.

Not only was barley essential for food, but it was also essential for the brewing of beer, a drink that held enormous importance during this period as it was drunk even more regularly than water. The people of Mesopotamia were remarkable engineers and had complex sewer piping systems under their streets several thousand years before many other parts of the world. From each household, waste traveled through underground pipes far away from the city—and then dumped into the river. This would undoubtedly have created a health disaster, with no source of reliable, healthy drinking water. Faced with a choice between dehydration or outbreaks of disease, the people of Sumer came up with an alternative option—drink beer. This meant that barley was the single most important source of sustenance, the center around which the entirety of Sumerian culture and civilization revolved.

As people developed a sense not only of individuality but of personal property, barley became an important source of wealth. Farming was a careful, precise undertaking, and if you had a good crop yield one year, you had the potential to become significant within society. Those who produced the most and the best quality barley would eventually accumulate the most wealth and importance. As wealth accumulated, people could afford to acquire larger plots of land for farming, producing even more barley, their social standing skyrocketing as a result. People would come to rely upon these individuals, and they would find themselves in the position to make important decisions. Over time, they would even hold enough wealth to pay others to work their fields for them, freeing up time to focus on their personal pursuits—the cultivation of the individual, and the individual's importance within the running of a city.

It was not merely barley that led to this change, of course. The fall of the "old ways" will have led to vacant spaces in society, and conflict between individuals to fill those spaces. The people of Sumer would have developed hierarchies based upon weakness and strength, and the ability to contribute to the running of society. These factors, among no doubt numerous others, coalesced to create tightly bound city-states governed largely by a wealthy class, the very early step toward the introduction of kingship in society. The sale of land increased, the trade of commodities and luxury goods grew dramatically, as wealthy individuals found themselves with time and resources to spare. Even though the temples maintained significant power in society over this period, the rise of a wealthy class created a new, more practical political body, rivaling and eventually surpassing the temples in importance.

The Lugal of Kish

The wealthiest of cities, which were typically those with the most fertile farmland, would also be the most common target for raiders from the steppe—the long belt of grassland extending from Hungary to Manchuria, over 5,000 miles. The steppe was a fantastic place for hunting and grazing livestock such as sheep and cattle, thus providing the cities on its border with a regular supply of meat. Raiders would come down from the hills to loot and pillage in the fertile, rich lands near the steppe, and it was the powerful city of Kish that was most often targeted.

The targeting of Kish was in part due to its location near where the two rivers were at their closest, and as such, the city controlled large amounts of fertile farmland. It was a rich city, and it was the problem posed by the raiders that would form one of the significant catalysts in the establishment of kingship. Rising to the top in Sumerian society did not come without obligations—as the old saying goes, with great power comes great responsibility. It was ultimately the leaders who were looked to for protection and guidance in times of conflict, and it was these leaders who, in time, would provide organized resistance against the barbarian raiders.

While small attacks could have been staved off by farmers and common folk wielding basic stone tools, larger parties were not so easily defeated and required the defense of organized, trained men with effective arms. The working class could never hope to organize such a defensive force, nor would they have the time to train while also maintaining the fields and looking after their families—a dedicated defensive force was necessary. It was the *Lugalene*, or the "big men" of the city, who would have the funds and the time to organize a defense. Some of the *Lugalene* would have even provided men from their households to act as standing soldiers for the city; over time these defensive groups evolved into genuine armies.

Eventually, one *Lugal* among the many would rise to the top and take his place as the effective 'warlord' of the city. Due to the pressure from the regular raids, it was Kish that became one of the earliest seats for a *Lugal*, rising to dominance through a standing army and immense wealth. Over time, the *Lugal* of a city would have turned away from merely defending and instead put his army to use acquiring territory and establishing dominance over other nearby cities and settlements. Kish in particular was known for its tendency to prevent its neighbors from growing too powerful. In fact, with Kish being the original seat of kingship and the dominant city of its time, the phrase "*Lugal* of Kish" became the accepted title used by those who wished to claim some form of hegemony over the region of Sumer. That said, other cities followed the example of Kish and quickly gained their own *Lugal* and armies. Before long, the city of Uruk gained enough manpower to rival and eventually overthrow Kish as the dominant city in Sumer.

From Lugal to Monarch

The passing of the kingship from Kish to Uruk signified an immense change in the political landscape of Sumer. The *Sumerian King List*, a document discovered in several editions across Mesopotamia and listing the rulers of Sumer from the establishment of Eridu to the kingship in Isin, lists a series of exchanges between cities as powerful *Lugal* challenge one another for regional dominance. Kingship had been bestowed from heaven upon Kish, but, not unlike the Chinese concept of the Mandate of Heaven, it appears the kingship could be rescinded and passed on to somebody else. Kingship descended from heaven to Kish, and then after a lengthy list of absurdly long-lived monarchs, Kish was defeated, and the kingship moved to Eanna (Uruk). From Uruk, the kingship was taken to Ur; from Ur, it went to Awan; from Awan, back to Kish.

So it went, according to the king list, for an absurdly long time—while some rulers of ancient Sumer ruled only for a short period, others ruled far, far longer. Etana of Kish, for example, "ascended to heaven and put all countries in order, became king; he ruled for 1,500 years" (Livius.org, 2020). The kingship in Kish is professed to have lasted 23,310 years, 3 months and 3 1/2 days, spread between 23 kings. This means that, on average, each king of Kish ruled for around 1,000 years.

The king list outlines the origins of Sumerian dynasties, although it is important to note that the rulers rarely shared common blood, and each dynasty was defined more by the city than by the family lineage. The idea of hereditary monarchs, or even designated heirs, came about much later. The struggle for power between cities and between the men who ran them was bitter and constant—political careers were short-lived, as were, at times, the politicians themselves.

One unique perspective held by the Sumerians, however, is that both politics and war were not human pursuits; they were instead under the jurisdiction of the gods. Each city had its own god: Eridu had Enki, Uruk had Inanna, Nippur had Enlil. Wars may have been fought between armies of men, but the disputes were between the gods, merely using men as a tool in their conflicts. As a result, when two cities fought, such as Lagash and Umar, who engaged in repeated warfare over disputed land, the disagreement was, in fact, one between Ningirsu of Lagash and Shara of Umar, each of whom felt it was their right to the land in question—and to dominion over Sumer as a whole.

The one big difference between warlords and monarchs, irrespective of the power they may wield or how they may wield it, is the way they are viewed by others. A warlord may be powerful, with large armies at his disposal, able to issue decrees when and where he should choose, but he is still very much a human figure. Warlords maintain positions of power simply because of their control—their resources, their armies, the fear they instill in those they rule over. A monarch, at least traditionally, based their rule on something more altogether otherworldly—a divine bestowal of power, a religious confirmation of their right to rule. The emperors of China ruled under the Mandate of Heaven, legitimacy affirmed by a spiritual or religious force; in Europe, the "divine right of kings" dictates the monarchic authority derives from God and cannot be questioned. People need a reason to believe that the ruler, whoever they may be, is legitimately better than everybody else and genuinely deserves the power they hold. As such, the monarch must give the people a sign that their authority is divine.

In Sumer, it was no different, although the actual details of this move from *Lugal* to divine ruler are uncertain. What we do know is that in the city of Ur, for a short period, human sacrifices were made in the tombs of the deceased rulers, with skeletons found scattered across the floor, surrounded by a wealth of treasures rivaling even the tomb of Tutankhamen. Whether these sacrifices were willing or forced is up for debate, though Sir Leonard Woolley, who was involved in their discovery, believed them to be willing volunteers. He described a procession, likely made up of the court of the deceased ruler, entering a huge open pit with walls and doors covered in mats. Men, women, and soldiers would have been included, from slaves to decorated military commanders. Brightly colored garments, often ordained with lapis lazuli, were worn—only the best for the city's ruler. Even musicians would have accompanied the procession, carrying their instruments. Soldiers would follow up at the rear, guarding the entrance. Each of the volunteers would have brought with them a small clay cup. It was probable there were words spoken, likely entreaties to the gods, and the musicians would have played, before each of the volunteers filled their cup with poison and consumed it willingly and joyfully, following their great ruler into the underworld.

It is important to note that Woolley was being somewhat creative with his account, visualizing possibility as opposed to describing something for which there was solid evidence. Even so, whether willing or not, human sacrifices in the tombs of rulers symbolize a significant transition from the rule of mortal, human figures to the rule of something divine. Convincing the populace to accept the killing of their friends, family members, or even simply other city dwellers is no easy feat, and is most often seen in religious ceremonies intended to appease deities.

To have them sacrificed and left in the tomb of a mortal human demonstrates a drastic change in the way the people of Ur thought about their rulers. The graves were representative of attempts by the leadership of Ur to demonstrate their divine status, to combine state power with some form of supernatural authority. In doing so, they were able to assert the legitimacy of their rule. As Ur was the dominant city of Sumer at the time, it set an example for others to follow—the practice must have had a profound enough effect to make a continuation of the practice elsewhere unwarranted. It is believed that this was the moment when the rulers of Ur, and in turn, the rulers of Sumer, moved from simply *Lugal* to monarchs—the moment when kingship truly descended from heaven.

CHAPTER 2
THE FIRST EMPIRE
(CA. 2350-2150 BCE)

Prelude: The Conquests of Lugalzagesi

Sometime around 2400 BCE, a new sort of ruler rose to prominence in the city of Lagash. Urukagina, usurping the throne during a time of internal dissatisfaction, had a new approach to ruling his subjects—one that was less about fear or worship, and more about love. Urukagina appeared to have one thing in mind—to reform the city of Lagash so dramatically that his people would love him with all their hearts. Whether his motive was one of securing power, or that he genuinely wanted to ensure his people were living happy, comfortable lives, it is hard to say. What is abundantly clear, however, is that upon his ascension, the bureaucracy in Lagash was corrupt and crumbling. Taxes were high. The previous ruler had confiscated large amounts of land for himself and his family. There were additional charges to almost everything, from divorces to the shearing of sheep, and those additional charges were pocketed by the ruler and his ministers. Even burial rites came at an absurd cost, over 400 loaves of bread and 7 jars of beer paid to the priest and his assistant. Needless to say, the people were not happy.

Urukagina's legitimacy as a ruler was based on the rescue of his people from the domination of both the temple and his predecessor. He uncovered and put a stop to corruption throughout the bureaucracy, dedicating his time not to conquests and regional domination, but the well-being of his subjects. It seems probable that Urukagina was a good man, well-loved and respected, and would have had a long and successful reign ahead of him, were it not for the ambitions of another new ruler in the neighboring city of Umma.

Lugalzagesi of Umma was an ambitious man. Umma and Lagash had long been rivals, engaging in warfare originally over disputed territory, and had traded blows often over the past century. It was during a lull in conflict, however, while Urukagina was reforming his city, that Lugalzagesi saw an opportunity to build up his forces and strike a decisive blow. Lagash had often bested Umma, and it was perhaps this bitterness that drove forward the city's new ruler. The story of Urukagina goes to show that simply being a good ruler does not protect you from conquest and destruction. Urukagina's reign over Lagash lasted only a short eight years.

The fall of Lagash was condemned by many. Urukagina had been considered a good man, and Lugalzagesi was cursed by many for his crushing blow over his rival. Kriwaczek (2010) records a lament from the time:

> The ruler of Umma has set fire to the temple of Antasurra; he has carried away the silver and the lapis lazuli... He has shed blood in the temple of the goddess Nanshe; he has carried away the precious metal and the precious stones... The Man of Umma, by despoiling Lagash, has committed a sin against the god Ningirsu... May the hand that he dared to raise against Ningirsu be cut off. There was no fault in Urukagina, King of Lagash. May Nisaba, the goddess of Lugalzagesi, ruler of Umma, make him bear his mortal sin upon his neck. (p. 100)

Lagash was merely the beginning. Lugalzagesi went on to conquer not only his neighbor but also the cities of Kish, Ur, Nippur, Larsa, and Uruk. He took the latter as his capital and declared hegemony over the states of Sumer. While his claims of controlling the entirety of the Fertile Crescent appear greatly exaggerated, there is little doubt that Lugalzagesi was the catalyst for something great. Little did he know that, upon deposing the ruler of Kish, he laid the foundations for the first empire in human history.

Sargon of Akkad

By this point in Mesopotamian history, there had been temple rulers, *Lugalene*, monarchs ruling from strength and fear, and even a monarch who sought the approval and love of his people. The trouble with all of these systems of leadership is that they could only succeed over a limited scope. Both love and fear go a long way, but perhaps not so far as to bind together a vast empire. As such, the regional rule of most previous kings had been limited to a selection of cities over a small area. Following the fall of Kish to Lugalzagesi, however, a new leader rose to prominence, and with him came a new form of leadership—one based on hero-worship rather than fear or love. This man was Sargon, and he founded the first empire in human history.

When one thinks of an empire, several things come to mind. Firstly, we think of emperors, usually monarchical rulers who appear in higher stead than a simple king or queen. Secondly, we think of vast swathes of land under the rule of a single governing body. The one thread that runs through all historical empires is that it contains not merely one culture or people, but many different groups, all brought together under a single administration. The Roman Empire ruled over many different cultures across Europe, Africa, and Asia; the Mongol Empire ruled an even greater number, stretching from the Far East to Asia Minor and ruling over China, Persia, and the steppe cultures. The British Empire ruled over even more cultures and peoples, stretching around the entire globe. To be the ruler of an empire is to rule over people who are not your own, alongside those who are.

Sargon was believed to be the cup-bearer to the Ur-Zababa, who ruled over Kish before the conquests of Lugalzagesi. Due to his quick rise following the deposition of his king, chances are that Sargon had long nurtured a desire for power. The role of cup-bearer was one of great importance and would have provided Sargon with the connections and funds needed to entice a considerable number of loyal followers. Whether he seized power and marched south under the guise of revenge, or if he was simply opportunistic, is difficult to say. Regardless of his apparent motivations, however, Sargon knew what he was doing, and before long he had captured Uruk and Lugalzagesi.

It was the conquest of Uruk that brought Sargon into power. However, despite vanquishing his opponent, he also had to contend with many Sumerian cities attempting to establish their freedom following the original conqueror's death. Freed from the yoke of Lugalzagesi, they hoped to maintain independence and saw the opportunity to do so. Sargon proved an efficient conqueror, however, and before long he had Sumer in the palm of his hand. In fact, not satisfied with ruling only Sumer, Sargon set about conquering neighboring territories, bringing the southern Sumerians and the northern Semites together under a single administration. He set out to build a vast empire, spreading far beyond the two rivers. It is said that he was victorious in 34 battles, even seizing the lands of the Elamites on the far bank of the Tigris, the city of Mari in north, and even pushing into the lands of the Amorites, whose connection to Mesopotamia would become significant hundreds of years later, as would the small city of Ashur, conquered on the northern banks of the Tigris. It is even suggested that Sargon of Akkad may have ventured into Asia Minor, although any success in the region would have been limited.

Sargon himself was, in fact, a Semite as opposed to a Sumerian, but as emperor over both peoples, he walked a lonely path between cultures. It was perhaps as a Semite living among Sumerians that Sargon had developed the mindset required to rule over many, the ability to understand people of various backgrounds and cultures. Whatever the case may be, Sargon knew that to establish himself as a new kind of ruler, to separate himself from both Ur-Zababa and Lugalzagesi, and to appeal not merely to the subculture of Kish but people the world over, he was required to create a new center of power.

Akkad (the Semitic name for the city; it was called Agade in Sumerian), founded by Sargon upon the establishment of his new empire, was to become the center of the Mesopotamian world. It was from Akkad not only that the name of the empire was derived (Akkadian Empire) but also that of the language spoken by many of its people, a language that was still spoken by inhabitants of the area many years later under the Assyrian and Babylonian empires.

For widespread appeal, Sargon was required to rethink kingship. The people of a nation or a city are typically bound to their ruler by a shared culture, language, or priority. To rule over many, a ruler had to establish themselves as universally acceptable, transcending typical ideas of belonging and culture. It could be a very lonely undertaking, requiring a lot of psychological fortitude, to no longer see yourself as part of a pre-established group. To make others see you that way as well requires a new kind of legitimacy, one that appeals to all.

The foundation of Akkad was the beginning of this separation, but it was to continue. Sargon had to cultivate an image of himself as a heroic figure, worthy of adulation and worship. While remaining a man, Sargon had to step into the role of a god, founding a city himself as opposed to inheriting one from a deity. Even his name was fabricated, meaning "true king"; his true name remains unknown. He created a backstory that accentuated his humble origins and avoided any particular political affiliations. In a story reminiscent of that of Moses, yet occurring much earlier, Sargon was said to have been conceived in secret by a priestess and then set upon a river in a basket of rushes, bore downstream until discovered by Akki, who raised him.

Regarded by later generations as semi-divine, Sargon's name was even called upon by later rulers to provide a sense of legitimacy to their rule. In fact, Sargon still offers a sense of legitimacy to this very day. In 1990, during the International Babylon Festival, Iraqi President Saddam Hussein celebrated his 53rd birthday in his home village with lavish festivities owing more than a little to the origin story of the great

Akkadian emperor. A wooden cabin was wheeled into the street, before which numerous people dressed in ancient Mesopotamian costumes prostrated themselves as the door opened to reveal a baby in a basket, floating down a stream. The baby was representative of Hussein, but it called on the legitimacy offered by a connection to Sargon of Akkad. The longevity of Sargon's importance serves to demonstrate just how significant he was in the history not only of Mesopotamia but of the world as a whole, providing a model for future nations and empires thousands of years later.

The Rise and Fall of Gods

To describe the Bronze Age Akkadian empire as supplanting the role of religion and the gods in Mesopotamian society may be going a stretch too far, but Sargon's conquests had significant, long-term effects on the practice of religion and worship across his empire and into the future. He did not try to frame himself as an actual deity, rather a semi-divine hero not unlike those we have seen in the Greek Bronze Age—Heracles, Perseus, Achilles—those who had created a cult-like following of worshippers in recognition of their inhuman achievements.

In fact, the Akkadian period holds many parallels to the Greek age of heroes, where the gods, who had been directly involved in the lives of humans, took a step backward, retreating to Mount Olympus, and yet remaining connected to the world usually through Demi-gods and heroes such as those mentioned previously. Sargon's role as city-founder, and the man who tied a multicultural empire together, usurped the role of the city-founding god or the collective deity. This is not to imply that the gods were no longer important in Mesopotamian society; more they were now less connected, ruling from afar—that the new Akkadian empire was an empire not of gods but men.

This new relationship between people and gods can be seen in the artwork produced during this time. In the Stele of the Vultures, an earlier piece of artwork produced before the rise of Sargon to recognize one of Lagash's victories over Umma (before the rise of Lugalzagesi), the gods play a central role: a row of soldiers, led by a *Lugal*, are dwarfed by the enormous figure of the god Ningirsu who holds the captured enemy forces in his net. By contrast, a later stele depicts Sargon's third successor and grandson, Naram-Sin, in his victory over the Lullubi people of Zagros. In this piece, it is Naram-Sin who takes center stage, even wearing the horned helmet representative of divinity. The gods, while still present, are represented by mere stars in the sky.

Another interesting feature of Naram-Sin's stele is the composition of the image. The Stele of the Vultures is organized not unlike a comic strip, a series of events to be read as though part of a story, moving across the page, divided to represent new lines of 'text.' Naram-Sin's stele is entirely different, reminiscent more of a photograph than a story, a snapshot in time, a unified composition—a picture. This dramatic change in depictions not only suggests actual writing may have supplanted artworks and steles as a means of recording a series of events, but provides a general example of just how much the culture had changed in the first hundred or so years of the Akkadian empire.

In the new world of Sargon and Naram-Sin, humanity was no longer the tools of the divine. No more were the feuds and disagreements of the gods seen as part of the 'real' world, humanity's squabbles a mere shadow. Humans filled the shoes of the gods, ruling their cities and making decisions, not for some deity, but themselves. The focus of life had firmly shifted to the human world, and it would remain that way far into the future.

Naram-Sin is often considered equal, if not greater, in importance to Sargon in the history of Mesopotamia. He was also the final great Akkadian ruler, in power from 2261 to 2224 BCE, and is the main character in numerous stories over the following millennia—one in particular, *The Curse of Agade*, depicting him not as a great ruler but as the destroyer of Akkad, inviting divine punishment through impious acts. While this is merely fiction, Naram-Sin was likely chosen as the main character of this legend in part due to this immense fame, and in part due to the empire's gradual collapse in the wake of his death.

It was during the rule of Naram-Sin that the Akkadian Empire reached its zenith, and the powerful ruler certainly acted the part. He is depicted as a proud, confident, and arrogant ruler, proclaiming himself the "King of all four corners of the universe" — a line borrowed from his grandfather, Sargon. That said, Naram-Sin went one step further and deified himself, even going so far as to sign documents with a god's seal. According to Kramer (1971):

> Naram-Sin... raised Agade to new heights of power and glory... His military successes were numerous and

prodigious: he defeated a powerful coalition of rebellious kings from Sumer and the surrounding lands; he conquered the region to the west as far as the Mediterranean Sea and Taurus and Amanus ranges; he extended his dominion into Armenia and erected his statue of victory near modern Dierbakir; he fought the Lullubi in the northern Zagros ranges and commemorated his victory with a magnificent stele; he turned Elam into a partially Semitized vassal-state and constructed numerous buildings in Susa; he brought booty from Magan after defeating its king Manium, whom some scholars have identified with the renowned Menes of Egypt. (p. 62)

Despite his successes, however, Naram-Sin would forever remain associated with the fall of the empire. Following his death in 2224 BCE, he was succeeded by his son, Shar-Kali-Sharri, who ruled for 25 years. As with his predecessors, Shar-Kali-Sharri began his reign by stamping out numerous revolts across the empire; however, unlike those who came before, he failed to maintain peace and order, and the empire's borders were constantly under attack.

Whether the collapse was due to Shar-Kali-Sharri's incompetence, or to the unfortunate state of the empire he had inherited, is up for debate. However, it does appear that bad luck played a significant role, with invasions, border-wars, climate change, and famine eventually inspiring *The Curse of Agade*, with Shar-Kali-Sharri most likely serving as the true inspiration.

His death in 2198 BCE spelled the end of the Sargonic dynasty and was followed by several years of conflict as four rivals fought for control over the empire. When the dust settled, a new king, Dudu, held power in Akkad, but the empire was greatly diminished. Dudu and his successor ruled between 2189–2154 BCE, but the glorious days of the Akkadian empire were well and truly over. Following the collapse, Mesopotamia found itself thrust into a dark age. The self-styled gods had fallen, their creation in ruins. This period of conflict and disunity lasted until 2112 BCE when a new dynasty rose from the ashes—the kingship had returned to Ur.

CHAPTER 3
SUMER RESTORED
(CA. 2119-2004 BCE)

More often than not, it is the most progressive societies that prove the most vulnerable. Progressive structures are essential for moving forward, for innovation, for creation, and for reform, but as they delve into unknown territory they encounter new problems for which there are no predefined solutions. Such was the case for the first empire in history. A combination of climate change and conflict put such pressure on the Akkadian borders that it simply collapsed in on itself. It was not designed with such struggles in mind.

During the dark age that followed, the most well-known ruler, Gudea of Lagash, did not take on the title of Lugal but instead referred to himself simply as an Ensi—a governor. He was a pious figure, building temples, bowing and scraping before the gods of old, demonstrating respect and recognition for the deities which came before Sargon and the Akkadians. While he was, by all accounts, a great man, Gudea of Lagash was also an ideal illustration of the attitudes of his time—and of all times following such a cataclysmic fall. Gudea represented the conservative attitude, a return to the old ways, the retreat into the safe burrow of traditional practices. He was no Sargon, no Naram-Sin. He returned to the old religion and restored the responsibility of war and politics to their rightful place: the gods.

It seems like a natural response to such trying times. Turning to gods, repenting the sins of the impious rulers, seeking a divine explanation for why such tragedy has befallen so many people. One need only look to The Curse of Agade to see this attitude made manifest. After all, if the gods bestow all rewards, if they sit in the heavens and make decisions about the world of men, they must also be responsible, and have reasons for, the tragedies and disasters that occur.

During this period, it was the Guti who ruled—barbarians from the Zagros Mountains who had seized upon the opportunity granted by a weak state and invaded from the east. The Sumerian King List suggests the Guti held power in Mesopotamia for several generations after the fall of Akkad.

They were likely driven down from their mountains by the same famines and climate changes that contributed so significantly to the weakening of Akkadian control on the region.

The Guti had failed to restore the old practices of statecraft and administration which had worked so well for the Akkadians, instead allowing the many facets of imperial bureaucracy to fall into disrepair. Weeds and grass grew over roads, towns, and cities were neglected. They certainly did not hold the same understanding of engineering and public sewer systems as the previous rulers had, and made no efforts to appease the local populations through religion. It was apparent that it would only be a matter of time before the civilized cities of the south amassed their strength and struck once again into the heart of Mesopotamia, clearing the land of the invaders.

It was Utu-Hegal of Uruk who claimed to rid Mesopotamia of the Guti once and for all. He most likely prepared his revolt against the new overlords for many months, perhaps even years, gathering supporters and enlisting the help not only of his people but of the divine. In fact, Utu-Hegal made sure to offer Enlil, the supreme god, much of the credit for the vanquishing of the Guti (although of course not all of it), and claimed Inanna as a patron-goddess. This was, after all, not the time for progressive gestures. Utu-Hegal, as the leader of Uruk, had a responsibility to appease the gods and the god-fearing among his people.

Upon gathering his forces, Utu-Hegal marched north. He paused on his way to receive envoys from the Guti, and subsequently placed them in chains, before routing the enemy and destroying their forces. The Guti king fled with his family to a nearby town, but he was captured and handed over by citizens who sensed a change in the god's favor. Utu-Hegal "put handcuffs and a blindfold on him. Before Utu (the sun god), Utu-Hegal made him lie at his feet and placed his foot on his neck... He brought back the kingship to Sumer" (Kriwaczek, 2010, p. 130).

The accuracy of this story remains uncertain. States, especially new or returned states, make efforts to legitimize their ruler through origin stories and propaganda. In fact, it is believed that the Sumerian King List, first compiled around this time, was created to assert the legitimacy of Utu-Hegal's rule, demonstrating his connection to a long line of Sumerian rulers back to and even preceding the Flood.

However, there is an alternative explanation for this story. Following the resurgence of Sumer, there appears to have been a hasty recording of stories, records, myths, and legends, leading some to suggest that the shock of the fall of Akkad and the conquests of the Guti made Sumerians realize the fragility of their traditions and history, until that point having been largely recited orally. This is suggested by the inclusion of, and focus on, many mythical heroes (such as Gilgamesh) and deities in the recorded documents from this time, as opposed to strictly factual, human accounts. This is reminiscent of the Quran, which was first written after many of those who had it memorized were killed. This would suggest not political persuasion, but preservation, may have been the guiding factor in the recording of not only Utu-Hegal's defeat of the Guti, but of many other texts first written around this time. Regardless of the motivations, we know one thing for certain—around the year 2100 BCE, Sumer began the process of putting itself back together.

Despite Utu-Hegal's efforts to rid Mesopotamia of the Guti, he was unsuccessful in establishing a dynasty or a lasting power base in his city of Uruk. When Utu-Hegal died (following a reign of between 7-427 years, depending upon what source you consult), powerful men took advantage of the power vacuum and seized control of the region. The kingship was taken to Ur.

The Third Dynasty of Ur

The third dynasty of Ur, or Ur III as it is often known, became the foundation for the emerging Sumerian empire, which ruled the region between 2112 and 2004 BCE. The empire, often referred to as the Neo-Sumerian Empire, not only signified the restoration of power to the old base of Sumer, nor even a golden age for the great city of Ur. The Neo-Sumerian Empire was one of the most unusual and surprising forms of administration in the ancient world, a great experiment of sorts that had more in common with the Soviet Union than it did with the Akkadians preceding it.

Founded by Ur-Nammu, the nephew of Utu-Hegal, Ur III controlled much of the Mesopotamian plain, with formally independent cities becoming provinces or vassal territories, paying taxes to the central administration. The Sumerian language once again became the language of administration, although Akkadian remained spoken on the streets of many cities.

Scholarship on the Neo-Sumerian period has often believed

the administration was entirely obsessed with bureaucracy, but this is largely to do with the locations of the archaeological excavations. Most of the digs have been pursuing rare and valuable items, and as such temples and palaces have been prioritized over other parts of cities. As such, it has had an impact on the portrayal of the empire, with ordinary, everyday life remaining unreflected. That said, the Neo-Sumerian Empire did indeed have an unusual, perhaps even radical, perspective on bureaucracy, which is even more surprising when you consider their place in history, long before even the early biblical tales of the origins of western society in Greece or Rome.

The structure of society in the Neo-Sumerian Empire was remarkably similar to that of Soviet or Maoist communism. It differed in many respects, especially regarding religious belief, but it was defined by the totalitarian ideologies used to justify economic and social arrangements. Put simply, the state took from each according to ability, and gave to each in accordance with need—although as usual, need and ability had to be decided by somebody, and more often than not one party or another would find themselves benefiting above others.

The individual had no voice, and society was structured not

around citizens but groups or small communities, largely defined by ethnicity, family, or belief. The state owned all land and the means of production, and each individual was obliged to serve the state for at least part of the year. Society revolved around the concept of Bala, whereby each province or city would pay a certain amount in grain or livestock to a central resource pool, from which each could then draw from as needed. The amount contributed could vary, but could at times exceed 50% of a province's production for a year.

In fact, the Neo-Sumerians went even further than the communists may have by keeping detailed records of each and every individual's contributions and rewards. Those of the lower classes, such as the slaves and workers of little skill, were considered to be state property. They had no purpose aside from providing labor to the city each and every day. Supervisors, on the other hand, had it very differently. Their performance was measured with extreme detail, and then scrutinized intensely. Their goods, materials, and labors, including metals, wool, and grains (all provided by the state), were measured and converted into equivalent "worker days." This was contrasted with the credit—namely, the production output, be that quality of flour, number of textiles woven; as it was different depending upon the team. Again, an equivalent in worker-days was calculated, even making room for time spent on side-projects such as repairs or urgent, external jobs, as well as the workers' yearly leave, averaging around 35 days a year for men and 55 for women.

The expected production was much higher than was possible, and surpluses were extremely rare. Many supervisors would end up with considerable debts to the state, which could have been called in at any point. If a supervisor was to die before paying up, his debts would fall to his descendants, who may have been required to sell themselves into slavery to raise the funds.

Another element of Neo-Sumerian administration that is particularly interesting is their use of invalids and the disabled. Everybody had their place in society, filling some role or another. This may have simply been an attempt to exploit every last possible means of production, but may also have been intended to offer a place in society to those who could not hope to otherwise compete or succeed.

The new style of government worked well for a time. Uniformity was established across the empire—a national curriculum was designed for scribal training, weights and measures were standardized and remained so for the rest of

Mesopotamian history. Even an imperial calendar was created, used for all administrative documents aside from purely local matters. Even an early code of laws was created, listing various crimes and disagreements and the resolutions or punishments for each. Capital crimes were listed as murder, robbery, the deflowering of another man's wife, or adultery (when committed by a woman), whereas other crimes had a prescribed quantity of silver to be paid, differing depending upon severity. While this legal system was not as complete as that of Hammurabi in the second millennium BCE, it went a long way toward standardizing punishments and bringing all cities and regions under a single law code.

Ideology and Personality

This ability to bring everybody together under one uniform banner was quite remarkable. The government in Ur managed to override local traditions across the empire and had a tight grip on institutions and practices throughout cities under its jurisdiction. They were obsessed with the regulation of everything in society. Society was structured to have a single, father-like figure on the throne, with everybody else spread out below him in the shape of a pyramid, a hierarchy based on and held together by the complex web of ability, contribution, and reward. Such a complex and inorganic state, however, needs something to hold it together, something beyond mere ideology. It is a common fact of life that humans tend toward the conservative, looking back on the societies of their youth as ideal and struggling to assimilate into new societies later in life. To overcome this tendency, the Sumerian king needed to create something that would bind his people together, something that would overpower this tendency toward social inertia.

The solution was to generate adulation and awe from the people of the empire. The truth is, states based on power can last for centuries without too much struggle, so long as they allow people to retain their culture and traditions. Ideological states, especially those that aim to control the economic structure of society, struggle to last even half that long. They become so obsessed with the control of the mindset of their population that they are unable to focus on defending themselves from outsiders, and the grip often falters first from the inside. To tie people together, a ruler needs to create a reminder of their power, legitimacy, and ideology.

Ur-Nammu, the first king of the Neo-Sumerians, came up with a plan to remind the people of his greatness on a daily basis. It is, in fact, one of the first things that springs to mind when one thinks of Sumer and Mesopotamia—the Ziggurat of Ur. Ziggurats were magnificent structures, smaller than the

Pyramids of Giza and yet no less impressive, rising high above the surrounding city and built in three immense levels. The lowest level was the widest, and a second, slightly smaller level was built above, leaving room for a walkway around the outside and terraces at each side. The third level was a temple, closest to the sky. The Ziggurat of Ur, and other ziggurats which came to rise from other cities across Sumer, were designed to momentarily bring the human and the divine world together. While the Ziggurat of Ur remained incomplete upon his death, Ur-Nammu had created a monumental reminder of his divinity, the sort of structure that would attract people from miles around and spark the imagination of men and women for many thousands of years into the future.

There was one other method of maintaining an ideological state that is not only noticeable in Neo-Sumerian records, but also the Soviet state of the 20th century. The cult of personality has been used, in varying ways, for centuries, but a comparison between the worship of rulers like Shulgi, the second king of Ur III, and the adulation afforded to Stalin or Lenin, demonstrates a similar tactic used for similar reasons millennia apart.

Shulgi, like Naram-Sin of the Akkadians, declared himself a

god during his reign. The actual purpose of this remains unclear, but it has been suggested that the deification was designed to create a figurehead to bind the people of the empire together. An ideological state cannot be maintained if the people are expected to believe in the concepts as they are. A populace tends to follow, or worship, a personality over an idea. The cults of Lenin and Stalin held the Soviet Union together, and while neither declared themselves to be gods as did Shulgi and his successors, their mummified bodies were kept on display, attracting pilgrims to this day. This form of worship amounted to a Soviet state religion, despite their atheistic ideology.

In Babylon, Kriwaczek (2010) presents two passages, one written as a chant in honor of Stalin in the 1930s, another for Shulgi in the third millennium BCE. Upon first glance, it is difficult to tell which passage is in honor of whom:

> Who is as mighty as you, and who rivals you?
>
> Who is there who from birth was as richly endowed with understanding as you?
>
> May your heroism shine forth, and may your might be respectfully praised! (p. 143)

And the second:

Thou who broughtest man to birth.

Thou who fructifiest the earth,

Thou who restorest the centuries,

Thou who makest bloom the spring,

Thou who makest vibrate the musical chords...

Thou, splendour of my spring, O thou,

Sun reflected by millions of hearts. (p. 144)

It may come as some surprise that it is the first, in its somewhat more humble phrasing, that was written in honor of Shulgi, king of Sumer. The latter, far more dramatic, was written for the "Great Stalin, O leader of the peoples" in 1935. Comparing these together, the Neo-Sumerian Empire, in all of its communist-like glory, appears more reasonable, humble, and human, despite existing many thousands of years ago. Either way, Shulgi, king of Sumer, was the Neo-Sumerian culture and ideology made human—the glue that bound the empire together.

The Fall

Nothing lasts forever, and most controlled, ideological states last for very little time at all. The collapse of the Neo-Sumerians was not only inevitable but happened remarkably quickly. What sparked the decline is not certain, but it appeared that upon the ascension of King Ibbi Sin, the provincial regions began to detach themselves from central control. Within the first two years of his reign, taxes had ceased from the most distant provinces, and outlying cities had stopped dating documents using the official imperial calendar. This was the case across the entire empire by his ninth year. The outlying provinces declared independence. Vultures circled. Enemies amassed on the borders.

Semitic peoples in the west, known as Amorites, began raiding the lands along the Euphrates. During times of stability, the western Semites would enter the empire peacefully and in small numbers, but during times of weakness, they came in numbers and were well-armed. They seized patches of territory in the empire's west, and their attacks drove the price of grain up enormously. When the king in Ur asked one of his generals to secure wheat and barley from the north, the general informed him that due to the danger posed by raiders, he was not going to return the grain to Ur.

The final blow came not from the west, but the east. Once under Sumerian control, the new leader of Elam had risen and marched into southern Mesopotamia. Ur fell quickly, and King Ibbi Sin was carted off to Elam and never seen again. The Elamites occupied Ur for seven years before being driven out, but by this time the damage was well and truly done. Sumer fractured into individual city-states, this time ruled largely by Amorite chieftains or Sumerian warlords.

Ur was forsaken, the kingship rescinded. Sumer would never again reign supreme.

CHAPTER 4
OLD BABYLON
(CA. 2000-1600 BCE)

Babylon is one of the most famous cities of the ancient world. Where places like Akkad, Kish, and Lagash are known almost exclusively to academics, with a few other Mesopotamian cities mentioned in the Old Testament, Babylon has secured a long-term position in the human imagination. Even those who do not know when Babylon flourished, or even why it is significant, still most likely recognize the name.

Babylon may have received its name from Bab-Ilu, the Gate of God. It is a city of biblical infamy, known for the exile of the Jews, described as the "mother of harlots and abomination of the earth" (Carroll & Prickett, 2008, Revelation 17:5). It is remembered by the Greeks as a city like any other, by the

Rastafarians as the ultimate symbol of the oppression of Black people, and by the British of the Victorian Era as one of the most magnificent cities of ancient history. It is remembered differently by different people, but there is no doubt that it is remembered.

The trouble with Babylon is that much of its history cannot be studied in archaeological sources. In the time since the Old Babylonian Empire, the water table has risen to the point of preventing excavation beyond the later period of its occupation. The Babylon of King Hammurabi is lost to us, possibly forever. Even so, we have enough information from surrounding cities, and later periods, to build a detailed picture of what life in Babylon may have been like.

Babylon was a city founded by the Amorites, those who had invaded the Neo-Sumerian Empire from the west at the end of the last reign of Ur. In this sense, they represent a continuation of an old pattern—the crumbling of the old Mesopotamian centers of power and the occupation by external forces. However, unlike the Guti of times past, the Amorites recognized the benefit in continuing the traditions and practices of the Sumerian culture preceding them. As such, they were well positioned to form a new, dominant power in the region.

This did not happen overnight. For several centuries following the fall of the Neo-Sumerian Empire, westerners poured into Mesopotamia. In Akkadian, they were called the Amurru, but they did not all come from the same location, being made up of at least two distinct Semitic peoples. In addition, there were also foreigners entering the region from the north and the east.

Power bases were established and collapsed, cities rose and fell, fighting for domination between the two great rivers. Chaos reigned. Some cities had three or four kings in a single year. Monarchs would emerge as if from the earth, only to return to it no less swiftly. One interesting story tells of King Irra-Imitti of Isin who, fearing bad omens, placed the gardener Enlil-Bani on the throne with the intention that the gardener should suffer whatever fate had in store. Enlil-Bani was to be removed from the throne and killed when the period of misfortune had passed; instead, King Irra-Imitti himself died and Enlil-Bani refused to relinquish power. He ruled for almost 25 years, making him one of the longest-reigning monarchs of this period.

We have unique insight into this period through documents

uncovered in Mari, a city captured by Hammurabi of Babylon before he established his empire. Thousands of clay tablets were uncovered, offering a glimpse of the thought processes and personalities of leaders of the time. One such man was Zimri-Lim of Mari, whose writings show us a man with a witty personality, a tendency toward the use of proverbs and social references as opposed to outright, crude humor. He was also a man with a vain streak, harassing servants for specific garments and fabrics, angered when his desires were not entertained. He was curious, traveling at length to neighboring regions, and was active in diplomacy and government affairs. Most significantly, however, Zimri-Lim of Mari was a pious man, with love for the gods and for religious festivals, and a keen interest in any signals the gods may have sent down to his realm.

This is just a small taste of the wealth of information the preserved tablets had to offer. Written largely informally, we can learn not merely of these people's day-to-day lives but their thoughts, feelings, vices, and values.

It was following the collapse of Mira, however, and presumably the death of Zimri-Lim, that the next great state revealed itself. Hammurabi, best known for his code of laws, was the sixth king in the first dynasty of Babylon but was to become the first king to rule over a Babylonian Empire proper following his conquest of southern Mesopotamian. As such, it was the Old Babylonian Era, led into glory and posterity by King Hammurabi, that emerged from the ruins left by the third dynasty of Ur.

King Hammurabi's Code

The code of laws attributed to Hammurabi was found not in Babylon, but the city of Susa. Upon the document, the king is shown to be receiving the laws from the god Shamash, whom to the Sumerians had been the sun god Utu, brother of Inanna. It begins with a preamble explaining the purpose of the document and proclaiming Hammurabi's greatness, "who like a father gave his people their birth" (Richardson, 2000, p. 123).

It is not a code of laws in the modern sense, rather providing a list of model cases, likely either drawn from real life or fabricated examples of crimes, covering upward of 280 judgments. Even commodities, prices, wages, and family law (including marriage, divorce, and incest) are included in the code. Considering our perspective on the ancient past, we may find some laws in Hammurabi's code to seem quite progressive, especially regarding women, as recorded by

Kriwaczek (2010):

> If a man wish [sic] to separate from a woman who has borne him children... he shall give that wife her dowry, and a part of the income from field, garden, and property, so that she can rear her children... She may then marry the man of her heart.

> If a woman quarrel [sic] with her husband, and says: "You are not congenial to me," the reasons for her prejudice must be presented. If she is guiltless... but he leaves and neglects her, then no guilt attaches to this woman, she shall take her dowry and go back to her father's house. (p. 169)

Hammurabi's laws differed from those of Ur-Nammu in that retribution is more obviously on display. Where Ur-Nammu's laws proclaimed fines of varying amounts for most crimes, Hammurabi has a more direct "eye for an eye" approach to punishment—quite literally: "If a man has destroyed the sight of another similar person, they shall destroy his sight. If he has broken another man's bone, they shall break one of his bones." (Richardson, 2000, p. 105).

Some of these punishments may come across as extreme, but at the same time, they were effective as universal punishments. Babylon was a multi-ethnic society, differing enormously from the Sumer and Akkad of old where most members of society belonged to a single cultural identity, or several similar subcultures. Value systems differed between cultural groups, and as such, the subtlety of traditional cultural punishments would not have been effective, and an easy-to-understand code of laws was required. Where some people may not understand the idea of paying a fine for causing physical harm, the philosophy of "an eye for an eye" is simple to grasp no matter where you are from.

A New Society

The old division of cities, with an individual god residing in each, was now long gone; the age of empires had begun. At this point in history, there were two major powers: Babylon ruled the south of Mesopotamia, while the city of Ashur dominated the north. In each, people from numerous backgrounds mixed, offering their culture to the enhancement of society. It is often easy to imagine multicultural societies as a modern phenomenon, but such a belief would be misplaced. The mixing of cultures has been practiced throughout history and often signals a period of prosperity, glory, and acceptance.

Babylon had taken a drastic new approach to society following the collapse of the Neo-Babylonian Empire. Gone was the Sumerian obsession with collectivism, the old semi-communist practices of Ur III nothing more than a memory. Individualization returned in the Babylonian Empire to the point that society itself seemed to be nothing more than a collection of individuals, each pursuing his or her own means. Compared to days past, people became detached from one another. Privatization became a central tenet to society. In fact, Babylon of old was not too different from a capitalist society today, with banks, trading companies, loans, shares, mortgages, and investments all becoming part of everyday life.

While this encouraged the vast economic expansion that characterizes the western world today, it also resulted in high levels of debt and a dramatic increase in the gap between the wealthy and the impoverished. It was not uncommon for people to sell themselves, their children, or their siblings into slavery simply to fund debt repayments. Aware of this, Hammurabi ensured his law code considered the issue, proclaiming that anyone sold into slavery over a debt would be set free after working for three years, debts forgiven.

The language of Sumerian ceased to be spoken on a day-to-day basis among the masses, and instead became what Latin is for us today—a language of religion and scholarship, written but rarely spoken. It remained in use for more than a thousand years after this point, disappearing only after the fall of Mesopotamian civilization around 700 BCE, but it never again served as the common tongue of an empire.

One other area of society that changed dramatically during the Old Babylonian Era was education and scholarship. Education was a secular affair, perhaps in part due to the multi-ethnic society, and it was also extremely accessible—assuming you could afford to send your children for education rather than having them help with day-to-day tasks. Most poor people remained uneducated, but among the merchant and wealthy classes, literacy, and numeracy levels grew dramatically. The Babylonians were a very concrete people, studying mathematics and even science in detail, but their achievements often instead heaped upon the Greeks of antiquity due to their more theoretical approach. Many of the practices we attribute to Ancient Greece were, in fact, inherited first from Babylon. The Babylonians insisted upon the importance of the concrete over the abstract; they valued practice over theory.

Omen tables, while easily dismissed at first glance, were, in fact, an early Babylonian attempt at understanding the world from a scientific perspective. They recorded important events and noted any unusual occurrences from beforehand, hoping to find connections between signs and outcomes. They saw the world as based on natural laws, logical, rational, and not dictated by the whims of a god or gods. Through studying omens, they were trying to understand cause and effect—if X happens, Y is going to follow. The diviners themselves, far from relying upon spiritual guidance, believed they were approaching the world from an empirical perspective. While we may now look at their practices and laugh, it remains clear that, from their perspective, they were uncovering worldly truths, not merely seeking guidance from spirits and deities.

In medicine, also, the Babylonians excelled. There were two types of physicians in the cities of old Babylonia—the ashipu, specializing in omens and exorcisms, and the asu, who made diagnoses and offered medications. Physicians were so important to the Babylonian society that Hammurabi's code went so far as to dictate the fees paid to physicians for their services—as well as the punishments for when they failed. As in mathematics, they focused on a practical medical approach, leaving little in the way of medical theory, and thus differ once again from the Greeks who followed.

That said, they appeared to have a very in-depth understanding of medicine and health, evolving their beliefs through several hundred years of careful observations and experiments. Their prescriptions for certain health issues, while perhaps lacking the scientific understanding we have today, were remarkably accurate and effective. For example, slices of liver would be prescribed as a cure for night-blindness (the inability to see at night, despite perfect sight during daytime). Today, we understand that this condition is caused by a lack of vitamin A—something the liver is rich in.

Some practices are even still in use today, such as the draining of lungs in pneumonia patients, following a remarkably similar procedure to modern times. They even had an understanding of the spread of diseases, as is demonstrated in another letter, noted by Avery (2016):

> I have heard that the lady Nanname has been taken ill. She has many contacts with the people of the palace… Now then, give severe orders that no one should drink from the cup where she drinks, no one should sit on the seat where she sits, no one should sleep in the bed

where she sleeps... This disease is contagious. (p. 7)

The Fall of Old Babylon

There is little in the way of recorded history during the time of Old Babylon, and even less so in the way of personal accounts. With such a focus on the practical, abstract ideas such as opinions and retellings were largely dismissed as unnecessary. That is not to imply that speculative thought was entirely lacking in the Babylonian mind, more that it is difficult for us to identify and interpret. The unfortunate consequence of this is that we know little about the fall of the Old Babylonian Empire, and what we can devise from the sources we have is lacking in substance.

What we do know is that following Hammurabi, there were five more kings in the first dynasty of Babylon, each of which reigned for upward of 20 years. However, as was the case following the reign of Shulgi of Ur, and even Naram-Sin of Akkad, controlled territory began progressively to shrink following Hammurabi's death, with cities and land being seized by outsiders. Once again, foreigners crossed the borders, and for some reason, people appeared to leave cities en masse. The de-urbanization was dramatic, with many significant Sumerian cities losing vast numbers of their populations. Even great cities like Ur lost the majority of their citizens.

The final blow to the Old Babylonian Empire came from the north—specifically Anatolia, which was ruled at the time by the Hittites. A Hittite force was sent south through Mesopotamia, reaching the city of Babylon and shaking it, bringing the dynasty to an end. The Hittites had no desire to rule from Babylon and so quickly left, leaving an enormous power gap that was soon filled by the Kassites. The Kassites were an eastern people, and held power in Babylon for over 400 years, during which little advancement occurred.

That said, Kassite Babylon by no means reached the previous lows seen during the Guti occupation following the fall of the Akkadians or even the years between the Neo-Sumerian and the conquests of Hammurabi. Kassite Babylon entered a sort of cultural stasis, retaining elements of the old culture but improving on them little. Meanwhile, it was the Assyrians, based in the northern city of Ashur, who would dominate Mesopotamia.

CHAPTER 5
ASSYRIA
(CA. 1800-700 BCE)

The great empire of Assyria is subject to some of the most negative perceptions in the history of the world. It has often been categorized alongside the Mongolian Empire or the Third Reich in terms of the violence it represents. The ancient city of sin may surely be Babylon, but it was Assyria that was considered the state of evil.

But is this perception a fair one? The Assyrians were surely no worse than the Romans, who were comfortable displaying rotting corpses for miles along the Appian Way in response to rebellion, or to any number of other nations and empires through history whose creatively gruesome methods of capital punishment shock us to this day. In fact, in a world where we can even entertain the idea of killing hundreds of thousands of civilians with atomic weapons, it seems somewhat hypocritical to crown Assyria as the empire of violence. The Assyrians contributed enormously to literature, science, theology, mathematics, and engineering, and are even believed to have been inspirations for the great Greek poets of antiquity such as Homer and Hesiod. Their empire provided the template upon which all future empires were built, and they even led the way toward a monotheistic society.

This is not to suggest they were a peaceful people. What started as a merchant state in the north of Mesopotamia was, over time, transformed into a highly militarized, aggressive society with a severe justice system and even more severe treatment of women. Nonetheless, we can follow the Assyrian story from its origins to its precipice, from mercantile to military, to understand the forces that led to their transformation from a small state to the largest empire the world had yet seen.

The Merchant State

In the early years of the Old Babylonian Empire, or perhaps even earlier, before the conquests of Hammurabi, people settled in the region near where today's Syria, Iraq, and Turkey meet. This was fertile land, with plentiful rain, far from the arid farmland of the south which required the building of dams and canals to water the fields. These people inherited their culture from Babylon to the south, but rather than building an impressive imperial base and conquering surrounding territory, they appeared to spend their time focusing on trade and sale, establishing a base in the city of Ashur along the banks of the Tigris.

Early Assyria was made up of mostly small farming communities, the only major city in the area being Ashur itself. Ashur was known simply as "The City" by many of its inhabitants, and thus conjures images of Constantinople during the medieval period in terms of significance and prestige. The fortifications were monumental, and yet Ashur was located in a particularly dangerous region, surrounded by three major empires—the Hittites and Mitanni to the north and northwest and Babylon to the south, with Egypt at this point working its way up the eastern coastline of the Mediterranean. While there was much exchange between the empires and Assyria in ideas and technology, their location prevented them from becoming powerful, constantly suppressed on all sides by great strength.

During this early Assyrian period, the Amorites ruled in Babylon but following their fall to the Hittites and the Kassites it was Assyria that held the mantle of Mesopotamian culture, and they were very aware of this. They retained innumerable practices, leaving the pantheon almost unchanged aside from the supplanting of Marduk, the city god of Babylon and successor of Enlil, with Ashur, for whom their capital city was named. Despite this cultural debt to the south, the relationship with Babylon was ofttimes strained, and sometimes outright violent. The two nations, Assyria small but rising, Babylon on the decline under its Kassite overlords, competed fiercely in trade and prestige, and the Assyrians even assaulted the city of Babylon on multiple occasions. Despite this, the Assyrians would often attempt to make reparations to Babylon, and it is believed that there may have been two major factions vying for power through much of Assyrian history—the nationalist, anti-Babylonian powers, and the traditionalists who remained aware of their debts to their southern neighbor.

It was business and mercantile practice that drove early Assyria forward, and during this time their culture was almost incomparable to what it would later become. Merchants would travel across Anatolia to the north and northwest, setting up trading settlements to work and trade with the local communities. The wealthy Assyrian families would send out representatives to these trading communities, receiving goods from home, which they would trade for silver. The silver would then be sent back to the city. Some men would marry local women, even father children, although they were permitted to divorce these women when their time at the communities came to an end, so long as they paid a fair compensation to the families and any possible children.

While private businesses had taken over from the old Akkadian and Sumerian state-based trading practices, there were still regulations on what could and could not be traded. Merchants would find themselves in trouble if they were caught transporting illegal goods. That said, the profits could be enormous, perhaps as a result of the risk involved in transporting goods across dangerous lands.

While Babylonian textiles were greatly desired and fetched a handsome price, their import from the south was not always reliable, and thus the Assyrians made efforts to create their own. Maintaining a high standard was of exceptional importance, as demonstrated by this letter from a merchant to his wife back in Ashur (Hirth, 2010):

> Concerning the fine cloth that you sent me: you must make more like that and send it to me via Ashur-Idi.

Then I will send you a half pound of silver. Have one side of the cloth combed, but not shaved smooth: it should be close-textured... The other side must just be lightly combed. If it still looks fuzzy, it will have to be close shaved, like kutanu-cloth. (p. 225)

Women played an important role in this mercantile state, in dramatic contrast to their treatment only a few hundred years later under a transformed Assyria. They would supervise the production, loading, and dispatch of goods, and were comfortable making their opinions and feelings clear when communicating with their merchant husbands via letter. In one uncovered tablet, a woman writes to her husband: "Why do you keep writing to me: 'The textiles that you send me are always of bad quality!' Who is this man who lives in your house and criticizes the textiles that are brought to him?" (Kriwaczek, 2010, p. 203). Despite their role in society, however, it appears women were often neglected by their traveling husbands, being left with little funds or food while they remained in Ashur, overseeing the production of their husbands' goods.

However, within a few generations, the Assyrian way of life changed dramatically. What had been up until then a relatively peaceful, moderately progressive merchant state, took a sudden U-turn toward nationalism, militarization, and expansionism. The trading life ceased, and Assyria transformed into the greatest of the Mesopotamian empires.

From Mercantile to Military

At some point around the middle of the second millennium BCE, catastrophe befell Assyria. The city was attacked by outsiders, rulers lost their territories and their bloodlines were extinguished. The subsequent years were defined by a series of illegitimate rulers rising from nowhere, as recorded in an unearthed list of Assyrian rulers: "Ashur-Dugul, son of a nobody, who had no title to the throne; he ruled for six years... the following six sons of nobodies ruled for periods of less than a year." (Kriwaczek, 2010, p. 204).

Assyria was too small and insignificant to stand up to the outside powers, especially Mitanni to the north, which sacked Ashur at one point and left with gold and silver doors to mount at the king's palace. The ruler of Assyria was forced into submission, and a long economic depression resulted. Through this period, the Assyrians came to understand the need to hold on to provinces and trading centers throughout their territory, lest their people and city fall into poverty. They came to see the world as a dangerous place, not least because they were crushed between four dangerous adversaries. It was the resulting anxiety and paranoia that would act as the catalyst in their transformation from an insignificant region, overshadowed by giants, to a regional superpower.

One of the ways we can observe this change is through the cylindrical seals used by the rich and powerful to identify themselves. While public presentation had always been significant in ancient Mesopotamia, cylindrical seals tend to show a more personal, honest representation of what an individual thought of himself (it was almost always men who used them). Seals from the early Assyrian period show men bowing before the gods and making offerings; later, these seals change to far more aggressive, dominant symbols which show men as impressive rulers or fighting with savage beasts that "fill the Assyrian seals with a world of fantastic vigour which seems untrammelled with any purpose to tell a story but only to picture the clash of mythological terrors against daemoniac champions of human kind." (Gadd, 1977, p. 47)

Assyria's lucky break ultimately came when the Hittites sacked the Mitannian capital, killing their ruler. As the empire fell, the Hittites and Assyrians divided up the land between them. This time, the Assyrians had no intention of losing their newly gained territory, their militarized psychology having developed through years of political and diplomatic paranoia. They had gained enough land to grant them a place on the international stage, and the Assyrian king, Ashur-Uballit, wrote to the Egyptian Pharaoh Akhenaten in the mid-1300's BCE, pronouncing his new power, as quoted by Spar (1988):

> Say to the king of the land of Egypt: Thus Ashur-uballit, the king of the land of (the god) Ashur. For you, your household, for your land, may all be well. I have sent my messenger to you to visit you and to visit your land. Up to now, my predecessors have not written; today, I have written to you. I send you a splendid chariot, 2 horses, and 1 date-stone of genuine lapis lazuli as your greeting gift. (p. 149-150)

Ashur-Uballit was polite, but there was little sign of the reverence usually offered to the Pharaoh of Egypt by other contemporary rulers. Later in his reign, Ashur-Uballit wrote again to the Pharaoh, in this letter referring to the ruler as his 'brother' and thus suggesting equal standing between them. The paranoia that had grown within the Assyrian state had left them extremely sensitive to even the mildest perceived slight, and they demanded equal standing among empires. When an insult was perceived, the Assyrian king was quite comfortable responding in kind, even to the most powerful ruler in the known world. "Is it from a great king, a gift such as this? Gold is dust in your land—one simply gathers it up... If in good faith your intention is friendship then send me much gold" (Kriwaczek, 2010, p. 207).

This newfound confidence was sure to raise eyebrows across the Middle East. In Babylon, the Kassite ruler was upset by the Assyrian contact with the Egyptian Pharaoh and made no efforts to disguise his displeasure. He demanded the Pharaoh reject the Assyrian envoys, claiming they were his own citizens and that he had not authorized their expedition to Egypt. That said, the Kassites in Babylon were clearly aware of the threat posed by their northern neighbor, managing to convince Ashur-Uballit to send one of his daughters south to marry the crown prince.

Years later, it was their son, half-Babylonian, half-Assyrian, who took up the throne in Babylon. However, Kassite nobles were apparently unhappy with the arrangement and revolted. Following the new Babylonian king's assassination, the king of Assyria rode south and seized the city, eliminating opposition and installing a puppet ruler. For the first time in history, it was now Ashur, and not Babylon, that held true power over Mesopotamia.

A New Culture

The struggle for preeminence in Mesopotamia lasted for many hundreds of years. It became somewhat simpler when the Hittites fell in the 12th century, and it was in 1120 BCE that the Assyrians reached their first peak when King Tiglath-Pileser I crossed the Euphrates to capture Carchemish. This victory was short-lived, however. Immense numbers of Aramaic-speaking camel herders and traders had been moving west, and around this time the numbers spiked further still. These immigrants seized land for themselves, carving slices from the edge of the Assyrian territory until, over time, the Assyrian empire was pushed all the way back to its homeland around Ashur. They remained confined in this point for nearly a century, and it was during this low point that the most dramatic changes in Assyrian society occurred.

Legal tablets dating from around the rule of Tiglath-Pileser show just how far the Assyrians had come from their peaceful, mercantile origins. The penalties laid out in these tablets are strikingly brutal, even when compared to Hammurabi's "eye-for-an-eye" policies from earlier in the millennium, and nowhere is this more apparent than in the treatment of women. Women were targeted harshly and punished severely, especially when compared with the punishments received by men. Gruesome death penalties, horrific mutilations, and savage beatings were common punishments for various crimes. The sudden rise of misogyny in Assyria is both fascinating and horrifying. According to one of the tablets, if a women made efforts to receive an abortion (specifically, if she induced a miscarriage), upon her conviction she would have been impaled upon stakes and left to rot in the Assyrian sun. If she had died in the process of the abortion, however, it was her body that would be impaled, and she would receive no burial. In the event that she had fought with a man and injured one of his testicles, her finger would be cut off; if she injured both of them, or if the second became infected as a result of the original injury, they would go a little further: her eyes would be gouged from her head. If she should commit adultery with another man, they would both simply be killed; however, if the husband chose instead to slice off his wife's nose, he could then choose to brutally mutilate the face of the guilty man, and make him into a eunuch.

Needless to say, the Assyrian treatment of women (and men, to a lesser degree) was extreme. It is difficult to say exactly how often punishments of this severity were actually practiced, but it is clear simply from the document's existence that the Assyrian attitude had changed dramatically.

Brutality, and especially that toward women, appeared to be a central virtue in society—"An inscription of Tiglath-Pileser, comparing the king to a hunter, who 'set out before the sun rose and marched three days' distance before dawn,' proudly claims that he 'cut open the wombs of the pregnant, he blinded infants.'" (Kriwaczek, 2010, p. 210). If anything, these horrific accounts appear to be tools of propaganda and manipulation, used to strike fear into enemies and the populace alike, not unlike practices used by the Mongols during their conquests in the 13th and 14th centuries CE where the horrific treatment of one city would encourage others to surrender without any resistance.

The treatment of women went further, in fact, and laid the foundations for some common practices across the region to this very day. It is at this point in history where we first encounter the veil, or specifically the forced covering of women in public in a style similar to today's hijab. Assyrian women of any respectable standing (such as a wife, widow, or daughter) were required to veil themselves in order to go out in public. They were permitted to use a shawl, robe, or mantle, so long as their hair and head was covered for modesty. Should a man's concubine go out into the street while accompanied by his wife, she would also veil herself, as would a prostitute whom a man had chosen to marry. A standard prostitute, however, was not permitted to wear a veil.

One major difference between Islamic and Assyrian practices is the division between those who must be veiled and those who must not. In Islamic tradition, all women wore veils, with no distinction between members of society. In Assyria, the wearing of a veil was restricted to 'respectable' women; those who veiled illegally were punished no less severely than those who should veil but did not. A female slave who veiled herself would be prosecuted and have her ears cut off. A veiled prostitute would also be arrested, have her clothing confiscated, and be flogged 50 times. A man who saw an illegally veiled woman was obliged to bring her in for prosecution, lest he also wished to be flogged, and more besides: "they shall pierce his ears, thread them with a cord, and tie it at his back. He shall do work for the king for one full month" (Kriwaczek, 2010, p. 211).

Women of the palace were under even tighter regulation. The king's wives and concubines would be locked up for the entirety of their lives, with the only visitors allowed being eunuchs, and even then only for a very brief time. The palace commander would have to grant permission and wait outside the entrance of the women's quarters to escort the eunuch when he had finished his business. A eunuch who overheard women arguing or singing would have one of his ears removed and would be beaten. If he spoke to a woman for longer than deemed necessary, he would be flogged and have his clothes taken. Anybody who spoke to one of the palace women without a chaperone, or anyone who was aware of a breach in the protocol but failed to report it, would be killed.

In this, Assyria became the model for many future societies, including Persian, Byzantine, and Islamic. But why was it that women's role in society changed so dramatically and so quickly? The answer is somewhat surprising and relates to another significant change in culture from around this time, specifically that of religious practice.

As the Assyrians grew in strength, and as their political paranoia shaped them into the ruthless nation they are known for today, there was a profound shift in the way one thought about the gods. For millennia, gods had been part of the world, the embodiment of natural forces—the winds, the rain, famine, rivers. At this point in history, however, when the individual was being reshaped by Assyrian ideals, the connection between the gods and nature fractured. Over time, the representation of the gods grew distant from the real world, eventually leading to their replacement by symbols over characters—stars, the sun, the moon, leaves, water, and numerous other representations. As time passed, the gods became transcendent as opposed to imminent; once a part of nature, they were now detached from it, above it.

As humanity had been made by the gods and in their image, the human relationship with nature shattered as well. Once awed by natural forces, now men were the master of nature, given "dominion over the fish and the sea, and over the fowl of the air, and over the cattle, and over all the earth, and over every creeping thing that creepeth upon the earth" (Carroll & Prickett, 2008, Genesis 1:26).

It was not so simple for women, however. In a world of transcendent religion, any connection with biology was frowned upon, considered to be inhuman. Women, unlike men, are bound firmly to the biological world, and according to the Assyrians, it was this that dictated their purpose and usefulness in life. Childbirth and menstruation were symbolic of a woman's inferior nature. Women were nothing more than a danger to men's semi-divinity. This attitude would stick for centuries, with its consequences still felt today. Women were largely excluded from religion until the rise of Christianity and their belief in Jesus, the son of God, being born from a woman.

An additional consequence of this theological change was the development of the very first monotheistic religion. The idea of transcendent, omnipresent deities is only a small step away from a single overarching deity, and before long the Assyrians considered Ashur to be the one true god, all others to simply be elements or interpretations of him. Those gods worshipped by outsiders were found to be reinterpretations (or misinterpretations) of Ashur. This was not to imply that the worship of other gods ceased entirely, merely that it was now recognized that these other gods were parts of Ashur himself, one of his many facets. Whether the monotheism of the Abrahamic religions stemmed from this origin or developed independently is difficult to say for certain, but it can be said with some certainty that their idea of a singular, overarching god was by no means a new one.

The Military State

Semitic arrivals from the west were a part of Mesopotamian history since the beginning. The Akkadians joined the Sumerians in prehistoric times, followed by the Amorites, who established the Old Babylonian Empire. The Arameans in the Assyrian days were simply the next in a long tradition. The reasons for this mass migration remain unclear, but we can deduce that there had been a motivational push from their old homeland, likely in the form of drought and famine. The lands of Assyria were not unaffected, but they remained at least somewhat fertile, and the rainfall was greater than on the eastern Mediterranean coastline. The Arameans probably moved into Assyrian land out of mere necessity, and upon their arrival they plundered and seized land, causing havoc across the western Assyrian borders.

Faced with this mounting threat, the Assyrians realized their best hope at survival lay in the development of an incontestable military. The ultimate solution to the Aramean problem was to build up military strength (a multi-generational process) and seize the Semitic homelands, forcing the population to remain. This goal was the final piece in the puzzle that would lead to Assyrian supremacy across Mesopotamia.

The cost of holding new territory, however, must be funded by the looting of even more lands further outside borders. The Assyrians quickly came to realize that the construction of an empire was not a simple undertaking and that it would take on a life of its own, swallowing up new territories simply to fund those already conquered. By around the 10th century BCE, the Assyrians began to swallow up not only their lost lands but also the lands of their neighbors, consuming the Aramean kingdoms in the west. By the rule of Tiglath-Pileser

III in the eighth century BCE, the Assyrians had created the largest empire yet known to humankind.

The key to their military success was their military might. The Assyrian army was the model from which all other armies were drawn right up until the invention of firearms. Where warfare had previously been unorganized, one chaotic mass fighting against another, the Assyrians were disciplined and efficient. They were the first fielded army to be equipped in iron, a far superior and cheaper metal than bronze, which had been the standard of the time. They were one of the earliest armies to employ horses not merely for the pulling of chariots, but for use as cavalry. Furthermore, they invented the military boot, replacing the sandal, which allowed them to fight on any terrain. Their armies had a highly developed command structure, which allowed discipline to be enforced. If one were to look out at an Assyrian army lined up before a city, they would see up to 50,000 armored men standing in perfect formation. The Assyrians, through several generations of hard work and social reform, had created a militarized state that would change the face of warfare forever.

They also knew how to use fear to conquer their enemies, and would proudly announce their most violent punishments in warning to others. One Assyrian king, quoted by Mark (2014), described in great and gory detail the punishments inflicted upon chieftains who had revolted during his reign:

> I built a pillar over against the city gate and I flayed all the chiefs who had revolted and I covered the pillar with their skins. Some I impaled upon the pillar on stakes and others I bound to stakes round the pillar... I made one pillar of the living and another of heads and I bound their heads to tree trunks round about the city. Their young men and maidens I consumed with fire. The rest of their warriors I consumed with thirst in the desert of the Euphrates. (para. 6)

Assyrian military conquests were focused on the capture of locations that either posed a threat or represented great strategic importance. Trade routes and towns were captured and held, as were the larger of Assyria's neighbors, while those who appeared to be insignificant were largely left to their own devices. As a result, the empire began to take on an unusual shape, with pockets of independence within its perceived borders. That said, while the Assyrians allowed some nations to retain their independence (within reason), should a state rise against them, they would wipe out the rebellious forces and annex the state immediately. Over time, more and more independent kingdoms were brought into the fold, plugging up the gaps within the Assyrian borders.

At its apex, the Assyrian Empire covered an enormous area of land stretching across the entirety of the Near East and even down into Egypt. Every free inhabitant within its borders was considered a free Assyrian citizen, for military might can only hold territory for a limited time. There was a firm ideology rooted in the Assyrian imperial structure, one that has remained largely unchanged throughout the millennia and to the empires of the 19th and early 20th centuries. This ideology, while not as extreme and brittle as that of the Neo-Sumerians, was strong enough to bind people together for many hundreds of years.

All Assyrian territory was part of Assyria. There was no differentiation between the original Assyrian lands and those conquered in Egypt or the south. This was important because it avoided a hierarchy based upon location, and decreased the chances of those in the provinces, far from the seat of power, feeling out of place and rising up against the imperial forces. In older empires, where individuals retained their own culture and ethnic identity, organized resistance was common and occurred whenever there had been a perceived weakness at the center of power. By treating all lands (perhaps aside from the city of Ashur) the same, the Assyrians were able to decrease the chance of rebellions and dissatisfaction.

All people were subject to the same laws, the same taxation, the same burdens, and the same rewards. This avoided a divide between the native Assyrian population and the conquered people, the "us-and-them" perspective, which would have encouraged organized resistance. Whether an individual was born in Ashur or born in Israel, in Babylon, or in Egypt, they were the same before the eyes of Ashur and before the king. To enforce this, many people from conquered territories were relocated across the empire, dispersed to new locations to separate them from their cultural identity. Over time, this would destroy their old identity and replace it with exclusive loyalty to Assyria.

The final piece of the Assyrian ideological web was the figurehead of the empire—both the ruler, the Assyrian emperor in Ashur, the empire personified; and the single god, Ashur, who existed within and behind all the primitive gods worshipped by newly conquered subjects and was accepted as the ultimate creator of all things—the Jehovah of the Assyrians.

This was the formula for an immensely powerful, long-lasting empire. However, as with all things of this scale, it had its flaws. The equality among all citizens of Assyria and the dispersion of people across the land would eventually lead to an imbalance in ethnicity. The immense influx of Arameans from the west, and the conquest of their cities and nations, led to the native Assyrians becoming a minority within their own empire. The Akkadian language was lost to all but the scholars, replaced by Aramaic, which would remain in use until being supplanted by Arabic in the seventh century. As such, this imperial principle of inclusion and equality would spell the end of a culture, or at the very least a millennia-old linguistic tradition, built upon the Sumerian and Akkadian languages. Mesopotamia had conquered the world (or a significant part of it), yet the world had then conquered Mesopotamia.

CHAPTER 6
THE END OF AN ERA (AFTER CA. 700 BCE)

The Decline of Culture

When one thinks of the fall of civilization, what most likely comes to mind is dramatic conquests, vicious battles, and crumbling cities. We tend to think of empires swallowed up, piece by piece, or even a foreign usurper taking up the mantle of power and enforcing their cultural practices upon the people of the city. After all, this is how Byzantine culture fell, and Roman, and countless others. In the case of the Assyrians, however, and the Mesopotamian tradition as a whole, the cause was something far more unusual—an alphabet.

To blame the fall of Mesopotamian culture on nothing but an alphabet may be an overstatement, but the introduction of a syllabic writing system was one of the largest contributors to the erasure of thousands of years of culture and tradition. Culture is, after all, rooted in language. A language combines and interprets common experiences and histories, creating terminology specific to one particular way of seeing the world. Our understanding of the world is limited by the language we can use to describe it, and as such the loss of a language means in turn the loss of a certain perspective, a way of understanding the world.

The mass migration eastward of the Aramean people would spell the end of Mesopotamian culture more completely than any military conquest ever could. The dispersal of Arameans throughout the empire, growing to become the majority in most areas, led in turn to the abandonment of both Sumerian and Akkadian as the imperial tongue. Even worse, however, was the invention of a syllabic alphabet, an entirely new way of recording information. This invention was not only going to eradicate a culture but also condemn information and accounts from the late Assyrian period largely to the dust.

The new alphabet had been developed for common people, designed with symbols representative of specific sounds to make the formation of words easy for even those with lesser education. This first alphabet, designed for use with the Aramaic language and not the Akkadian of the empire, was so easy to learn and use that it encouraged the adoption of Aramaic empire-wide. To make matters worse, the Aramaic alphabet was written using inks on papyrus or animal skins, biodegradable materials that would rarely last longer than a century or two before rotting away to nothing. The quick adoption of this new form of writing, and the language which it was designed for, resulted in a dramatic decrease in the number of cuneiform tablets produced and thus preserved from this era. As a result, much information is lost to the dark recesses of history, and what we do know either comes from the rare uncovering of a cuneiform tablet or the writings of those who came later, tending toward bias and incorrect information.

While it is difficult to make many bold statements about the late Assyrian period, we have evidence to suggest the Assyrians were aware of their impending fate and were making efforts to preserve their culture while they had the chance. Ashurbanipal, king of Assyria from 669-631 BCE, during which time he ruled from his capital, Nineveh, is considered the last great king of Assyria. During his reign, Ashurbanipal set about creating a collection of writings from across his empire, including Sumerian, Akkadian, Babylonian, and Assyrian cuneiform tablets, storing them in his library in Nineveh—perhaps the first organized library in history. What is of interest here is not so much the collection itself, but the urgency with which Ashurbanipal set about compiling it. He collected tens of thousands of tablets, including religious texts, stories, and handbooks, and was constantly on the lookout for new additions. Kriwaczek (2010) quotes a letter he sent to a city governor requesting documents:

> You shall search for and send to me... rituals, prayers, stone inscriptions, and whatever is useful to royalty such as expiation texts for cities, to ward off the evil eye at a time of panic, and whatever else is required in the palace, all that is available, and also rare tablets of which no copies exist in Assyria. (p. 234)

Ashurbanipal's timing could not have been more prudent. In the year 612 BCE, the city of Nineveh was sacked and destroyed by a joint force of Babylonians, Medians, and Scythians, sealing the fate of the Assyrian Empire. The penultimate king of Assyria, Sinsharishkun, was killed in the battle, and the library was destroyed. Thankfully, due to the hardy nature of clay tablets, the destruction of Nineveh resulted in the preservation of Ashurbanipal's collection under the rock until it was rediscovered in the 1800s. Ashurbanipal's hope of preserving his nation's culture and knowledge for future generations had succeeded, after more than 2,500 years.

The Decline of Power

The destruction of Nineveh, alongside that of Ashur, spelled the end of the Assyrian empire after long years of conflict with Babylon. Babylon had held a complicated position in Assyrian history, largely due to the cultural debt owed by the Assyrians to the Old Babylonian empire. During most of the Assyrian Empire's rule, Babylon was held under its sway, but there remained a king in Babylon, often assigned by the ruler of Assyria himself. The fall of Assyria was an unfortunate side effect of the long-standing imperial attitude toward their neighbors and client states— "It was the almost inevitable consequence of the imperial policy of Oderint dum Metuant, let them hate so long as they fear. For when the fear is overcome, the hatred remains" (Kriwaczek, 2010, p. 237).

The fall of Nineveh was so complete that, according to the Greek writer Lucian, there was "no trace of it left, and one can't even guess where it was" (Vlaardingerbroek, 2004, p. 233). This was not quite the end of the Mesopotamian story, however. There would be one final power in the land, ruling for no longer than the Soviet Union held power in the 1900s.

The Neo-Babylonian Empire, sometimes referred to as the Second Babylonian Empire, remerged from the sacking of Ashur and Nineveh around 612 BCE. Following the death of Ashurbanipal, the Babylonians had revolted against the new Assyrian kings, who had proven weaker and incapable of holding on to their territory in a changing age. The Neo-Babylonian Empire represented the first time in more than a millennium that Babylon had been the seat of power in Mesopotamia. The empire itself only lasted until around 539 BCE, and it ruled over the end of an era.

There was an increasing awareness among the people of Mesopotamia that the world as they knew it was coming to an end. Kabiti-Ilani-Marduk wrote a text during the last days of the Neo-Babylonians, known as The Myth of the Pest-God Irra, The King of All Habitations, that tells of the impending fall of Mesopotamian civilization. He tells of the plague-god, Irra, persuading the gods to allow him to lay waste to the lands of Sumer and of Akkad. His alleged motivation is the lack of piety among the people, a common explanation offered for the waning of empires and reminiscent of the attitudes following the fall of Akkad.

According to Kabiti-Ilani-Marduk, however, this was not the end. The actions of Irra were not intended merely to destroy the world and its people; rather, they were to clear away the old and make room for a new era. It is representative of the age-old idea, whereby destruction of the old is necessary for progress; that destruction is the ultimate creative force behind history.

In 549 BCE, the Median Empire, which stretched across modern-day Iran and up into Anatolia, was conquered by Cyrus the Great of Persia. Cyrus was considered by many to be a reasonable ruler, and the Persians were known for letting their subjects rule themselves as long as their kings paid homage to Cyrus and his successors, the King of Kings, ruling from Persepolis. Following the fall of Medes, it was inevitable that Babylon would follow, and in 539 BCE, this inevitability became reality. Babylon was attacked during a festival day when the populace was unprepared to defend the city. They opened the sluices and lowered the river, marched across, and occupied the city with relative ease. According to Herodotus (2015):

> ...if the Babylonians had only been given forewarning of what Cyrus was up to, or fathomed it for themselves, then they could have turned the entrance of the Persians into their city so completely to their own advantage as to have annihilated the invaders utterly... However, the enemy was upon them before they knew what had hit them... Such was the size of the city that those who lived in the centre of Babylon had no idea that the suburbs had fallen. (p. 191)

Babylon fell to the Persians; the age of Mesopotamia had come to a close.

There are multiple accounts of how the Persians may have been received by the Babylonians. According to some, they were caught unawares and thus had no option but to surrender, but others suggest the Babylonians welcomed Persian rule with open arms. It was agreed that Cyrus was a worthy king, and the previous ruler of Babylon had not been well-loved. An unearthed tablet from around the time, however, shows a receipt for 7 weeks worth of work on one of the city walls, suggesting that perhaps the conquest was not so easy as it may have been implied by later sources.

It was believed by the Babylonians that the conquest of Persia would not spell the end of their culture. After all, many outsiders had entered the land between the two rivers in the past and set themselves up as rulers, adopting local customs themselves. It was most likely assumed by many that this would be no different, particularly considering their culture was the oldest and most respected in the region.

This belief was terribly mistaken. While Cyrus and his successors adopted elements of Mesopotamian culture for their own, this was no different from the open attitude displayed to all conquered nations. Persia was built upon a selection of cultural practices taken from all their conquered states and kingdoms, and Mesopotamia was no more or less important than the others. Furthermore, unlike earlier conquerors and invaders, the kings of Persia chose not to rule from one of the great Mediterranean cities but remained in Persepolis. Rule from the outside would remain for millennia. The consequences of this were immense. Mesopotamia, once the cultural beacon of the east, had lost both its self-confidence and centrality, reduced to a mere province. This was not effective immediately, of course—cultures do not die out overnight, rather wither away slowly, almost unnoticed, supplanted by more modern practices.

The rise of Persia represented not so much a new age, but more a period of transition. The world was now opened up to new ideas, peoples, and cultures—a sign of things to come. The true transition into a new era occurred when Alexander the Macedonian, ruler of the first great western power, rolled his war machine eastward and burnt Persepolis to ashes in 330 BCE. This Hellenistic era, with Greek ideas and practices spreading from Italy to India and beyond, was the beginning of the modern age, the new world in which we ourselves live. But Mesopotamia, the colossus of the ancient past, had by this time shriveled and collapsed, buried under the rubble of a bygone age.

PART II: THE MYTHOLOGY

CHAPTER 7
ENUMA ELISH

*T*he Enuma Elish (meaning "when on high," taken from the opening lines) is a Babylonian creation myth telling of Marduk, the champion of the gods, and his victory over the forces of Tiamat. Being of Babylonian origin, it is believed that the original story from which this is derived will have featured either Enki or Enlil in the major role. It appears to have been told in such a way to justify the reign of Marduk, the Babylonian supreme god, over all the previous deities of Sumer and Akkad. Tablets telling this story have been found in the excavation of Ashur, Kish, and the Library of Ashurbanipal in Nineveh, and date to ca. 1200 BCE, although the original myth is believed to be much older.

In the beginning, there is water, and that water is swirling in chaos. The water parts into two distinct entities—the god Apsu, freshwater; and the goddess Tiamat, saltwater. Upon their separation, the two deities come together, mixing their waters to create a new generation of gods.

However, the young gods are loud and irritating, as children tend to be. Apsu, their great father, finds it difficult to sleep during the night, and even more difficult to work during the day. On the suggestion of his vizier Mummu, Apsu does what any loving father would in such a situation: he decides to have them killed.

Tiamat, aware of her husband's intentions, is rightfully upset at the idea of her children being murdered. They are loud and obnoxious, but they are also young, and she had brought them into the world—she is duty-bound to protect them. As such, Tiamat seeks Enki, her great-grandson, and tells him of his father's terrible plan.

Enki is shocked. The other gods, upon being told of their father's murderous intentions, are similarly taken aback, uncertain of how to act. After a good deal of contemplation, Enki comes up with a masterful plan.

Late one night, he sneaks into Apsu's abode and pours sleep upon him. Mummu, who tries to wake Apsu and warn him, is instead captured and chained up. With his father incapacitated, Enki removes his crown and places it upon his own head, before slaying Apsu where he lies.

In a stroke of genius, Enki decides to create a dwelling for himself and his fellow younger gods within the corpse of their father. In the subsequent excitement and celebration, Enki and his wife Damkina come together and bear a son, Marduk, whose greatness and splendor exceeds even the greatest among the younger gods.

Meanwhile, Tiamat grieves the loss of her husband. She may have warned Enki of Apsu's plans in the first place, but she had never intended to simply swap out one death for another. In her grief, Tiamat gathers an assembly of great allies, with her son Kingu at its head. She creates 11 terrible chimeras, horrendous, disgusting monsters the likes of which the world had never before seen, and bestows upon Kingu the Tablets of Destiny, legitimizing his rule over the entire universe. Her army assembled, Tiamat declares war upon the younger gods, seeking terrible vengeance for the death of her first husband, Apsu.

The war does not go well for the younger gods. Many fearsome battles ensue, and there are numerous turncoats, gods who abandon Enki and instead support Tiamat. With her great army and her 11 monsters, Tiamat is believed to be invincible.

Enki, fearing for the worst, speaks to his grandfather, Tiamat's son Anshar. He tells Anshar of their terrible odds, and of Kingu, wielding the Tablet of Destinies, leading the 11 monsters into battle. Anshar, concerned, seeks out his son, Enki's father Anu, and asks him to go to Tiamat and to appease her. Anu sets off, but the closer he comes to Tiamat, the greater his fear. In a moment of weakness, Anu turns back, returning to his father in shame.

The younger gods are running out of options quickly. In a desperate last attempt, Anshar suggests Marduk, son of Enki, serve as their champion. Marduk is brought before them and he asks which god he will be fighting.

"You will fight no god," they tell Marduk. "You will be fighting the goddess, Tiamat."

Marduk, apparently feeling confident, declares that he will fight and defeat the goddess Tiamat, but only on one condition—upon his victory, he is to be proclaimed the supreme god, ruler over even Enki, Anu, and Anshar. The younger gods have little choice—they must either accept Marduk's terms, or submit to the murderous wrath of Tiamat. In the end, there is no decision to be made at all. Even Lahmu and Lahamu, Tiamat's firstborn children, are eventually convinced of Marduk's worthiness, although not without first drinking themselves into a stupor. Marduk will be the supreme god.

The younger gods provide Marduk with a throne that sat above all other gods. They make him a scepter and provide him with a wide array of weapons with which to fight Tiamat—a bow and quiver, a mace, bolts of lightning, and four winds. The gods kneel before him, proclaiming "Lord Marduk, your word is the first among all gods. If you command destruction, it shall be so; if you command creation, it shall be so."

Marduk, proclaimed supreme god and equipped with every weapon he could want for, sets out to capture and slay his great-great-grandmother, Tiamat. Using the four winds, he traps her, and then approaches in a chariot, condemning her for the trouble she had created. Enraged at such treatment,

Tiamat makes the mistake of joining Marduk in single combat.

Marduk throws a net over Tiamat, and try as she may, she is unable to escape. In her rage, she opens her mouth to swallow Marduk whole, but instead, he fills her mouth with the *Imhullu*, the evil wind. Dazed and confused, the evil wind raging inside her, Tiamat becomes incapacitated and Marduk takes the opportunity to fire an arrow into her heart. Tiamat, the mother of all gods, is slain.

In one last act of defiance, he smashes Tiamat's head in with a mace, and from her crushed eyes flowed the waters of the Euphrates and the Tigris rivers. Splitting his mother's corpse in two, Marduk creates the sky from one half, the earth from the other, and in the skies creates a place for himself, his grandfather Anu, his father Enki, and Enlil.

As the supreme god, Marduk sets about putting his realm in order. He creates constellations and uses them to define the days of the year. He creates the moon, weather, and the day and night cycle. Finally, he seeks to create humankind, subjects, and servants for the gods. Consulting his father, it was decided that a god must be sacrificed from whose blood humans would be created. It did not take long for them to settle on a suitable candidate—Kingu, who had remained under lock and key since Tiamat's defeat.

In one last major act, Marduk divides the gods into two realms—those who will reside in the heavens, and those who will reside on the earth, thus arranging the pantheon and his realm. The gods, in honor of Marduk, decide to construct him a shrine; he instead tells them to construct the great city of Babylon. In the city, the gods build the *Esagila*, the Temple to Marduk, and make it an earthly abode for Marduk, Enki, and Enlil.

CHAPTER 8
THE MYTH OF ADAPA

The Myth of Adapa is the Mesopotamian myth explaining why humans are mortal. It tells of Adapa, the first man created by Enki, being tricked into declining the gift of immortality. A comparison can be made to the story of Adam and Eve in Genesis when Yahweh banished the pair before they could eat from the Tree of Life. The myth is believed to have originated in the Babylonian Kassite period, and was retold in the third century BCE by Berossus, who used the name Oannes in place of Adapa.

Adapa, the first man created by Enki, the god of wisdom, is a man of many qualities. The great god has seen fit to endow him with great wisdom and intelligence, strength, and bravery, and yet has left him mortal.

One day, Adapa is fishing in the gulf when a strong southerly wind caused his boat to capsize. Adapa is hurled into the ocean, and, spluttering and choking on the salty water, rages at the south wind, breaking its wings so that it can no longer blow. Anu, the sky god, is furious and sends for Adapa, demanding the man explain himself.

Before heading to confront Anu, Adapa is taken aside by Enki, who counsels him on how to behave before the gods. Enki was the father of men, and as such, Adapa trusted him more than any other, listening intently to Enki's advice.

"Firstly," Enki tells him, "you must flatter Tammuz and Gishida, the guardians at the gates. Tell them you remember them from another time, that you are familiar with their names and importance. This will please the guardians, and they will speak favorably of you to great Anu.

"When you come into the presence of Anu, you must refuse all food and drink you are offered. The food that Anu offers you will be the food of death, a punishment for your transgressions against the south wind. That said, you must accept any oil to anoint yourself with, and any clothing that is offered to you."

Adapa is sure to do exactly what Enki tells him. He honors both Tammuz and Gishida respectfully at the door, and, while anointing himself and accepting a robe, declines all food he is offered. Anu asks him to explain his actions, and Adapa does, admitting he acted rashly and out of anger.

However, Adapa does not realize he has been tricked; for Enki feared that Anu may offer Adapa the food of eternal life, and having made Adapa wise and brave already, had to ensure his creation remained tethered somehow, unable to rise and challenge him. As such, Enki had deceived Adapa, convincing him to decline the food he was offered, and as such ensuring that humans would never gain immortality. Anu, perplexed by Adapa's refusal to eat the food of life, sends the man back to earth to live out his life as a mortal.

Anu meant no harm to Adapa, and in his offering of the food to Adapa, had been attempting to find a solution to one of the fundamental existential questions of life: if you are born only to die, and you live knowing you will soon die, what point is there to living? The remainder of this tale is too damaged to recount, but it appears that Anu, Enki's father, summons his son and chastises him for deceiving Adapa and preventing him from tasting the food of life.

CHAPTER 9
THE MYTH OF ETANA

According to the Sumerian King List, Etana reigned as the king of Kish early in the third millennium BCE. Etana was a well-known and respected individual and was likely chosen as the main character of this myth for that very reason. The myth's central message is one of piety, of loving, and of obeying the gods. While the date of composition is unknown, the British Museum holds fragments of the myth dated from Ashurbanipal's Library, almost certainly a late copy of the original story.

Shortly following the emergence of order from chaos, and the birth of humanity, the gods created the great city of Kish. Having built magnificent walls to protect the inhabitants of the city from the dangers outside, the gods select a king from among the people. Etana is chosen as king by the goddess

Ishtar, and he immediately sets about building a shrine to the god Adad.

Beside the shrine, there grows a poplar, and within the poplar tree, an eagle and a snake make their homes. The two creatures both swear an oath of loyalty before the sun god, Shamash, promising to watch over one another, to watch over the other's children. This is a fruitful arrangement, and both the eagle and the serpent live in comfort and happiness until, one day, while the snake is out looking for food, the eagle consumes his children, breaking his oath.

The snake returns home from his hunt to find his nest destroyed and his children gone. Around the nest, the footprints and feathers of an eagle lie scattered, and the snake makes the obvious conclusion. Lifting his head to the sky, he calls to the sun god, crying out for justice.

Shamash, far above, takes pity on the snake. He tells the snake to hide inside the carcass of a wild beast and wait for the eagle to arrive to feed. When the eagle arrives, the snake is instructed to seize him, pluck his features, sever his wings, and toss him into a pit. The snake does as Shamash instructs, and soon the eagle lies broken at the bottom of the pit, punished for the breaking of his oath sworn before the sun god.

At the bottom of the pit, the eagle looks up to the sky and cries out to Shamash. Shamash looks down upon the eagle with pity, and he tells the eagle, "what you did was a terrible thing. You broke your word, a sacred oath sworn before me. But I will have mercy on you, and I will send Etana, the king of Kish, to help you."

It is no coincidence that Etana himself was, at that very moment, also petitioning Shamash. Etana had learned his wife was barren, and he feared dying without an heir to the throne. Shamash tells Etana to go to the pit and rescue the eagle. Upon retrieving the eagle, Etana nurses the bird back to health, and the two grow close.

While Etana nurses him back to health, the eagle repays the king's kindness by interpreting his dreams. In one dream, Etana ascends to the heavens riding upon an eagle and is offered the plant of birth by Ishtar, who had been the one to select him as king. The eagle concludes that this dream is a message, an instruction for them to attempt this very journey.

His wings stronger, and his feathers having grown back, the eagle carries Etana into the sky.

Clutching tightly to the underbelly of the eagle, Etana is carried so high that when he looks down, he can no longer see the city, or in fact the entire earth. Etana grows afraid, and cries out to the eagle: "I cannot see the land, nor can I see the sea! We are up so high! Please, my friend, I do not want to go to heaven. Return me to my city!" Etana, so desperate to return to the safety of solid ground, lets go of the eagle and plummets. The eagle, shocked, dives after Etana and manages to catch him before he hits the earth. The two of them decide it is probably best if they return to the city.

Shortly after their return, both Etana and his wife begin to have similar dreams. The eagle, interpreting the dreams once again, tells Etana that the gods wish him to make a second attempt, to once again ascend heavenward. Harnessing every ounce of courage, Etana clings to the eagle, and they ascend, and this time they reach heaven without incident.

Unfortunately, the tablets we have uncovered are cut off at this point. It is understood, based on the Sumerian King List, that Etana had a son, Balikh, who succeeded him and reigned for 1,500 years. As a result, it is fair to assume they were greeted warmly by the gods, and that Ishtar gifted Etana the Plant of Birth, with which he and his wife were able to conceive a son.

CHAPTER 10
THE ATRAHASIS MYTH

*T*he Atrahasis Myth tells of the great flood unleashed upon the earth by the gods. The story itself is very similar to the flood story in the Epic of Gilgamesh, only in this edition it is not Utnapishtim, but Atrahasis, who builds the ark. It is also almost identical to an older story, the Eridu Genesis, of which we have only uncovered fragments. In real life, the flood itself was likely caused by natural, local events, but the tale shows it being of epic proportions. The Atrahasis Myth was likely written sometime in the 17th century BCE, during the reign of Hammurabi's great-grandson Ammi-Saduqa.

Following the creation of the earth, but before the first human beings, the gods work on the land, digging out the Euphrates and Tigris river beds, laying the foundations for cities. However, the younger of the gods begin to rebel against this intense labor, and so Enki, the god of wisdom, decides to create a new race of creatures who will do the work for them. The god We-Ilu offers himself up as a sacrifice, and the goddess Nintu mixes his body and mind with clay to create seven male and seven female humans.

The creation of humanity is a huge relief to the gods, who no longer need to labor long hours, leaving the work instead to their new servants. In time, however, the people grow too loud, always shouting and fighting and singing, preventing the gods from sleeping. Enlil, the supreme god, finds it particularly irritating, and decides something must be done.

Looking down at their creation, the gods consider what to do. The humans had clearly been of great use, but it was clear now that their creation had been a mistake. Enlil proposes a cull, lowering the population below by unleashing drought, disease, and famine upon the earth.

This does not have the desired effect. Instead of lessening their noise, the disasters sent by Enlil only serve to make the humans louder. They cry up to the gods, and to Enki in particular, to relieve their suffering. Enki offers guidance, but Enlil's patience has worn thin, and so he persuades the other gods to join him in summoning a terrible flood to wipe humanity from the earth.

Enki looks down at the humans, his creation, and feels pity for them. He knows he cannot save them all, so he descends to the earth and warns Atrahasis, a kind, loyal, and wise man, of the impending flood.

"Build an enormous ark," he tells Atrahasis, "and within it, bring two of every animal. Only this way will life be preserved."

Atrahasis does as he is bid, and no sooner than he completes his work, the great clouds gather in the sky, and the deluge pours across the land. The storm is terrible, and even the gods are afraid, and they weep as they look down upon the terrible destruction and suffering. As the sky clears, even Enlil, who had proposed the flood, realizes his mistake. He is repentant, wishing he had never brought such a terrible catastrophe upon the people below. He knows, however, that what is done is done, and that there is no way to undo it.

It is at this point that Atrahasis, far below, finds land and opens his ark. Having witnessed such a humbling ordeal, and eternally grateful to the gods for his family's survival, he immediately sends up a sacrifice to the heavens. Enlil is caught off guard, confused as to how there could be sacrifices still ascending even after he had just killed off all the humans.

Enki comes forth and explains himself before the gods. At first, Enlil is furious, and despite his prior regret, he berates Enki for going behind his back. Enki proposes a new solution to the problem, however, one that will prevent the population of humans from ever growing too great again.

"We will create new humans," he says, "humans that are not as fertile as the last. We can prevent them from overpopulating by creating women who cannot bear children, others who will remain virgins and spend their lives in the temples. We will bring forth demons who will steal infants away, who will cause miscarriages. This way, we will never need to worry about the humans growing too noisy, and we can live our lives in peace."

The gods all agree that this is a fantastic plan, and so set about creating their new race of humans. The new humans populate the world below, inhabiting the ruins of the cities and building them up to their former glory. Atrahasis, however, is taken by the gods and lifted away to a new paradise, far from the new race of humans, where he lives in peace and comfort for eternity.

CHAPTER 11
THE EPIC OF GILGAMESH

The Epic of Gilgamesh is the best-known ancient Mesopotamian epic and tells the story of the mythical king of Uruk, Gilgamesh, and his quest for immortality. The tale was no doubt shared orally at first, and as a result, it is difficult to date the original work. That said, numerous copies have been unearthed over the last two centuries, with the most complete version being told over 12 clay tablets and dating from around the 12-10th century BCE. The original epic is told over about 1,950 lines.

Gilgamesh, king of the city of Uruk, is a man of the greatest wisdom, bravery, and strength. One-third human, two-thirds god, Gilgamesh constructed the great walls of his city to keep enemies and invaders out, and to protect his people from any threat. There is, however, one threat he is unable to protect them from—himself.

Despite his great qualities, Gilgamesh is an oppressive ruler. He exhausts the men of the city through tests of strength and forced labor, but the greatest of his crimes was that of the "lord's right" to sleep with brides on their wedding nights, a right that Gilgamesh enjoys to the detriment of his people. Upset and angry, his people cry out to the gods, desperate for release from their king's oppressive reign. Upon hearing the pleas of the Urukian people, the gods decide to create a man equal and yet opposite to Gilgamesh, to balance out his strength and put him in his place. The man they create is Enkidu, a 'wild-man' who lives out in the forests among the beasts, attacking shepherds and eating their sheep. The people of Uruk suffer as Enkidu consumes their livestock, uproots their game traps, and ruins their fields.

A plan is devised by which Enkidu could be tamed, transformed into a civilized man. A temple prostitute, Shamhat, is sent beyond the walls of Uruk to track down Enkidu and to tame him, for it was known that upon union with the temple prostitute, Enkidu will lose his wild nature and instead learn the ways of civilization. Shamhat finds Enkidu and seduces him, and after laying together for six days and seven nights, Enkidu discovers that the animals of the forest find his new behaviors to be strange and shun him.

Shamhat teaches him the common practices of civilization, and together the two of them return to the city of Uruk.

Upon their return to the city, Shamhat and Enkidu find Gilgamesh attending a wedding. It is, of course, Gilgamesh's right to bed the bride on her wedding night, and he had come for this very purpose. Upon learning of Gilgamesh's intentions, Enkidu is disgusted, demanding Gilgamesh forfeit his right to the bride. He blocks the bedchamber entrance and challenges Gilgamesh to a duel. Should Gilgamesh make it past Enkidu, he could enter the chamber and claim the woman; however, if Enkidu should defeat him, Gilgamesh must forfeit his right to new brides.

Gilgamesh accepts the challenge, and the two of them fight late into the night until eventually, Gilgamesh overcomes his rival, and Enkidu concedes. Despite his victory, Gilgamesh spares Enkidu's life and honors his wishes, forfeiting the right to sleep with the bride. They return to the palace as friends, and Gilgamesh follows Enkidu's lead by learning the virtues of mercy and humility, working hard to be a more reasonable ruler for his people. In time, the two of them grow very close, becoming almost inseparable.

Many years pass and Gilgamesh grows bored and lazy. Seeking new adventures, he suggests the two of them should travel to the Cedar Forest and defeat the great beast, Humbaba. Humbaba is said to be part demon, part ogre, and is the protector of the Cedar Forest. While Enkidu objects to the plan at first, he finds it is impossible to change Gilgamesh's mind and eventually agrees to join him on the adventure.

The two of them set off across the desert, but each night Gilgamesh finds himself experiencing terrible nightmares. In one, he sees Enkidu lying still on a bed, unmoving; in another, he sees a giant stone monster, clasping Gilgamesh around the waist, squeezing him. Gilgamesh confides in Enkidu, who offers encouragement, assuring him that the dreams are merely signs of their victory. It means that they will return home safely, he explains, and that Gilgamesh's legacy will be lifted to the heavens.

Arriving at the Cedar Forest, Enkidu and Gilgamesh proceed to cut down the surrounding trees. The loud sound of falling trees quickly attracts the attention of Humbaba, who attacks the two men. A great battle ensues, during which Gilgamesh bribes the creature, offering his sisters to Humbaba as wives, in an attempt to trick Humbaba into giving up its layers of armor. Finally, Gilgamesh is victorious. The monster, clinging to life, begs mercy of Gilgamesh, who falters, uncertain of how to proceed. Seeing Gilgamesh's uncertainty, Humbaba takes the chance to curse the two men, and so Gilgamesh kills it.

The two men cut down the tallest tree of the forest, and from it, they construct a magnificent gate to set in the walls of Uruk. Cutting down several other trees, they lash the trunks together to form a raft and use it to carry their great gate downriver toward Uruk.

Upon their return, Ishtar, goddess of love and war, daughter of the sky god Anu, expresses sexual desire for Gilgamesh, but Gilgamesh rejects her advances. Ishtar is taken aback, upset, and offended, and so convinces her father to send the Bull of Heaven down the Uruk to punish Gilgamesh for shaming her. With the Bull comes great plague, a famine which sweeps across the land, and terrible drought. Enkidu and Gilgamesh, worried for their people, fight and slay the bull, offering its heart to the god Shamash, and bringing the plague and drought to an end.

As the city celebrates the great victory of their ruler and his right-hand man, Enkidu falls unwell and begins to suffer from nightmares, not unlike Gilgamesh had done on their way to the Cedar Forest. In the nightmares, the gods curse Enkidu for the killing of the Bull and Humbaba, the demon-ogre of the forest. Enkidu, afraid, curses the day he met Shamhat, wishing he had instead remained in the forest, where he could have avoided the curse of the gods.

As he dies, Gilgamesh remains beside his bed, watching over him. He listens as Enkidu tells him of the House of Dust, the underworld where the dead are clad in feathers, eat stone, and where no light ever shines. He tells of the skulls of kings in enormous piles. Upon his death, Enkidu leaves Gilgamesh terrified and distraught. Gilgamesh, deep in mourning, begs the gods to allow him to walk beside Enkidu in the afterlife. He stays beside the corpse, unmoving, wretched, until Enkidu's body begins to decay and has to be taken away.

Without his friend, Gilgamesh falls into depression, terrified of the afterlife Enkidu had described as he died. He vows to never enter the House of Dust, and so sets out to find Utnapishtim and his wife, the only humans ever granted immortality by the gods.

Gilgamesh sets out from Uruk, battling great monsters and overcoming terrible odds, and eventually reaches Mt. Mashu, the twin peaks at the end of the earth, where he finds the path blocked by two great scorpions. They laugh at Gilgamesh, telling him he cannot hope to achieve his goal and that immortality is impossible, but he convinces them of his desperation, and so they let him pass regardless. Gilgamesh continues beyond the mountain to a great tunnel through which the sun travels at the end of each day. Entering the tunnel, Gilgamesh treks for 12 leagues before finally emerging in a beautiful paradise.

As he wanders through the paradise, taking in the sights, Gilgamesh stumbles upon the wine-maker Siduri. Siduri, seeing his disheveled appearance, mistakes him for a murderer or a thief, but Gilgamesh manages to explain himself, and she directs him to the ferryman, Urshanabi, though not without first reminding him of the pointlessness of his quest.

Upon reaching the water's edge, Gilgamesh finds his way blocked by two great stone monsters. Believing them to be a threat, he fights and slays them both. At this point, Urshanabi arrives, and informs Gilgamesh he has made a terrible mistake—the stone creatures he killed were the only beings in existence who could help them cross the Waters of Death, beyond which he would find Utnapishtim. To pass, Urshanabi tells him, he will need to cut down 120 trees and shape them into punting poles, for as each touches the water, it will dissolve.

Gilgamesh sets to work and has soon fashioned 120 trees into the poles required for the crossing. They set out, traveling through a thick, dark mist, and eventually arrive at a small island whereupon Utnapishtim and his wife live.

Gilgamesh drops to his knees before Utnapishtim and recounts his story, begging for his help in achieving immortality. Utnapishtim admonishes Gilgamesh, telling him that immortality would do little more than wiping the joy from one's life, that the inevitability of death was what gave life purpose and meaning. Gilgamesh, not to be put off, asks Utnapishtim how he gained immortality, and Utnapishtim tells Gilgamesh the story of the flood.

The gods had a secret council, he explains, and decided to send a terrible flood to earth to wipe out humanity. Enki, however, feared for humanity and so snuck down to the earth and found Utnapishtim, telling him to build a boat, upon which he would take his entire family, his craftsmen, and all the animals he could find. Utnapishtim set to work, and had soon built an enormous ark, in which his family and animals resided as the storm approached. Even the gods cowered in fear as the great black clouds rolled across the land, and for six days and nights, a terrible storm ensued, with water pouring across the earth in great waves. The storm finally subsided, and the boat struck a mountain, becoming lodged in the rocks. Utnapishtim sent out birds, and when they failed to return, he opened the boat and released all the animals onto the land. He made a sacrifice to the gods, and Enlil, realizing there had been a survivor, was enraged. He descended to strike Utnapishtim down, but Enki and Ishtar intervened, condemning his terrible flood, and Enlil saw reason. He instead decided to bless Utnapishtim and his wife, as the first people of a new world, with immortality.

And so, Utnapishtim explains, immortality was a special, one-time gift. It was not something that could be accessible to anybody who desired it, and nor should it be, for it was no less a curse than a blessing.

Upon hearing this tale, Gilgamesh remains determined. Utnapishtim decides to test Gilgamesh's resolve and challenges the king to remain awake for six days and seven nights. Gilgamesh, however, falls asleep almost immediately, and Utnapishtim asks his wife to bake a loaf of bread for each day he sleeps. Upon waking, Gilgamesh denies having slept at all, but Utnapishtim shows him the loaves of bread, each in a different state of decay, and explains that one was baked on each day that he slept. Seeking to overcome death, Gilgamesh was unable even to overcome sleep.

Utnapishtim sends Gilgamesh back across the Waters of Death, and exiles Urshanabi alongside him. Just as they are parting, however, he takes pity on Gilgamesh and tells him of a plant in the deepest part of the ocean which, when one consumes it, will make him young once again. Intrigued, Gilgamesh travels to the ocean and ties rocks to his feet, descending to the depths in search of the plant. He finds it, and upon returning to the surface decides to test it on an old man when he returns to Uruk, so as not to unwittingly poison himself.

Unfortunately, as they travel toward the great city, Gilgamesh leaves the plant unguarded for a time and a snake consumes it. Gilgamesh finds the plant gone, and the snake has shed its skin, and so realizes that not only did the plant work but that he had just lost his one last chance at immortality. Weeping, he returns to Uruk with Urshanabi, and before its walls he drops to his knees, praising the immense walls of Uruk as his greatest achievement. He realizes, kneeling in the dust before his city, that eternal life is not a natural path for men, and that the walls, his greatest achievement, will stand for centuries after his death, thus preserving his name and legacy for eternity. It is not eternal life, he explains to Urshanabi, but eternal legacy, leaving a mark on the world, that grants a person true immortality.

It is here that the Epic of Gilgamesh ends, although in some cases a 12th tablet has been uncovered, apparently added at some point later and telling of events that appear to have no direct link to the original epic itself. In this additional tablet, Enkidu is once again alive, and Gilgamesh sends him down into the underworld to retrieve lost possessions. While in the underworld, Enkidu makes a series of mistakes that result in him being trapped, but Gilgamesh appeals to Enki and Shamash, who open up the earth and allow Enkidu to go free.

CHAPTER 12
THE DESCENT OF INANNA

*T*he Descent of Inanna is a Sumerian poem, written sometime around 1900-1600 BCE. The story tells of Inanna, Queen of Heaven, traveling from the sky down into the underworld to visit Ereshkigal, her sister, whose husband had recently died. The story is one of injustice and the unfairness of life, with Inanna's bad choices leading to the suffering of others.

Inanna, clad in her finest clothes, the crown of heaven shining brightly upon her head, stands before the gates of the underworld. Pausing before she enters, she turns to her faithful servant Ninshubur, and imparts instructions on how to rescue her, should she fail to return. Ninshubur bows his head respectfully, and Inanna steps forward, knocking loudly on the ancient gates.

Behind the gates, Neti, the gatekeeper, appears and demands to know who seeks entrance to the underworld.

"It is I," she answers. "Inanna, Queen of Heaven."

Neti frowns.

"Why would you want to enter a land from which none return?"

"Because," she replies, "My sister Ereshkigal has been widowed. Her husband, Gugalanna, has died, and I have come for the funeral."

Neti asks Inanna to wait while he consults Ereshkigal. Upon learning of her sister's arrival, Ereshkigal seems uncomfortable, falling silent for a long time. Eventually, she tells Neti to bolt the seven gates dealing into the underworld, and then let Inanna in one gate at a time, removing a royal garment for each she passes.

Neti does as he is bid, and he allows Inanna to enter the underworld. At each gate, he requests she remove a garment or item. She first removes her crown, her beads, her ring, and her scepter. Even her clothing is removed, and by the time she enters the last gate, Inanna is entirely naked. She turns on Neti, demanding an explanation for this undignified treatment.

"Do not question the ways of the underworld," he replies. "They are perfect."

Inanna enters the throne room and bows before Ereshkigal, bare and humbled. As she approaches the throne to speak to her sister, the underworld's judges, the Annuna, quickly surround her, holding her in place. Together, they pass judgment upon Inanna, for it was she who caused the death of Gugalanna, the Bull of Heaven, for she had sent him down against the king of Uruk, Gilgamesh, after he had spurned her advances, and Gugalanna had been killed.

Ereshkigal bears down upon Inanna, cursing her for her selfishness, proclaiming her guilt. She strikes her sister, killing her, and mounts her corpse from a hook on the wall.

Meanwhile, Ninshubur had been waiting for his mistress to return. When three nights and three days have passed, Ninshubur ascends to heaven and seeks Enki, Inanna's father, begging for help. Enki, worried about his daughter, sends two *galla*, creatures neither male nor female, down into the earth to find Inanna. The two *galla* enter the underworld as if flies. As they approach Ereshkigal, the Queen of the Underworld begins to suffer greatly, experiencing pains as if in childbirth. The *galla* express their sympathy for her pain, and the Queen, grateful, offers them a gift of their choosing.

"We want nothing more than the corpse that hangs from the wall," they tell her, and she gives it to them willingly. The *galla*, having found Inanna, resuscitate her with the food of life, and she rises from the dead.

Leaving the underworld, however, is not easily done. Having entered the realm of Ereshkigal, one can only depart if their place is taken by another. The *galla* ascend with Inanna and try to find a substitute for her, first seeking Ninshubur, and then her sons Shara and Lulal. Inanna, however, is having none of it, for Ninshubur and her sons are dressed in the clothing of mourning, believing her to be dead.

When she comes across Dumuzi, her lover, she finds him dressed in rich clothing and jewels. Inanna, hurt and angered that he is not mourning her as are the others, demands the *galla* seize him as her substitute in the underworld. Dumuzi, panic-stricken, appeals to the god Utu and is turned into a snake. He tries to slip away but is caught, and carried into the underworld to remain forever. Before he can arrive, however, the *galla* are stopped by his sister, Geshtinanna, who volunteers to share his fate, each spending half a year in the underworld and half a year in the heavens. It was by this bi-annual cycling that the seasons were created, as Geshtinanna was the goddess of agriculture and fertility, and could bless the earth for only half the year. Inanna, meanwhile, returned happily to her old life in the heavens, most probably unrepentant for the suffering she had inflicted upon those around her.

CHAPTER 13
THE CURSE OF AGADE

The Curse of Agade (Akkad) dates back to the Neo-Sumerian period and tells of the Akkadian king Naram-Sin and his confrontation with displeased gods. Naram-Sin was considered to be one of the greatest Akkadian rulers, and while the text appears to offer a mythological explanation for the collapse of Akkad and the empire, the king was likely chosen more for name recognition than because any of the events were true. If anything, it is probable that his successors were the true inspiration for the tale. The text focuses on the relationship between kings and gods, and warns about the consequences of impious behavior.

The great city of Akkad is the center of the world. Ruled by the magnificent Naram-Sin, the descendant of Sargon himself, the gates of Akkad are constantly flowing with wealth, taxes and tribute, gems and treasures. However, upon seeing the riches pouring into Akkad, the goddess Inanna (later Ishtar) feels that she and the other gods ought to be honored by those in the city—temples should be built, festivals held, sacrifices offered.

The supreme god Enlil does not agree. Enlil had destroyed Kish and placed the great Sargon on the throne of Akkad, leaving the goddess Inanna to watch over him and the city. However, now that Naram-Sin is king, Enlil is no longer pleased with the city, for what reasons, he will not say. He instructs the gods to withdraw from the city and no longer offer blessings to its inhabitants.

Naram-Sin, king of Akkad, dreams of a grim future for his city and empire. He sees cities burned to rubble, he sees floods and famine and invaders from outside lands. Naram-Sin decides to enter a period of mourning and prayer lasting seven years, waiting for the gods to offer counsel. However, no gods come to Naram-Sin, and, fearing for the future of his people and city, he decides he must do something to draw their attention.

Naram-Sin marches on the city of Ekur, the home of Enlil, and he puts the temple to the flame. The house of Enlil is turned to rubble, the inside on display for all to see. This act is the worst of transgressions, the greatest desecration possible. So great had been Naram-Sin's anger that he had turned to vandalizing the house of the supreme god. The other gods now come to Enlil's side—he may have been unreasonable before, but Naram-Sin's actions were unforgivable. The king had entered into a battle he could not possibly hope to win, and he was to suffer the greatest of punishments. As the empire is overrun by famine and foreign invaders, Enlil curses Akkad, driving out all who lived within its walls and leaving it barren. Naram-Sin had, at the cost of thousands of lives, learned his lesson—one must never turn his back on the gods.

CONCLUSION

On October 3rd, 1932, Iraq shed the chains of British rule and gained independence. While perhaps lost on many, the significance of this moment was immense. This was the first time in 2,470 years (to the month) that Mesopotamia gained independent rule. From the conquest of Babylon by Cyrus in October 539 BCE, Mesopotamia had been reduced to a client state or province for numerous successive empires and powers. Following the fall of Persepolis to Alexander the Great, Mesopotamia became Hellenic; it was subsequently fought over by the Seleucids, the Romans, the Parthians, the Byzantines and Sassanids, the Muslims and Mongols, until eventually coming under the rule of the Ottomans. When the Ottomans fell in the 1920s, the British held sway over the Mesopotamians. Come 1932, they were, at long last, free.

It seems fitting that Mesopotamia gain its independence again at this time. The fall of Babylon to Cyrus represented the transition from the ancient era to the modern, from the age of the Near East to that defined by Hellenism, Roman expansionism, Islam and Christianity, the west and the east. It is the era we live in to this day, but it is also an era that is slowly drawing to a close.

From the founding of Eridu in the sixth millennium BCE to the fall of Babylon in the first, the story of Mesopotamia spans almost 5,000 years—double the time that has passed since its fall. It is a length of time that is almost impossible to comprehend, especially in a world that is advancing exponentially. But the same changes we see in Mesopotamians near the end of their era are rearing their heads in our own time—a profound uncertainty about the future, a growing obsession with the past, and the dramatic development of a new culture and language—a digital revolution, an entirely new way of looking at the world that far surpasses the cultural changes following the introduction of the Aramaic alphabet during the Assyrian period.

As such, the lessons of the past have never been more relevant. Despite the yawning chasm of time between their time and our own, there are certain things about human psychology that have not changed, and our responses to change will surely be similar to those of our ancestors, two and a half millennia ago. As we look back at the past from a great distance, we can see its sweeping patterns, the paths, and connections that one could never hope to see when immersed in their own time.

From nomadic groups and agricultural communities dotted along the banks of the Tigris and the Euphrates, a culture and civilization as yet unsurpassed emerged. The advances they made, from simple baked-brick cities to towering ziggurats; from flimsy, local theocracies to semi-totalitarian communist states and sweeping military empires; from simple, recited tales to sweeping epics and great myths which explored the nature of the world, the place of humans in it, and laid the foundation for the Greeks and Romans that followed; technology, law, education, mathematics, science; the Mesopotamians laid the foundation for the entirety of human civilization as we know it today. Without the contributions of the Sumerians, Akkadians, Babylonians, and Assyrians, we would never have reached the heights we have. We owe everything to that civilization, many thousands of years ago.

They were a civilization of immense creativity, innovation, and longevity. Empires rose and fell, cities were reduced to rubble, but the culture itself continued, inherited by locals and newcomers alike, each carrying the torch for future generations. When disaster struck, the Mesopotamians returned to their smaller cities and clung to their culture as if their lives depended upon it. When they found glory, they spread their beliefs and knowledge across the known world, with a reach and influence beyond any contemporary. They were a truly multicultural society, providing a template, and perhaps a lesson, to those of us today who are divided by ethnic, social, and national differences. Without the interaction and co-operation of so many ethnicities and backgrounds, their civilization could never have flourished as it did.

It was, from one perspective, not only the earliest but also the greatest civilization in history. It is an immeasurable tragedy that the stories, the history, the names of great *Lugal* and emperors, are known by so few today. The culture of Mesopotamia is not one we can afford to lose, and its memory is important now more than ever before. History repeats itself, forming great, arcing patterns imprinted across the canvas of time, and we still have so much more to learn from the ancient past. As we piece together their stories, and as we come to understand their principles, practices, and beliefs, we can slowly but surely bring history to life.

ROMAN EMPIRE

RISE & THE FALL. EXPLORE THE HISTORY, MYTHOLOGY, LEGENDS, EPIC BATTLES & THE LIVES OF THE EMPERORS, LEGIONS, HEROES, GLADIATORS & MORE

HISTORY BROUGHT ALIVE

INTRODUCTION

Author Bio

History Brought Alive is a company that specializes in writing expertly crafted works on ancient world history and mythology. The books we write are informative, factual, and ideal for anyone wanting to learn more about the past and the world we live in. Our books aim to teach the eager reader, to open your mind, and to challenge your assumptions about history in ways you never thought of before. This book is a timeless reference you will want to use over and over! These lovingly constructed works are written to endure. The legacy they produce will last through the ages and entertain, satisfy and empower generations of readers.

Roma Victrix

In AD 27, an empire was born. A tiny settlement on the banks of the Tiber River developed and grew into a colossal, unstoppable force, a power unrivaled in the ancient world. At its peak, the Roman Empire dominated the world from continental Europe, Britain, Western Asia, North Africa, and many other territories. Modern language, religion, culture, and way of life all sprang forth from this empire. "SPQR" was the motto of the Roman Empire: *Senatus Populusque Romanus* (meaning the Senate and the Roman people). This motto stood for the entirety and inevitability of the Roman state, the two aspects of her greatness: both her people and her government (or Senate). Rome's greatness was not only evident in her military might, but also in her technological advancements, her progressive way of life, and her hegemony over the cultures of the world. At that time, Rome was at the forefront of the advancement of civilization, and her rule was total.

The study of Roman history is vast and complex. We can break the study of Ancient Rome into different areas that will make it easier to analyze. Much like the Ancient Romans themselves, to study this civilization, we have to adhere to the principles of order, structure, and discipline. First, we have the timeline of Roman history. How did it all begin? What were the factors that led to the rise and founding of Rome? What were the factors that led to its eventual decline? Important events are easier to understand if they are enumerated in chronological order. We can view the most important events in Roman history as they occurred, and we can easily see the context surrounding these events.

Next, we have the lay of the land itself. What was Rome built on, literally? What was the topography and geography of Ancient Rome? Important topics to consider when thinking about the geography of Ancient Rome are the way the mountains surrounding the city played a role in its development. These terrain features weren't only used for the defense of the city and the empire; how the Ancient Romans used the environment also played a role in their development as a civilization. The geography of the region itself was inextricably linked to the culture and the history of the empire.

The characters of Ancient Rome made it what it is, a political and social theatre of intrigue. Much of Roman life centered around the figures in authority at that time. Any serious study has to begin with a look at the emperors themselves. Not only that, but what has to be examined is also the way in which the Senate played its role in the empire. Beyond the nature of government in Ancient Rome, there are the playwrights, wordsmiths, scholars, poets, philosophers, warriors, and the ordinary men and women who made up the empire. Every single one of these people shows a different aspect of Ancient Rome as a whole. They are a microcosm of what the society must have been like, and their stories are fascinating to behold. The beating heart of Ancient Rome was its people.

How did Romans survive in everyday life? Roman life became amongst the most advanced of any civilization anywhere in the world. Rome was the educated world, the civilized world and the beacon of light people saw in an otherwise dark and uncivilized society. Rome survived because it implemented a way of life that was successful for everyone in the society at the time. The rigidity of the society as a whole bred a sense of duty and patriotism towards the empire and to Rome herself. People knew what was expected of them on any given day. Loyalty was the currency of the realm. The Roman way of life was structured in such a way that the civilization as a whole, thrived and grew.

When people think of Rome, they think about the military first and foremost; and with good reason. The Roman military was amongst the most powerful in the world. How did they get that way? From a small army of men to one of the greatest fighting forces the world has ever seen, the Roman army was the gold standard for centuries because of their discipline, dedication, ruthlessness, and skill. Backed up by a thorough training regimen, Roman soldiers were considered to be amongst the best in the world at what they did. And what they did was to conquer the known world and spill blood. The process of how they developed into this fighting force is a fascinating journey to discover.

Roman mythology contains a plethora of fascinating and complex characters. Just as the Greeks had their pantheon of gods, so the Romans had their own pantheon. Every aspect of society was covered by a specific god. The leader of the pantheon of their gods was known as *Jupiter* or *Jove*. Other notable Roman gods include Minerva, Juno, and Mars. The name "pantheon" is borrowed from the Greek name for a collection of gods in a culture.

The way of the Roman Empire did not last. Due to numerous issues, the empire eventually fell due to poor governance, a weakened military, and outside influence from barbarian invaders. The fall of the Roman Empire in the West led to the Dark and Middle Age periods of which few written records remain.

Roman history is a journey of discovery, and it needs to be approached with an open mind. By doing so, we can begin to unlock the secrets of the empire and what it meant in the context of world history.

CHAPTER 1
TIMELINE

The Three Periods of Ancient Rome

Roman civilization can be divided into three distinct periods. These periods encompass the complete progression of the empire, from its birth in 700 BC, to its decline and fall in around 600 AD. The names of these periods are disputed amongst historians. According to *The Roman Empire: A Brief History* (n.d), the three periods (apart from the founding itself) are the Period of Kings, Republican Rome, and Imperial Rome.

The Founding of Rome

According to *This Day In History* (n.d) there are two versions of the founding of Rome: one mythological, or legendary, version and one historical account. According to mythology, Rome was founded by Romulus and Remus on the Tiber River in about the 7th century AD. The origin of the exact date of Rome's founding can be attributed to Roman scholar Marcus Terentius Varro in the 1st century.

The Legend

Legend holds that Romulus and Remus were twin sons of the mythical figure Rhea Silvia, the daughter of King Numitor. Silvia and Numitor lived in Alba Longa, a city in the Alban Hills, situated southeast of Rome itself. Numitor was deposed by his younger sibling Amulius. The evil Amulius tried to force Rhea Silvia to become a vestal virgin, thus depriving her of the ability to have sons who could one day challenge him for the throne. However, Mars, the god of war, impregnated Rhea Silvia and she gave birth to twin sons Romulus and Remus. While the villainous King Amulius ordered the babies to be killed by drowning them in the Tiber River, they survived and were later found and suckled by the she-wolf at the foot of Palatine hill. A shepherd, Faustulus, then rescued them, or so the story goes. Faustulus raised the boys until they became hardy and strong. Forming a band of warriors with other men, they attacked Alba Longa and killed Amulius, passing the throne back to their grandfather while establishing a town on the banks of the river where they were discovered. However, things did not end well for the family. Some time later, Romulus and Remus had a disagreement, and Remus was killed in the scuffle. Romulus then took over the settlement on the river and named it after himself, Rome.

How Rome Was Born

As legend suggests, Rome was indeed founded on the banks of the Tiber River in 700 BC. According to Joshua J. Mark (2009), Rome began as a small town that grew in strength and stature. She was ruled by seven kings for a period of about 200 years. Having observed the nearby Greek way of life, the small tribe began to mimic the neighboring society's improvements in culture and architecture. The Roman tribe looked at the stronger Etruscans of the north and noted their lifestyle and technological advances. Etruria was already a well-established settlement and seemed to have a significant impact on the development of the Roman settlement at this time. The positioning of Rome to the river meant that trade could flourish, agriculture growth thrived, and water was readily available. This mirrors how the mighty Egyptian Empire itself had come to be many, many thousands of years earlier - by relying on the strength of the Nile River. As Rome grew stronger, she came into contact with neighboring settlements. From her earliest years, she proved to be great at learning from the tribes around her, and by around 600 BC, she was a thriving and prosperous city. A tiny town no more, the seeds of what would eventually become the mighty kingdom of Rome had already been sown. In around 500 BC, the last of the seven kings of Rome was deposed, namely, Tarquin the Proud. A man named Lucius Junius Brutus then abolished the monarchy and established the very first Roman Republic.

Expansion

Rome had yet to realize the full potential of her military might in the earliest years of the empire, although it was beginning to show signs of branching away from trade and towards a more expansionist mindset. According to Wasson (2016), "the history of the city is mired in stories of valor and war." After the fall of Tarquin the Proud, the last king of Rome, the rest of the 5th century BC was marked by struggle. Many significant events were to shape the growth of the realm. After the fall of the monarchy in 509, little is known about the next 70 years, as few written records survive. The city was starting to become the dominating force on much of the Italian peninsula, but it was not without sacrifice. Other neighboring tribes noted the lack of leadership and control over the city itself, and they sought to besiege it.

According to *Roman Republic (509 BC - 27 BC)* (n.d), many people within the city itself were divided between wanting to return to the monarchy and wanting to remain a republic, which led to conflict within the republic itself. Rome had to contend with neighboring tribes who wanted to put an end to the fledgling state, threatened by her dominance. Notable battles at this point included the Pyrrhic Wars, the battle of Regallus, and conflicts against Greece, the Samnites, and the Etruscans themselves.

The legal system of Ancient Rome was beginning to be established, and the seeds were being sown for what would later become the mightiest empire the world has ever known. In 450 BC, the Law of the Twelve Tables was drafted (in Latin, Lex XII Tabularum). This is amongst the earliest iterations of Roman law, and it laid out how citizens were to be treated, with both fairness and equality. These bronze tablets formed the foundation for future Roman legal doctrine. According to *The Twelve Tables* (n.d), the tablets contained statutes for all kinds of legal situations, from public laws to matters of justice. The codification of these tablets was a sign that Rome was moving towards a more structured form of society, one that would endure through the ages.

The Seeds of the Empire

By the time 27 BC arrived, Rome was advanced both technologically and in terms of its civilization and society. Rome was ready to become an empire. But, to do so, Romans would need to expand and grow further and further. The republic was in political turmoil and there was unrest in the streets, namely at the battle of Gallia Aquitania, wherein General Agrippa won a great victory over the rebels.

Many felt that Rome was about to fall due to this unrest created by the civil war between different factions within the republic. The Roman citizenry was falling victim to the corruption and vice that was plaguing the city (Wasson, 2016). A kind of evil was springing up caused by moral decay and reckless living. The event that eventually led to the formation, or transition, from republic to empire was the creation of the triumvirate, an alliance between three major figures in Roman history: Julius Caesar, Crassus, and Pompey, all of whom had agendas for ruling Rome. These three men took power away from the Senate and leveraged it to themselves. Because the Senate had been in charge of Rome when it was a republic, it was previously up to the Senate to decide the direction the government took and to oversee transitions of power, but the triumvirate severely weakened the Senate's role. This newfound dictatorial power gave the new triumvirate political leverage over the plebeians (or, common folk). Over time, one of these men would grow more influential than the others, and would eventually become a dictator over all of Rome. His name, of course, was Julius Caesar, the first of the great political figures in Ancient Rome, and probably the greatest Roman ruler who ever lived. At the time, though, the three men consented to put their differences aside and rule the fragmented Republic. The beginnings of this alliance had been sown many years earlier, however.

Caesar, Pompey, and Crassus

Ten years earlier, a man by the name of Spartacus, a gladiator from the arena, had led a rebellion through the streets of Southern Italy. The rebels' motivation was simple: they no longer wanted to be slaves. The revolt carried on for so long that the Senate sent Crassus to put down the uprising; however, he did not receive the due credit for doing so because Pompey, returning from Spain, had claimed the glory for crushing the rebellion himself. The two men continued to view each other with distrust, but both were named co-consuls in around 70 BC for their part in that victory over the rebels.

In 67 BC, Rome was facing a food shortage. Rampant piracy had meant that trade routes were being affected, and widespread shortages of precious resources resulted. Pompey was tasked with dealing with these pirates and also a man named Mithridates, ruler of the kingdom of Pontus who kept besieging Roman provinces. After Mithridates was defeated and the pirate threat was similarly extinguished, Rome enjoyed a period of relative calm. However, Pompey's campaigns in the Mediterranean were to fundamentally change the nature of the empire and redraw the map to the east of the empire. By the time he returned in 62 BC, Pompey's vision had changed, and he desired land for his military veterans. This was not to be forthcoming from the Senate, but it did highlight Pompey's agenda: to rule over a territory of his own.

What is clear is that each member of the triumvirate had their reasons for wanting to rule Rome. Pompey hoped for military glory and living space for his soldiers. Caesar wanted to attain the role of "Consul" and therefore a share in the ruling powers of Rome. Crassus desired to benefit financially and economically. Caesar was already a military man, having returned from Spain in triumph. He had something that the others lacked: charisma. However the three men might have felt about each other, they elected to remain as a three-pronged ruling party, keeping power away from the people and the Senate. Caesar succeeded in uniting Crassus and Pompey in an uneasy truce due to their differences of opinion on policy. In 59 BC, Caesar was elected Consul of Rome, one of the most powerful positions in the land, as it was the ruling head of the Senate. In this position, he was able to exert influence over the other two members of the triumvirate. He increased the number of members of the Senate to 900 and began to command the loyalty of the army itself. The Senate, now extremely fearful of Caesar's influence, ordered him to release command of the army, but Caesar refused.

The Rule of Caesar

Although Julius Caesar did not rule for a long time, his impact on the Roman world and the course of history cannot be denied. After his election to Consul, he attempted to consolidate his rule and expand the empire at the same time. One of his notable achievements was the conquest of Gaul in around 58 to 50 BC. Caesar was noted as being an astute and ruthless general, having been involved in the military all his life while in Spain. However, he had made many enemies during his time in the upper political echelons of Rome. What happened next was to further damage the fragile relationship between the triumvirate: Crassus was killed in the battle of Carrhae in 53 BC. This left the less popular Pompey and the immensely popular Caesar. By this time, Caesar was the sole Consul of Rome, and Pompey lived in Caesar's shadow. It was clear that there was only going to be one ruler of Rome and that Pompey would have to wait. Pompey grew increasingly jealous of Caesar and his increasing influence, and the relationship between the two men soured. Caesar then started a civil war in 49 BC, leading an army across the river Rubicon, going against the wishes of the Senate. In the years that followed, political resistance to Caesar's rule was swiftly extinguished and a period of relative stability followed. Caesar was now the sole dictator of Rome, unchallenged in terms of his power.

The Assassination of Caesar

Julius Caesar's rule did not last long. Despite the reforms that he had brought to Rome and the changes he had wrought in society, a group of his political enemies got together in March of 44 BC and assassinated him. It was a seemingly premature end to one of the world's great rulers. His legacy cannot be overstated. He ended the line of republican rulers, took power away from the Senate, expanded the empire greatly, introduced societal change, and introduced Rome to a new era: the era of the emperors. From this time forward until her eventual decline 400 years later, Rome would always be ruled by an emperor.

The Time of the Emperors

The Second Triumvirate

After Caesar's death, a new triumvirate was formed. When Caesar died, Marc Antony took over the leadership of the empire, but he still had to deal with Caesar's killers. To placate these men, an arrangement was made between Antony and the plotters of Caesar's downfall, Brutus and Cassius. They were made governors of provinces in the empire, but this angered Caesar's adopted son Octavian, according to *Second Triumvirate* (n.d). After stirring up several disgruntled Roman war veterans against Antony, Octavian attempted to lead a revolt at Modena. After defeating Antony in battle, Octavian returned to Rome and demanded to be made Consul - forming an alliance with none other than Antony himself. Backed up by another influential figure in what was once Caesar's army, Marcus Aemilius Lepidus, the three decided to form the new collective dictatorship of Rome. The three rulers collectively made decisions on behalf of Rome and made reforms to weaken the Senate, provide farmland for Caesar's soldiers, execute a slew of political opponents, and, at Phillipi, defeat the forces responsible for the plot to murder Caesar. Brutus and Cassius killed themselves during the battle.

Battle at Sicily

Enemies of the regime banded together at Sicily under the leadership of the son of Pompey, Sextus. In 36 BC, Sexus was defeated in battle at the battle at sea. This incident also led to the end of the triumvirate, as Lepidus was relieved of his powers after angering Octavian by demanding that Octavian leave Sicily. Half of Lepidus' army defected to Octavian's side, showing his influence. Five years later, Antony and Octavian went to war because Antony had fallen in love with the stunning Ptolemaic queen Cleopatra. Deciding that Antony was divided in his loyalty to the empire, Octavian attacked and defeated Antony with the help of the skilled general Agrippa. Octavian then assumed sole leadership of Rome, united the empire, and was considered one of Rome's greatest leaders until his death in 14 BC. In fact, his reforms lead to Rome becoming as powerful as she would ever be due to one small phrase: Pax Romana.

Pax Romana

With the quelling of the civil unrest, Rome had entered a new phase of world dominance. No more was she to be on the offensive. Rome was beginning to embrace the idea of consolidating its power in the lands that she already owned. The next 200 years were spent in peaceful imperialistic conquest, marked by fewer wars than there had been previously. The empire grew and was strengthened. Although there were a number of revolts, the Roman government was able to quell these incidents and keep the peace. Trade and industry with neighboring countries was enhanced. This period lasted until around 180 AD according to *The Pax Romana* (2021).

After the battle at Sicily, Octavian returned to Rome and set himself up as the sole ruler of the empire. However, he was careful not to flex his authority to the Senate as Julius Caesar had done, according to *The Pax Romana* (2021). He was careful to maintain a balance between his absolute power and the traditional structures of the republican government. The Senate took kindly to Octavian and bestowed the honorary title "Augustus" on him when he attempted to voluntarily give up his powers in 27 BC. The term Augustus means "the majestic one" in Latin. And Augustus certainly was a great ruler deserving of the name. In his 41 years as ruler of Rome, the empire experienced stability as it had not experienced before.

One of the key areas in which Rome became more and more powerful was in the field of technology. The discovery of concrete enabled them to build massively powerful buildings and structures and led to the formation of roads, which at that time were not the most developed part of any region's communication structures. The building of mighty monuments, such as the Pantheon, out of concrete solidified the idea that Roman culture was dominant. Such structures were symbols of the rule of law and order within the empire. Some of the greatest literary minds in world history were born during this period: the likes of Virgil, Ovid, Livy, and Horace.

One could say that the Roman way of life became entrenched in society, and, for much of the world, Rome was seen as the bastion of law, order, and civilization in the West. It was impossible to imagine the world without Rome. All was not perfect, however. The empire still had some growing pains. Not all emperors could be trusted.

Caligula

For example, one of the great tragedies in Roman history came after the death of Augustus in 14 AD. The emperor that came after him was the evil Caligula, a sadistic man who took pleasure in the sufferings of others. He was so awful that the Senate turned against him and had him executed in 41 AD by his own Praetorian guard.

Christianity in Ancient Rome

It is important to be aware of the social and political issues that Rome faced during her rise, development, and eventual decline as a world power. In an empire where loyalty to Caesar was seen as the highest honor a civilian could give, personal and religious views were sometimes seen as threats because they challenged the assumptions that Rome was built on - the notion that Caesar was a god and that Rome was all-powerful. Nowhere is this more clearly demonstrated than in the instance of the rise of Christianity as a popular belief system.

When the personal beliefs of citizens collided with their duty to Rome, there was often conflict between them. Founded by Jesus Christ and later expanded on by the Apostle Paul, the message of Christianity started spreading at around 40 AD. Despite attempts by the government to control it, the message continued to grow even to the furthest corners of the empire. This naturally caused a huge divide amongst the Christians of Rome (this was the name that the scornful Romans had given those who believed in the teachings of Christ), and the people who worshipped the local Roman deities. According to *Rome And Christianity* (2015), those who followed Christianity were frequently the poor and slaves. They were often badly treated and in 64 AD, the evil emperor of the time, Nero, blamed the Christians for setting the great fire which destroyed much of the Circus Maximus. From this moment on, Christians were even more persecuted than they had been, and they were executed at every opportunity. This persecution led to what must have been a common practice for people fearing for their lives and safety during that time: Christians decided to operate underground in the catacombs and waterways under Rome where their activities would not be discovered. This persecution of Christians would continue until the Emperor Constantine removed the restriction on practicing religion in 313 AD.

The Five Good Emperors

Not all Roman emperors were morally corrupt. What largely contributed to the stability of the Pax Romana was the succession of wise and stoic Roman emperors after the death of Caligula. These emperors were: Nerva, Trajan, Hadrian, Antoninius Pius, and Marcus Aurelius, the final upright emperor of the Pax Romana. According to *Five Good Emperors* (n.d), there were small signs of weakness in the empire at this point, but they went largely unnoticed for many, many years. The evil Emperor Commodus, however, put an end to this era of Roman peace. Troubled times were to follow. In the early part of the 2nd century, however, things seemed to be going well. Rome was at the peak of her powers under the great Emperor Trajan. Her empire stretched to the fullest extent that it could, from Scotland in the north and west, to Babylonia in the east. This was in the year 117 AD.

End of the Pax Romana

In 180 AD, Marcus Aurelius died, leading to a succession of civil wars within the empire that only ended with the death of the evil Commodus in 193 AD. Much damage had been done to the empire at this point. Septimius Severus was the new ruler of Rome and inherited an empire burdened by strife and division. He entered the Senate in 173 AD, and became consul in 190 AD, after a turbulent number of years in the empire. He was the son of an equestrian and was from the Roman colony of Leptis Magna, an ancient Libyan City. The reign of Severus (from around 193 AD to 211 AD) was marked by his constant military campaigns and control over his political rivals. Severus is noted for his favorable treatment of soldiers and veterans and his improvement of their lives. They were given land and special favors and were even allowed to marry while in military service.

During Serverus' time as emperor, it was also notable that he "orientalized" the Roman monarchy, to an extent. This is seen in his priorities, such as establishing more outposts on the Eastern frontier and re-establishing the province of Mesopotamia when he overthrew the Parthians in battle at Ctesiphon. Serverus also oversaw the repair of the Pantheon after it was damaged during the civil war which took place until 197. In 211 AD, Severus died while he was in Britain. For the last few years of his life, he had been battling against the Caledonians there. According to an article entitled "Lucius Severus Septimius" (n.d), there was a rumor that Severus advised his sons to favor the military and army veterans while he was on his deathbed. How true this admonition is, though, is uncertain. What is known, however, is that Rome was entering a newer and more uncertain era. The Severan dynasty following the disastrous era of Commodus is considered to be the beginning of the end of Rome's golden age. The empire would still exist for many hundreds of years, but the tranquility and stability which had been present for so long was now at an end.

The Third Century

The third century in Roman history was a period from 201 AD to around 300 AD. It was a period marked by the beginnings of chronic political instability, economic depression, and major divisions within the empire. Rome was still the major world force, but it was starting to reach the limits of its power. Barbarian tribes from the north and other regions were starting to sense weakness, and much of the 3rd century was marred by fighting. The reign of Aurelian from 270-275 AD brought some measure of stability for a time, but overall, this was a turbulent period in Roman history.

Emperor Diocletian further divided the empire during his period of rule in around 280 AD. Each part of the empire was controlled by a separate ruler called a tetrarch. The Tetrarchy, however, did not survive for very long due to Diocletian's sudden resignation due to illness. He retired peacefully to his vegetable garden in Dalmatia and there lived out the rest of his days. However, trouble was brewing. Diocletian's withdrawal once again threw the empire into chaos. The slight period of calm that Aurelian had brought was soon forgotten as fresh divisions, factions, and political unrest started to emerge once more.

East and West

In the great city of Naissus in 272 AD, the legendary Constantine was born. Raised under the leadership of Flavius Constantius, one of the leaders of the infamous Tetrarchy, he soon established himself as a divisive figure due to his political and religious leanings. His Greek mother, Helena, was not well-educated or well-known, but Constantine himself was to become one of the great rulers of the struggling Roman Empire, and his time as ruler from 308 to 337 AD was significant for many reasons. Rome was now a fragmented empire and had been so since the rule of Diocletian some years earlier. Constantine managed to unite the factions within the empire once again, although Rome would always now be divided between East and West. By 324, things were once again returning to normal in the Roman Empire, and stability and peace were prevailing. However, the great city of Rome itself was no longer seen as the jewel in the crown. Constantine turned his gaze eastward. Sensing that in the coming years there would be barbarian invasions that Rome would not be able to deal with, Constantine founded the great city of Constantinople in the eastern part of the empire.

Constantinople was a much more easily defensible position than the exposed Roman coastline in Italy. Constantinople was to become a mighty fortress in the years to come, a symbol that Roman strength would always be there, even if it was entrenched in the east and not the west.

The First Christian Emperor

Constantine was unique in that he was the first emperor to embrace Christianity, which up until that point, had been seen as a challenge to the traditional Roman values of worshipping Caesar, the State, and the Roman pantheon. Constantine, on the other hand, did not see things the same way. In 313, he introduced the Edict of Milan, a document that afforded Christians freedom from persecution and freedom to practice their belief system anywhere that they wanted to. This action on the part of the emperor marked a sharp change from what had existed before. Without the fear of death hanging over them, many Christians became even bolder and more active in sharing their faith and beliefs with others.

This did not, however, mean that Christians were more popular amongst the civilian population. The vast majority of Roman citizens still believed in their traditional gods. There were still clear divisions amongst those who believed in the glory of the empire and those who did not. This division between Christian Rome and Pagan Rome would last until the fall of Paganism in around 230 AD.

The 4th Century and the Decline and Fall of the Empire

The 4th century marked the beginning of the end for Rome as a world power. This decline had been many years in the making, but when it did happen, it was a swift process. Constantine the Great, the ruler of the western half of the Roman Empire, was content to let others take rulership of the eastern half. In 316 AD, eastern Emperor Licinius who had been sharing power with another Roman ruler, Maximinus, took sole ownership of the eastern half of the Roman Empire. In 324 AD, Constantine fought and defeated Licinius and to reunite the empire once again. This action led to the founding of the city of Constantinople (formerly known as Byzantium). The dedication of the city in 330 AD marked the official division of the Roman Empire for the first time in its history. It was known as the "Second Rome" (Nicol, n.d).

Constantine died in 337 AD after falling ill in Persia. His legacy is found in his Christianization of the Roman Empire and his reforms that established religious freedom rather than in any kind of major legislative overhauls. Constantine's inclusion of Christianity amongst the religions of Rome formed a new cultural outlook in which the Pagan gods of Rome were worshipped alongside the new Christian God. His establishment of the Nicene Creed in 325 AD led to the belief in Jesus as a divine being and is still adhered to this day. His reforms led to the emergence of a new Rome as a Christian state. Politically, he left three sons to carry on his dynasty.

After Constantine, few rulers wanted to take on the challenge of ruling the entire empire alone. It was too vast and too easily attacked by the increasingly emboldened barbarian tribes. Both the eastern and western empires were now coming under increasing pressure from these invaders. According to *Byzantium: The New Rome* (n.d), Italy was invaded by the Ostrogoths, Spain was invaded by the Visigoths, the provinces of North Africa fell to the Vandals, and Gaul fell to the Franks, all at different times during the 4th century.

One of the last rulers to attempt to unite the empire was Theodosius (379 to 395). His ban on Pagan religion helped to entrench the ideals of Christianity within Roman society at that time. When he died, Theodosius bequeathed the empire to his two sons: Honorius in the western half of the Roman Empire and Arcadius in the east.

Because of its more entrenched urban structure and culture, and its more easily defensible position, the eastern Roman Empire fared better in the 3rd and 4th centuries. They were able to use their considerable resources to buy time from the invaders and to placate them with gifts of useless land on the borders of the empire. They hoped that over time, the barbarians would eventually become like the Romans themselves, naturalized citizens. This tactic seemed to be working for a time. But some barbarian rulers were not satisfied with meaningless trinkets of land. They wanted Rome herself.

The Invasion of the Huns

One of the Romans' principal foes during this period was a particularly dangerous foe known as the Hunnic tribe. Led by a great warlord calling himself Attila the Hun, they ransacked and pillaged much of what remained of the western Roman Empire and continuously threatened the eastern Roman Empire. While he was emperor, Theodosius had attempted to bribe the Huns with the aforementioned useless trinkets of land. The Huns continued to ask for tribute, however. After Theodosius' death, the new Emperor Marcian refused to pay the Hunnic tribute. However, by this time, the barbarian king had focused his attention on what was going on in the west. In

453 AD, Attila died and much of the Hunnic Empire collapsed, leading to fighting amongst various factions in the tribe.

The Decline, Invasion, and Fall of Rome

What happened in the 5th century was to shape the future of the world for hundreds of years to come. In 476 AD, the western Roman Empire ceased to exist, crushed beneath the weight of ceaseless invasions and sackings. Weakened by economic turmoil, economic hardship, and fragmented military presence, Rome was unable to cope any longer. Odoacer, a Germanic leader, deposed the final Roman ruler of the western Empire, ironically entitled Romulus. It had begun with Romulus, and now it was ending with Romulus. The thousand-year reign of order that the western empire had brought to the world was over.

Life After the Empire

The western Roman Empire was divided up amongst the barbarian tribes. T*he Fall Of The Roman Empire* (n.d) states that waves of barbarians feasted upon the remains of the dying empire. Vandals, Visigoths, Angles, Saxons, Gauls, Lombards, Ostrogoths, and many others took their turn at claiming Roman land. The Angles and the Saxons took over the previously held British Isles, and the Gauls invaded Gaul, or what is today known as France.

CHAPTER 2
THE GEOGRAPHY OF ROME

Rome's Place in the World

Rome was located in the middle of several different countries. It was bordered by Switzerland and Austria to the north, France and the Tyrrhenian ocean to the west, the Mediterranean sea, Greece and the Aegean to the southeast, and Slovenia and the Adriatic to the east. Rome was open to many kinds of trade during times of peace, but it was also vulnerable during times of war because of its exposed coastline.

The Boundaries and Divisions of Rome

Ancient Italy was divided into 3 parts: northern, central, and southern. The northern part of Italy was considered to run from the Alps to the River Macra in the west, to the Rubicon in the east. Southern Italy completed the rest of the "boot" of Rome, comprising four different countries: Lucania and Bruttium in the west, and Apulia and Calabria to the east. Central Italy made up the part of the northern peninsula which was between the Rubicon and the Macra. It comprised the territories belonging to the Samnites, the Etrurians, Campania, and what was known as the Sabellian country.

The Geography of the City

The Location of Rome

The city of Rome was located around the center of Italy on the banks of the Tiber River. Surrounded by hills, the city of Rome was the hub of communication, trade, industry, and culture during the time of the Roman Empire. Roman roads gave easy access to the city and the surrounding areas, facilitating this trade. Rome was located near many shallower rivers that were not difficult to traverse. However, because Rome was not situated on the coastline itself, it did not have as developed of a navy as other more advanced naval civilizations such as the Greeks. Early Rome was vulnerable to attacks when they were in the water because of these perceived weaknesses.

Geographical Features That Allowed Rome to Thrive

The fact that Rome was far inland was also a strength, because it meant that Rome could not be attacked from the sea. The fact that the Tiber River was present was hugely influential in Rome's rise. According to *The Geography Of Rome* (n.d), the river provided easy transportation and had many acres of land available for farming, although it was prone to flooding and was also quite marshy. This allowed the agricultural sector of Rome to flourish in its early years. The Alps and Apennines Mountains offered some protection for the empire and were of strategic value when enemies tried to attack the city.

Rome's central location allowed them to exercise strategic trade initiatives with the Greek and Phoenicians. Trading with these nations helped to keep Rome afloat during her formative years and long after them as well. Rome looked at what the surrounding nations around her were doing and copied them. From the Phoenicians, they learned how to ship-build and manage their navy more effectively. Rome's strength lay in their ability to adapt and modify the technologies of the countries around them, and to improve on them. As the Romans found themselves increasingly in need of contact with the sea, they built a harbor at Ostia. During the day, wheeled vehicles were not allowed inside the city of Rome due to the large pedestrian presence there, but by nightfall, carts and wagons poured in from Ostia carrying goods and precious resources.

The Role of the Environment in the Early Development of Rome

In her early years, Rome was primarily a farming and fishing community. This was because of her distance to the river and the fact that large amounts of farmland surrounded the city on the seven hills themselves. This proximity to important natural resources enabled the city of Rome to develop quickly. It was the perfect base from which to begin imperialist conquests later. Once Rome was established on the peninsula, she had all the resources she needed and she was in the perfect position to capitalize on these resources. Being a farming community, grazing was readily available on the hills. Fish were available in the rivers for people to eat. Finally, the hills around the city offered natural protection from any enemies who wanted to attack Rome.

Rome's climate was perfectly suited to agriculture, being that it was mild and temperate. Rome had hot summers and moderate winters which meant that the risk of frost on crops was lessened. They did not experience the severe weather patterns of other nations. The soil in the region of the Tiber

River valley was flat, but it was also fertile, allowing for easy distribution and raising of crops and livestock. The plains that were especially beneficial were found in the Po river valley and Campania according to *Geography Of Ancient Rome And Italy* (n.d). A burgeoning population also meant that Rome had a workforce with which to start building its city. Some of these workers were slaves from the local populace and surrounding areas. Central Italy did experience rare snowfall, but it is not known whether the Romans experienced any significant hardship as a result. For the most part, the Roman climate was stable and ideal for an agrarian economy.

The Mountains Of Rome

Rome was built on seven hills. The names of these hills were: Aventine, Palatine, Caelian, Esquiline, Quirinal, Viminal, and Capitoline. It is also worth noting that Italy itself was 80 percent mountainous according to *Geography of Ancient Rome And Italy* (n.d). There was an extraordinarily varied amount of mountainous and hilly terrain in Rome, all of which offered defensive tactical advantage, or stone for masonry that was used in the construction of buildings for many hundreds of years.

Some of the mountains bordering Rome include the Apennines, the Alps, the Matterhorn, Mt. Blanc, the

Dolomites, and many others. Rome was also home to two of the world's most well-known and fierce volcanoes: Mt. Vesuvius and Mt. Etna. Vesuvius is of course infamous for being the volcano that buried an entire city, namely Pompeii, and it is still very ferocious to this day. The Romans were noted for making use of the softer volcanic rock in their buildings and constructions as well. Here, it is important to know exactly what the Romans did with the volcanic material that they gathered. Concrete was one of the great secrets of the Roman Empire and, to this day, it is still considered one of the great advancements of the ancient world. The Romans used to mix volcanic ash and lime fragments to bind rock fragments together to form a kind of self-healing material. Roman concrete was able to repair itself, to an extent, through the process of crystallization. This substance was impacted by the saltwater of the ocean which changed the structure via chemical reaction, rendering it impenetrable to most ancient devices that could attack it. It is a marvel of ancient engineering. Scientists are still poring over exactly what made Roman concrete such an amazing tool back in the day. All this aside, it was the proximity of these volcanic beasts that enabled Rome to take advantage of their materials. Rome was extremely adept at making the most of the environment they found themselves in.

The Strategic Advantage of Topography

Rome's defensive strength lay in the fact that she could not be easily attacked due to the hilly and mountainous terrain that lay on all sides of her. As an example, one needs to look no further than the battle of Hannibal. In 219 BC, Hannibal of Carthage attempted to overthrow the Roman ally of Saguntum which led to a predictable aggressive response from the Romans.

These conflicts began what is known as the Second Punic War. Hannibal led a massive army through the rocky terrain and into central Italy. Fighting against the shrewd and dangerous Roman general Publius Cornelius Scipio, Hannibal did not find the mountain crossing easy, and lost many of his troops to the climate and the harsh terrain. Hannibal eventually prevailed against Scipio but was later defeated; the challenge of overcoming the Roman army in their own lair was too great. This exemplified the fact that crossing the mountains with an army of any size was a large undertaking for even the most skilled of commanders. The hilly terrain Rome was faced with saved her on numerous accounts in battle. During her early years, it likely saved her from being overwhelmed by the larger and much more powerful tribes that surrounded her such as the Samnites, Etruscans, and Greeks.

Roman Roads

The geography of Ancient Rome enabled her to more effectively trade with the nations around her. As Rome became more sophisticated, roads were developed. The purpose of these roads was to facilitate movement in and out of the city daily. Troops could be maneuvered more quickly in a hurry, food supplies could be easily shifted, and people themselves could more effectively move around the city. Rome's central position meant that her roads could be connected to ports and other cities more efficiently. Rome was ahead of the curve in this regard. Because of the development of these roads, the empire was able to expand and develop at a faster pace. Men and materials could be transported more easily, and the furthest reaches of the empire could be patrolled and garrisoned more regularly. Rome grew culturally and economically stronger due to the improved systems of communications between the provinces. A journey on horseback might have taken several weeks to tramp across rough terrain. With the aid of a road, it became a much more streamlined process.

Types of Roads

Roman roads were divided up into three specific categories. There were the *via publica (via munita), via vicinalis,* and *via privata*. The *via publica* were the public roads, as the name suggests. They were used for wheeled, mounted, and pedestrian traffic and could be thoroughfares, but they could also be cul-de-sacs (*diverticulum*) ("Via Publica," 2019). The other term used was *via munita,* but over time, this came to mean the same thing. The *via vicinalis* were roads designed for general use within the provinces and sometimes running across private land. *Via privata* were small roads constructed without the aid of the government that ran across an individual's property, and they were also known as country roads. The public could still access these roads if they needed to. The *Via Militaris* was a specific road used by military units and troops that ran across the northern border of the empire along the length of Danube. It was of vital importance because of the need to funnel troops to this far-off area quickly if the situation demanded it. A road in this part of the empire made the process of transporting troops, supplies, and equipment a lot more efficient.

Roman roads had specific names if they were used for a particular purpose or had cultural and historical significance. One of the most famous roads in all of Rome was the *Via Appia* or, *Appian Way,* as it is known in English. It was one of the first Roman roads to be constructed in around 312 BC, and its length was about 560 km. It led to the development of further roads, and at the height of the empire's power, almost

80,000 km of roads had been developed. According to *The Roman Empire, c125 CE* (n.d), the Romans also built the world's first dual carriageway which was named *Via Portuensis*. It connected the Roman harbor at Ostia to the city itself and made transporting precious materials, cargo, and supplies much easier. At the center of Rome itself was a monument known as the *milliareum aureum* or the "golden milestone." It was said to be the central point from which all Roman roads originated. When the western Roman Empire collapsed, the system and network of roads collapsed along with it. The Roman network of roads and transportation systems is an indicator of how they approached life. Their ways of construction were just another sign of the manner in which the empire was organized, which in turn led to their success through the ages.

Management of Roads

Roman roads were set up for efficiency. Traveling speed was enhanced by placing stables every 15 km or so along the routes with fresh horses should travelers need them. Refreshment stations existed along these routes for the benefit of weary travelers and those traveling with their families. It was estimated that the average traveler could manage about 40 km in a day and thus the stations were set up at these intervals. However, this was not a hard and fast rule. Many travelers and courier services could travel further distances if they needed to. Many people preferred to travel longer distances via ships, as they were less taxing, although they were also more expensive. Overall, roads were an important part of the geography of Rome because they showed how Romans overcame the terrain and obstacles that they were faced with, turning the land into an advantage while expanding the empire.

CHAPTER 3
THE MAIN FIGURES IN ROMAN HISTORY

Political Figures

Emperors

The very first thing people think of when they hear the term 'Ancient Rome' are the leaders, both good and bad, of this great nation. After she became a monarchical dictatorship, leaving behind the ideas of state and Senate, these men determined the fate of Rome. It is worth noting that every ruler of the Roman Empire had something about them that was unique to that particular ruler.

The greatest of these leaders was the mighty Julius Caesar. He was a renowned military man, a charismatic speaker, and a great leader of men. Born in 100 BC, he rose to power and through the ranks as a Roman general. He took on the governorship of Hispania in 61 BC. After his pact with Pompey and Crassus in 59 BC, Julius Caesar assumed the role of Consul of Rome. His next eight years were spent in conquest of Gaul and he eventually assumed the role of absolute authority in the Roman hierarchy. Julius Caesar was also a very complex character and one who has been analyzed throughout history. His intelligence and craftiness helped him to gain the edge in tactical and military situations. He was an expert strategist and was able to get out of seemingly disadvantageous situations using his amazing powers of negotiation. One such example of this is when he found himself captured by pirates while on his ocean travels. According to *Julius Caesar* (2019), he convinced his captors to raise his own ransom and then organized a naval force to attack and kill them.

Julius Caesar's status rose even further when he attacked and defeated Mithridates IV of Pontus who had laid siege to several Roman cities. Soon after these military conquests, he cunningly arranged an agreement with two other powerful Roman allies which allowed him to maintain a foothold in power, where he stayed until he could eventually assume total control of Rome.

The reign of Caesar came to a premature end in 44 BC. His mistake was trusting others with his life. He allowed the wrong types of people into his circle: Brutus and Cassius. While Caesar might have known that his life was in danger, he was unable to determine who wanted to kill him. He was betrayed by those he trusted, and this trust was, in the end, a fatal character flaw.

The assassination of Caesar during the Ides of March is considered to be one of the landmark events in Ancient Roman history. It cemented what was already a firm transition to the new era of the emperors and marked further movement away from the idea of a republic.

Furthemore, one great Roman Emperor (and some might say the greatest) was the man known as Octavian, or otherwise known as Caesar Augustus. Augustus was the term given to him by the Senate as a way of honoring him. During his time in power, Augustus treated the Senate fairly and made sure to never promote himself, like Julius Caesar had. One senses this was a wise decision as it seemed to make him a popular figure.

In the article "8 things you may not know about Augustus" (2018), we learn that he was born in 63 BC, around the time that his adoptive father Julius Caesar was preparing to take full ownership of Rome. He is considered the very first emperor of Rome.

Augustus lived in more modest quarters than other Roman emperors. He refused to refer to himself as a monarch and appeared more reasonable and humble than many other Roman rulers. His power, however, was greater than any other ruler before him.

A noted tactician, Augustus was able to expand Rome's borders greatly. As a teenager, he went to war against Mark Antony and defeated him, and later expanded the Roman influence north into Germania across the Rhine, and also south into Egypt and North Africa. However, Augustus did suffer some major defeats. In 9 AD, three divisions of Roman legions were destroyed when they were attacked by barbarian tribes across the Rhine. Augustus was so broken that he banged his head against the wall and cried "give me back my legions," a now-famous line quoted in many works of literature.

Another great and interesting Roman emperor was Antoninius Pius (86 AD to 161 AD). He was unique in his way of ruling Rome because he did not leave the country once. He promoted arts, music, books, culture, museums, science, and the glory of Rome, and there are also no records of any sign of military campaign or war during his reign. This also made him one of the only Roman emperors to not engage in conflict with the surrounding nations. Antoninius Pius rewarded those who practiced the arts and honored those who taught rhetoric and philosophy. He was also involved in the construction of several temples, mausoleums, statues, and theatres. In Roman times, theatres were somewhat different from how we experience them today. They were large, open stone structures where the seating was arranged in a circle, and the performance would take place in the center of the ring.

Hadrian was another very interesting character within the Roman dynasty. Fascinated with the culture of Greece, he attempted to bring some of their ideas to the Roman world. Even though he was never technically given the status of "heir to the throne" by his predecessor Trajan, his wife declared that he was the emperor of Rome not long before Trajan died. Hadrian's rule was marked by his building of the wall, a defensive fortification on the northern borders of the empire. It is marked as the furthest point north that Rome managed to expand. These fortifications still exist to this day and are considered to be one of the landmarks that noted where the borders of the Roman Empire once lay. Hadrian also rebuilt the Pantheon and constructed the temple of Venus and Roma. Overall, he is noted for his more humble personage which is evidenced by reports that he used to camp out with the soldiers after dark instead of lying in state in his luxurious palace.

Marcus Aurelius might be one of the most tragic figures out of the line of Roman Emperors. His rule was a difficult one, coming in during a period of instability and civil unrest. He battled the Parthians in the east, defeated the Marcomanni, Quadi, and Sarmatians in the Marcomannic wars, and generally did his best to try and stave off civil war for as long as possible. Marcus Aurelius was a serious man and was partial to philosophy and pursuing ancient wisdom. What was unique about him could be said to be his desire to write. His book "Meditations" is still published and read to this day. It was written while he was on campaign between 170-180 AD and describes the nature of service to Rome, duty, and maintaining one's dignity even amid hardship and turmoil. After his death, his nickname stuck with him, "The Philosopher."

The next interesting character, Emperor Trajan, presided over what was the height of Roman world dominance. Under him,

Rome reached its peak. His reputation as a governor of Rome still endures to this day. Trajan's reforms, actions, and words were all respected by opponents, the Senate, the people, and the army. He was one of the most universally popular rulers in Roman history and with good reason. His rule was philanthropic, and he sought to create a peaceable system of imperialist expansion rather than conquering through all-out war. After Trajan died, Rome never again reached the heights of dominance that it once did. His reign was the zenith of Rome's world rule.

Other emperors were interesting but not for popularity or fame. They got their reputation of violence and lawlessness from their inability to think and rule. One of these awful rulers was the villainous Commodus, who ruled after Marcus Aurelius until he was assassinated in 193. His lust for power and popularity was insatiable. Commodus could not follow in the footsteps of his wise father. Instead, he destroyed his legacy in a few bloody years in the throne that left Rome reeling. His decisions led to the destruction of Roman currency and the weakening of the empire which had taken others before him so long to build. Dio Cassius, a Roman scribe wrote that Commodus turned Rome from a kingdom of gold to one of rust. Much of the administrative work of running the empire was left to servants and co-rulers.

Commodus preferred to spend his time watching and organizing the Roman games where he would hunt and kill animals for sport. He would also fight in the arena itself, although the men he fought were often handicapped themselves, making his victory inevitable. Eventually, his colleagues grew tired of his rule and he was assassinated while he was in the bath in 193 AD.

Famous Writers

Roman writers were a diverse and interesting crowd. Spanning hundreds of years, their works continue to be relevant even to this day. Roman writers covered a vast range of subjects including their own versions of the history of the empire, politics, religion, philosophy, science, the natural world, culture and poetry, and many more topics. Roman poets belong to their own specific special grouping, as their form of literature is unique and fascinating. Roman poetry incorporates the mythology and lore of the time. As the periods shifted and seasons changed, the focus of these writers' work also altered. The subject matter tells us what was influential during these periods.

Some 1st Century Roman Writers

Valerius Maximus was a writer that lived during the time of the Emperor Tiberius. His work dealt with famous deeds, battles, and the achievements of Rome. His work seemed to be primarily focused on the realities of Rome rather than fictional constructions.

Aelius Saturninus was another Roman writer living in the first century who was noted for having written some scurrilous documents about the Emperor Tiberius. His punishment was to be thrown from the Tarpeian Rock.

Scribonius Largus was a medical writer who lived under the reign of Emperor Claudius. His works are interesting primarily because they highlight the Roman approach to medical science at this early point in history. His work *De Compositione Medicamentorum Liber* is a long list of medical compositions dealing with medical recipes, herbs, and remedies.

Lucius Junius Moderatus Columella was a former soldier turned farmer. His works deal with agriculture, plants, and different kinds of trees which were common to the region and further afield in the empire. He wrote about this in *De Re Rustica* and *De Arborius*.

Publius Cornelius Tacitus is considered by many to be one of the greatest, if not the greatest, Roman writers and historians. Born in 56 AD, he became a notable Roman orator and public speaker. But it was his written work that caused the biggest stir. Amongst Publius Cornelius Tacitus' works, *Germania, Historiae,* and *Annals* are widely regarded as some of the finest specimens of Ancient Roman literature dealing with a wide range of topics from Roman politics to popular subjects of the time. However, it is his work written about Jesus Christ that is still his most valuable writing. Although much of what was written was lost, some fragments remain. Within the text *Annals* there is a specific reference to Christ and his followers ("Tacitus on Christ," n.d). Tacitus tells of a man named *Christus* who was executed under the orders of Pontius Pilate. His teachings, however, continued to cause division and unrest within the Roman capital.

This source highlights the fact that there was a man named Christus or Christ and that his followers were being persecuted during the time of the Emperor Nero who blamed them for the Great Fire in 64 AD. Extra-Biblical texts like this are incredibly valuable to Christian scholars, those who study the scriptures, and Biblical archaeologists.

The works of Tacitus are also noted for their commentary on Roman society at the time. His histories cover the times of Nerva, Trajan, Nero, Tiberius, and Caligula. Much of his work has been lost in the mists of time, however.

Plinius Maior, known as Gaius Plinius Secundus, or more popularly known by the name Pliny the Elder, was a writer, philosopher, and commander of the Roman fleet. His most famous work is the *Naturalis Historia*, a work dealing with all kinds of subjects relating to natural history such as mining, astronomy, botany, farming, and art.

Some 2nd Century Roman Writers

Quintus Septimus Florens Tertullianus, better known by his common name Tertullian, was a well-known Roman Christian writer from the 2nd century. His works of theology are still popular even to this day. It was his work *Apologeticus* that led to the modern Christian discipline of Apologetics, or the defense of the Christian faith by upholding its values and precepts.

Vibia Perpetua was a Carthaginian writer and noblewoman who was captured and imprisoned in Carthage during the reign of Severus in around 200 AD. She was both a Christian and a slave, and she kept a diary of her experiences called *Passio Sanctarum Perpetuae et Felicitatis,* or The Passion of the Saints. She was martyred on the emperor's birthday in 203 AD.

Pliny the Younger was another well-respected Roman author from the second century who was the adopted son of Pliny the Elder. He was a lawyer and an administrator in Rome who wrote a series of letters to friends and colleagues which would later become noteworthy. As he rose through the ranks of Roman society to eventually become Consul, Pliny the Younger gained much exposure to the ways of Roman politics and also everyday life. His viewpoints on life at the top echelons of Roman society have become critical to our understanding of the reasons why the Romans thought and acted the way that they did during this time period. Pliny the Younger's relationship with the Emperor Trajan and also with Tacitus himself were significant because they gave him insight into the workings of both the common man and those at the very top of the hierarchy. Some of the contents of his letters detail the eruption of Mt. Vesuvius, other letters are addressed to Trajan asking for advice on what to do regarding the policies relating to Christianity, a rising new belief system at the time. His letters were also known as *Epistulae* in Latin.

One of the greatest Roman minds of the 2nd century was a man by the name of Marcus Tullius Cicero, or simply Cicero for short. According to *Cicero (106-43 B.C.E)* (n.d), he was a gifted orator and speaker, and perhaps one of the most influential figures of the first century behind Julius Caesar himself. Cicero's death coincided with the fall of the Roman republic, and he was there to witness its transition into the era of the emperors. His writings always placed value on political matters over those of the philosophical, and given his station as a lawyer and orator, this is hardly surprising. Although much can be said about the life, thought, writings, ideas, and activities of Cicero, the most significant aspects of his life was his influence on future philosophers such as Augustine.

Some 3rd Century Roman Writers

Apicius is most likely brought up when referring to Ancient Roman cuisine, as his works deal with recipes and dishes of the time. When he was born is not entirely certain, but he is most well-known for his work *De Re Coquinaria*. However, there is confusion over the exact ownership of this work. It is ascribed to Apicius because of the heading on one of the two remaining manuscripts which reads API CAE. According to "List of Roman Authors" (n.d), some of the recipes may be attributed to Apicius and but not exactly written by him. There may have been several people called by this name, and no one is quite sure of the origins of the book. It is known, however, that many Roman celebrities liked to put their names to specific recipes as a mark of honoring themselves.

Pontius of Carthage, also known as Pontius the Deacon, was a deacon serving in the employ of St. Cyprian (Cyprianus). After Cyprianus was arrested and martyred, Pontius wrote *Vita Cypriani,* a work on the life and times of Cyprianus.

Novatian was a religious figure and writer during the rule of Emperor Elagabalus (Heliogabalus). He was a controversial figure in the Catholic Church because he was an antipope (someone who attempts to usurp the Pope despite the office already being filled). He wrote extensively on restrictions within the Biblical Old Testament, public games, and the importance of remaining chaste and pure.

Some 4th Century Roman Writers

In the years after Constantine the Great, many Roman writers turned to Christianity, and this is evident through many of the philosophical texts at the time.

Eusebius Sophronius Hieronymus, also known as Hieronymus or St. Jerome, was a secretary or assistant to Pope Damasus the 1st. He is most notable for his work on translating the Hebrew scriptures into Latin. This is known as the Vulgate translation and is held as canon by the Catholic Church to this day. He wrote notes on the Biblical gospels, commentaries, letters and a work containing information on 135 other Christian authors called *De viris illustribus*.

Augustinus, also known as St. Augustine of Hippo, was a philosopher and thinker in the latter part of the empire's years. He was a writer, theologian, and Christian bishop from what is modern-day Algeria. His influence is still felt to this day, and his grace, humility, and wisdom continues to inspire many.

Aurelius Prudentius Clemens was a poet, jurist and writer, and governor from northern Spain. His work *Psychomachia* is a commentary on the spiritual struggle Christians sometimes experience in their daily lives, but he also wrote numerous hymns and songs.

Poets, Artists, and Musicians

Famous Roman Poets

Virgil, Ovid, and Horace are names that often come to mind when people think of the most notable Roman poets. But throughout the history of the empire, we find that the culture of poetry appreciation was flourishing in Roman society from its beginning to end. Many minor names are becoming more appreciated contemporarily as people delve into the depths of Ancient Roman prose and verse.

One of the most famous of the poets, of course, is Virgil who wrote *The Aeneid*, a poem about a Trojan hero named Aeneas. It is also a commentary on the history and reality of Rome up to the point that it was composed.

Horace was another legendary Roman poet who wrote the *Odes*, *Satires*, and *Epistles*. His style of poetry can be described as lyric poetry.

Ovid's most famous work is known as *Metamorphoses* which details the fictional account of Julius Caesar and his rise to godhood. Ovid is also known for writing numerous love poems.

Roman poets sometimes put their words to music and created compositions and songs. Often, they would create simple notations that other musicians could use to play along with the words of their poems and songs.

Roman Music

Music is as engrained in Roman history and culture as it is in our own modern-day culture and history. Roman music is depicted in literature, art, and on mosaics as using woodwind instruments, pan flutes, small stringed instruments, cane reed instruments, and harps, amongst others. The Romans also made use of percussion and brass. In the desolate ruins of Pompeii, modern-day archaeologists found remains of shell trumpets, bone flutes, and bronze horns ("Music in Ancient Rome," n.d). Little is known of the system of Roman musical notation itself. But who were the most effective exponents of these musical instruments?

Music was popular amongst the emperors themselves. Roman Emperor Titus (81-79 AD) was greatly interested in music according to Ancient Roman writer Suetonius ("Music in Ancient Rome," n.d). According to Suetonius, Titus played the harp skillfully and used to amuse his secretaries with his fast finger work with shorthand writing.

Hadrian was also fascinated by music and was very proficient at the flute in particular. He was also good at singing according to *Music in Ancient Rome* (n.d).

Nero, the great and evil emperor of the 2nd century, was said to have played the lyre while Rome burned in the Great Fire of 64 AD. While this may or may not be entirely accurate, it seems that he did have a definite interest in music.

As for celebrity musicians in Rome, there doesn't seem to be much material surviving from that period that would suggest certain people were particularly well-known for their performances. However, there is evidence of plays and dramas incorporating music into them. One such example is the famous dramatist Terence. Born in North Africa, he was taken as a slave to Rome by Terentius Lucanus. His stage plays are noted for being models of "pure Latin" according to

Terence (n.d). What this shows is that Rome is noted for having talented musicians, poets, and orators of all races and creeds. Their diversity is surprising. Anyone could become a playwright or a famous poet in Ancient Rome if they had the skill and the knowledge to do so.

Famous Military Figures

One would be remiss to analyze a list of the Roman characters in history without looking at the military leaders and players in the Roman army. The Roman military is the central conversation in any discussion about Ancient Rome. Their leaders at the time of the empire were some of the most noteworthy in history, and some have been given a god-like status.

Much has been said about Julius Caesar already, but his prowess as a military leader cannot be understated. His conquest of Gaul was no easy feat. He was by no means the only military leader, though.

One of Rome's greatest (and underrated) generals was a man by the name of Nero Claudius Drusus, who showed brilliant promise early in his career. He was the only Roman general who managed to beat back the Germanic tribes living beyond the Rhine. After being elected to the position of Consul, he rode out once again to battle the Germanic tribes on the Rhine but suffered a terrible fall from his horse and never recovered. His loss was a massive blow for Rome.

Agricola was another of the mightiest generals Rome had ever known. He was most known for being the Roman general who conquered the British isles, or Britannia as they were known at the time. Sent by the Emperor Vespasian, he subdued Britain, led his army all the way to the north of Scotland, built 1300 km of roads, and built up to 60 forts across much of the country. Roman dominance over Britain ensured that she was able to establish Roman culture there which would last for many hundreds of years and still holds true even to this day. Agricola also made sorties around the British coastline under instruction to find out whether Britain was part of the mainland or whether it was in fact an island. In many senses, the battle for Britain was an important step in the development of the Roman Empire, as it established their superiority not only as a military force on land, but also on the water. Agricola was a huge part of this evolution.

Scipio Africanus was a Roman general most noted for his actions in North Africa and at the battle of Zama. His tactical acumen was well-known throughout the empire during a critical time in Roman history. Born in 236 BC, Scipio quickly rose through the ranks of the Roman army. During the Second Punic War against the legendary general Hannibal Barca, he demonstrated his ability to survive during the Roman failures at Cannae and the battles of Trebia and Ticinus. In 211 BC, Scipio's uncle and father were killed during battle, and he became the new leader of the Roman army. In the years that followed, Scipio managed to capture Carthago Nova in Hispania. This became his new base for operations. Scipio is noted for being a humble man, returning a captured slave woman to the chieftain of her tribe. The leader of the tribe was so grateful that he offered to lend Scipio some troops. Scipio then used his reinforced army to fight and defeat Hasdrubal, destroying the Carthaginian cavalry in the process. In 205 BC, Scipio was made consul of Rome. It was at this point that he fought one of the most famous battles in Roman military history: the battle of Zama.

In 202 BC, both Rome and Carthage were vying for control of the Roman peninsula and the territory that Rome had won in North Africa and Europe. After victories on the Iberian peninsula, Scipio arrived at the ancient city Zama (also known as Xama) in Tunis. Hannibal himself was there with about 6,0000 troops and 6,000 cavalry. Scipio had around 3,4000 troops and about 9,000 cavalry. Scipio was supported by Numidian leader Masinissa, who had a specific kind of cavalry trained to counter the fearful Carthiginian war elephants (they had been trained to get used to the smell and therefore did not panic during the heat of battle). While Hannibal instructed his heavy troops to try and punch holes in the Roman lines, Scipio created gaps for the opposition to funnel through and then used these areas as killzones, creating chaos and confusion by having the Roman troops blow trumpets. Having confused, panicked, and disorganized the enemy, Scipio routed the left flank of the Carthaginian army and routed their cavalry along with the famed war elephants. Hannibal's army was then bested in a hand-to-hand battle with the stronger Roman legionaries. Scipio received great acclaim when he returned to Rome, not only for his military conquest but also for his restraint in not completely destroying the city of Carthage. He was honored with the title "Africanus" for his role in the victories in North Africa.

Gnaeus Pompeius Magnus was a Roman general better known by the name "Pompey." While he is known for being one of the leading figures in the early part of the Roman Empire, he was also a respected general, leader, and tactician. Pompey impressed the Roman ruler Sulla and fought campaigns in Sicily, North Africa, and Numidia. After the death of Sulla in

78 BC, Pompey was sent to Hispania where he was tasked with bringing the resolute King Sertorious to heel. After a protracted struggle, Sertorious was eventually assassinated by one of his own men, and Pompey returned to Rome to quell another attack, this time led by Spartacus. Having successfully accomplished his mission by capturing 5000 of Spartacus' men, Pompey then fell out of favor with his other partner in the soon-to-be triumvirate, Crassus, who felt that Pompey was taking an unfair share of the glory for triumphing in the battle. Nonetheless, the two men would go on to form a powerful alliance with Julius Caesar. In 70 BC, Pompey was elected Consul of Rome and joined with Crassus. For the next 10 or so years, they ruled Rome together until Julius Caesar joined the party in around 60 BC. Pompey had further successes in the 50s, but disaster struck when Crassus was killed in battle at Carrhae. Julius Caesar's influence was becoming more and more evident, and in 49 BC, civil war broke out between the two factions. From this point onward, the legend of Pompey seems to be overshadowed by the more illustrious reign of Caesar.

Another notable Roman general was Germanicus Julius Caesar. Born in 15 BC, he quickly established himself as a top Roman general and made great strides into subduing the barbarian tribes around Germania, hence his name "Germanicus" which was given to him as a mark of honor.

Marcus Vipsanius Agrippa was the key military advisor to the great Caesar Augustus, or Octavian as he was sometimes known. He was most notable for naval battles against Sextus Pompey and for the construction of a harbor at Portus Julius. This harbor linked Lake Avernus and Lucrinus Lacus so that Roman ships could be properly defended in the battle with Sextus. He was responsible for repairs to much of Rome after numerous and costly battles, and he took an interest in improving the city itself and creating festivals for the enjoyment of citizens in the city. Overall, he was a skilled commander and a dutiful servant to Rome.

Aetius was one of the last great western Roman Empire generals. He was born in the 5th century and was a young, daring, and skilled military leader whose speciality was dealing with the threat of the barbarians who now harassed the borders of the Roman Empire on every available occasion. He was tasked with repelling the invasion of the Huns in around 451 AD. Aetius mustered a massive Roman force at the Battle of the Catalaunian fields, made alliances with other barbarian chieftains, and successfully managed to stall the Hunnic invasion of the western Roman Empire at the time. It was one of the bloodiest battles in Roman history, and Attila the Hun's army was broken - as were the Romans. However, Aetius retired from active military service soon after, and the Huns returned not long after that. This time Aetius was not available to save the empire.

In the case of each one of these military commanders, they realized their duty to Rome and fulfilled their calling with distinction. That is why they are remembered throughout history as Rome's finest fighting men.

Gladiators

We have all seen images of gladiators in the arena through TV, movies, and books. These men continue to inspire courage in us through their acts of bravery in the arena.

Roman gladiators and gladiatrices were men and women from all walks of life taken as slaves for every part of the empire. Tasked with entertaining the masses, they were the celebrities of the Ancient Roman world. If they survived, they were treated like royalty. For those not so fortunate, severe injury might have been the best thing that they could hope for. Many were maimed or killed in the arena. What follows is a discussion of some of the most well-known names of men who took on the arena and managed to not only survive, but thrive.

Carpophorus

Carpophorus was the kind of gladiator who takes on wild animals or beasts, also known as a *bestiarii*. The men who were responsible for looking after the beasts were also known as *bestiarii*. Often when man and animal met, there was only one winner. The vicious creatures gave their tired, hungry, and worn out opponents little chance. However, Carpophorus embraced the challenge and became a living legend. Roman writer Martial states that Carpophorus once killed 20 animals at one time and regularly took on bears, lions, and leopards (Bestiarius, n.d). According to *Top 10 Famous Roman Gladiators* (2020), Carpophorus once saw off a rhino with nothing more than a spear. He was one of the most anticipated gladiators to ever set foot in the arena. The Roman people loved to root for a particular class (or type) of gladiator. Many were trained to use specific weapons depending on their skill and body type. Romans liked to see specific kinds of gladiators pitted against each other and would pay large sums of money betting on who was going to win.

Flamma

Flamma was a slave from Syria who was forced to fight in the arena. His real name was Marcus Calpunius, but he was renamed *Flamma* or "flame" for the arena. He was a class of gladiator known as a *secutor* meaning he carried armor, a heavy shield, and a short sword or gladius into the fights. He won 21 fights and lost about four. He was awarded his freedom but elected to stay and fight in the arena. He died at around age 30 in his final battle. Deaths in the arena were common, but they were sometimes avoided if at all possible. These men were celebrities, and their deaths would send the wrong signals to people watching. Training a gladiator was costly and good money was paid for people to see specific gladiators. The loss of a gladiator through death or injury would have hurt the popularity of the arena games.

Gannicus

Gannicus was considered to be one of the most able gladiators of his generation. Originally hailing from the British Isles, he was noted for his incredible speed, athleticism, and agility. He was able to more easily evade his enemy attacks, and this made him a formidable opponent in the arena. His body was covered in tattoos, one of which represented invincibility. The Romans enjoyed watching agile gladiators as they made the games more exciting. Men like Gannicus would have received top billing.

Spiculus

Spiculus is most known for having ties with the evil Emperor Nero. He was both loyal and supportive of Nero even when it seemed all others were deserting Nero at the time. This impressed the villainous emperor and he granted Spiculus his freedom.

Marcus Attilius

Marcus Attilius is an unusual addition to this list because he might be one of the few gladiators to voluntarily sign up to fight in the arena. He was a free born Roman, not a slave. He was regularly able to hold his own against far more skilled and experienced opponents, and this was evident from early on in his gladiatorial career. He also overcame other notoriously difficult opponents such as Raecius Felix (who had won 12 fights in a row) and Hilarus (another gladiator favored by Nero). Attilius fought in the *murmillo* class using a short sword and a longer shield.

Commodus

Commodus was the tyrannical emperor from the latter part of the 2nd century, but he was also noted for his prowess facing gladiators in the arena. However, how skilled he was is difficult to tell because he would often disable or cripple opponents before getting into the arena with them. Opponents would fight with small wooden swords while Commodus had the real thing. He also enjoyed killing animals which drove down his popularity as a result. His style of fighting was considered unfair amongst the Roman public and he was often jeered. The Romans had a great sense of fairness, and Commodus' actions only served to harm his cause even further.

Tetraites

Tetraites was another gladiator in the *murmillo* class who won notoriety by beating a fellow celebrity gladiator Prudes. He was considered to be one of the strongest gladiators of his generation, and his victory against Prudes is immortalized in graffiti discovered in the ruins of Pompeii back in 1817. Tetraites used to enter the arena without a shirt, but wearing a helmet, and carrying a short sword and a rectangular shield. This would have been considered against type, as most gladiators would armor up as much as possible, depending on what kind of fight they were going to undertake.

Priscus and Verus

Priscus was a Celtic gladiator and was both skilled and powerful in the arena. His partner Verus was also one of the most influential gladiators of his generation. The two used to make a headline act for the games, especially on the opening of the Colosseum. The games themselves consisted of mock naval battles, animal fights, and gladiatorial battles. Under the rule of the Emperor Titus (around 81 AD), these spectacles were intended to try and appease the Roman masses before the entertainment began. Priscus and Verus did end up fighting each other, but such was the respect between these two men that they laid down their arms and did not injure or kill each other. This is still noted as a spectacular development in the history of Roman gladiatorial games, and it is recorded as such. Over time, the two men began to be referred to as a collective rather than as individuals. Roman crowds loved to see a spectacle so the more spectacular the bout, the more people would come to watch the games. Two men fighting on a team would have definitely attracted the attention of the crowds in what was usually a single combat sport.

Crixus

Crixus was a gladiator from Gaul, noted for his size and strength. He trained together with Spartacus at the gladiatorial school known as *Lentulus Batiatus*. A large number of the gladiators, about 70 in total, escaped the school due to the harsh training from their *lanista* (or trainer). They formed a factional group, and under the leadership of Spartacus, attempted to overthrow the Roman government. He was killed during the rebellion.

Spartacus

Spartacus was considered to be one of the greatest, if not the greatest, gladiators of all time. He was a Thracian-turned-Roman-soldier, eventually joining the training school at Capua. His biggest legacy is rebelling against Rome in 71 BC and incurring the wrath of Crassus who arrived bringing 5,0000 troops to crush the revolt. He was killed in the battle of Sicily and his followers were executed in large numbers.

What made these men so great was that they were willing to put their lives on the line in order to impress the mob that was the Roman people. Their bravery and their heroism stands out. Not all great Roman gladiators survived, and many were mortally wounded doing what they felt called to do.

CHAPTER 4
ROMAN LIFE

Romans lived very differently than how we do today, and with very good reason. Their customs, tastes, ways of viewing the world, and their political, economic, cultural and military situations were very different to our modern ways. Their ways of living were dictated by economic prosperity (or lack thereof), whether the empire was doing well and was stable, who was in charge in Rome, and many other factors.

Roman Food and Cooking

Roman Food Habits

Romans ate little food during the day and had a large meal in the evenings. Dinner was the main meal of the day, and preparations would begin at around three in the afternoon. It was as much a time for the family to come together as anything else. Romans did try to eat three meals a day, if possible. This could change depending on what the makeup of a day looked like. If they were richer and had many social events, they may have more meals. If they were poorer and of a lower social status, they might be lucky to eat at all. For the purposes of consistency, most Romans tended to stick to the three meals a day structure with lighter snacks and beverages in between if needed, much the same as we do today. The first meal was called *ientaculum*. Lunch was known as *prandium* and dinner was known as *cena*.

Dinner was an event that the Romans looked forward to each day, as it gave them the opportunity to rest and relax from the hard labors of the day. How long each meal took depended on the status of the meal. If it was an important meal, it could carry on for several hours, intersected by dancing, speeches, singing, and many other activities. Meals for simple folk took only as long as they needed before they had to resume important activities.

Middle and upper-class Romans tended to recline on couches while they ate at more formal events. This was considered the more comfortable way to eat, and there were no such thing as high tables or they were very rare. Romans typically made use of a low table that they all lay around.

For less formal meals, Romans would stand while they ate or sit on high stools (Ancient Rome: Food and drink, n.d).

Romans did not make much use of knives or forks while eating. Typically they used a spoon for lifting food to the mouth. Forks were sometimes used for spearing food on the table and knives were used for cutting food into more manageable portions much as it is today. Romans also ate with their hands a great deal.

Everyday Foods

One of the most common foods in Ancient Rome was of course bread. This was eaten with every meal of the day. Fruits of all kinds were typical. Vegetables, beans, legumes, cheese, honey, and many other kinds of foods were common. For breakfast, fruit with bread was often eaten early on in the day. Dates, honey, and light wheaten cakes could also form part of this meal, depending on the social status of the eater. Certain foods were easier to access if the person or family happened to be wealthy.

Prandium took place at around 11am. It could consist of fish, vegetables, soup, bread, cheese, or cold meat. Leftovers from the previous day's *cena* might also be served alongside the meal.

Cena was held much later on in the day, and it was at this meal that the most exclusive and expensive food was served. If the family had guests, usually the best food would be served to them at this meal. The same was true in the case of celebratory events such as holidays and feast days. The main meal consisted of three different courses: *gustatio* or *promulsis*, *prima mensa,* and *secunda mensa. Gustatio* was an appetizer that could consist of light seafood, eggs, fish, cheese, bread, and vegetables. *Prima mensa* was the main course within the primary meal of the day. It could consist of cooked vegetables, sauces, and meats such as pork, chicken, lamb, beef, and wild game amongst others. More wealthy Romans ate more expensive delicacies such as dormice with honey, peacock tongues, and also strange dishes which might seem unappealing to the modern reader. The more wealthy Romans could afford to be more expansive in their tastes and eating habits than the average Roman citizen. The *secunda mensa* was the dessert course, and it could consist of sweet tarts with honey, fruit, nuts or cakes.

Roman Drinks

Wine was drunk with every meal that the Romans ate. It appeared in many different forms and varieties and was often diluted with water in order to make it last. For example, Romans enjoyed a drink made with warmed wine mixed with different kinds of spices. They also liked *mulsum,* a type of wine mixed with honey. Poorer people drank what they could find, either water or cheap beer. Beer was common in Ancient Rome and was enjoyed by all sectors of society. Coffee did not exist within the Roman world and tea was also non-existent, as herbal infused drinks only made their appearance in modern Europe.

Popular Dishes

Romans enjoyed many kinds of sausages, as they could be customized to the taste of the person making them. One particular variety that seems to have stood out in history as being a favorite was the Lucianian sausage. Made with cumin, rue, parsley, seasonings, bay berries, garum, fat, and finely ground meat, this sausage was brought to Rome by the soldiers who had served in Luciana. It was thinly rolled and then smoked.

The Romans also loved eggs. One particular dish that was popular was boiled eggs in various kinds of sauces. They were popular as a snack or an appetizer. One recipe has them served alongside a pepper, lovage, and pine nut sauce.

A common Roman condiment was called *garum*. It can be classified as a type of fish sauce, but it was not like the fish sauce we see in stores today. It was made with the entrails of fresh fish, salt, and herbs such as celery, mint, or oregano. It was diluted with olive oil, vinegar, wine, or water to make it spread further ("What is garum," 2019).

Romans were extremely fond of seafood, and this is evident in their love of mussels. One specific dish that catches the attention is made with leek, *passum* or raisin wine, cumin, and wine. The mussels were cleaned and then cooked within the wine itself until tender.

Roman desserts do not get a lot of attention, but one popular dish was called "pear patina." As the name implies, it is a dessert made with ground pears, cumin, honey, *passum*, *garum*, and olive oil, made into a *patina* (or a small flat dish), combined with eggs and pepper.

Libum was a type of Roman cheesecake made with flour, ricotta cheese, eggs, and honey and scented with bay leaves. Dishes such as this one were often cooked covered using a dish or cover known as a *testo* (Raimer, 2000).

Food for the Rich

Apart from the more standard fare, richer Romans ate strange and innovative foods such as peacock and nightingale tongues, snails, geese, dormice, ducks, pheasants, pigeons, thrushes, finches, and wild game such as boar and deer. Wealthy Roman parties were often festivals of innovation to see who could produce the most outlandish dishes.

Food for the Poor

Poorer Romans tended to eat what they could find, which was usually ground meal made of different types of grain, and a dish called *puls*. This was a dish made with ground wheat and water. They tended to eat bread and vegetable soup, cheese, fruit, and olives. Meat was a rarity unless they could go hunting for it. While they did drink wine, it was more out of necessity, and there was a distinct lack of experimentation in their diets.

Ways of Cooking

Uncovered Ancient Roman kitchens within the ruins of Pompeii showed what Roman cooking was once like. Romans cooked their food over specially made long troughs in which flaming hot coals were placed. Meat, fish, vegetables, and poultry were laid on grills over the troughs in order to cook. Stews were cooked in large open pots over fires. The pots were mounted on tripods over the fire (Mandal, 2016).

Roman Jobs

Romans had many different kinds of occupations throughout the empire. Manpower was needed to keep the order and structure of daily life running and to maintain the stability of the empire.

Many Roman citizens were farmers. Their job was vital, as they had to prepare and harvest crops with which to feed civilians and the military. They harvested wheat, barley, fruits and vegetables. Wheat, the most common crop, was used to make bread and other baked goods.

Rome had the sturdiest military in the ancient world. It was made of brave men who risked their lives in battle. The military was made of poorer people who wanted to earn a livable wage. Anyone could enlist the Roman army if they were over the age of 17 and were physically fit enough to handle the hardships.

Merchants were the people who were responsible for the sale of goods and services. They operated in open air markets and were responsible for keeping the economy stable and strong. They sold all manner of goods from weapons and armor, to food, fabrics, linens, dishes, currency, and many more.

Craftsmen were the people responsible for producing the goods sold by merchants. They did all the small jobs people didn't want to do or were too busy. They made pots and dishes, jewelry, swords, leather goods, baskets, art and toys, musical instruments, and many other objects that were of use to people. Some honed their skills in a particular area like making clothes or mending shoes. Either way, they were vital to the expansion of the empire because they fulfilled the small roles that people didn't often see.

Musicians and entertainers were essential to the lifeblood of the empire because they kept people entertained and distracted. They took many forms. Some played music in the streets. Some were tasked with entertaining emperors and people in positions of authority. Others were more skilled at playing certain kinds of musical instruments or at using their bodies to entertain, shock and amuse. Either way, they added color and spice to life throughout the empire.

Lawyers, teachers, and engineers were the intellectual hub of the empire. They often occupied positions of power and had high status roles in finance and legal positions. Teachers were tasked with educating the younger generation and those wanting to further themselves in specific disciplines. Engineers were tasked with designing and developing more efficient transport networks, bridges, roads, and buildings. Lawyers were excellent orators and philosophers and were tasked with giving legal counsel.

Government consisted of the most wealthy and powerful men and women in society. This included rulers, emperors, Senate leaders, judges, wealthy public speakers, orators, governors, and all those in positions of authority within the empire. Many other kinds of people were required in the more complex jobs in order to keep the empire running smoothly such as bankers, tax collectors, creditors, debtors, clerks, and many more. Senators were considered some of the most important people in society.

A Typical Day

Life in the City

Most Romans in the city would start their day by waking up at first light, washing and doing their ablutions, and then sitting down to whatever breakfast happened to be available at the time. Then they would go about their daily work, whatever that happened to be. They would work until the early afternoon and then have a light meal which would keep them going until *cena*. After their afternoon meal, they would head off to social activities or to the local baths. The evening *cena* was an event that most Romans looked forward to as it gave them a chance to relax from the activities of the day and to communicate with family and friends. Life in the city was marked by a cycle of social life mixed with business and tending to one's friends and family. Community was important to city Romans. A lot of the wealthier people tended to live in the city as well, which made it easier to connect with people of a higher status.

Life in the Country

Daily life in the country was dictated to by what needed to be done and the basic needs of people. Their livelihoods determined what they needed to do each day and how much time they had for the daily tasks that had to be done such as eating and taking care of themselves. One imagines that daily life in the country would begin at the crack of dawn with doing their daily chores and then sitting down to breakfast, which would be simple fare. Farmers worked about seven days a week and rarely got time to take a break, depending on the season. Farmers enjoyed fishing, hunting, riding, and many other outdoor activities that might not have been possible if they were staying in the city. Wealthier Romans who lived in the countryside might have gone for walks, rode horses, and visited with friends who were staying at nearby villas.

Family

Family structure was important to the Romans. Wives were generally treated with respect and had a say over the finances and the running of the household. Fathers were referred to as *paterfamilias* and were responsible for earning money in their various trades to keep the family strong and stable. They were seen as the head of the *domum* or house. Children in wealthy families had the best education money could buy, while those who were not wealthy would have to be educated at home.

School

The kind of education most families could afford depended on their social status and financial position. The wealthier could attend more expensive schools and later on, specialized classes in order to improve in a specific discipline or trade. Many of the tutors within the system were freedmen or slaves. The school systems used in Rome itself were implemented throughout the empire in order to build a consistent educational culture. That is to say, the same ideas were taught everywhere. Some of these educational systems still hold sway to this very day, such was their quality.

Roman schools were tiny, with only one room and a single teacher or tutor. Schools were divided into both boys and girls. There were no desks, and only the teacher was allowed to sit on a chair with a back. Reading, writing, speaking, mathematical systems, military history, simple geography, and many other important subjects were taught. It was important for students to learn about the glory of the empire itself and to be educated in the Roman way of law, order, and discipline in whatever field they chose to study. Children from wealthier families were educated privately, and this was often a lot more expensive as the tutors or teachers were trained more thoroughly in their specific disciplines. An emphasis seems to have been placed on speaking well, as this is the stated goal in analyzing many Ancient Roman historical records. Overall, the system was influenced by Grecian practices that the Romans had learned from observing the Hellenic culture. As with many societies, those on the bottom of the Roman social pyramid or those who were poorer had to educate themselves at home and could not afford the very best in education. The Roman way of life and Roman culture was embodied within their educational systems; children were taught about the values that they needed to know growing up so that they could become effective men and women serving in the empire in whatever role they were required to.

Clothing

Roman clothing depended vastly on the occasion of the day. For those attending special or celebratory events, sophisticated dress was worn. The toga was most commonly worn for public use. The more ornate versions were worn at formal events and by those in positions of authority. They were difficult to wear and in later years within the empire, the tunic with a cloak was preferred as it was more comfortable overall. Depending on the weather, the tunic could be removed if it was too hot or put on if it was cold. Tunics were like a form of shirt that could be worn by rich and poor alike, but they were mostly favored by the poor. Most Romans wore sandals but there are records of more elaborate footwear amongst the wealthier.

Entertainment

Entertainment was important to both the Roman people and to the Roman government as a whole. According to *Roman Entertainment* (n.d), the government knew that if people were unoccupied, they would cause trouble, so they made great efforts to try and appease the masses by providing different outlets for amusement around the city. These forms of entertainment were mostly free. Most notable amongst these was of course the Colosseum where people watched all kinds of combat, executions, chariot races, recreations of naval battles, and many other often violent activities.

The Circus Maximus was a noted public entertainment venue where people could watch chariot races, gladiatorial fights, and other sporting events.

The Campus was a converted military base on the banks of the Tiber that was used for sports and recreation. Men from all over Rome competed in wrestling tournaments, javelin, archery, boxing, and many other kinds of shows where they could exercise their physical prowess.

There were many other activities for people to take part in such as going to museums to view Roman art, visiting the baths, going to zoological gardens to view rare and interesting animals, and many others.

CHAPTER 5
MYTHOLOGY

Roman mythology refers to the body of stories that make up the origins of the Roman Empire. It refers to the creation of Rome, their gods and goddesses, mythical creatures, aspects of culture, the rationale for Roman beliefs, and deals with the existential elements of how the Roman Empire came to be and what their purpose or positioning was in the world. Rome was a complex and multilayered society whose place in the world was seen as a dominant force. She was both the oppressor and the law-giver. What people believed about Rome affected the way that they acted and carried themselves in public life, in their daily lives and in battle.

The Mythological Origin of Rome

It is worth noting that Romans were proud of their legends and tales about the empire. They took pride in the fact that these stories existed and passed them down through generations in both written and verbal mediums.

Roman Gods

Roman gods were divided up into the major and minor deities. Each god represented a different aspect of Roman society and culture. Every facet of Roman life was represented in these gods. Before the advent of Christianity in Rome, it was an exclusively Pagan society. The gods themselves were characters within Roman history, and much of the influence on Pagan Rome came from the influences of the surrounding Greek culture.

Jupiter was the alpha Roman god who controlled everything. He was the king of all the Roman gods, and his equivalent in the Greek culture was Zeus. He could summon thunder and lightning like Zeus.

Juno was the Roman equivalent of Hera. She was Jupiter's wife and was considered Rome's protector. She was the queen of all the gods and held great power within the pantheon.

Mars was the Roman god of war. He was also the son of Jupiter and Juno. He was the leader of the military legions and also the agricultural guardian initially. He changed to his familiar warlike role later on and was second only to Jupiter in terms of his power amongst the pantheon of gods.

Venus was the Roman goddess of love, beauty, and romance. She also represented all aspects of sexual desire, lust, fertility, prosperity, and victory. Additionally, she was the goddess of fields and gardens.

Mercury was the god of trade and industry. He is portrayed as being fleet of foot and is synonymous with speed, fertility, luck, and prosperity. Popular sculptures of Mercury have him with wings on his heels, which suggests he also fulfilled the role of the messenger of the gods.

Neptune was the god of the sea. He was the patron of horses and the brother of Jupiter. Before the Romans became a sea-going people, Neptune was confined to being a god of the rivers and streams. It is an example of how perspectives of cultural deities can change over time. As people understood more about their environment, they worshipped their gods in different ways.

Apollo was the god of music, arts and culture, and prophecy and was brother of Diana. He also inspired medicine, health, vitality, and well-being.

Diana was the goddess of hunting, skill, and archery. She also represented animals and living creatures that could be hunted.

Minerva was the goddess of wisdom. She was a parallel of the Greek goddess Artemis.

Ceres was the goddess of agriculture and the harvest. She also represented the climates and seasons. It is from her name that we get the modern term "cereal," which is often a food product made with harvested items such as grain and other similar items.

Vulcan was the Roman god of fire. He was also commonly associated with forging and metalwork.

Bacchus was the Roman god of wine and orgies. He also represented the Roman theatre. Bacchus was associated with fertility, too. The Romans had many fertility gods and would pray and make sacrifices before the harvests were sown in order that they might be more productive and fruitful before the harvest season.

The greatest of the Roman gods was actually Caesar himself. A group calling themselves the Imperial Cult made the worship of Caesar, starting with Julius Caesar, their number one priority. All of the Roman emperors were worshipped except the evil or morally corrupt ones. As the empire grew and developed, emperor worship became formalized. The Roman Emperors of course encouraged this worship as this made their subjects easier to rule and less likely to revolt. On the opposite side of things, if an emperor became unpopular, they were less likely to be viewed as a god and they were more likely to be assassinated and killed as a result.

The character of the Roman deities reflects different aspects of Roman society and even the different personalities of the Roman Emperors themselves. From the more warlike gods to the more peaceful ones, it is clear that the nature of these gods were based on real life people and their personalities in specific cultural moments. One could say that Roman gods were really more like deified men.

Other Cultural Myths

As in many other cultures, the Romans believed in a natural order of things. They believed in gods and goddesses that ruled over various aspects of the natural world and over Roman life. There was a great deal of interest in the supernatural. Pagan Rome was all that existed before the advent of Christianity during the time of Constantine the Great. Roman culture and belief were also heavily influenced by the cultures around at the time, particularly the Grecian or Hellenic culture. Even the structure of their pantheon of gods was similar with many Roman gods being parallels of their Greek equivalent.

Heroism was a common trait within Roman folklore and mythology. It carried over into Romans' real life adventures as well. Romans were expected to be able to cope with all kinds of situations. There was a great deal of emphasis placed on strength and ability, as well as intellectual capability. What follows are some accounts of Roman heroes as they appeared in different parts of literature. Each story is part of the broader tapestry that helps us to understand the Roman Empire and how it functioned. We understand the empire better when we see these stories both individually and collectively.

The story of Aeneas was told in many forms of Roman literature including the Iliad by Homer and The Aeneid by Virgil. Aeneas was a Roman and Trojan hero who was also the ancestor of Romulus and Remus. After Troy was defeated, Aeneas fled to Rome carrying several statues of Trojan gods which he planted in Italy. He then came into contact with Dido, the queen of Carthage and they fell in love. It was Dido's intention that they rule over the city of Carthage together but Venus, the goddess of love caused their relationship to break up.

To honor his late father, Aeneas arranged a series of funeral games in the gladiatorial style. When he was killed during the games, he descended down into the underworld and met his father and Dido. Aeneas found out from his father what the line of succession in Rome would be. Thus, the line of kings and emperors was established. This story was a favorite of Roman orators over the centuries and it was retold from generation to generation.

The Romans liked to use examples from nature in order to tell their stories. One such example is called "Jupiter and the Bee." This story carries a moral lesson about vengeance and how dangerous it can be to have a vengeful attitude.

One day, after humans had taken away the honey from inside her hive, the queen of all the bees grew enraged. She decided to pay a visit to Jupiter and offered him fresh honey. He was so delighted at the taste of the honey that he offered to give her anything she wished. She asked him only for a stinger that she could use to harm and kill any mortal that tried to approach her hive. Jupiter was annoyed with her request because he loved the human race and did not want to see them suffer. However, he also did not want to deny her request after having promised her something. So he ended up giving her a stinger in her tail which, while wounding the mortal that came near her, would also result in her death. The moral of the story is do not wish for that which can kill you. Rather, forgive.

Apollo is one of the most well-known gods in the Roman pantheon. He appears in both Grecian and Roman mythology. Apollo had fallen in love with the beautiful daughter of King Priam. In order to bind her to himself, Apollo promised her the gift of prophecy if she would agree to his wishes. Upon their union, she immediately reneged on their deal, causing

Apollo to burst into flames. Enraged, he cursed her so that no one should believe her prophecies. As a result of this, no one believed what she had to say about the Greeks invading the Trojans, and they were destroyed as a result.

A priestess called Io was one of the lovers of the mighty Jupiter, and in order to be closer to her, Jupiter made himself into a dark cloud so that he could hide his activities from his wife Juno. But Juno, being too wise, saw through the disguise. Jupiter then descended to earth and disguised Io as a white cow so as to protect her. Juno discovered the cow and placed it under the care of Argus, a god with 100 eyes. In order to rescue Io, Jupiter sent his son Mercury to Argus in order to bore him to sleep with many stories. When Mercury was successful in freeing Io, Juno became enraged and sent a large poisonous fly to sting Io for eternity. Only when she vowed never to pursue Jupiter again was Io set free and departed to go to Egypt where she was worshipped as a goddess.

Pluto was named after the Roman god of death. The Roman process of death itself is that one has to cross the river Styx where they pay the undead ferryman with coins that they are buried with. The coin has to be inside the mouth of the person being ferried or the ferryman, Charon, will not transport them. The river was considered bad news to even the strongest gods. Anyone coming into contact with it would lose their voice for nine whole years. As an aside, the Greek god of death, or the underworld, was called Hades. As you can tell, the Greeks and Romans had many parallels in their culture.

One of the greatest Roman and Greek heroes of all time was the mighty Heracles, or Hercules. He was considered to be half man and half god, and was capable of feats of extraordinary strength. He was capable of wrestling with and overcoming supernatural beings of extraordinary strength. One of the most popular stories surrounding Hercules, or Heracles, is the legend of the twelve tasks. He had to perform these tasks in order to appease the goddess Hera, or Juno in Roman lore.

Janus was the Roman god of beginnings and endings. He had two faces, signifying the past and the future. He was responsible for the changes in times and seasons. In Roman mythology, there is a story about a woman who was captured by Romulus and had to be rescued. Janus saved the woman and drowned the kidnappers under hot lava. He was in control of the natural world and all the elements.

Paganism in Ancient Rome

Paganism in Ancient Rome lasted up until the advent of Christianity under Emperor Constantine the Great who outlawed all such practices. In the 4th century, he began to remove all traces of Pagan objects from the Roman Senate house and from the temples themselves. All traces of Pagan Rome were eventually stripped away to make way for a more Christianized Rome. But, what was the nature of Paganism in Rome? What did people believe? It's important to see how Paganism had an impact on their daily lives. How did their beliefs lead to the myths that we know today?

Paganism involved the worship of the natural world and the observable universe around the Roman Empire. People had to make sense of what they saw, and they invented stories to do it. Gaps in the Roman oral tradition were filled in by influences from other cultures, and this is evident when studying Ancient Roman literature and the stories that were handed down for generations.

CHAPTER 6
ROMAN MILITARY

The Roman army was the strongest of its time. With capable military leaders, sophisticated weapons and tactics, and a motivated and disciplined force, they were the strongest fighting force of their age and time period. This fighting force enabled the Romans to maintain control of the known ancient world for many hundreds of years. What made the Roman army different from other armies at the time? What weapons, tactics, and strategies did they employ that made them the envy of the world? The Roman army was a reflection, in many ways, of the nature of the empire itself. When it was strong, Rome was strong. When it was divided, fragmented, and leaderless, it showed in the way that the empire was being governed. It was an inseparable part of the strength and glory of the empire.

Structure

The Roman army was made up of smaller and larger units. The smaller units were known as cohorts. Cohorts fit together into the larger structure known as legions, which will be addressed in more detail later. Each legion had 59 governing centurions. A cohort was made up of about 480 men. There was one centurion for every 80 men within a cohort.

Each legion had around 120 *alae* or cavalry. These units were also known as belonging to the unit *Eques Legionis*. They were used not as heavy cavalry, but as reconnaissance troops and units for harassing enemy supply chains. They were also utilized as messengers that could quickly and quietly slip through enemy lines or between outposts to deliver news or important information.

Each centurion, cohort, and legion had its own symbol, banner, and a flag which was held up on a long pole. These were carried into battle.

The commanding officer of a legion was called a legate or *Legatus Legionis*.

Logistics

The Roman army was known for its supreme discipline and fortitude. They had to make forced marches, sometimes as much as 20 miles or 30 kilometers a day, carrying heavy sacks on their backs. When they were in the field, they had to handle not only their weapons and armor, but also their clothes, pots and pans, and other cooking utensils. They carried everything they needed in order to survive in the field. According to *The Roman Army* (n.d), the Romans would share a tent while in the field. While on the move, mules were used to move heavy loads such as the tents and other large packs that would have weighed the infantry down. While the Roman soldiers themselves were sturdy enough, carrying too much weight would have slowed the entire advance of the army, and thus pack animals were used for a large portion of the work.

Depending on the conditions of battle and who and where they were fighting in the world, the Romans would make extensive use of conscripts who had better knowledge of the terrain than they did. These auxiliaries were paid less than the Roman soldiers themselves, but also received other rewards for their service; they were offered the opportunity to become Roman citizens once the war was over. To become a Roman citizen in those days was a huge reward for any man, as it brought with it a host of privileges.

Under the command of a Roman Emperor Gaius Marius, the Roman army was reformed and became even more battle-hardened in around 100 BC. Roman soldiers were often referred to as "Marius mules" due to the amount of equipment they had to carry. Such equipment included their food, weapons, rope, sickles, shield, pick-axe, and many other items that were needed in battle and in the field. The men also had to travel long distances in a day. It was a test of endurance. Roman soldiers would march, fight, build bridges, and break into fortresses, sometimes all in one day. At the end of the day, the camp consisting of heavy wooden logs had to be built, and trenches had to be dug around the perimeter. In the morning, it had to be uprooted again.. This all was arduous and back-breaking work. Punishments were often harsh for soldiers who fell asleep or who broke the rules.

Legions

The Roman army consisted of two groups: auxiliaries and legionaries. Legionaries were soldiers younger than 45. Auxiliaries were soldiers who were not Roman citizens, conscripted from other tribes. Rome had conquered many territories and had a lot of manpower if they needed additional soldiers for their military forces. Each legion consisted of ten cohorts. The first cohort consisted of 800 men and the other nine consisted of 480 men each.

Training

A Roman soldier was a trained fighting machine, equipped to deal with the most extreme of battle situations. Only men were allowed to enlist in the army, and those who were under the age of 17 or were too weak or physically unfit were rejected. A term of about 25 years in the army was the standard contract for most Roman soldiers. If they survived their time, they were rewarded with gifts of land, and they were allowed to retire in peace. Older soldiers sometimes lived together in towns called *colonia*. Training itself lasted for about four months. Soldiers were put through a series of tests. If they failed, they would be put onto specific diets or receive specific kinds of training.

The army education was divided up into individual training, collective training, as well as combat and non-combat training (survival). Individual training was all about whether the soldier could keep themselves fit and mentally alert. This also included practice with both melee and ranged weapons. The soldiers were put through a range of physical exercises every day which included swimming, jumping, running, lifting heavy objects, and other kinds of physical activity.

Collective training dealt with the tactical aspects of warfare and understanding how to work as a group. Roman soldiers did not train solely for the purposes of improving their physical condition or to improve morale, or for collective pride and belief. They trained because they knew that they were going to go into real-life situations and they would need to employ the skills that they were learning. The reality of life in the Roman Empire was often savage and cruel, and they needed to be prepared. Aspects of collective training included how to march and parade as a unit, keeping their rank and file, and how to construct military buildings, palisades, and dig ditches. They would have practice fights against members of their own units with wooden swords. These fights would be to see who could dislodge the other unit's formation first.

Every so often, infantry and cavalry would go on route marches together. These were tests to see who could apply their skill while they were out in the field. There was no combat involved, but was still rigorous. It allowed the soldiers to put into practice what they had learned: camping drills, building exercises, and crossing rivers. The cavalry would also undertake the maneuvers they had learned while at the school.

Large scale military drills were also practiced, and it was not uncommon to receive a visit from the emperor himself on occasion. Hadrian was one of the emperors most noted for visiting troops in the field and on the frontline. He gave praise, criticism, and remarked on the training and discipline of the troops.

Training Infrastructure

Roman soldiers lived and trained in tents for the most part. To ensure that training was done correctly, the proper buildings needed to be in place. Training was usually conducted outside, but in the case of rainy or inclement weather, it could be moved indoors if necessary.

There were different kinds of camps for differing units and various kinds of training. There were areas for training on how to build bridges and forts; there were siege workshops, ranges for practicing archery and artillery maneuvers, and there were areas where infantry formations could be practiced. This meant that Roman training camps tended to be very large and established institutions. They were expensive to maintain and were considered to be well-respected.

There were many kinds of people running these camps. For example, there were *campidoctores*, or drill instructors, whose job it was to ensure that the standards of the troops never dropped. A *doctor armorum* was considered to be an expert in the use of weaponry of all kinds. A *doctor cohortis* was the drill instructor for an entire platoon or cohort. They specialized in larger scale maneuvers. *Exercitatores* or *magister campi* were the specialists in cavalry related moves and formations.

Romans Soldiers in Everyday Life

Roman soldiers weren't only used for fighting. They had many practical advantages outside of the military. Soldiers could be used to build entire cities and structures. They helped with the building of roads, schools, bridges, encampments, and many other types of structures. When on the front line, the infantry who were building towers and military outposts were often guarded by the cavalry.

Benefits of Roman Army Training

Some historians have noted that the training that the Romans went through really helped soldiers when they were on the field of battle. Being in the outdoors constantly prepared the Roman soldiers for the reality of battle and for long, drawn-out campaigns. Being constantly tired, thirsty, and hungry while having to face extreme conditions was enough to acclimatize them for the conditions they had to face in the theatre of war. Constant exercises with other soldiers helped to build up a sense of camaraderie between the troops. This bond between Roman soldiers made them a more effective fighting unit in the heat of battle. The understanding that they had and the friendships that they built while in the field were effective motivators. The mental and physical resiliency that they had built up while doing their training could sometimes be the deciding factor in swaying close battles.

Navy

Initially, up until around the 3rd century, the Roman army was not noted for being a naval civilization. Their prowess on land was usually enough to crush the armies of most civilizations, but they tended to struggle as soon as they got onto the open ocean. However, over time, this changed. During the first Punic war in around 264 BC, they came up against a fantastically organized naval power in Carthage, and this proved to be the catalyst for their embracing of naval strategy. Up until this point, Carthage had been the world power when it came to ocean-going endeavors. The Romans knew that this would have to change if they were going to consolidate the power that they had won. In order to overcome Carthage, Rome would need to rebuild their navy from scratch, build harbors, and learn the basics of naval warfare. It was a momental ask.

To begin, Rome tried to level the playing field by making use of its greatest strength at sea: the infantry. In order to engage the enemy at sea, the Romans invented the aforementioned *corvus*, a device that enabled the infantry to get across a flat platform in order to attack enemy troops on their ships. Unfortunately the *corvus* did have some drawbacks, namely the fact that it could not be used on rough seas due to its inflexible nature. It would cause more damage to both ships than was necessary. In an age where ship building was expensive and time-consuming, the Romans could not afford to lose so many vessels. Over time, the *corvus* was phased out and replaced with more efficient ancient warfare tactics. By the time the *corvus* had disappeared from use, the Roman army was already a highly effective naval superpower and had no further use for it.

During the imperial period of Roman history, there were no enemies left to fight save for a few pirate raids which were easily dealt with, although they were a nuisance. For the most part, the Roman navy was only used to transport grain and industrial materials without seeing anything of war.

Weapons and Tactics

Weaponry

Roman soldiers used a great variety of weapons on the field of battle. Which weapons were preferred depended on the nature of the battle. If it was a siege, siege equipment would be used to crack open stubborn enemy cities. If a defensive wall was needed, more armored troops would be called into play. According to *Ancient Rome: Roman Army* (n.d), Romans soldiers used a variety of different kinds of weapons including daggers, short swords, spears (for thrusting), javelins, and (depending on their station) a bow and arrow as well. The Roman short sword, or the gladius, proved effective in close quarters of battle and enabled them to destroy the Grecian army during their invasion and occupation of Greece. The short sword was cheap and efficient to manufacture, and it offered improved mobility, although it was not a substitute for heavier forms of weaponry of course.

Roman siege equipment was amongst the best in the world. The siege weapons they developed were adapted from what they learned from the Hellenic siege culture in the early years of the empire. The siege weapons the Roman army used included the *ballista,* the onager, the battering ram, *scorpio*, and various kinds of artillery. There were also Roman siege divisions tasked with designing, constructing, and operating the siege equipment, digging underneath walls, and planning the strategy for invading fortified towns.

Siege Equipment

One of the most well-known tools that the Roman army used was the battering ram. It was a large, heavy, wheeled beam-like construction that was covered with sheets of iron to make it as heavy as possible. Men inside the ram would push it into enemy structures (while remaining safe from enemy arrow fire). It was used on slow-moving and stationary targets.

Another effective Roman weapon was the *ballista*. It was a form of ancient artillery that could launch large projectiles, bolts, or arrow-like weapons at masses of units. It was considered to be extremely accurate on the battlefield. The *ballista* was a fixed construction on the ground which was operated by drawing a drawstring back and letting it go, much the same as would have happened with a bow and arrow. They were made use of by Julius Caesar during his battles in Britain and during the battle in Gaul at Alesia.

Siege towers were large, tall, wheeled structures that could be used to aid infantry and soldiers in accessing walls and other towers. They gave a bird's eye view of the battle and offered the advantage of height to troops that were in the tower. Arrows, rocks, and other projectiles could be launched from these towers, and they were also resistant to archer fire. Siege towers contained structures which could raise or lower them to the height of the wall if it was required. They were used at the siege of Masada in 74 AD and at the siege of Yodfat in 67 AD, amongst other campaigns.

Mines were tunnels that were dug under enemy fortifications such as walls and towers. They also weakened the walls and caused structures to collapse or made them easier to knock down. Special teams of engineers called sappers created tunnels filled with resin, sulfur, and incendiary materials in order to destroy these tunnels and whatever structures happened to be on the ground above them. The use seemed to be a specific Roman tactic and a terrifying one for people inside the cities who could hear the Romans slowly but surely advancing underneath them, while the battle raged outside.

In naval battles, the Roman army made use of something known as a *corvus* in order to board enemy ships. It was a siege engine but it was also a plank-like bridge with a spike in it that was affixed to a Roman vessel via a pole. The plank could be raised or lowered by a series of pulleys, and when it was dropped on the deck of an enemy ship, the spike would embed itself in the deck of that ship and was impossible to remove. Once the ships were latched together, they could not be maneuvered properly, nor could they be disentangled easily. Roman soldiers could then board the opposing ship and set fire to it or slaughter the people on board. Soldiers would advance on the opposing ship with their shields in front of them to avoid being struck by enemy projectiles or swords.

The *scorpio* was a device that looks like a crossbow with wheels on either side. It could be moved into position using these wheels. They were an anti-personnel weapon rather than a weapon that could break down fortifications. *Scorpio* were easier to move into position than ballistae or similar types of weapons, due to their smaller size. But even though they were small, they were still able to do major damage to armored troops.

Onagers or catapults were large, heavy, wheeled, projectile-throwing weapons that could launch weighty objects long distances. They were intended for firing on masses of units causing widespread destruction. But their primary purpose was for destroying walls and fortifications that would otherwise be impervious to other siege weapons. The projectiles that they launched were large rocks or heavy objects doused in a flammable material and set on fire.

Tactics

The Roman way of operating was to dominate the battlefield and to control the outcome of battle. Romans would advance into the midst of battle under the cover of their shields in order to protect themselves from enemy archer fire. Their defense was strong, and they counterattacked the enemy from their fortified position. The Roman army had many different shield formations that they used depending on the situation they found themselves in. These formations could be adjusted during the course of a battle so that they could gain the advantage. One of the most common Roman military maneuvers was known as the *testudo*. This was a formation that was based on a tortoise's shell; the formation itself was designed to protect the soldiers inside from enemy fire. Soldiers held their shields over their heads and crouched inside the formation or block while advancing or holding a defensive position.

Another popular formation was the wedge. It was created to drive at enemy formations and break them open; thereafter, the Roman soldiers would create havoc inside enemy lines and destroy them. Legionaries would form a triangle-shaped formation and charge the enemy with their gladiuses drawn.

Initially, the Romans had employed the phalanx formation themselves during the early years of the empire. This was a formation that required soldiers to move forward as a unified block and to throw the enemy off balance by counter punching their way to victory. It was popularized in Hellenic culture and was taken forward by these early Roman armies. The long-handled spears were most effective in this formation at driving into the enemy lines and breaking them apart while being very defensively rigid. However, the Romans discovered in their battles against the more nimble Samnites that this formation wasn't so effective on terrain that was more rocky; and thereafter, they modified the way that they handled combat.

When the Romans did eventually meet the Greeks in battle during the wars 146 BC, they came up against the phalanx themselves and trounced it. A new brand of warfare had come to the ancient world based on mobility and speed, rather than relying solely on heavy armor. The Roman's ability to utilize their short swords in small spaces completely confused the Greeks heavier, but slower armored units. They were cut to pieces in a short time during these wars. The Romans introduced the idea of infantry being organized into small groups depending on their function within the battle. Each unit functioned as part of the larger whole. The names of these groups were: *velites, hastati, principes,* and *triarii.*

Velites were young and inexperienced soldiers whose role was to hold the front line of the Roman army as they marched into battle. They were meant to press the enemy early on in battle. When they were recalled after the first phase of the battle was over, they returned to the front line and the next zone or group of Roman soldiers took their place. These were known as the *hastati*. These men were responsible for the next phase of action: the javelin phase. When they were about 35 yards or 32 meters from the enemy, they stood with their javelins facing towards the opposition. When their commander gave the order, they threw their javelins at the enemy, injuring or killing those in the front line or disabling enemy cavalry. Once they had launched their javelins, they rushed towards the opposition with their swords ready while the soldiers behind them threw their javelins over their own heads and into the ranks of the enemy. If the charge of the *hastati* was unsuccessful, they would reform at the back of the column and the next phase of Roman soldiers would take their place: the *principes*. As the name implies, these were the best soldiers that the empire had to offer. They were often the most skilled and made their presence felt on the battlefield when the enemy was disorganized and ravaged from the previous two attacks. If the previous attacks were unsuccessful, historical records indicate that this was usually the attack that completely routed the enemy. If for some reason the enemy was more resilient than usual, the *principes* would be withdrawn and the next and final phase of the column would be brought to the front to engage the enemy, the *triarii*. These were usually the heaviest of the infantry and the unit was made up of older and wealthier men. They were usually the last resort when the Roman army had exhausted its first three options.

If the enemy retreated, Roman cavalry would be brought up. While the Romans were not a noted cavalry civilization, they still made extensive use of these units in order to ensure that they were not outflanked by the enemy. Once the danger had passed or the enemy had fled or been routed, the cavalry would be brought up to mop up what remained of the enemy. As previously noted, the Romans were not naturally drawn towards the use of cavalry, a fact which would become significant later on during the final years of the empire's history. However, during the majority of their history, the cavalry units in the Roman army were made up of more skilled conscripts from North Africa and Gaul, according to *Military Tactics of the Roman Army* (n.d).

The Romans paid careful attention to how their cavalry was stationed or where they decided to fight their battles. If the battles were against strong cavalry-oriented armies, the Romans tried to lure the enemy onto rough or mountainous terrain. They also tended to prefer fighting with the wind instead of against it. Launching of projectiles was made more effective depending on which way the wind was blowing and what the speed of the wind was.

As previously mentioned, the Romans made effective use of siege tactics to break down stubborn enemies. Such tactics also included the filling in of defensive ditches with soil or concrete. They would make use of battering rams to weaken the defensive structure of a wall and they also made use of wooden beams with hooks on the end. These hooks would be used to yank the mortar and bricks out of a wall to terminally weaken it and cause it to collapse or to create breaches that Roman troops could pour through into the city. To protect themselves while going into the breach, the Roman troops would make use of the *testudo*. The Romans also invented a kind of crane that could lift groups of men up and over the wall to attack specific enemy positions.

Famous Battles

Rome saw many battles over the years. Some were great victories and others were great defeats. The legacy of these conflicts shaped the world for centuries to come, leading to the extinction of some civilizations, and the birth of others. These battles fundamentally changed the course of human history.

Punic Wars

The Punic wars were some of the most significant land and sea battles fought in the history of the Roman Empire. The battle between Rome and Carthage was between two of the main competing world powers at the time. One such battle was the battle of Cannae, fought near a small village in central Italy. It was considered one of Rome's worst ever defeats. A smaller force of Carthiginians surrounded a much larger force of

Roman infantry and cavalry, under the command of Lucius Aemilius and Gaius Terentius Verro, and destroyed them. The scale of Roman life lost equated to the more modern battles of World War 1. So great was the destruction of the Roman army that it was noted as being one of the darkest moments in Roman military history. Out of the 86,000 troops that started the battle, only about 15,000 survived, and these were most reserves.

In the aftermath of this battle, Roman was shaken to the core. They suffered a second massive defeat that year at the battle of Silva Litana but refused to give in to the Carthiginians. They would battle for 14 more years before Rome was finally victorious at the battle of Zama, which would mark the end of Carthiginian superiority and the downfall of their empire.

Teutoburg

This great battle between the Romans and the Germanic people of Saxony and the North Rhine took place in 9 AD in the Teutoburg forest around the Limes Germanicus. It is referred to as the Varian Disaster because it was led by the ill-fated general Publius Quinctilius Varus. The Germanic warriors and their allies ambushed a group of Roman legions and their auxiliaries in the forest while they were marching out of formation on the muddy trails that led into the forest.

The Romans seemed to have been taken by surprise. The leader of the Germanic tribe, Arminius, had lived in Rome and knew about Roman tactics and ways of fighting. Because they were so dispersed, the Roman soldiers had little defense against the numerically superior Germanic army and found themselves with little space to maneuver. When they attempted to break out, they walked into a trap at the base of Kalkriese hill with only narrow passages between the mountain passes that they could cross. Without being able to move easily and establish a defensive position, Germanic troops attacked them from above and slaughtered them, leading to the death of Varus and several other Roman army leaders. It turned into a rout for the Roman army. In the aftermath of the battle, the Germanic tribe attempted to cross the Rhine into Gaul but was eventually repelled by the Roman defenses there.

Catalaunian Fields

The battle of the Catalaunian fields was fought in the declining years of the empire, when they were under constant threat of invasion by barbarian tribes. The main figures in this battle were the brilliant young Roman general Flavius Aetius and the barbaric warlord king Attila the Hun. By way of context, Attila had been menacing the western and eastern Roman Empire for many months and sought to take the ownership of Rome for himself by claiming Honoria, Emperor Valentinian's sister, as his bride. Attila had already attacked large areas in Europe and devastated them. However, the Hunnic way was not to hold territory, but to raid and take what they could, moving on to other areas when they had bled the land dry.

The battle on the Catalaunian fields was one of the last major battles of the western Roman Empire before their eventual collapse in 476. It took place in around 451 AD and was fought between the weakened western Roman Empire's forces and their allies and the ferocious Huns and their own allies. The Roman army was composed largely of auxiliaries and was therefore not at its usual strength. Aetius' regular Roman army was stationed largely in Gaul and was thus rendered largely inoperable at this time. The Roman army started the more aggressive and dominant of the two armies and pushed the Huns back. In the midst of the battlefield was an elevated piece of land that the Huns attempted to take but were beaten to the chase by the Romans. One of the Roman allies' leader, Theodoric the Goth, was killed by a leader of the opposing barbarian tribes.

As night fell, the tide of battle changed slightly, and Aetius became separated from his troops. Not being able to see where they were going in the dark, his ally Thorismund accidentally entered the Hunnic camp while wandering around, and they were ambushed. Fleeing, wounded but still alive, Thorismund withdrew from the battle. The next morning, Aetius and what remained of his Roman and allied forces investigated the battlefield and found it piled high with bodies. Assuming that Attila was low on supplies, Aetius besieged the Hunnic encampment but refused to completely destroy them for fear that he would lose his only bargaining chip in the wars with other barbarian tribes in the future. He withdrew with the outcome of the battle inconclusive and hoped that he had done enough to safeguard the future of Rome. Attila had suffered huge losses. He died two years later in 453 AD, and the Huns ceased to be a serious threat after that. The battle of the Catalaunian fields is considered by many Roman historians to be one of the most violent and brutal conflicts in the history of Roman warfare. It stretched an already depleted western Roman Empire to its breaking point.

Actium

The Roman battle of Actium was a naval battle that took place in around 31 BC, in the final years of the Roman republic. It was fought between the legions of Octavian, or Caesar Augustus, and the forces of Marc Antony who represented Ptolemaic Egypt. Under the command of the skillful general Agrippa, the much smaller force of Octavian was able to overcome the larger force of Antony (about 500 warships to 250). Octavian kept the majority of his ships out of the range of the more effective Ptolemaic warships and as a result, was able to bait them into making a mistake and becoming isolated from one another. With disorganization present within their ranks, the forces of Marc Antony were made to withdraw.

Corinth

Another amazing battle between the Romans and the Hellenic forces took place at Corinth in 146 BC. This battle was decisive because it led to the ending of the Achaean war and the beginning of Roman hegemony over Greece. In the aftermath of this battle, the Romans completely annihilated Corinth and no part of it is left standing today. A few weeks prior to the battle, the Roman army had destroyed Greek forces at Scarpheia and Boeotia. The battle began when the Grecian forces attacked a Roman encampment containing auxiliaries not expecting an attack from the smaller Greek forces. Because of this carelessness, the Romans were caught by surprise. Their response to this incursion was swift and tragic for the Greeks. The Roman army counterattacked and then faced them on the battlefield outside the city the next day. Initially, the Greek cavalry was able to hold their own lines against the Roman infantry, but when a handpicked brigade of about 1,000 men attacked their flank, they broke ranks and tried to flee back into the city. The Roman army followed and destroyed them as they fled.

In the resulting carnage, the Romans completely ransacked the city of Corinth and destroyed it, leaving no buildings standing.

CHAPTER 7
DECLINE AND FALL OF THE ROMAN EMPIRE

The Beginning Of The End Of The Roman Empire

All empires must eventually draw to an end or change in some way as the balance of power shifts or the world evolves. New powers rise and grow more rapidly than these empires can manage, or the empires themselves are weakened from within. The Roman Empire was never going to remain as the world's leading power because of the shifts in times and season. All over Europe, other powers were rising. But what led to the eventual fall and disappearance of half of the empire responsible for bringing law and order to the known world for 1,000 years? Such a thing would seem impossible, and yet, it happened.

Factors That Led to the Empire's Decline

Initially, for the first few hundred years of its empire, the Romans had traditionally had the upper hand over the barbarian tribes, especially in Germania and across the Danube and the Rhine. Although they had not had much success in subduing those civilizations completely, they had maintained steady control over these regions and prevented the barbarians from crossing the Rhine. By the 4th century, however, the barbarians had begun to encroach beyond the Roman borders and make inroads into the empire. Although they did not come close to intruding on the empire itself, there were definite warning signs at this point that all was not right within the empire Other barbarian tribes had improved significantly, copying the Roman playbook and developing technologically at a commensurate rate. All of these factors led the opposition north of the Danube to be significantly more troublesome than its predecessors. Combined with a Roman army which did not have the strength of its former legions, it spelled trouble for the Roman Empire as a whole. In 410 AD, the Visigoths sacked the city of Rome, and it was raided again in 455 AD.

Economic troubles also afflicted the Roman Empire right up until it eventually fell and ceased to exist. Increased taxation and rising inflation had led to a widening gap between the haves and the have-nots. In order to escape the rapidly increasing taxation on them, many people who lived in the city fled to the country instead. This led to decreased urban development and the beginnings of urban decay. A reduced labor rate meant Rome had to induct foreign people into its workforce. As they lost territory, they were unable to conscript slave labor in order to keep the empire thriving. They were dealt a further setback in the 5th century when the Vandals claimed North Africa, leading to a further slave shortage. With pirates hindering them on the ocean, supplies and trade were also affected, leading to agricultural concerns and food shortages throughout the empire.

The rise of the eastern Roman Empire was a key factor in the eventual decline of the west, strange as it seems to say. In the 3rd century, the Emperor Diocletian divided the Roman Empire into two halves, western and eastern, claiming that it was too unruly for one person to rule alone. It did make the empire easier to govern, but because they developed at different rates, there was a widening gulf between the more financially wealthy east and the increasingly problematic west. While the east was fortified and guarded carefully, the west was left open to barbarian invasion. Over time, the west became increasingly fragmented and disconnected as one by one, their territories fell.

Over-expansion of the empire eventually led to its weakening. The terrority Rome held sway over was too vast and too difficult to control. Had the Roman Empire settled for a smaller, but more stable empire, it might have stood a better chance against future invasions. Even with the efficient Roman road system, they were unable to effectively communicate with their holdings throughout the empire. Outposts were often too far away from each other to relay important messages in time. This lack of communication meant that if something went wrong, as it often did, help would not be forthcoming for a long time. Local rulers often suffered from rebellions or attacks in their towns. In order to repel the constant stream of invaders which now regularly threatened the peace and stability of the empire, Rome was forced to station troops in these areas and to build defensive fortifications which were often expensive. The increase in military spending led to shortfalls elsewhere in the empire which meant Rome regressed technologically.

Corruption and instability were rampant in the latter years of the empire. An oversized empire was difficult enough to deal with even without ineffective leadership. Once the leadership itself started to weaken, the rest of the empire quickly crumbled. Rome's strength had always been her leadership, and throughout the long years of the empire, this had been what had seen her through numerous challenges. With the leadership gone, the structures underneath them also crumbled. The Roman Senate was most to blame for its culture of excess. Numerous high ranking politicians were regularly being assassinated, and the culture of fear and paranoia led to constant bickering and infighting in all sectors of government. The emperors themselves were often models of wastefulness and excess, and this filtered down through government.

The Huns were considered one of the arch-enemies of Rome during the 5th century. They differed from the other barbarian tribes in that their intention was not to invade and settle, but to raid lands wherever they could and to take what they had stolen back to their own homesteads. They were a nomadic people who reached new strength under the leadership of Attila the Hun, a great warlord and chief of the tribe. They were not the only barbarian tribe vying for control of the Roman peninsula, though. Other tribes were also on the move across Europe in search of new lands, and they crossed paths with the Roman army as they did so. One of these tribes was the Visigoths, who were grudgingly permitted to stay in the

Roman Empire. They were treated with extreme cruelty by the Roman soldiers and eventually revolted against Roman rule in the battle of Adrianople in 378 AD. The unprepared Romans negotiated peace with the Goths at that time, but it was broken in 410 AD when Alaric the Goth sacked Rome. At the same time, the Vandals, Gauls, and Saxons were able to take vast swathes of Roman territory.

The rise of Christianity was another critical factor in the weakening of the Roman Empire. When Emperor Constantine the Great legalized Christianity in around 313 AD, it weakened the traditional values that Rome was built on. The Pagan values that they held on to for many years began to fail as a result. Christianity took credit away from the idea that the emperor himself was a god. It eroded trust in the state. Other political actors began to interfere in state affairs, such as the pope and the church. Historians are divided on much Christianity actually contributed towards the decline of the empire. Some feel that it had little impact, while others state that it had a great deal of impact (Andrews, 2019).

The weakening of the Roman military was definitely one of the presiding factors over the fall of the empire. When Rome was prosperous, the government had more and more money to spend on strengthening the military. When the empire started to struggle financially and economically, it also struggled to find enough soldiers to cover the vast spaces of the empire. Rome was forced to employ mercenaries from all over the empire and its other territories. These men were not as loyal or well trained as the Roman soldiers were, and their performance in battle showed as a result. Rome also had many defectors during this time. Many of the barbarians who fought against Rome were once Roman soldiers themselves (Andrews, 2019).

The Timeline for the Decline

When it eventually did happen, the fall of the Roman Empire was fairly swift, taking place over a period of about 70 years. Although the seeds had long been sown beforehand, when they eventually did produce fruit, it was a quick process. From the period marked as the official end of the western Roman Empire in 476, Roman culture slowly died out over the next 100 years.

The Visigoths sacked Rome in 410 AD after a campaign that lasted for nearly nine years starting in 401 AD. This was one of the first (but not the only) major signs that the Roman Empire was near its end.

From 429 to 435 AD, the Vandals attacked Roman grain supplies in North Africa, leading to a shortage of food in the empire and cutting off a valuable supply line.

From 440 to 454 AD, the Huns attacked and ransacked both the western and eastern Roman Empire. They were paid off in gold from the eastern Roman Empire but they continued to attack and attack until their efforts were thwarted at the battle of the Catalaunian fields in 451 AD. Shortly after that, their ranks fell into confusion.

In 455, the Vandals plundered Rome but they were turned back after a hasty consultation with Pope Leo the First.

The Fall of the Empire in 476

In 476, the empire fell. The ex-Roman barbarian leader Odoacer deposed the last western Roman Empire Romulus Augustulus and established the Kingdom of Italy. What had led up to this was the Vandal invasion of the 50s. When Rome's weaknesses were exposed, other barbarian tribes began to rise up in revolt. Tribes in Gaul, Spain, and other territories began to rebel against what they perceived were their often unjust overlords. At the end of this turbulent process, and through a painful battle of succession, Romulus

Augustulus was crowned emperor in 475. Ruling in his son's stead, Romulus' father Orestes made an enemy of an auxiliary general named Odoacer who fomented revolt around the city of Rome and Italy itself. Fleeing to Pavia, Orestes was pursued by the invading barbarian forces and executed. Odoacer was given the title of *patrician* by the Roman Senate, which, fragmented as it was, still held some power. Romulus was sent into exile. Odoacer proclaimed himself king, although not of the whole of Italy, and united the barbarian tribes. He, however, was murdered by an Ostrogoth while enjoying a meal at a banquet in 493 AD. The conqueror of the Roman Empire had been conquered.

Aftermath

The aftermath of the events of 476 was a bloody war of succession over who would take which territories on the Roman peninsula. Odoacer was unable to completely rid Rome of the Ostrogoths who had threatened to overrun it. The eastern Roman Emperor Justinian fought the Ostrogoth menace for nearly 20 years, eventually overcoming them. The Roman reconquest of the peninsula was halted by the invasion of Italy by the Lombards. Every single territory that the western Roman Empire had won over its 1,000 year history was lost including the British Isles, Greece, North Africa, and many others. All that was left were the territories belonging to the eastern Roman Empire in Anatolia and Turkey. It would continue to exist until 1453, nearly 800 years later. It was overrun by the Ottoman Turkish Empire.

Overall, the western Roman Empire ceased to function as a state and was overrun by tribal invasion after tribal invasion until all traces of its former glory and culture had either been assimilated or ceased to exist.

What followed in the next several hundred years was that the world changed from being one focused on a single world power to being individual territories governing themselves. Never again would the world see such an influential power.

CONCLUSION

Ancient Rome was an empire that grew from nothing on the banks of the Tiber River to become the greatest empire the world has ever seen. Starting as a small town, evolving to a large prosperous city and eventually to a state, then a kingdom, then a republic, and eventually an empire, it continued to grow and grow. The seeds of this growth were found in the adaptability of the people, their solid leadership, and their determination to rise above the difficult circumstances that they found themselves in. They eventually succeeded in making a name for themselves.

The rule of Julius Caesar was the landmark moment between the transition from republic to empire. He was the catalyst that led to the formation of the Ancient Roman world. The development and rise to power of the Roman juggernaut taught us that it is not what you have been given that makes you great, it is what you do with what you have been given.

The Roman people made the most of their resources in a way that led to them becoming as powerful as they did.

The Roman military was the greatest standing army the world has ever seen. Their discipline, courage and resilience has been the inspiration for many fighters who came after them, many thousands of years later when the dust from the empire had long since settled.

The Roman gladiators taught us that self-sacrifice is a prize that no one is exempt from and that no one is too poor to buy. They taught us the value of living and dying nobly. A dignified life and death is not something many aspire to in today's world. The empire was not only the envy of the ancient world but continues to inspire and educate us even to this day. Countless books, plays, movies, songs, and poems have been written or sung about this glorious period in world history. What studying this period in ancient history has taught us is that every empire has a beginning and an end. Ancient Rome had many problems: corruption, greed, excess, and every kind of evil. It was a great empire, but it was a brutal one. We learned that nothing lasts forever, no matter how strong or solid it may be. Even the greatest empires may crumble if they depart from the principles that made them great. Change is not evil but is a necessary part of life.

The Roman Empire fell in 476 and disappeared, but the lessons they imparted and the legacy that they left behind still exist to this day. One can view the statues of Ancient Roman Emperors and learn from their stories. This book has demonstrated that vast and ancient civilizations are more than just the people who rule over them. They are made and constructed by the people who lived in them. The battles that they fought, in both victory and defeat, are the stuff of legend and continue to bring hope to us even today. The Roman people faced insurmountable odds, at times, in their fight to stay relevant in the ancient era. The people of the Roman Empire were a microcosm of the empire itself: strong, tough, and resilient.

This book has provided the basis for a careful analysis of these people and their role in history. The intention of analyzing these stories and the history behind them was to examine the assumptions up which Ancient Rome was built. It examined the good and the bad, and sometimes even the ugly. From its rise to its end, the most significant parts of what made the Roman Empire special are the times when it inspires us to go beyond what we are capable of doing and to stretch ourselves to heights we never knew were possible. The world's greatest empire teaches us that the limits of human potential are without end when we truly believe that we can do the impossible.

ABOUT THE AUTHOR

At History Brought Alive, we share one passion: ancient history and mythology. And we have one mission: to present you, the reader, with meticulously researched, expertly crafted, and thoroughly enjoyable works that will ignite that same passion in you! We curate the information in our books not only to provide you with the essential facts but to create an *experience*. We want you to see, feel, and hear as the history and mythology of ancient civilizations are "brought alive" in your mind's eye. Our books will become welcome additions to your library collection, trusted works to which you will return time after time. And future generations will be informed and entertained by these timeless histories and mythologies of long ago.

REFERENCES

ANCIENT EGYPT: DISCOVERING FASCINATING HISTORY, MYTHOLOGY, GODS, GODDESSES, PHARAOHS, AND MORE FROM THE MYSTERIOUS ANCIENT EGYPTIAN CIVILIZATION

Adams, J. (2021). *Africa during the last 150,000 years*. Ornl.gov. https://www.esd.ornl.gov/projects/qen/nercAFRICA.html

Bell, B. (1970). The Oldest Records of the Nile Floods. *The Geographical Journal, 136*(4), 569. https://doi.org/10.2307/1796184

Brier, B. (1999). *The history of ancient Egypt: Course guide*. The Great Courses. http://www.thegreatcourses.com

Brier, B., & A Hoyt Hobbs. (2013). Ancient Egypt: Everyday life in the land of the Nile. Sterling.

deMenocal, P. B., & Tierney, J. E. (2012). Green Sahara: African humid periods paced by earth's orbital changes. *Nature Education Knowledge, 3*(10), 12.

Edwards, A. B. (2014). *A thousand miles up the Nile* (2nd ed.). Big Byte Books.

Eltahir, N. (2021, January 4). Egypt eyes slow return for

tourism after revenues dive in 2020. *Reuters.* www.reuters.com

Feeney, J. (2006). The last Nile flood. *Saudi Aramco World*, *57*(3), 24–33. archive.aramcoworld.com.

Geggel, L. (2017, March 17). *"Gilded Lady" and other exquisite mummies on display in NYC.* Live Science; Future Plc. http://livescience.com

Gemmill, P. F. (1928). Egypt Is the Nile. *Economic Geography*, *4*(3), 295. https://doi.org/10.2307/140298

Godfrey Mugoti. (2009). *Africa (a-z)*. Lulu Com.

Haney, L. S. (n.d.). Egypt and the Nile. *Carnegie Museum of Natural History.* Retrieved September 18, 2021, from http://www.carnegiemnh.org

Harari, Y. N. (2014). *Sapiens: A brief history of humankind*. http://www.amazon.ca

Harvey Gallagher Cox. (2013). The secular city: Secularization and urbanization in theological perspective. Princeton Univ. Press.

Heath, J. M. (2021). Before the pharaohs: Exploring the archaeology of stone age Egypt. Pen and Sword Books. http://www.amazon.ca

Herodotus: II 19-31. (2020). Uoregon.edu. https://darkwing.uoregon.edu/~klio/tx/gr/H-NILE.HTM

Hymn to the Nile flood. (2002). Www.ucl.ac.uk; University College London. https://www.ucl.ac.uk/museums-static/digitalegypt/literature/floodtransl.html

Keding, B. (2000). New data on the Holocene occupation of the Wadi Howar region (Eastern Sahara/Sudan). *Studies in African Archaeology, 7*, 89–104.

Liu, S., Lu, P., Liu, D., Jin, P., & Wang, W. (2009). Pinpointing the sources and measuring the lengths of the principal rivers of the world. *International Journal of Digital Earth, 2*(1), 80–87. https://doi.org/10.1080/17538940902746082

Mark, J. J. (2016a, April 14). *Egyptian Gods - The Complete List*. World History Encyclopedia. https://worldhistory.org/article/885/egyptian-gods----the-complete-list/

Mark, J. J. (2016b, October 13). *Ancient Egyptian Government*. World History Encyclopedia. https://www.worldhistory.org/Egyptian_Government

Marlow, H. (2007). The Lament over the River Nile—Isaiah xix 5-10 in Its Wider Context. *Vetus Testamentum*,

57(2), 229–242.
https://doi.org/10.1163/156853307x183721

Maslin, M., & Leakey, R. E. (2019). The cradle of humanity: How the changing landscape of Africa made us so smart. Oxford University Press.

Mertz, B. (2009a). Red land, black land : Daily life in ancient Egypt. HarperCollins e-books.

Mertz, B. (2009b). *Temples, tombs, and hieroglyphs: A popular history of ancient Egypt* (2nd Revised, Updated Ed.). HarperCollins e-books.

Mousterian Pluvial. (2021, February 17). Wikipedia. https://en.wikipedia.org/w/index.php?title=Mousterian_Pluvial&oldid=1007401031

Pinch, G. (2004). Egyptian mythology: A guide to the gods, goddesses, and traditions of ancient Egypt. Oxford University Press.

Sandford, K. S., & Arkell, W. J. (n.d.). *Prehistoric survey of Egypt and western Asia: Paleolithic man and the Nile-Faiyum Divide* (J. H. Breasted, Ed.; Vol. 1). The University of Chicago Oriental Institute Publications. http://www.oi.uchicago.edu (Original work published 1929)

Shaw, G. J. (2014). The Egyptian myths: A guide to the

ancient gods and legends. Thames & Hudson.

Shaw, I. (Ed.). (2000). *The Oxford history of ancient Egypt.* Oxford University Press.

Smithsonian's National Museum of Natural History. (2010, March). *The Smithsonian Institution's Human Origins Program.* The Smithsonian Institution's Human Origins Program. http://humanorigins.si.edu

Stanley, J.-D., & Wedl, S. E. (2021). Significant depositional changes offshore the Nile Delta in late third millennium BCE: relevance for Egyptology. *E&G Quaternary Science Journal, 70*(1), 83–92. https://doi.org/10.5194/egqsj-70-83-2021

Taylor, J. H. (2001). *Death and the afterlife in ancient Egypt.* University Of Chicago Press.

Terra Amata (archaeological site). (2021, June 5). Wikipedia. https://en.wikipedia.org/w/index.php?title=Terra_Amata_(archaeological_site)&oldid=1027028445

University of Cologne. (2021, June 14). *Climate conditions during the migration of Homo sapiens out of Africa reconstructed.* Sciencedaily.com; ScienceDaily. http://www.sciencedaily.com/releases/2021/06/210614153909.htm

Vermeersch, P. M., & Van Neer, W. (2015). Nile behaviour and Late Palaeolithic humans in Upper Egypt during the Late Pleistocene. *Quaternary Science Reviews*, *130*, 155–167. https://doi.org/10.1016/j.quascirev.2015.03.025

Wilkinson, Toby. (2015). The Nile: Travelling downriver through Egypt's past and present. New York Vintage Departures.

Wilkinson, R. H. (2003). The complete gods and goddesses of ancient Egypt. Thames & Hudson Inc.

Wilkinson, T. H. (2013). *The rise and fall of ancient Egypt.* Random House Trade Paperbacks.

GREEK MYTHOLOGY: EXPLORE TIMELESS TALES OF ANCIENT GREECE, THE MYTHS, HISTORY & LEGENDS OF THE GODS, GODDESSES, TITANS, HEROES, MONSTERS & MORE

Adkins, A. W. H., & Richard, J. (2018). Greek mythology | Gods, Stories, & History. In *Encyclopædia Britannica*. https://www.britannica.com/topic/Greek-mythology

Ancient Greek Mythology. (2015). *Sacred places*. Ancient Greek Mythology. https://welcometothegreekreligion.weebly.com/sacred-places.html#:~:text=The%20Parthenon%20on%20the%20Acropolis%20in%20Ancient%20Athens%2C

Ancient Literature. (2020, November 6). *Artemis' Personality, Character Traits, Strengths and*

Weaknesses. Ancient Literature. https://www.ancient-literature.com/artemis-personality/

Baring the Aegis. (2020). *The festivals of early Boedromion*. The Festivals of Early Boedromion. https://baringtheaegis.blogspot.com/2013/09/the-festivals-of-early-boedromion.html

Britannica. (2018a). Hermes | Greek mythology. In *Encyclopædia Britannica*. https://www.britannica.com/topic/Hermes-Greek-mythology

Britannica. (2018b). Aphrodite | Mythology, Worship, & Art. In *Encyclopædia Britannica*. https://www.britannica.com/topic/Aphrodite-Greek-mythology

Britannica. (2018c). Ares | God, Myths, Siblings, & Family. In *Encyclopædia Britannica*. https://www.britannica.com/topic/Ares-Greek-mythology

Britannica. (2018d). Apollo | Facts, Symbols, & Myths. In *Encyclopædia Britannica*. https://www.britannica.com/topic/Apollo-Greek-mythology

Britannica. (2018e). Zeus | Myths, Wife, Children, & Facts. In *Encyclopædia Britannica*. https://www.britannica.com/topic/Zeus

Britannica. (2019a). Panathenaea | Greek festival | Britannica. In *Encyclopædia Britannica*. https://www.britannica.com/topic/Panathenaea

Britannica. (2019b). Artemis | Myths, Symbols, & Meaning. In *Encyclopædia Britannica*. https://www.britannica.com/topic/Artemis-Greek-goddess

Britannica. (2020). Nymph | Greek mythology | Britannica. In *Encyclopædia Britannica*. https://www.britannica.com/topic/nymph-Greek-mythology

Campbell, M. (2007, February 12). *Meaning, origin and history of the name Poseidon*. Behind the Name. https://www.behindthename.com/name/poseidon

Cartwright, M. (2012, July 29). *Greek Mythology*. Ancient History Encyclopedia; Ancient History Encyclopedia. https://www.ancient.eu/Greek_Mythology/

Cartwright, M. (2018). *Trojan War*. World History Encyclopedia. https://www.worldhistory.org/Trojan_War/

Davis, E. (2018). *characteristics and symbols*. Athena. https://elissadavis.weebly.com/characteristics-and-symbols.html

Decibelboy. (2012, November 16). *Mythology, does it explore or hide?* Decibelboy. https://decibelboy.wordpress.com/mythology-does-it-explore-or-hide/

Dilouambaka, E. (2014). *A Brief History Of The Temple Of Poseidon, Sounion*. Culture Trip. https://theculturetrip.com/europe/greece/athens/articles/a-brief-history-of-the-temple-of-poseidon-sounion/

Encyclopedia.com. (2019). *Satyr | Encyclopedia.com*. Www.encyclopedia.com. https://www.encyclopedia.com/literature-and-arts/classical-literature-mythology-and-folklore/folklore-and-mythology/satyr

Gill, N. S. (2003a, October 8). *What You Need to Know About the Greek God Zeus*. ThoughtCo; ThoughtCo.

https://www.thoughtco.com/profile-of-the-greek-god-zeus-111915

Gill, N. S. (2003b, October 17). *Hermes Greek God.* ThoughtCo; ThoughtCo. https://www.thoughtco.com/hermes-greek-god-111910

Gill, N. S. (2019a). *Greek Winter Solstice Celebrations in Honor of Poseidon.* ThoughtCo. https://www.thoughtco.com/greek-winter-solstice-celebrations-120989

Gill, N. S. (2019b). *Pregnant King Carries Baby in His Head: The Birth of Athena.* ThoughtCo. https://www.thoughtco.com/athena-the-greek-goddess-of-wisdom-111905

Goddess Guide. (2008). *Athena The Greek Goddess.* Goddess-Guide.com. https://www.goddess-guide.com/athena.html

Greek Boston. (2016, November 22). *Children of Zeus and Hera in Greek Mythology.* Greekboston.com. https://www.greekboston.com/culture/mythology/children-zeus-hera/

Greek Gods and Goddesses. (2014, September 19). *Poseidon • Facts and Information on Greek God Poseidon.* Greek Gods & Goddesses. https://greekgodsandgoddesses.net/gods/poseidon/

Greek Gods and Goddesses. (2016). *Centaurs • Facts and Information about the Greek Mythological Creature.* Greek Gods & Goddesses. https://greekgodsandgoddesses.net/myths/centaurs/

Greek Gods and Goddesses. (2017). *Hera • Facts and Information on Greek Goddess Hera.* Greek Gods & Goddesses. https://greekgodsandgoddesses.net/goddesses/hera/

#:~:text=Hera%20is%20the%20Queen%20of%20the%20Gods%20and

Greek Gods and Goddesses. (2017). *Typhon - The Father of All Monsters | Greek Myths and Monsters*. Greek Gods & Goddesses. https://greekgodsandgoddesses.net/gods/typhon/

Greek Mythology. (2017). *Poseidon :: Greek God of the Sea*. Www.greekmythology.com. https://www.greekmythology.com/Olympians/Poseidon/poseidon.html#:~:text=Poseidon%20is%20the%20violent%20and%20ill-tempered%20god%20of

Greek Travelers. (2019, December 19). *30 of the Most Famous Tales from Greek Mythology*. Greektraveltellers.com. https://greektraveltellers.com/blog/30-of-the-most-famous-tales-from-greek-mythology

Greekgod.info. (2019). *Greek god Zeus, the King of the Gods and Ruler of Mankind*. Greek-Gods.info. https://www.greek-gods.info/greek-gods/zeus/

Greekgods.info. (2019). *Greek God Hermes, the God of the Trade and Messenger of the Gods*. Www.greek-Gods.info. https://www.greek-gods.info/greek-gods/hermes/#:~:text=Appearance%20of%20Hermes%20Hermes%20was%20depicted%20as%20a

GreekMythology.com. (2017, May 26). *The Creation II - Greek Mythology*. Greekmythology.com; GreekMythology.com. https://www.greekmythology.com/Myths/The_Myths/The_Creation_II/the_creation_ii.html

GreekMythology.com. (2018a, March 13). *Hera - Greek Mythology*. Greekmythology.com; GreekMythology.com. https://www.greekmythology.com/Olympians/Hera/hera.html

GreekMythology.com. (2018b, March 13). *Theseus - Greek Mythology.* Greekmythology.com; GreekMythology.com. https://www.greekmythology.com/Myths/Heroes/Theseus/theseus.html

GreekMythology.com. (2018c, May 20). *The Creation - Greek Mythology.* Greekmythology.com; GreekMythology.com. https://www.greekmythology.com/Myths/The_Myths/The_Creation/the_creation.html

GreekMythology.com. (2018d, November 14). *Eros and Psyche - Greek Mythology.* Greekmythology.com; GreekMythology.com. https://www.greekmythology.com/Myths/The_Myths/Eros_and_Psyche/eros_and_psyche.html

Hellenion. (2021). *Skiraphoria / Skira – Hellenion.* Skiraphoria. https://www.hellenion.org/festivals/skiraphoria/

Hellenismos and Me. (2019). *Mounukhion.* Hellenismos and Me. https://hellenismosandme.tumblr.com/post/48532766292/mounukhion

Hill, B. (2015, May 30). *Cerberus: Legendary Hell Hound of the Underworld.* Ancient Origins; Ancient Origins. https://www.ancient-origins.net/myths-legends-europe/cerberus-legendary-hell-hound-underworld-003142

International Olympic Committee. (2021, April 27). *Welcome to the Ancient Olympic Games.* International Olympic Committee. https://olympics.com/ioc/ancient-olympic-games

Ivy Panda. (2019). *Political and cultural impact of Alexander the Great's conquests - 1355 Words | Essay Example.* Ivypanda.com.

https://ivypanda.com/essays/political-and-cultural-impact-of-alexander-the-greats-conquests/

Legends and Chronicles. (2019). *Hydra | Mythological Greek Hydra | Greek Hydra Mythology*. Legendsandchronicles.com. http://www.legendsandchronicles.com/mythological-greek-creatures/hydra/

Lloyd, J. (2015). *The Anthesteria*. World History Encyclopedia. https://www.worldhistory.org/The_Anthesteria/

M. A., L., & B. A., L. (2016). *How Did the Norse Believe the World Was Created?* Learn Religions. https://www.learnreligions.com/creation-in-norse-mythology-117868

Nangia, N. (2020). *The Original Story Of Pandora's Box*. Onehowto.com. https://education.onehowto.com/article/the-original-story-of-pandora-s-box-12643.html

Need for Science. (2020, September 7). *Alexander the Great: Life and Conquests | Need For Science*. Alexander the Great: Life and Conquests. https://www.needforscience.com/history/alexander-the-great-life-and-conquests/

Opsopaus, J. (1996). *Ancient Greek Samhain Festivals*. Opsopaus.com. http://opsopaus.com/OM/BA/GSF.html

Pagan Paths. (2020). *Greek paganism (Greco pagan)*. Pagans and Wiccans Welcome. https://paganpaths.weebly.com/greek-paganism-greco-pagan.html

Reference.com. (2020). *What Is a Physical Description of Aphrodite?* Reference.

https://www.reference.com/world-view/physical-description-aphrodite-271879e15f37534e

Singing for Her. (2016, May 27). *Plunteria*. Singing for Her. https://singingforher.wordpress.com/2016/05/27/plunteria/

Smith, G. (2020). *Why Ancient Greek Mythology is Still Relevant Today*. Corespirit.com. https://corespirit.com/articles/why-ancient-greek-mythology-is-still-relevant-today

Tales Beyond Belief. (2017a). *Demigods* ***. Talesbeyondbelief.com. http://www.talesbeyondbelief.com/greek-gods-mythology/demigods.htm

Tales Beyond Belief. (2017b). *Temple of Zeus* ***. Www.talesbeyondbelief.com. http://www.talesbeyondbelief.com/greek-gods-mythology/temple-of-zeus.htm

The Brittish Museum. (2019). *Ancient Greece - Festivals and Games - The British Museum*. Ancientgreece.co.uk. http://www.ancientgreece.co.uk/festivals/home_set.html

The trials of Apollo. (2018). *Zeus*. Riordan Wiki. https://riordan.fandom.com/wiki/Zeus#:~:text=Zeus%20is%20very%20tall%2C%20imposing%2C%20and%20very%20muscular%2C

Theoi. (2020). *Nymphs | Theoi Greek Mythology*. Www.theoi.com. https://www.theoi.com/greek-mythology/nymphs.html

Thought Co. (2019). *Greatest and Mightiest Heroes of Greek Mythology*. ThoughtCo. https://www.thoughtco.com/greatest-greek-heroes-118992

Violatti, C. (2014, May 27). *Ionia*. Ancient History Encyclopedia; Ancient History Encyclopedia. https://www.ancient.eu/ionia/

Wikipedia. (2018, December 3). *Apollo*. Wikipedia; Wikimedia Foundation. https://en.wikipedia.org/wiki/Apollo

THE MYTHOLOGY OF MESOPOTAMIA: FASCINATING INSIGHTS, MYTHS, STORIES & HISTORY FROM THE WORLD'S MOST ANCIENT CIVILIZATION. SUMERIAN, AKKADIAN, BABYLONIAN, PERSIAN, ASSYRIAN AND MORE

Avery, J. S. (2016). *Science and society*. World Scientific.

Carroll, R. P., & Prickett, S. (2008). *The Bible: Authorized King James version*. Oxford University Press.

Gadd, C. J. (1977). Assyria and Babylon c. 1370-1300 B.C. In Edwards, I. E. S., Gadd, C. J., & Hammond, N. G. L. (Ed.), *The Cambridge Ancient History, Volumes 2 Part 2: The Middle East and the Aegean Region c. 1380-1000 B.C.*(3rd ed., pp. 21-48). Cambridge University Press.

Herodotus. (2015). *The histories*. (T. Holland, Trans.). Penguin Books.

Hirth, K. (2020). *The organization of ancient economies: A global perspective*. Cambridge University Press

Kramer, S. N. (1971). *The Sumerians*. University of Chicago Press.

Kriwaczek, P. (2010). *Babylon: Mesopotamia and the birth of civilization*. Thomas Dunne Books.

Lerner, G. (1986). The origin of prostitution in Ancient Mesopotamia. *Signs,* *11*(2), 236-254. https://www.jstor.org/stable/3174047

Livius.org. (2020, September 24). *The Sumerian king list*. Livius.org. https://www.livius.org/sources/content/anet/266-the-sumerian-king-list/

Mark, J. J. (2014, July 9). *Ashurnasirpal II*. World History Encyclopedia. https://www.worldhistory.org/Ashurnasirpal_II/

Richardson, M. E. J. (2000). *Hammurabi's laws: Text, translation and glossary*. T&T Clark International.

Spar, I. (1988). *Cuneiform texts in the Metropolitan Museum of Art volume I: Tablets, cones, and bricks of the third and second millennia B.C.* The Metropolitan Museum of Art.

Vlaardingerbroek, M. (2004). The founding of Nineveh and Babylon in Greek historiography. *Iraq, 66*, 233–241. https://doi.org/10.1017/s0021088900001819

ROMAN EMPIRE: RISE & THE FALL. EXPLORE THE HISTORY, MYTHOLOGY, LEGENDS, EPIC BATTLES & THE LIVES OF THE EMPERORS, LEGIONS, HEROES, GLADIATORS & MORE

Adhikari, S. (2019a, February 11). Top 10 Interesting Roman Mythology Stories. Ancient History Lists. https://www.ancienthistorylists.com/rome-history/top-10-interesting-roman-mythology/

Adhikari, S. (2019b, April 9). Top 10 Famous People in Ancient Rome. Ancient History Lists. https://www.ancienthistorylists.com/rome-history/top-10-famous-people-ancient-rome/

Adhikari, S. (2019, April 29). Top 10 Greatest Emperors of Ancient Rome. Ancient History Lists. https://www.ancienthistorylists.com/rome-history/top-10-greatest-emperors-ancient-rome/

Alexander Hugh McDonald. (2019). Tacitus | Roman historian. In Encyclopædia Britannica. https://www.britannica.com/biography/Tacitus-Roman-historian

Ancient Roman Entertainment. (2020). Wabash. http://persweb.wabash.edu/facstaff/royaltyr/Ancient Cities/web/bradleyj/Project%201/Games.html#:~:text=Men%20all%20over%20Rome%20enjoyed

Ancient Roman Recipes. (2000, November). PBS. https://www.pbs.org/wgbh/nova/article/roman-recipes/

Ancient Roman statutes : translation, with introduction, commentary, glossary, and index. (2019). Yale; Austin : University of Texas Press, 1961. https://avalon.law.yale.edu/ancient/twelve_tables.asp

Ancient Rome: Food and Drink. (2019). Ducksters. https://www.ducksters.com/history/ancient_rome/food_and_drink.php

Andrews, E. (2018, August 29). 8 Reasons Why Rome Fell. HISTORY. https://www.history.com/news/8-reasons-why-rome-fell

Arnott, G. (2019). Terence | Roman dramatist | Britannica. In Encyclopædia Britannica. https://www.britannica.com/biography/Terence

Augustus. (2018, August 21). HISTORY. https://www.history.com/topics/ancient-history/emperor-augustus

Battle of Actium. (2021, April 26). Wikipedia. https://en.wikipedia.org/wiki/Battle_of_Actium#Battle

Battle of Cannae. (2020, March 4). Wikipedia. https://en.wikipedia.org/wiki/Battle_of_Cannae

Battle of Corinth (146 BC). (2021, April 9). Wikipedia. https://en.wikipedia.org/wiki/Battle_of_Corinth_(146_BC)#Battle

Battle of the Catalaunian Plains. (2021, April 25). Wikipedia. https://en.wikipedia.org/wiki/Battle_of_the_Catalaunian_Plains#Battle

Battle of the Teutoburg Forest. (2021, April 22). Wikipedia. https://en.wikipedia.org/wiki/Battle_of_the_Teutoburg_Forest#Battles

Beneš, C. E. (2009). Whose SPQR?: Sovereignty and Semiotics in Medieval Rome. Speculum, 84(4), 874–904. https://www.jstor.org/stable/40593680?seq=1

Byzantium: The New Rome. (n.d.). Lumen Learning. https://courses.lumenlearning.com/boundless-worldhistory/chapter/byzantium-the-new-rome/#:~:text=One%20of%20Constantine

Cartwright, M. (2013, October 22). Roman Warfare. World History Encyclopedia. https://www.worldhistory.org/Roman_Warfare/

Cartwright, M. (2014, April 13). Roman Naval Warfare. World History Encyclopedia. https://www.worldhistory.org/Roman_Naval_Warfare/

Cicero. (n.d.). Internet Encyclopedia of Philosophy. https://iep.utm.edu/cicero/#H3

Constantine the Great: History of York. (n.d.). History of York. http://www.historyofyork.org.uk/themes/constantine-the-great

Daily Life in the country. (n.d.). Rome. https://rome.mrdonn.org/countrylife.html#:~:text=In%20the%20country%2C%20they%20enjoyed

Dattatreya, M. (2016, August 8). Restored Pompeii Kitchens Glimpses Into Ancient Roman Cooking Styles. Realm of History. https://www.realmofhistory.com/2016/08/08/restored-pompeii-kitchens-roman-cooking/

Deposition of Romulus Augustus. (2020, December 15). Wikipedia. https://en.wikipedia.org/wiki/Deposition_of_Romulus_Augustus

Flavius Aetius. (2021, April 4). Wikipedia. https://en.wikipedia.org/wiki/Flavius_Aetius

Geography of the Roman World. (n.d.). Students of History. https://www.studentsofhistory.com/geography-of-the-roman-world

Greenspan, J. (2018, August 30). 8 Things You May Not Know About Augustus. HISTORY. https://www.history.com/news/8-things-you-may-not-know-about-augustus

Hannibal. (2018, August 21). HISTORY. https://www.history.com/topics/ancient-history/hannibal

Hays, J. (n.d.). MUSIC IN ANCIENT ROME. Facts and Details. http://factsanddetails.com/world/cat56/sub399/entry-6333.html

Hays, J. (2018). GEOGRAPHY AND CLIMATE IN ANCIENT ROME. Facts and Details. http://factsanddetails.com/world/cat56/sub401/item2048.html

History of Ancient Rome for Kids: Roman Food, Jobs, Daily Life. (2018). Ducksters. https://www.ducksters.com/history/ancient_rome_food_daily_life.php

History of Ancient Rome for Kids: Roman Gods and Mythology. (2019). Ducksters. https://www.ducksters.com/history/ancient_roman_gods_mythology.php

History of Ancient Rome for Kids: The Roman Army and Legion. (n.d.). Ducksters. https://www.ducksters.com/history/ancient_rome_a

rmy_legions.php#:~:text=The%20Roman%20soldiers%20used%20a

Imperial Roman Army – Training. (2016, April 29). Military History Visualized - Official Homepage for the YouTube Channel. http://militaryhistoryvisualized.com/imperial-roman-army-training/

Julius Caesar. (2017, November 30). Biography; A&E Television Networks. https://www.biography.com/political-figure/julius-caesar

Kemezis, A. (2014). From Antonine to Severan (A. M. Kemezis, Ed.). Cambridge University Press; Cambridge University Press. https://www.cambridge.org/core/books/greek-narratives-of-the-roman-empire-under-the-severans/from-antonine-to-severan/31ADC6E1D2C80976502676EEFC264BB4

List of Roman Authors. (n.d.). Latinitium. https://www.latinitium.com/blog/list-of-roman-authors/#3rdcenturyad

Lloyd, J. (2013, April 13). Roman Army. World History Encyclopedia. https://www.worldhistory.org/Roman_Army/

Mark, J. (2008, September 2). Ancient Rome. World History Encyclopedia. https://www.worldhistory.org/Rome/

Marrison, R. (2020, August 24). Top 10 famous Roman Gladiators. History Ten. https://historyten.com/roman/famous-roman-gladiators/

Military Tactics of the Roman Army. (n.d.). Spartacus Educational. https://spartacus-educational.com/ROMmilitary.htm#:~:text=The%20combat%20formation%20used%20by

National Geographic Society. (2018, July 6). Rome's Transition from Republic to Empire. National Geographic Society. https://www.nationalgeographic.org/article/romes-transition-republic-empire/

Paganism and Rome. (2019). University of Chicago. https://penelope.uchicago.edu/~grout/encyclopaedia_romana/greece/paganism/paganism.html

Pliny the Younger - Ancient Rome - Classical Literature. (n.d.). Ancient Literature. https://www.ancient-literature.com/rome_pliny.html

Ricketts, C. (2018, August 18). 5 Key Works of Roman Literature. History Hit. https://www.historyhit.com/key-works-of-roman-literature/

Roe, I. (2012, January 19). 7 Greatest Roman Generals. Listverse. https://listverse.com/2012/01/19/7-greatest-roman-generals/

Roman Empire. (2020, November 21). Wikipedia. https://en.wikipedia.org/wiki/Roman_Empire#Fall_in_the_West_and_survival_in_the_East

Roman Empire (27 BC – 476 AD) - History of Rome. (2019). Rome. https://www.rome.net/roman-empire

Roman geography. (n.d.). Ancient Roman Civilization. https://galligan18.weebly.com/romangeographyregionlocation.html#:~:text=Geography%2Flocation

ROMAN MEALS: An Introduction. (n.d.). Carroll. https://www.carroll.edu/sites/default/files/content/academics/philosophy/msmillie/foodilap/introRommeal.htm

Roman navy. (2021, March 2). Wikipedia. https://en.wikipedia.org/wiki/Roman_navy

Roman Navy - Know the Romans. (n.d.). Know the Romans. https://www.knowtheromans.co.uk/roman-army/roman-navy/

Roman Republic (509 BC – 27 BC) - History of Rome. (2019). Rome. https://www.rome.net/roman-republic

Rome founded. (2019, February 20). HISTORY. https://www.history.com/this-day-in-history/rome-founded

Rome Timeline. (n.d.). World History. https://www.worldhistory.org/timeline/Rome/

Second Triumvirate - Livius. (2003). Livius. https://www.livius.org/articles/concept/triumvir/second-triumvirate/

Septimius Severus. (n.d.). Encyclopedia Britannica. https://www.britannica.com/biography/Septimius-Severus

Simkin, J. (2014). The Roman Army. Spartacus Educational. https://spartacus-educational.com/ROMarmy.htm

Tacitus | Encyclopedia.com. (2018, August 18). Encyclopedia. https://www.encyclopedia.com/people/history/historians-ancient-biographies/tacitus

Tacitus and Jesus. Christ Myth refuted. Did Jesus exist? (n.d.). Tektonics. https://www.tektonics.org/jesusexist/tacitus.php

The Bestiarius and the Ludus Matutinus. (n.d.). University of Chicago. https://penelope.uchicago.edu/~grout/encyclopaedia_romana/gladiators/bestiarii.html

The Geography of Ancient Rome. (n.d.). Scott Devlin. https://sites.google.com/site/romescottdevlin/the-geography-of-ancient-rome

The Geography of Transport Systems. (n.d.). The Geography of Transport Systems. Retrieved April 27, 2021, from https://transportgeography.org/contents/chapter1/emergence-of-mechanized-transportation-systems/roman-empire-c125ce/

The Roman Empire: in the First Century. The Roman Empire. Emperors. Julius Caeser | PBS. (2019). PBS. https://www.pbs.org/empires/romans/empire/julius_caesar.html

The Roman Republic. (n.d.). Khan Academy. https://www.khanacademy.org/humanities/world-history/ancient-medieval/roman-empire/a/roman-republic#:~:text=Rome%20was%20able%20to%20gain

The Roman Tortoise. (2013). Primary Homework Help. http://www.primaryhomeworkhelp.co.uk/romans/formation.html

Tilburg, C. (2019). Via publica. The Encyclopedia of Ancient History, 1–1. https://doi.org/10.1002/9781444338386.wbeah06342.pub2

Trueman, C. N. (2015, March 16). Rome and Christianity. History Learning Site. https://www.historylearningsite.co.uk/ancient-rome/rome-and-christianity/#:~:text=Rome%20had%20a%20large%20number

US history. (n.d.). The Pax Romana. US History. https://www.ushistory.org/civ/6c.asp

US history. (2019). The Fall of the Roman Empire. US History. https://www.ushistory.org/civ/6f.asp

Wasson, D. (2016a, March 20). First Triumvirate. World History Encyclopedia. https://www.worldhistory.org/First_Triumvirate/

Wasson, D. (2016b, April 7). Roman Republic. World History Encyclopedia. https://www.worldhistory.org/Roman_Republic/

What was life like in the Roman army? (2019, November 14). BBC Bitesize; BBC. https://www.bbc.co.uk/bitesize/topics/zwmpfg8/articles/zqbnfg8

Williams, N. (2016, December 16). Geography and Topography of Rome and the Roman Empire. Humanities LibreTexts. https://human.libretexts.org/Bookshelves/History/World_History/Book%3A_World_History_-_Cultures_States_and_Societies_to_1500_(Berger_e t_al.)/06%3A_The_Roman_World_from_753_BCE_to_500_BCE/6.05%3A_Geography_and_Topography_of_Rome_and_the_Roman_Empire

Zoccali, N. (2019, June 20). What is garum? Gourmet Traveller. https://www.gourmettraveller.com.au/recipes/explainers/what-is-garum-17421

OTHER BOOKS BY HISTORY BROUGHT ALIVE

- Ancient Egypt: Discover Fascinating History, Mythology, Gods, Goddesses, Pharaohs, Pyramids, and More from the Mysterious Ancient Egyptian Civilization.

Available now on Kindle, Paperback, Hardcover & Audio in all regions

- Greek Mythology: Explore The Timeless Tales Of Ancient Greece, The Myths, History & Legends of The Gods, Goddesses, Titans, Heroes, Monsters & More

Available now on Kindle, Paperback, Hardcover & Audio in all regions

- Mythology for Kids: Explore Timeless Tales, Characters, History, & Legendary Stories from Around the World. Norse, Celtic, Roman, Greek, Egypt & Many More

Available now on Kindle, Paperback, Hardcover & Audio in all regions

- Mythology of Mesopotamia: Fascinating Insights, Myths, Stories & History From The World's Most Ancient Civilization. Sumerian, Akkadian, Babylonian, Persian, Assyrian and More

Available now on Kindle, Paperback, Hardcover & Audio in all regions

- Norse Magic & Runes: A Guide To The Magic, Rituals, Spells & Meanings of Norse Magick, Mythology & Reading The Elder Futhark Runes

Available now on Kindle, Paperback, Hardcover & Audio in all regions

- Norse Mythology, Vikings, Magic & Runes: Stories, Legends & Timeless Tales From Norse & Viking Folklore + A Guide To The Rituals, Spells & Meanings of Norse Magick & The Elder Futhark Runes. (3 books in 1)

Available now on Kindle, Paperback, Hardcover & Audio in all regions

- Norse Mythology: Captivating Stories & Timeless Tales Of Norse Folklore. The Myths, Sagas & Legends of The Gods, Immortals, Magical Creatures, Vikings & More

Available now on Kindle, Paperback, Hardcover & Audio in all regions

- Norse Mythology for Kids: Legendary Stories, Quests & Timeless Tales from Norse Folklore. The Myths, Sagas & Epics of the Gods, Immortals, Magic Creatures, Vikings & More

Available now on Kindle, Paperback, Hardcover & Audio in all regions

- Roman Empire: Rise & The Fall. Explore The History, Mythology, Legends, Epic Battles & Lives Of The Emperors, Legions, Heroes, Gladiators & More

Available now on Kindle, Paperback, Hardcover & Audio in all regions

- The Vikings: Who Were The Vikings? Enter The Viking Age & Discover The Facts, Sagas, Norse Mythology, Legends, Battles & More

Available now on Kindle, Paperback, Hardcover & Audio in all regions

FREE BONUS FROM HBA: EBOOK BUNDLE

Greetings!

First of all, thank you for reading our books. As fellow passionate readers of History and Mythology, we aim to create the very best books for our readers.

Now, we invite you to join our VIP list. As a welcome gift, we offer the History & Mythology Ebook Bundle below for free. Plus you can be the first to receive new books and exclusives! Remember it's 100% free to join.

Simply click the link below to join.

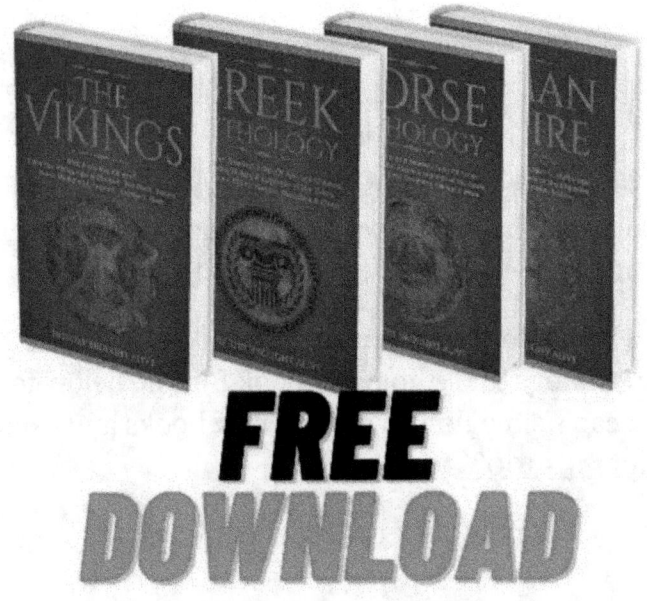

Keep up to date with us on:

YouTube: History Brought Alive

Facebook: History Brought Alive

www.historybroughtalive.com

www.ingramcontent.com/pod-product-compliance
Lightning Source LLC
Chambersburg PA
CBHW071552080526
44588CB00010B/875